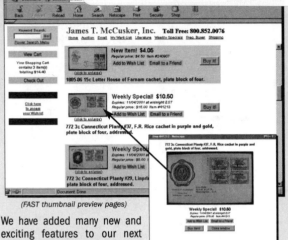

1A

SCOTT 2002 U.S. FIRST DAY COVER CATALOGUE & CHECKLIST

BY MICHAEL A. MELLONE

Complete Up-to-date Catalogue

EDITOR	James E. Kloetzel
ASSOCIATE EDITOR	William A. Jones
ASSISTANT EDITOR/NEW ISSUES & VALUING	Martin J. Frankevicz
VALUING ANALYSTS	Leonard J. Gellman, Rich Wolff
EDITORIAL ASSISTANT	Beth Brown
DESIGN MANAGER	Teresa M. Wenrick
GRAPHIC DESIGNER	Cinda McAlexander
SALES/MARKETING DIRECTOR	William Fay
ADVERTISING	Renee Davis
CIRCULATION/PRODUCT PROMOTION MANAGER	Tim Wagner
EDITORIAL DIRECTOR/AMOS PRESS INC.	Michael Laurence

4A

CONTENTS

cover binders

Padded, durable, 3-ring binder will hold up to 100 covers. Features the "D" ring mechanism on the right hand side of album so you don't have to worry about creasing or wrinkling covers when opening or closing binder.

Item	Description	Retail
CBRD	Cover Binder - Red	$7.95
CBBL	Cover Binder - Blue	$7.95
CBGY	Cover Binder - Gray	$7.95
CBBK	Cover Binder - Black	$7.95

Cover pages sold separately.

T2	Cover Pages Black (25 per pckg)	$4.95
CBBL	Cover Pages Clear (25 per pckg)	$4.95

The cover binders and pages are available from your favorite stamp dealer or direct from:

ACKNOWLEDGEMENTS

Appreciation and gratitude go to the following individuals who have assisted us in preparing information included in this catalogue. These individuals have generously shared their knowledge with others through the medium of this work. Those whose names follow have provided information that is in addition to the many dealer price lists and advertisements, as well as auction results, which were used in producing the Scott U.S. First Day Catalogue. Support from these people goes beyond data leading to catalogue values, for they also are key to editorial changes: Alan Berkun, Larry Graf, Scott Pelcyger, William Geijsbeek, Edward Siskin and Jim Bingle.

THE "COVERS" ON THE "COVER"

Winning covers from the 10th Annual Cachetmakers' Contest, sponsored by the American First Day Cover Society, are shown on the cover of this catalog. The front cover features three FDCs with original artwork. The Literary Lion cachet is by Dave Bennett. The cachet for the Los Angeles Class sub issue features the first U.S. submarine and its builder, John Holland. This cachet is by Doris Gold. The Library of Congress cachet by Jeannie Horak is hand painted using watercolors, acrylics and pastels.

The back cover features six more winners from the AFDCS Cachetmakers' Contest. Shown at top is a Year of the Dragon cachet by Alex Rogolsky. The all-over White House cachet is a design created using computer graphics by Barry Southard. The 2001 Federal Duck Stamp cachet is by Fred Collins. The Year of the Dragon cachet with the Isle of Jersey souvenir sheet has a cartoon cachet by Dave Bennett. The cachet for the Escaping the Gravity of Earth holographic souvenir sheet is by the 2001 AFDCS Top Cachetmaker, David Peterman.

In a year in which there were no Christmas adhesive postage stamps issued in the U.S.A., the final First Day Cover says, "I'm dreaming of a White House." This is a cachet by May Day Taylor. Information on all of these cachetmakers can be obtained from the American First Day Cover Society publication, *The 2002 AFDCS Current Cachetmakers Directory*.

The American First Day Cover Society is a nonprofit, noncommercial, international society and the world's largest society devoted to First Day Cover collecting! Through the American First Day Cover Society publications and activities, you'll understand that FDC collecting is a hobby of personal involvement. We encourage the individual collector to fully develop their range of interests so that their collection is a reflection of personal tastes—a unique collection!

Membership in the American First Day Cover Society entitles you to a fantastic array of exclusive benefits to help you enjoy First Day Cover collecting. As a member you will receive a FDC collecting kit including AFDCS publications, 5 free FDCs, and a one-year subscription to FIRST DAYS, winner of the Boehert Award for the best philatelic periodical of the year 2000. Each issue is packed cover to cover with departments and features including the AFDCS Mentors Program. Without any charge or obligation to you, our mentors will answer your questions on all aspects of FDC collecting, including autographs, cachets, local FDC chapter activities around the US and on the internet, international FDC information, youth activities and much more!

For more information about the annual Cachetmakers' Contest or membership in the American First Day Cover Society, contact our membership chairman, Mrs. Monte Eiserman, 14359 Chadbourne, Houston, TX 77079 or visit us on the web at www.AFDCS.org

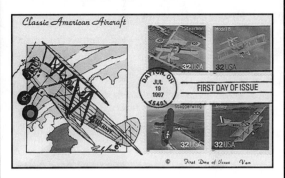

HOW TO USE THIS CATALOGUE

Sample Listing and Headings

SCOTT NUMBER	DESCRIPTION	UNCACHETED SINGLE	UNCACHETED BLOCK	CACHETED SINGLE	CACHETED BLOCK

1923

	610	2c **Warren G. Harding,** 9/1/23, DC..30.00 ..35.00
		Marion, OH (5,000) ....20.00 ..22.50
		Brooklyn, NY; Mt. Rainier, MD;
		Caledonia, OH (Unofficial cities) 37.50
		Pre-date, 8/31/23, DC,(1known) 250.00
		1st George W. Linn cachet
		(1st modern cachet) 850.00

The first number is the Scott catalogue number. This is followed by the denomination and subject. Next is the official first day (FD) date, 9/1/23, and the official FD city, Washington, D.C. which normally is listed only as "DC."

Marion, Ohio is another official FD city. Some issues have more than one official FD city. The number after Marion, Ohio, is the approximate number of covers canceled there on the FD. There's no number after the Washington, D.C. listing because it is not known.

Listed next is "Caledonia, Ohio, unofficial." This listing is for a cover postmarked on the first day of issue in Caledonia, Ohio, which was not an official FD city. Often collectors have purchased stamps in the official FD city and taken them to other cities to create "unofficial" FDCs.

Unofficial cities from which cancellations are obtained on the FD normally add to the value of the FDC, when the value is compared to that of the official city. Often a special slogan cancel, related to the new stamp, will be available on the FD. Even when these are from the official city, they are valued as unofficials on FDCs since 1940.

A Pre-dated FDC or Pre-FDC is a stamp or stamps on cover with a postmark before the official first day of issue

A **1st Cachet** is simply the first cachet that a particular cachet maker has produced. Only the most prominent are listed in this catalogue. The total number could exceed 2,000.

First day ceremony programs (CERM PROG) are produced and distributed at ceremonies dedicating a new stamp. The programs normally are produced by either the U.S. Postal Service or a local sponsoring group.

Formats of the programs vary greatly. They can be as simple as a single sheet of paper or an elaborate work of graphic art. A common element is that most programs contain the words "First Day Ceremony Program" and contain a listing of the ceremony order of events.

CATALOGUE VALUES

Catalogue Values shown in this book are retail prices. A value represents what you could expect to pay for the cover. The values listed are a reference which reflects recent actual dealer selling prices drawn from retail lists and auction realizations.

A catalogue value in italics suggests that not enough information was available to establish a firm value, and the italicized number is as close an estimate as we could ascertain.

Use this catalogue as a guide in your own buying and selling. The actual price you pay for a cover may be higher or lower than the catalogue value because of one or more of the following: the amount of personal service a dealer offers, increased interest in the cachet maker or time period when the stamp was issued, whether an item is a "loss leader," part of a special sale, or otherwise is being sold for a short period of time at a lower price, or if at a public auction you are able to obtain a cover inexpensively because of little interest in the cover at that time.

Minimum catalogue value

The minimum value for an item in this catalogue is one dollar. For items where the stamp or item of postal stationery has a face value of 25 cents or more, the minimum value is $1.25. In all cases, the minimum value is designed to reflect the cost of purchasing a single item from a dealer.

Values by year range

Values for pre-1920 first day covers (FDCs) are for uncacheted FDCs with single stamps, unless otherwise stated. Many early FDCs or earliest known use (EKU or eku) covers are unique. A dash in the value column means that FDCs are seldom found in these categories, or that no market value has been determined through recent sales of the covers.

Before 1920, stamps were not regularly released with an official first day of issue observance. In many of these cases, the catalogue shows the earliest known postal use of the stamp.

Regular issues of 1922-26, Scott 551-600, are valued as uncacheted FDCs with singles and blocks of four stamps or as singles and pairs of stamps.

During the issues of 1923-35, Scott 610-771, cachets on FDCs first appeared. Values are arranged in four columns, giving values for singles and blocks both as uncacheted and cacheted FDCs. FDCs with plate blocks from this period sell for two to three times the price for singles.

From 1935 to date, values are given for common cacheted FDCs with singles, blocks, and plate blocks. Coils are valued as common cacheted FDCs with singles, and pairs (Pr), line pairs (Lp), and plate number coils (PNCs) where appropriate. **Uncacheted covers sell for about 10-15 percent of the catalogue value of common cacheted covers.**

Cacheted FDCs, 1950 (Scott 987) to date, values are for clean unaddressed FDCs with printed cachets. **Addressed FDCs usually sell for about 50-75 percent of catalogue value.**

Values for Cacheted FDCs in this catalogue are for common mass-produced commercial cachets. Specific cachets may sell for several times catalogue value. Values for many various cachets can be found in our Cachet Valuing Calculator section of this book.

Values for Ceremony Programs

Values for material from 1940-1957, unless otherwise stated, are for programs without stamps and first-day cancels. Programs containing stamps and first-day cancels usually sell for twice the stated value.

Values for material from 1958 to date, unless otherwise stated, are for programs with stamps and first-day cancels. Programs without stamps and first-day cancels usually sell for half the stated value.

17A

cover box

10.5"

4.25"

7.5"

Keep your collection organized in this handsome and durable cover box. Box will hold hundreds of covers. Available in classic marble styling.

Item	Description	Retail
CVBOX	Marble Cover Box	$6.95

INTRODUCTION TO FDC COLLECTING

This introductory material is presented as a grouping of individual essays.

• First is a nuts-and-bolts discussion of
First Day Covers,
including definitions and concepts.

• Following is the classic
Cram Course
by the late Prof. Earl Planty, which will get you in a proper frame of mind to enjoy this hobby.

• Next is B. Wayne Caldwell's article,
"How to Make Your Own First Day Covers."
Completing this introduction is an "Introduction to Cachet Collecting"

and the
"Cachet Calculator"

WHAT IS A FIRST DAY COVER?

When a new stamp is issued by the U.S. Postal Service (USPS), it is offered for sale in (usually) only a single city on one day and then throughout the country on the second day and thereafter. That date of sale in a single city is designated as the "official" First Day of Issue. It is permissible to purchase stamps at that official city and have the stamps canceled elsewhere on that day, which lead to "unofficial" first day cancellations.

The USPS requires that cancellations may be applied only to those covers which contain enough postage to at least meet the current First Class Mail rate. For newly issued stamps which individually do not meet that rate, multiples of that stamp to "make rate" or that stamp coupled with other stamps to reach the minimum are required.

Figure 1. The first official First Day of Issue machine cancel used for the Ordinance of 1787 commemorative (Scott 795) issue July 13, 1937, in Marietta, Ohio, and New York, New York.

A special cancel is applied to the new stamp in the official city. These cancellations can never again be duplicated after the grace period allowed by the USPS to secure such postal markrags.

In the 1920's and 1930's, FDCs were canceled with everyday working postmarks. The post office first used an official FD postmark with the words "First Day of Issue," in killer bars, for the 1937 Ordinance of 1787 Commemorative (Scott 795). An official "First Day of Issue" machine cancel has been supplied for almost every new issue since.

An official "First Day of Issue" hand cancel was first

used for the first stamps released in the Famous Americans Series, the 1-cent and 2-cent Authors, Washington Irving and James Fenimore Cooper (Scott 859-860), both issued January 29, 1940.

Figure 2. The first official First Day of Issue hand cancel used for the 1-cent and 2-cent Famous Americans Authors (Scott 859-860), issued in Cooperstown or Tarrytown, New York, on January 29, 1940.

Figure 3. The first official pictorial First Day of Issue cancel used for the Horticulture commemorative (Scott 1100) issued on March 15, 1958, in Ithaca, New York.

A third type of official FD cancel has been available for many U.S. new issues. In the 1940's and 1950's this third type of cancel was a short-bar hand cancel. Now it is a bull's eye, which is usually identical to the town machine cancel, without the killer bars or "First Day of Issue" slogan.

Sometimes the stamp with FD postmark can be found on some other object: postcard, souvenir, piece of wood, bark, or cloth, or anything that will accept a stamp and postmark.

Most often an FDC is an envelope. Some are just plain white envelopes. Some bear elaborate and attractive cachets.

WHAT IS A CACHET?
(pronounced ka-SHAY)

A cachet is a design of words and/or pictures which refers specifically to the new stamp on the FDC. Designs are usually found on the front, left side of the envelope. They can be printed, rubber stamped, individually hand created, or pasted-on. The purpose of a cachet is to enhance the meaning and appearance of the cover.

WHY COLLECT CACHETED FDCs?

For a long time, collectors wanted an example of every stamp issue on a FDC. They did not really care if the FDC was uncacheted or cacheted, or who made the cachet. If they could find one with an attractive cachet, all the better, but any FDC to fill the space in the collection would do.

Today, many (if not most) collectors don't want just any FDC. They are looking for cacheted FDCs. There are several reasons for this.

Information about cachet collecting has been published and promoted in many places and in many ways. The American First Day Cover Society has promoted FDCs through its magazine First Days for more than 25 years. More recently, several cover-oriented columns have appeared in the philatelic press, helping to generate additional interest. And, there has been a steady upsurge in mass-produced FDCs offered on a subscription basis, each with its own cachet series.

The real reason for the great increase in interest is the collector himself. Collectors have become much more knowledgeable about FDC cachets. They have been captured by the quest for new cachets and information about them.

WHAT TO SEEK WHEN BUYING FDCs

When you are buying an FDC, look at the whole cover. It should be in good condition, without tears, wrinkles, stains, or wear. The stamp should not be torn or damaged. The postmark should be legible and it should have the correct FD date.

Many collectors prefer unaddressed FDCs because they are perceived as neater and more attractive. Often the specialist will want to see an address on a cover because it can sometimes help identify the cachet or the servicer of the cover. Occasionally collectors put their own name on previously unaddressed FDCs.

Just because this catalog emphasizes cacheted FDCs does not mean that uncacheted FDCs are not collectible. A number of the important early FDC servicers, — Adam Bert, C.E. Nickles, and Edward Worden — made many uncacheted FDCs which remain valuable.

Only a small percentage of all pre-1930 FDCs that exist are cacheted, because most collectors and dealers of that period were happy enough to have an uncacheted FDC. Some collectors today prefer uncacheted FDCs because they look more like legitimate pieces of mail than elaborately cacheted covers. Thus, the choice is left to the collector.

When buying cacheted FDCs, seek unusual looking cachets when you can. You will always be able to find the mass-produced commercial cachets for your collection. If you bypass an unusual cachet, however, you may not ever see that cachet offered for sale again.

If you generally collect one of the mass-produced commercial cachets, the same rule applies. Keep your eyes open for unusual color or text varieties.

WHAT ARE THE SPECIALISTS COLLECTING?

Specialists collect in many ways: by cachet maker, by issue, by set, by years or periods of years, and by topic. They collect first cachets, combination FDCs, unofficial FDCs, and hand painted cachets.

If you find a cachet maker whose work you particularly like, you can try to put together an entire run of FDCs. For example, Anderson, Artcraft, and House of Farnam all started producing cachets before 1940. While you may not have too much trouble finding most of the cachets, it will be a challenge to fill in some of the early cachets of any of these three makers. It will be particularly hard to find some of the early cachet color varieties of Anderson and Artcraft.

Some specialists pick out a particular issue or set that they like and try to make a complete collection of cachet varieties. This can be a modern issue, such as a space issue, a Kennedy issue, or an older issue that is of special interest to you. Pick out a stamp issued in your home state, or issued for your profession, or one that is related to one of your other hobbies.

Check the new issue information in any of the stamp periodicals. If there is a new stamp for which the first day of issue is near your home, you might enjoy going to a FD ceremony, collecting all the cachets you can find on that issue, and perhaps producing a cachet for that stamp that you design yourself.

Figure 4. An example of a combination FDC.

Collectors sometimes seek groupings: all FDC cachets of the 3-cent purple-colored stamps of the late 1930's, all cachets of the 28 stamps issued in 1948, and so on. Some specialists collect early uncacheted regular issues or commemoratives by set or for FD postmark varieties.

People also collect by topic - masonic, military, or

professional topics, women's history, national or local history, sesquicentennials, bicentennials, or just about anything else that interests them.

First Cachet collecting has become very popular with FDC specialists. A "first cachet" is simply the initial effort a particular cachet maker has produced. First cachets have been researched, documented, and firmly established for hundreds of cachet makers.

For other cachet makers, the search for the first cachet is still going on. First-cachet collecting is just one of many areas in FDC collecting where the knowledgeable collector can find desirable cachets in dealers' boxes. Very often first cachets are priced the same as the more common mass-produced commercial cachets because the former are not recognized for what they are.

Listings for many first cachets appear under the appropriate Scott number in this catalogue.

A combination FDC is one which has other stamps or labels along with the new stamp. Together the stamps help to tell a more complete story about the new issue.

The stamps or labels should be related thematically, usually by the history or topic of the stamp. For example, a stamp with a bird on it could be accompanied by other U.S. or foreign stamps with birds, or perhaps a wildlife conservation label.

A new stamp issued for an anniversary of statehood could be used in combination with older issues related to the state's history, or other stamps that had FDs in the state. The possibilities are only limited by imagination.

An unofficial FDC is one canceled on the official FD date, but not in the official FD city. An unofficial FDC can be canceled in any city as long as it has a postmark showing the FD date. An unofficial FDC is more meaningful when the city is related to the new issue. These relationships may be historically significant or by name only.

In 1926, Edward Worden prepared a truly classic unofficial FDC for the 13-cent Harrison stamp (Scott 622). He took 500 stamps from Indianapolis, Indiana, one of the official FD cities, to North Bend, Ohio, Harrison's home town.

On the Battle of Fallen Timbers stamp of 1929 (Scott 680), unofficial FDCs are known postmarked in Fallen Timbers, Pennsylvania. The only connection here between the stamp and the unofficial FDC is the town name. There are a number of issues from the 1920's and 1930's which have 50 or more unofficial FDCs known. While all of these unofficials are not related to the new issue, they are still eagerly collected.

A **semi-official FDC** is canceled in the official city, but with something other than the usual first-day-of-issue slogan or bull's eye cancels. Often these are pictorial cancels, perhaps from a stamp show where the show cancel is used rather than the FD cancel.

Hand-painted cachets are collected because they often have attractive and colorful original artwork. Each FDC represents a lot of time, effort and talent on the part of the cachet maker. Hand-painted FDCs are often difficult to find in dealers' boxes, because they are usually produced in limited quantities. Some of the well-known commercial cachet designers also make handpainted cachets. Ralph Dyer, who designed cachets for Artcraft during the 1930's, produced hand-painted cachets for several decades after that.

HOW TO LEARN MORE ABOUT FDCs

The best way to learn about FDCs is to be in touch with other FDC collectors. Visit them or write to them to exchange information and opinions on covers.

Join the American First Day Cover Society (AFDCS), which publishes the journal First Days eight times per year. The journal contains new issue information, free cover exchange ads, several columns on modern FDCs, and detailed research articles on cachet makers.

The AFDCS also has regular FDC auctions, an annual convention, periodic regional get-togethers, an FDC Expertizing Committee and numerous slide shows on FDCs available on loan. For additional information write AFDCS, P.O. Box 65960-S, Tucson, AZ 85728.

HOW TO ACQUIRE CURRENT FDCs

There are several ways that a collector can obtain current FDCs. The collector may service his own FDCs by sending envelopes to the FD city postmaster as new stamps are released. Different unserviced cacheted envelopes can be purchased from local or mail order cover dealers. Or the collector may choose to join a cover club or service offered by many cover dealers, and automatically receive each new FDC.

HOW TO SERVICE YOUR OWN FDCs

Many collectors believe that servicing their own FDCs is what FDC collecting is all about. There is a tremendous feeling of involvement and accomplishment. You may service your own FDCs by purchasing the new stamp when it is available at your local post office, affixing the stamp to your envelope and forwarding the envelope for servicing to the FD post office within 30 days of the issue date.

Your local post office has bulletins on upcoming stamps, their date of issue, and FD city, along with an illustration of the new stamp.

A detailed procedure for servicing your FDCs is outlined below:

Method 1: You affixing your stamps

1. Purchase the new stamp at your local post office as soon as it becomes available, which usually will be one or two days after the FD date. If you cannot obtain the

stamp at your local post office, you may need to visit your nearest post office with a Philatelic Center.

2. Affix the stamp(s) to the upper right corner of the envelope, 1/4-inch from the top and 1/4-inch from the right edge. Pencil address your cover or affix an addressed peelable label near the bottom of the envelope.

3. Send your cover(s) in an outer envelope to the FD city within 30 days after the first day of issue. No payment is necessary.

Method 2: How to join a FDC service

A more convenient method of obtaining current FDCs is to join a FDC new issue service, usually that of a cachet maker, or purchase the FDCs separately from dealers. By subscribing to a service, there is no chance of missing upcoming issues due to oversight. Uncacheted First Day Covers are now available through the USPS Philatelic Fulfillment Service Center.

The postal service will no longer affix stamps to envelopes sent in to FC cities.

There are over 200 different cachet makers who sell their cacheted FDCs for current issues. Some cachet makers produce individually hand-painted cachets in very limited quantities. Also, there are "comic" cachets, "silks" and many others. Some collectors purchase current FDCs from several different cachet makers, adding variety to their collections.

Most cachet makers stock FDCs of past issues, allowing you to add to your collection.

For a booklet of cachetmakers, send $4.00 and to: Michael Mellone, C/O AFDCS Cachetmaker List, P.O.B. 65960, Tucson, AZ 85728.

CRAM COURSE IN FIRST DAY COVERS
by Professor Earl Planty & Michael Mellone

Introduction

To meet the needs of newcomers to First Day Cover (FDC) collecting, we have produced this very simple cram course on getting started in, and enjoying, FDCs. There is plenty of research and writing by and for advanced collectors. There is an abundance of giant advertisements designed to hard sell a particular cover or set of expensive covers, mostly aimed at beginners and laymen. But little exists to guide the new collector before, and even after, he starts buying.

It tells simply what the first day cover pros have learned over years of experience, and it is knowledge which has been held a little tightly among the pros, or at least not written and published extensively.

Lesson I
Getting To Know FDCs

Your first step in all this is to visit local and nearby stamp dealers. Include all of them within a reasonable radius of your city, or further out if you are isolated in a small town or city. Visit them on business trips and vacations, too.

Make up a list of dealers from the telephone yellow pages. Then check off each stop as your visit there is completed—perhaps, with notes on the dealer's stock, how you were received, etc.

Visit each dealer several times. Stock changes from day to day. I have found some of my best covers in cupboards that were bare in my previous stop. Perhaps phone before going out to learn what first-day stock the dealer has and his open hours.

Once in the store, ask to see the dealer's stocks of first-days, those in his boxes, albums, collections and even good single covers from the safe.

Handle them very gently, study them, stare at them. Look at the details of the cachet and its workmanship, color, message and total impact upon you.

Then study the stamp, the envelope, the cancel, corner card, address and backstamp, if any.

At the store, don't hurry; instead, browse, linger, browse some more and compare. Look at a multitude of covers—at least 10,000 during this course.

But don't tie up a busy dealer. Come back at a slower time. Talk with the dealer. Make up and take along a list of questions for him.

Get answers from all whom you visit. Note the variety of their responses. Recognize that the field of first days is still growing and expanding rapidly.

Collecting practices are not yet firmly fixed and not wholly agreed upon. You will learn this from the variety and even contradictions among dealers' responses.

So, don't look for final answers. Expose yourself to many viewpoints and then decide for yourself which path and preference you wish to follow.

If a dealer asks what you want to see, be bold. Reply firmly, "Covers from 1940 to 1950, or recents." The 1940s are easily available, moderately priced and of great variety and interest.

They are starting to move up in price, too, but are still available at two to three dollars. But restrain yourself. You have not completed the course yet and have not graduated.

You are not a competent buyer or collector now. You will buy later, when you are more prepared. But perhaps you could buy a very few just to feel the thrill of purchase and possession, and to actually start you on collecting.

While in the shops with the covers and their cachets before you, appreciate them, feel for them as you would paintings in a gallery. These cachets are really little pictures to be understood and treated as such.

Note that a visit to them is free with no admission charge to these philatelic galleries. It's great for beginners or even seniors who are short on enough bread and bucks to buy in today's inflated market.

On your monopoly of the dealer's time: you'll repay him in a few weeks when you are an established collector, having fun with the hobby and spending money freely with him.

Lesson II
Learning At Bourses & Shows

The next assignment in this course takes you to shows, expositions, bourses and flea markets. At these places, dealers and collectors rent booths and tables and display stock for sale. These are mostly held on weekends.

Many shows are advertised in the classified sections of city newspapers, placed near the antique and hobby columns.

The pace may be a little fast and crowded here, but stock is good and often cheaper than at established dealers who have high rents and taxes.

Besides, at shows and bourses, dealers come to sell, to clean up remainders and overstocks. They price accordingly. Bargaining is in order, too. At the shows and bourses, repeat the learning exercises previously described for your searching in dealers' shops.

Linn's Stamp News, Box 29, Sidney, OH 45365, and other publications list upcoming shows and bourses faithfully for you each week, sometimes even six months in advance.

To find where and when to go, use these publications at

your local library, or buy a copy from a local dealer until you learn the publications to which you wish to subscribe.

Lesson III
Contacting FDC Mail Order Dealers

The next lesson in this cram course is a postcard campaign to mail-order dealers in first days. Buy 25 cards and request from those dealers their very helpful, educational, regularly issued lists and catalogs. Many mail-order dealers have advertisements in this publication.

This is particularly useful to collectors who live in places isolated from dealers. Some mail-order dealers may be small, relatively new and committed to collector services as well as their own profit.

Large or small, mail-order dealers usually are well-stocked, helpful, service-oriented and moderate in price. Their educational catalogs describe, picture and price their offerings.

Begin your collection of first-day literature by obtaining and saving these catalogs and lists for future reference.

Buy a few covers, too, and more as you advance in knowledge and confidence.

Lesson IV
Collecting The Newer FDCs

Probably, you have asked by now about servicers. FDC servicers are those who will, for a moderate deposit, send you one or more FDCs, issue by issue, as they are released. No fuss, no bother, they just keep you up to date. Servicing is for those who want recents. Most collectors eventually prefer earlier issues, as it is with collectors of coins, books and automobiles. Use of servicers is neat, assuredly regular, easy and almost effortless on the beginning collector's part.

Did we say "collectors?" Well hardly. Buying is not collecting. Collecting means searching out, finding, discovering, choosing from a great many, negotiating and then buying.

In servicing, you go through the buying process only once. You buy for 10 to 50 future issues at once. You also miss the pleasant practice of hunting bargains and negotiating on price.

Your range of cachets is usually very limited. Mostly, you choose from two to six cachets that the dealer services—a few offer up to a dozen different ones.

Buy from them for a wider choice among cachets, of which 50 to 75 different are usually made for each issue. If you buy a service, rotate cachet makers until you have bought and seen them all.

There is a wide variety of cachets available. A cachet can be very beautiful, educational or even comical.

Servicers as well as individual cachetmakers are well advertised in the classified and display sections of the philatelic press, and in "First Days" Magazine, the Journal of the American First Day Cover Society.

The servicers fill a good need for some. They help beginners who do not have time or inclination to follow this cram course or who do not have access to it.

They also serve those who have a casual interest, who want to see a little of what's regularly coming out in first day covers, but nothing more.

There are many good and great cachets too numerous to mention. Of the most heavily advertised cachets, perhaps 60,000 to 150,000 are issued per stamp. But some cachet makers restrict their issues to 2,000 or 3,000 copies. Others, especially hand-painted to 100 or less.

As you graduate here and move on to upper levels of instruction, you will hunt out these limited producers, if scarcity and advancement potential interest you.

Some servicers sell postally unused, cacheted envelopes for future stamp issues. The collector buys these and services them himself.

The process is simple and rewarding. It gets you into the act a little more than merely buying a service. But service a variety of cachets for each issue so you may learn about different cachets and choose among them for concentration.

The current edition of the "Directory of Cachet Makers" is available from the American First Day Cover Society for $3.00 and a SASE. The address is Box 65960, Tucson, AZ 85728.

This directory lists all known current participating cachet makers' names and addresses, where to write to purchase their cachets and the number of issues they produce.

Lesson V
Starting With The Currents, and
Working Your Way Back

To the degree that you are not interested in profit making or even getting your money back, collecting of recents that come out in such great numbers becomes more attractive.

Surely, the current cachets, disregarding age and romance of the earlies, are more professional than in the classic period. And, if you start on currents, you can easily work back to earlier ones. Most collectors do. Visit the local dealer and stamp shows first just to get oriented to the field.

Will you have to choose between earlies and recents? Handling both to any degree of completeness is costly in time and money. But you could easily carry both for a year or two while you are making a choice. The recents are easier because they are easily available. The early ones have to be hunted, i.e. collected.

What will you do for an album? Nothing. It's too early yet. Albums tie down and imprison your covers. You can't handle them, rearrange them and shuffle them in an album.

You can't hand a cover to a friend to be felt physically as well as psychologically. Go to a haberdasher. Get empty shirt or shoe boxes for your files.

Do encase your covers promptly in glassine or poly envelopes costing a few cents each and regularly advertised in the philatelic press.

Keep a record. Make up a marketing code to tell you what you paid for each cover. Mark the price lightly in pencil on the back. In a marketing code, letters stand for numbers thus: B (1) U (2) Y (3) I (4) N (5) G (6) F (7) D (8) C (9) S (0) (BUYING FDCS). Thus, a cover costing $1.75 would be marked $B.FN.

Lesson VI
Deciding Upon And Buying Catalogs

You'll need a First Day catalog. It is a guidebook and road map to the territory you will travel. The definitive first day catalog (the one you have in your hand now) debuted at the American Stamp Dealer's Association's 1979 show.

The book originally was called *Discovering the Fun in First Day Covers,* by Michael Mellone. It lists and prices all FDCs from the start of United States stamps in 1847 to date. It was the poor man's first-day Bible, listing everything in first days. This had never been done in one volume.

In 1983, that publication was retitled *Scott's U.S. First Day Cover Catalogue and Checklist.*

Also available is a *Photo Encyclopedia of Cacheted First Day Covers,* in 10 volumes. The encyclopedia covers the years 1901-39 and pictures, numbers, describes, and prices all known first day cachets on U.S. covers of that period. Some of these varieties may be unknown in your own collection and unidentified in dealers' boxes you will be searching.

The *Encyclopedia* also identifies hundreds of cachet

makers never known before. It also does the same for more than 1,000 cachet maker's and their first cachets. The encyclopedia also is a Bible on what to collect, where to find it, how much to pay for it and how to appreciate it fully. The encyclopedia was 50 years in the making but the first printing sold out in eight months.

Other specialized photo cachet catalogues cover the period from 1940-69 in seven volumes, consisting of over 15,000 photos of FDCs and values. For descriptive information send a SASE to the publisher of this catalogue. The address of which is printed on the title page.

Lesson VII
Specializing in various FDC Specialties

You begin to specialize a little bit now. Various collecting interests include cachets on the recently issued Marilyn Monroe stamp; cachets on stamps of various states; baseball cachets; and cachets on larger than standard-size envelopes.

In first days, there are over 200 different specialties, enough to fit each collector's whim or fancy. A few include all the covers of a particular year or decade; all cachets of two or three preferred makers; all airmails; special deliveries; registered; booklet panes; sets; back of the book; regular issues; or commemoratives.

Some collectors like to collect only hand-painted cachets. There are many beautiful hand-painted cachets produced today. Some are illustrated on the cover of this catalogue.

There are stamps and first-day cachets dealing with law, agriculture, science, education, environment, minorities, flowers, animals, state, presidents, space, military, polar, ships, railroads, transportation, art, books, music, Olympics, major historical events, opening of the country, emancipation and the Old West.

Explore these topics freely in dealers' boxes. Pick a few specialties that please you.

When is graduation? When does the course end? Like education, it never does. You continue learning doing the same things discussed in this section, but you also may wish to join the American First Day Cover Society. The membership address is Box 65960-S, Tucson, AZ 80728. Ask for membership information. Your membership includes a free subscription to the award-winning Journal, *"First Days."*

Lesson VIII
Graduation

When is spring training over and time for the game to begin? When may we buy a little more freely? You may begin to buy when you feel you don't know as much about the game as you thought you did. Buy when you are a little cautious, perhaps confused by it all. Confused enough to be careful about what you buy or sign up to buy.

When you see a glimmer of an attractive path ahead, an area and a direction in first days that fits your purse and personality, move on more freely.

When you just can't get enough to read or find enough shows to attend, then open your pocket and spend a little more—discreetly. Then you are a graduate and this Cram Course pedagogy is behind you.

Good luck, and happy collecting. Enjoy this fascinating hobby of ours.

HOW TO MAKE YOUR OWN FIRST DAY COVERS
by B. Wayne Caldwell

A great deal of the fun I have with First Day Covers is making my own limited edition FDCs. While this information is presented to help you prepare your own cachets for the first day of issue of a stamp, the process also is valid for any event for which you would like a postal cancellation as a commemoration. Two of my favorite FDCs are the Barrymores (Scott 2012), issued June 8, 1982, and the Knoxville World's Fair (Scott 2006-2009), issued April 29, 1982.

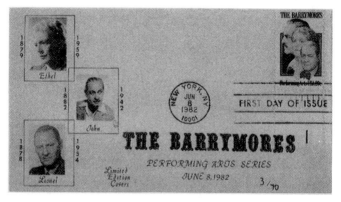

Here are the steps I follow:

1. First decide how many FDCs you want to make. I prefer to make 100. You may want to do more or less. There are no requirements here. I have chosen 100 as a base because at that level I have found average cost per cover to be reasonable.

The USPS charges for canceling more than 50 covers at a time with handstamp cancels. You may wish to investigate this charge if you choose to prepare covers in such a quantity.

2. Buy a box of No. 6 3/4 envelopes. A nice quality envelope can be purchased reasonably at a paper company or an office supply store.

3. When you purchase the stamps you will be using on the envelopes, be sure to buy a few more than you will need. You may not want to break up the plate number block or any of the other marginal blocks.

4. Make arrangements to have the envelope stamped (you can request this) on the day and in the city where the event took place. If you are not able to attend the event personally, you can provide a return envelope for all the covers you are having canceled. Explain that you want to print on them and do not want any smudges or stains on them.

If you are not able to have the covers returned in a single package, you will need to use a peel off label on each prepared cover with your return address on it. These can be purchased from a stamp shop or office supply store or ordered through the classified ads of the philatelic newspapers.

5. While you are waiting for the envelopes to be returned, decide what you want as the envelope cachet. You are free to use whatever means you want, q.v., commercial printing, hand drawing (color if you want), collage, or even a computer-generated piece of art or art and text. I recommend that you number your "limited-edition" covers, which adds to the later appeal.

6. If you choose to go with a commercial printer, or

even a hobbyist with a printing press, you will need to make your arrangements while the envelopes are being canceled. (Of course, if you prefer, you may wish to have the cachet prepared far enough in advance to send the finished envelope for cancellation. Before committing to a commercial printer, be certain he is able to print on the canceled envelopes. Most of the printers I talked to assure me they can.

When you have completed all of these steps, you will have a group of cachets for your own collection, to trade with others, or to sell. An increasing number of FDC collectors are choosing this route to having an enjoyable time with First Day Covers.

INTRODUCTION TO CACHET COLLECTING

As more and more FDC collectors turn to collecting FDCs by cachet varieties, the question is asked, "Who makes this cachet?" Included in this introduction to cachet collecting is a mini-identifier, with several popular cachet makers of the past 40 years.

Sixty cachet makers are identified and priced in *The Cachet Identifier*, available for $11.95 post paid from FDC Publishing, Box 206D, Stewartsville, NJ 08886, or from your local dealer.

C. Stephen Anderson

C. Stephen Anderson produced cachets for every issue between 1933 and 1979. Anderson cachets are easy to identify. They usually are signed "C. Stephen Anderson" or "CSA" and contain an illustration and some historical information in the text. His cachets are usually one color, with the earliest ones printed in black. Later purple, and then other color varieties, were printed. Many cachets were printed in several different colors.

Figure AND-1
THE FIRST ANDERSON CACHET was prepared for the Oglethorpe Issue of 1933. Anderson cachets can usually be identified by the lettering style and use of scrolls. Most are signed "C. Stephen Anderson" or "CSA."

Artcraft Leo August - Washington Stamp Exchange

Leo August of Washington Stamp Exchange traces the history of Artcraft cachets back to the World's Fair Issue of 1939. The earliest Artcraft cachets were not signed, but can be identified by their usual high quality engraving. Some early Artcraft cachets exist both unsigned and signed with the familiar Artcraft pallet with brush trademark. Most Artcraft FDC cachets since 1940 are signed.

The first Artcraft cachet is not the first cachet produced by Leo August. August started to service FDCs in the late 1920's, and he started producing cachets in the early 1930's. Washington Stamp Exchange cachets of the 1930's were designed by J.W. Clifford, John Coulthard and Ralph Dyer. Many of these cachets are signed by the cachet artist, and occasionally with "WSE."

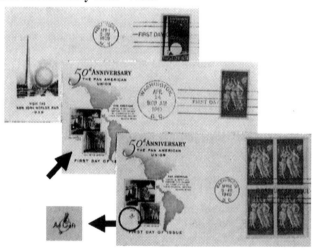

Figure ARC-1
THE FIRST ARTCRAFT CACHET was prepared for the New York World's Fair commemorative issue. This is an engraved cachet, printed in blue. Also shown are two Artcraft varieties for the 1940 Pan American Union commemorative. As with a number of early Artcraft FDCs, the cachet exists both with and without the Artcraft trademark.

Artmaster

Artmaster cachets have been created by Robert Schmidt of Louisville, Kentucky, since 1946. The firm is currently owned and operated by his nephew, Mike Zoeller. The first Artmaster cachet was prepared for the Honorable Discharge Emblem commemorative.

Artmaster cachets can be easily identified because they are high quality engravings signed "Artmaster."

Figure ARM-1
The first Artmaster cachet.

W.G. Crosby

A typical Crosby cachet has a small photo pasted on the cover. Crosby thermographed the text and frames found around the photos, which resulted in an unmistakably heavy raised printing. Crosby often produced several cachets for each issue, and occasionally produced cachets without a photo. Crosby cachets without photos can be identified by a similarity in text and cachet design. Crosby cachet photos are not to be confused with Ioor's, since Crosby's are actual photos that have been pasted onto the envelopes after the cachet was printed, and Ioor's are printed on the envelopes.

A few of Crosby's covers are signed. The trick is to see his name, which he had printed in the upper right-hand corner, right where the stamp is affixed. To see his name, one must hold the cover up to a bright light.

Crosby made cachets for ship covers in the early 1930's. He died in 1947, but his wife continued to make the Crosby covers through the Annapolis Tercentenary issue of 1949.

Figure WC-1
Most Crosby covers contain a pasted-on photo, making them easy to identify.

It was not uncommon for Crosby to have more than one cachet for a stamp issue. There are some issued where he created as many as 20 different designs.

Notice that one of the cachets for this issue does not contain a photo. However, the cachet does contain the same familiar raised print.

Figure WC-2
A few Crosby cachets are signed with a fine-line Crosby advertising imprint. This imprint is found in the upper right-hand corner of the envelope or, occasionally, on the back.

House of Farnam

House of Farnam cachets have been produced for nearly every issue since the TIPEX Souvenir sheet of 1936. Many Farnam cachets are signed "HF" or "House of Farnam." The early unsigned Farnams are usually small, simple, one-color designs found in the upper left-hand corner of the envelope. They are printed from steel-die engravings with slightly raised printing.

Figure HF-1
THE FIRST FARNAM CACHET is an unsigned design prepared for the 1936 TIPEX Souvenir sheet. Also shown is a typical unsigned early Farnam and a signed Farnam from the 1980's.

Dr. Harry Ioor (pronounced EYE-or)

Dr. Ioor's cachet career spanned the period from 1929 to 1951. His cachet designs fall into three different patterns.

Figure OR-1
Two early Ioor's, including the first Ioor cachet prepared for the George Rogers Clark commemorative of 1929. Notice that both cachets contain fine line drawings.

Early Ioor cachets (1929-1933) followed no particular pattern except that many are fine line drawings. Several are printed in black and light pink ink. In some cases the covers are addressed to Ioor, which allows for easy identification.

Figure OR-2
From 1934-1940 Ioor's covers followed a definite pattern. Almost all of them contained a printed photo as part of the cachet. These photos are printed on the envelopes and are not to be confused with Crosby's cachets, where the photos are pasted on the envelope. During this period, Ioor often produced several cachet varieties, using different black and white photos, with different colors around them.

Figure OR-3
Harry Ioor died before the completion of the Famous American series of 1940. His sister complete the series and then continued to produce cachets with a different design pattern. This particular period of Ioor is easy to identify since most of the covers are signed.

F.R. Rice

Rice cachets are undoubtedly one of the easiest cachets to identify. Most are signed and have a definite and consistent style. Rice's career spanned from 1932 to 1940.

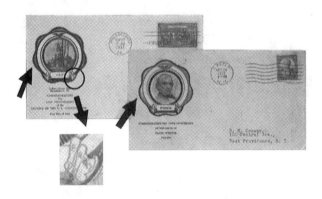

Figure RI-1
Rice used different illustrations or text inside this common border for about 75 percent of his cachets.

SCOTT

CACHETMAKER DIRECTORY

Check the following
Cachetmaker Directory
pages to find the
names and addresses
of the
finest Cachetmakers
in the U.S.A.

WRITE OR CALL
them for full details
on the services
they offer.

CACHETMAKER'S DIRECTORY

cover sleeves

Protect your covers with 2 mil crystal clear
polyethylene sleeves. (Sold in packages of 100.)

U.S. Postal Cards

Item		Retail
CV005	5 7/8" x 3 3/4"	$3.95

U.S. First Day Cover #6

Item		Retail
CV006	6 3/4" x 3 3/4"	$3.95

Continental Postcard

Item		Retail
CV007	6 1/4" x 4 1/4"	$4.95

European Standard Envelope

Item		Retail
CV008	7 1/4" x 4 5/8"	$4.95

European FDC

Item		Retail
CV009	7 " x 5 3/8"	$4.95

#10 Business Envelope

Item		Retail
CV010	10 1/8" x 4 1/2"	$5.95

SCOTT

P.O. Box 828 Sidney OH 45365-0828

to order call 1-800-572-6885

51A

CACHET CALCULATOR

As discussed in the introduction, values in this catalogue are for an average market FDC. Many FDCs, depending on the cachet, sell for many times the catalogue value.

Below is a list of cachet makers, the dates they serviced FDCs and a multiplier. By taking the multiplier range listed below and multiplying it by the catalogue value for a cacheted **commemorative** FDC *single*, you will get the **approximate** catalogue value of the specific cacheted FDC.

First cachets of all makers are in great demand and usually sell for a substantial premium.

Cachet Maker Dates	Pricing Multiplier	Cachet Maker Dates	Pricing Multiplier
Adelphia Stamp Shop		**Andrews**	
1932-1939	2 times	1978	6 times
Aero Print		1979-1982	2 times
1931-1932	3 to 4 times	**Animated (Ellis) Covers**	
1933-1934	1 to 2 times	1968-1969	6 times
Apage Cachets		1970-date	3 to 4 times
1984-date	5 times	**Annis, D. R.**	
Albers Cache		1938-1939	2 to 4 times
1966-1974	2 times	**Ardee Covers**	
Alexander, George A.		1975-date	3 to 4 times
1981-1984	6 to 12 times	**Aristocrat**	
America		1936-1937	4 to 4 1/2 times
1975-1980	3 times	1938-1940	1 to 2 times
1981-1988	2 to 3 times	1941-date	1/2 to 1 time
Anagram hand colored Cachets		**Artcraft**	
1987-date	6 to 15 times	1939	4 times
Anderson, C.		1940-1945	1 1/2 times
1933-1934	1 to 1 1/2 times	1946-date	1 time
1935-date	1/2 to 1 time	**Artique**	
		1974-date	3 to 4 times

Cachet Maker Dates	Pricing Multiplier	Cachet Maker Dates	Pricing Multiplier
Artmaster		**Beverly Hills**	
1946-1950	...1 to 1 1/2 times	1933-1937	.......3 to 4 times
1951-1986	...............1 time	**Bi-Color Craft**	
1989-date	..........1 1/2 times	1945-1947	.......3 to 4 times
Artopages		**Bickford, C.L.**	
1962-1969	.... 4 times	1931-1932	...............2 times
1970-date	.........2 to 3 times	**Bill Ressl Cachets**	
Aubry		1977-date	.........2 to 3 times
1936-1938	...............2 times	**Bittings**	
Ayerst Laboratories		1979-date	................2 times
(Artcraft variety)		**Black Heritage**	
1965-circa		1978-1984	...............4 times
1970's	.....................5 times	**Boerger (ABC)**	
Barcus, Norman		1952-date	.........2 to 3 times
1931-1939	...............5 times	**Border Craft**	
Baxter, James H.		1966-1968	.....8 to 12 times
1929-1932	.......2 to 3 times	**Broadway Stamp Co.**	
Bazaar		(Max Sage)	
1971-1972	...............2 times	1923-1929	...............5 times
1973-date	..1 to 1 1/2 times	1930-1937	.......4 to 5 times
Beardsley, Waiten S.		**Brookhaven**	
1933-1939	.......4 to 5 times	1933-1938	.......5 to 6 times
Beazell, R.		**Buchanan, Bradie**	
1929-1934	.............15 times	1927-1939	.......1 to 2 times
1935-1937	.............25 times	**Burfeind, George H.**	
Beck Printing Co. Inc.		1928-1934	...............3 times
1930-1931	.......2 to 3 times	**Burroughs, E.L.**	
Bert, Adam		1940-1941	.......2 to 3 times
1929-1933	.1 1/2 to 2 times	**Cachet Craft**	
Bennett, Ira		Pre-1950	..........2 to 4 times
1948-1949	... 10 to 15 times	1950-1972	.......2 to 3 times
Bernet Egon & Fred		**Calhoun Collectors Soc.-Gold**	
1929-1941	.......4 to 5 times	1978	........................3 times
Bernet-Reid W. Sheetlets		1979-1986	.......1 to 2 times
1938-1939	...............3 times	**Carrollton**	
1940-1945	...............4 times	1977-date	................2 times
Betts W.W.		**Cascade Cachet**	
1928-1931	..1 1/2 to 2 times	1958-1968	.......2 to 4 times

Cachet Maker Dates	Pricing Multiplier	Cachet Maker Dates	Pricing Multiplier
Chambers Gold Bond		**Crosby, W.**	
1935-1953	4 times	Pre-1939	5 to 8 times
Clifford, J		1940-1948	6 to 10 times
1936-1944	2 times	**Curtis, D**	
Clinton Classics		(Transcendental Arts Council)	
1984-date	2 to 3 times	1998-date	3-5 times
Collins, F., hand painted		**Cuscaden**	
1978-date	8 to 20 times	1978-date	2 times
Colonial		**Czubay, W.**	
1974	5 times	1936-1954	6 times
1975-1983	1 to 2 times	**DRC hand painted**	
Colorano "silks"		1979-1984	8 to 15 times
1971-1973	15 to 20 times	**DYS**	
1974-1976	4 to 5 times	1978-date	2 to 3 times
1977-date	3 to 4 times	**David "C" Cachets,**	
Colorano (Levine, Steve)		**hand painted**	
Press sheets		1966-1980	7 to 8 times
1998-date	5 times	1980-date	5 times
Com Cut		**DeRosset hand painted**	
1932-1939	1 to 2 1/2 times	1986-date	4 times
1940-1948	2 to 3 times	**Doak Ernest L.**	
Combo Cover Co.		1978-1950	5 to 8 times
1975-date	2 times	**Dome**	
Comic Cachets		1983-date	5 to 8 times
1977-1982	2 times	**Doris Gold Cachets**	
Copecrest Woven Cachets		1977-date	2 to 4 times
1969-1974	6 to 8 times	**Double A**	
Cos-Art Covers		1981-1987	3 to 4 times
1944-1950	1 to 2 times	**Dragon Card**	
Coulson Cachet		1983	2 to 3 times
1972-1977	2 times	1984-date	3 times
Coulthard, John		**Dyer R.**	
1936-1948	2 to 3 times	1928-1938	1 1/2 to 2 times
Cover Craft		**Dyer, R hand painted**	
1964-1966	5 times	1950-date	80-125 times
1967-date	1 1/2 to 2 times	**Dynamite Cover**	
Covered Wagon		1994-date	4-6 times
1931-1934	3 to 4 times	**Dysinger, M.**	
		1975-1979	2 times

Eagle Cover Service
1933-1936 ....1 to 2 times
Eastern Covers
1983-date.........2 to 5 times
Edgerly, Robert K.
1932-1948 ....2 to 4 times
Edken
1989-date.........3 to 6 times
Egolf
1928-1931 ....2 to 3 times
Edminston, Florence,
hand painted
1936-1939 ...10 to 20 times
Elliott
1929-1931 ....2 to 3 times
Emblem Cachet
1982-date.........2 to 3 times
Emeigh
1929-1930 ....1 to 3 times
Emerson
1925-1932 ....2 to 4 times
Espenshade
1935-1942...............2 times
Evans, C. M.
1929-1932 ....2 to 3 times
Evans, Glen L.
1935-1942 ....3 to 4 times
Fairway
1931-1940 ....1 to 2 times
Fawcett, James W.
1934-1936 ....2 to 4 times
Ferryman F.R.
1938-1940...............4 times
Fidelity Stamp Co.
1937-1950..1 to 1 1/2 times
First Rank First Day Covers
1979-date.........2 to 3 times
Fleetwood
1941-1947 ....3 to 6 times

1948-1960 ....2 to 3 times
1961-date.........1 to 3 times
Flok
1954-1955 .....6 to 10 times
Fluegel, I.
1945-1959 ....6 to 8 times
1960-1964 ...10 to 15 times
Folio-Print.......3 to 4 times
Fox Jack
1928-1930 ....2 to 4 times
Fulton Stamp Co.
1947-1949 .1 1/2 to 2 times
Gamm
1977...............8 to 10 times
1978-date. ...... 4 to 6 times
Geerling hand painted
1984-date .....20 to 25 times
George, C. W.
1927-1931 ....3 to 4 times
1931-1950 ....2 to 3 times
Gilbert, John C.
1937-1939 ....2 to 3 times
Gill John
1932-1933...............2 times
Gill Craft
1980.......................10 times
1981-date.........2 to 4 times
Glen
1974.........................3 times
1975-date..........1 1/2 times
Glory
1962-1963 ....3 to 4 times
Gold Bond
1935-1950 ....3 to 5 times
Goldcraft
1959-date....1 1/2 to 2 times
Gorham, A.
1932-1938 ....2 to 3 times

Cachet Maker Dates	Pricing Multiplier	Cachet Maker Dates	Pricing Multiplier
Grandy, W.		**House of Farnam**	
1935-date	2 to 4 times	1936-1939	3 times
Griffin, H. H.		1940-1960	.1 to 1 1/2 times
1926-1933	3 to 4 times	1960-1977	1 time
Grimsland, H.		1978-date	2 times
1932-1934	.1 1/2 to 2 times	**Horseshoe hand painted**	
1935-1952	1 to 2 times	1983-1987	3 to 6 times
Gundel, T.		**Hubbard**	
1929-1941	6 to 7 times	1935-1937	2 to 3 times
HM Cachets		**Hunt Harris R.**	
1977-date	6 to 10 times	1927-1930	3 to 4 times
HS Color Tint		**HUX**	
1954-circa		1928-1950	.1 1/2 to 2 times
1960's	2 to 4 times	**Imperial**	
Habbert, George Lewis		1934-1940	4 to 5 times
1927-1929	5 times	**Info Cachets**	
Hacker, E.		1992-date	3 to 8 times
1931-1938	4 to 5 times	**Info Handpainted**	
Halvorsen, Ejgil J. S.		1993-date	8 to 15 times
1926-1930	2 to 4 times	**Info Gold**	
Hammond Maxi		1996	5 times
1957-1972	2 to 4 times	**Intercity Stamp Co.**	
HAM hand painted Cachets		1939-1948	3 to 5 times
1977-1978	80 times	**Ioor, H.**	
1979-date	15 to 30 times	1929-1931	3 to 4 times
Heartland FDC		1932-1939	1/2 to 1 time
1984-date	2 times	1940 & later	1 to 2 times
Heritage Cachets		**Jackson, Gladys**	
1994 to date	5-8 times	1948-date	2 to 3 times
Hist-O-Card		**Janis, C. W.**	
1952-circa		1935-1936	3 to 4 times
1970's	2 to 4 times	**Jewelar**	
Hobby Cover Service		1998-date	5 to 8 times
1932-1933	2 to 3 times	**Jeweled Envelopes**	
Hobby Life-WCO		1935-1939	2 to 3 times
1945-1950	2 to 3 times	1940-1948	4 to 6 times
		J. Tournas	
		1997-date	5 to 8 times

Cachet Maker Dates	Pricing Multiplier	Cachet Maker Dates	Pricing Multiplier
Joseph, N.		**LEB Cachets**	
1929-1933	4 to 6 times	1981-date	3 to 6 times
Judith Fogt hand painted		**LRC Cachets**	
1982- date	15 times	1975-date	3 to 6 times
Justice Covers		**Laird**	
1979-date	1 1/2 times	1935-1937	1 to 2 times
Kapner		**Linprint**	
1934-1937	.1 to 1 1/2 times	1932-1941	1 time
Kee Ed		**Linto, Williams S.**	
1933-1935	1 to 2 times	1937-1940	8 to 10 times
Kirk Kover		1940-1959	10 to 15 times
1947-1949	4 to 7 times	**Ludwig, Oswald A.**	
Klotzbach		1937-1949	2 to 3 times
1929-1935	2 to 3 times	**MacDonald, Barbara**	
KMC Venture		(watercolored)	
1978	10 times	1990s-date	8 to 10 times
1979-date	2 1/2 times	**Mannino, Guy T. (GM)**	
Knapp, Dorothy, hand painted		(original art, hand painted)	
		Multiplier	1 to 25 times
1941-1945	300 to 400 times	**Marg**	
1945-1952	200 to 300 times	1962-1964	6 times
Knoble, Dr. Ross M. hand painted		1965-date	2 times
		Mauck	
1952		1927-1930	2 to 3 times
1960's	15 to 25 times	**Minkus, J.**	
Kolor Kover		1940's	1 time
1948	10 times	**Munprint**	
1949-1960	8 times	1936-1941	2 to 4 times
1960-1973	7 times	**Nickles, C. E.**	
Kraft B, hand painted		1925-1929	1 time
1982-date	4 times	**Nix**	
Kribb's HD/HP Kovers/Kards		1934-1958	3 to 5 times
		Nu-art	
1978	15 times	1945-1946	3 to 5 times
1979-date	5-8 times	**Orbit Covers**	
Kurkjian, S.S.		1962-1967	3 to 10 times
1927-1929	3 to 4 times	**Overseas Mailers**	
		1953-1977	6 to 10 times

Cachet Maker Dates	Pricing Multiplier	Cachet Maker Dates	Pricing Multiplier
Panda Cachets		**Rank II (flocked)**	
1982-date	5 to 8 times	1955-1959	5 to 10 times
Parsons, Albert B.		**Riemann**	
1933-1936	2 to 4 times	1947-1986	10 to 15 times
Paslay Classic hand painted		**Rice, F. R.**	
1982-date	10 to 20 times	1932-1941	1 to 3 times
Pavois		**Risko Art**	
1937-1940	1 time	1935-1938	10 to 15 times
Pent Arts		**Roessler, A. C.**	
1943-1958	1 to 11/2 times	1925-1931	2 times
Phoenix Insurance Overprint		1932-1938	2 to 3 times
1937-1956	2 to 5 times	**Ross Foil**	
Pilgrim		1971-date	2 to 3 times
1937-1941	6 to 10 times	**Rothblum**	
Plimpton		1929-1934	2 to 3 times
1936-1939	1 time	**Roy J.A.**	
Plotz David O.		1934-1937	2 to 3 times
1926-1927	2 to 3 times	**S & T (black & white)**	
Pontiac Press 1944		1990-date	2 to 4 times
1960's	3 to 10 times	**S & T (color)**	
Post/Art Engraved		1991-date	4 to 8 times
1980-1981	5 times	**Sadworth G.V.**	
1982-1986	3 times	1940-1952	2 to 8 times
Post/Art hand painted		**Sanders, Michael**	
1983-1985	10 to 20 times	1933-1939	2 to 3 times
Postmasters of America		1940-1952	2 to 5 times
1976	3 times	**Sarzin Metallic**	
1977-date	1 time	1964-1970	5 to 8 times
Pugh hand painted Cachets		1970-1977	4 to 6 times
1979-date	15 to 25 times	**Scatchard, Norwood B.**	
Quadracolorplus		1935-1938	3 to 6 times
1977-1987	3 to 5 times	**Scenic Craft**	
Raley		1940-1948	3 to 6 times
1932-1938	2 to 3 times	**Serug Cachet**	
		1944	2 to 3 times
		Shockley	
		1929-1930	1 time

Cachet Maker Dates	Pricing Multiplier	Cachet Maker Dates	Pricing Multiplier
Sidenius		**Texture Craft**	
1932-1939	3 to 4 times	1955-1957	4 to 6 times
Smartcraft		**TM Historical Covers**	
1942-1952	.1 to 1 1/2 times	**(black &white)**	
Softones		1977-1983	10 times
1978-1980	2 to 3 times	**TM Historical Covers (color)**	
Spartan		1977-1983	15-20 times
1948-1950	3 to 4 times	**Top Notch**	
Spectrum		1934-1937	.1 1/2 to 2 times
1977	6 times	**Trancsendentia Arts**	
1978-1983	2 to 3 times	**Counsel (hand printed)**	
Staehle, L. W.		1990s	5 to 8 times
1938-1940s	8 to 20 times	**Tri-Color**	
Steelcraft		1958-1960	2 to 4 times
1952-1953	2 times	**Truby**	
Sudduth		1931-1934	5 to 6 times
1936-1937	.1 to 1 1/2 times	**Tudor House**	
Sun Craft		1977	3 times
1947-1948	2 times	1978-date	1 1/2 times

cover box

10.5"

4.25" 7.5"

Item	Description	Retail
CVBOX	Marble Cover Box	$6.95

Cachet Maker Dates	Pricing Multiplier	Cachet Maker Dates	Pricing Multiplier
Uladh Covers		**Warneford**	
1977-date	2 to 3 times	1937-1940	3 to 4 times
Ulrich Frank J., hand painted		**Washington Stamp Exchange**	
1960-1968	15 to 50 times	1931-1939	3 to 6 times
Urie, C. W.		**Weaver, Howard M.**	
1926-1929	2 to 3 times	1928-1934	2 to 3 times
Vaughn Hord hand painted Cachets		**Weddle, T. M.**	
1983-date	20 to 30 times	1977-1981	15 to 25 times
Velvatone		1981-date	10 times
1947-1970	5 to 10 times	**Western Silk Cachets**	
Vintry House		1978	4 times
1992-date	3 to 5 times	1979-1983	2 to 3 times
Von Ohlen, William J.		**Wilson Covers**	
1937-1945	3 times	1989-date	3 to 5 times
1945-1969	5 times	**Wright, William N. hand painted**	
WCO		1945-1950	40 to 75 times
1946-1949	3 to 7 times	1951-1959	40 times
Wanstead & Co.		**Zaso**	
1935-1937	2 to 4 times	1977	6 times
		1978-1983	1 1/2 to 2 times

Cachetmakers

Editors Note: Cachetmakers wishing to be listed in the cachet calculator should send three original samples of their work along with current price list/auction realization showing the value of their work on the secondary market. The dates they started, printing method and quantities produced must also be included. Send information to the editor at Box 206, Stewartsville, NJ 08886.

COMMEMORATIVES AND REGULAR ISSUES

Editor's Note:

All listings prior to Scott 551 are considered 'Earliest Known Uses' (EKUs), unless otherwise specified as a 'First Day Cover'. An EKU is defined as a cover that has either received a valid certificate of authenticity from a recognized expertizing service, or has been examined by acknowledged experts in the field.

The editor wishes to thank Edward J. Siskin for his help in compiling the earliest-known use (EKU) dates.

Since EKUs can change as new discoveries are made, with a few exceptions, no prices are given for these covers. As a general rule, an EKU is worth a premium over the 'on cover' price found in the 'Scott Specialized Catalogue of United States Stamps', published by Scott Publishing Company. Collectors are urged to document covers with earlier dates than those listed here, and share their discoveries with the editors, so that we may update future listings.

1	2	230	231

SCOTT NUMBER	DESCRIPTION	UNCACHETED SINGLE

1847

☐ 1	**5c Benjamin Franklin**, 7/7/1847, New York, NY, eku....................	—
☐ 2	**10c George Washington**, 7/2/1847, New York, NY, eku	130,000

1851-57

☐ 5	**1c Benjamin Franklin**, 7/5/1851, eku...	—
☐ 5A	**1c Benjamin Franklin**, 7/1/1851, First Day Cover (1 known), Boston.	120,000
☐ 6	**1c Benjamin Franklin**, 4/19/1857, eku...	—
☐ 7	**1c Benjamin Franklin**, 7/1/1851, First Day Cover (1 known).........	50,000
	on printed circular dated 7/1/1851 without postmark (4 known) .	4,000
☐ 8A	**1c Benjamin Franklin**, 4/8/1857, eku...	1,300
☐ 9	**1c Benjamin Franklin**, 6/5/1852, eku...	—
☐ 10	**3c George Washington**, 7/1/1851, First Day Cover, any city	
	(43 known)...	12,500
☐ 11	**3c George Washington**, 10/6/1851, eku..	—
☐ 12	**5c Thomas Jefferson Ty I**, 3/24/1856, eku.....................................	—
☐ 13	**10c George Washington Ty I**, 11/14/1855, eku	4,000
☐ 14	**10c George Washington Ty II**, 5/12/1855, eku...............................	3,750
☐ 15	**10c George Washington Ty III**, 5/19/1855, eku..............................	5,500
☐ 16	**10c George Washington recut Ty IV**, 7/10/1855, eku	—
☐ 17	**12c George Washington**, 8/4/1851, eku..	4,000
	The 4 varieties of the 10c 1855, Sc 13-16, all came from one plate, but to date, only Scott 14-15 are known used in May, 1855.	

1857-61

☐ 18	**1c Benjamin Franklin**, 1/25/1861, eku...	—
☐ 19	**1c Benjamin Franklin**, 8/1/1857, eku...	7,500
☐ 20	**1c Benjamin Franklin**, 7/25/1857, eku...	625.00
☐ 21	**1c Benjamin Franklin**, 9/19/1857, eku...	4,000
☐ 22	**1c Benjamin Franklin**, 7/26/1857, eku...	—
☐ 23	**1c Benjamin Franklin**, 7/25/1857, eku...	2,500
☐ 24	**1c Benjamin Franklin**, 11/17/1857, eku...	—
	Listed above are the earliest-known uses for the 1c 1857 varieties. These varieties are found on a number of plates, hence the different earliest-known use dates.	

	25	3c George Washington, 2/28/1857, eku............................	—
	26	3c George Washington, 9/14/1857, eku............................	—
	26a	3c George Washington, 6/11/1857, eku............................	6,500
	27	5c Thomas Jefferson Ty I, 10/6/1858, eku......................	6,500
	28	5c Thomas Jefferson Ty I, 8/23/1857, eku......................	4,500
	28A	5c Thomas Jefferson Ty I, 3/31/1858, eku......................	—
	29	5c Thomas Jefferson Ty I, 3/21/1859, eku......................	—
	30	5c Thomas Jefferson Ty II,5/8/1861, eku.......................	—
	30A	5c Thomas Jefferson Ty II, 5/4/1860, eku......................	—
	31	10c George Washington, Ty I, 9/21/1857, eku	6,500
	32	10c George Washington, Ty II, 7/27/1857, eku	6,500
		The four varieties of the 10c 1857, Scott 31-34, all come from one plate, but to date, only Scott 32 is known postmarked July 27, 1857.	
	33	10c George Washington, Ty III, 10/15/1857, eku..........................	6,500
	34	10c George Washington, Ty IV, 9 or 12/5/1857, eku..................	—
	35	10c George Washington, 4/29/1859, eku............................	—
	36	12c George Washington, 7/30/1857, eku............................	5,000
	36b	12c George Washington, 6/1/1860, eku.............................	—
	37	24c Benjamin Franklin, 7/7/1860, eku.............................	—
	38	30c Benjamin Franklin, 8/8/1860, eku.............................	—
	39	90c Benjamin Franklin, 9/11/1860, eku...........................	8,500

1861-66

	62B	10c George Washington, 9/17/1861, New York, NY, eku	3,000
	64	3c George Washington, 8/17/1861, First Day Cover (1 known)	17,500
	64b	3c George Washington, Rose Pink 8/17/1861, First Day Cover (1 known)................................	23,000
	65	3c George Washington, 8/19/1861, eku............................	1,100
	67	5c Thomas Jefferson, buff, 8/19/1861, eku	—
	67a	5c Thomas Jefferson, (brown-yellow), 8/21/1861,eku	1,300
	68	10c George Washington, 8/20/1861, eku...........................	1,500
	69	12c George Washington, 8/30/1861, eku...........................	475.00
	70	24c George Washington, 1/7/1862, eku............................	3,750
	70c	24c George Washington, 8/20/1861, eku...........................	13,000
	71	30c Benjamin Franklin, 8/20/1861, eku...........................	1,000
	72	90c George Washington, 11/27/1861, eku..........................	—
	73	2c Andrew Jackson, 7/6/1863, eku...............................	5,000
	75	5c Thomas Jefferson, 1/2/1862, eku	—
	76	5c Thomas Jefferson, 2/3/1863, eku	—
	77	15c Abraham Lincoln, 4/14/1866, eku	5,000
	78	24c George Washington, 10/29/1862, eku..........................	—

1867 Grilled Issue

	79	3c George Washington, A Grill, 8/13/1867, eku...................	2,000
	83	3c George Washington, C Grill, 11/19/1867, eku..................	1,000
	85E	12c George Washington, E Grill, 2/15/1868, eku..................	4,500
	92	1c Benjamin Franklin, F Grill, 8/11/1868, eku	3,500

1869

	112	1c Benjamin Franklin, 4/1/1869, eku............................	10,000
	113	2c Post Horse & Rider, 3/20/1869, eku	12,500
	114	3c Locomotive, 3/27/1869, eku	—
	115	6c Washington, 4/26/1869, eku	1,450
	116	10c Shield & Eagle, 4/1/1869, eku	—
	117	12c S.S. Adriatic, 4/1/1869, eku	—
	118	15c Landing of Columbus Ty I, 4/2/1869, eku	1,700

SCOTT NUMBER	DESCRIPTION	UNCACHETED SINGLE
☐ 119	15c Landing of Columbus Ty II, 4/5/1869, eku	—
☐ 120	24c Declaration of Independence, 4/7/1869, eku	—
☐ 121	30c Shield, Eagle & Flags, 5/22/1869, eku	—

1870-71

☐ 133	1c Buff Re-issue, 10/5/1880, eku	3,500
☐ 134	1c Franklin, 4/9/1870, eku	—
☐ 135	2c Jackson, 7/14/1870, eku	—
☐ 136	3c Washington, 3/24/1870, eku	—
☐ 138	7c Stanton, 2/12/1871, eku	—
☐ 139	10c Jefferson, 6/2/1870, eku	3,500
☐ 140	12c Clay, 2/10/1872, eku	—
☐ 141	15c Webster, 6/2/1870, eku	5,000
☐ 142	24c Winfield Scott, 7/11/1872, eku	—
☐ 143	30c Hamilton, 8/23/70, eku	—
☐ 145	1c Franklin, 5/7/1870, eku	4,000
☐ 147	3c Washington, 3/1/1870, eku	5,000
☐ 148	6c Lincoln, 3/28/1870, eku	—
☐ 149	7c Stanton, 5/11/1871, eku	—
☐ 150	10c Jefferson, 5/25/1870, eku	—
☐ 151	12c Clay, 7/9/1870, eku	—
☐ 152	15c Webster, 6/24/1870, eku	—
☐ 153	24c Scott, 11/18/1870, eku	8,000
☐ 154	30c Hamilton, 7/13/1870, eku	—
☐ 155	90c Perry, 9/1/1872, eku	—

1873

☐ 156	1c Franklin, 8/22/1873, eku	—
☐ 157	2c Jackson, 7/12/1873, eku	—
☐ 158	3c Washington, 7/17/1873, eku	—
☐ 159	6c Lincoln, 6/8/1873, eku	—
☐ 160	7c Stanton, 9/10/1873, eku	—
☐ 161	10c Jefferson, 8/2/1873, eku	—
☐ 162	12c Clay, 1/3/1874, eku	—
☐ 163	15c Webster, 7/22/1873, eku	—
☐ 165	30c Hamilton, 10/14/1874, eku	2,000
☐ 166	90c Perry, 6/25/1875, eku	5,000

1875

☐ 178	2c Jackson, 7/15/1875, eku	—
☐ 179	5c Taylor, 7/10/1875, eku	1,000

1879

☐ 182	1c Franklin, 1/3/1879, eku	—
☐ 183	2c Jackson, 12/18/1878, eku	325.00
☐ 184	3c Washington, 8/3/1878, eku	—
☐ 185	5c Taylor, 2/26/1879, eku	—
☐ 186	6c Lincoln, 7/1/1879, eku	—
☐ 187	10c Jefferson, 9/5/1879, eku	—
☐ 188	10c Jefferson (w/secret mark), 10/5/1878, eku	—
☐ 189	15c Webster, 5/29/1879, eku	—
☐ 190	30c Hamilton, 8/8/1881, eku	1,600
☐ 191	90c Perry, 6/24/1882, eku	—

1881-88

☐	205	5c Garfield, 2/18/82, eku	—
		The designated first day for Scott 205 was 4/10/1882, but stamps were legitimately sold as early as 2/18. Curiously, no 4/10 covers are currently known. ....
☐	206	1c Franklin, 11/2/1881, eku	500
☐	207	3c Washington, 8/7/1881, eku	500
☐	208	6c Lincoln, 6/1/1882, eku	1,500
☐	209	10c Thomas Jefferson, 5/4/1882, eku	—
☐	210	2c Washington, 10/1/1883, any city, First Day Cover (80-100 known)	2,000
☐	211	4c Andrew Jackson, 10/1/1883, First Day Cover, no solo usage known	—
☐		Scott 210 & 211 on one cover (1 known)	35,000
☐	212	1c Franklin, 7/15/1887, eku	—
☐	213	3c Washington, 9/21/1887, eku	—
☐	214	3c Washington, 10/18/1887, eku	—
☐	215	4c Jackson, 1/18/1889, eku....................	3,000
☐	216	5c Garfield, 3/15/1888, eku	2,500
☐	217	30c Andrew Jackson, 9/7/1888, eku.............	8,000

1890

☐	219	1c Franklin, 2/27/1890, eku....................	2,000
☐	219D	2c Washington, 2/22/1890, First Day Cover (1 known)	12,500
☐	220	2c Washington, 4/29/1890, eku	—
☐	221	3c Jackson, 2/28/1890, eku....................	—
☐	222	4c Lincoln, 7/16/1890, eku	—
☐	223	5c Grant, 6/14/1890, Haddonfield NJ, eku..........	—
☐	224	6c Garfield, 5/30/1890, eku	—
☐	225	8c Sherman, 5/21/1893, eku	—
☐	226	10c Webster, 4/7/1890, eku	—
☐	227	15c Clay, 2/25/1890, eku.....................	—
☐	228	30c Jefferson, 4/14/1890, eku.................	5,000
☐	229	90c Perry, 2/7/1892, eku	10,000

1893

☐	230	1c Columbian, 1/1/1893, First Day Cover	4,000
☐	231	2c Columbian, 1/1/1893, First Day Cover	3,500
☐	232	3c Columbian, 1/1/1893, First Day Cover	6,000
☐	233	4c Columbian, 1/1/1893, First Day Cover	9,000
☐	234	5c Columbian, 1/1/1893, First Day Cover	15,000
☐	235	6c Columbian, 1/2/1893, First Day Cover	18,000
☐	236	8c Columbian, 3/18/1893, First Day Cover	18,000
☐	237	10c Columbian, 1/1/1893, First Day Cover	7,500
☐	238	15c Columbian, 1/26/1893, eku..................	8,000
☐	239	30c Columbian, 2/8/1893, eku	—
☐	240	50c Columbian, 2/8/1893, eku	—
☐	241	$1 Columbian, 1/21/1893, eku..................	—
☐	242	$2 Columbian, 1/2/1893, First Day Cover	52,500
☐	243	$3 Columbian, 3/24/1893, eku	15,000
☐	244	$4 Columbian, 3/24/1893, eku	15,000
☐	245	$5 Columbian, 1/6/1893, eku...................	—
		Since Jan. 1, 1893 was a Sunday, few post offices were open. January 1st and January 2nd are both collected as First Day Covers. Several values are known with Dec. 30 or Dec. 31, 1892 pre-dates.

1894-95

☐	246	**1c Franklin (ultramarine)**, 10/17/1894, eku	1,200
☐	247	**1c Franklin (blue)**, 11/11/1894, eku	—
☐	248	**2c Washington**, 10/16/1894, eku	—
☐	249	**2c Washington**, 10/11/1894, eku	—
☐	250	**2c Washington**, 10/17/1894, eku	600.00
☐	251	**2c Washington**, 2/16/1895, eku	800
☐	252	**2c Washington**, 4/5/1895, eku	—
☐	253	**3c Jackson**, 11/15/1894, eku..	—
☐	254	**4c Lincoln**, 12/5/1894, eku..	—
☐	255	**5c Grant**, 10/23/1894, eku	—
☐	256	**6c Garfield**, 8/11/1894, eku	—
☐	257	**8c Sherman**, 5/8/1895, eku	2,000
☐	258	**10c Webster**, 11/19/1894, eku..	—
☐	259	**15c Clay**, 12/6/1894, eku	—
☐	260	**50c Jefferson**, 1/15/1895, eku..	—
☐	261	**$1 Perry, (Ty I)**, 1/18/1895, eku..	6,000
☐	261A	**$1 Perry (Ty II)**, 3/22/1895, eku...	6,000
☐	262	**$2 Madison**, 7/18/1895, eku...	7,500
☐	263	**$5 John Marshall** unwatermarked dark green, 7/6/1896, (not known on cover) eku..	9,000
☐	264	**1c Franklin** watermarked blue, 5/16/1895, eku	1,500
☐	265	**2c Washington** watermarked carmine Type I, 5/2/1895, First Day Cover (1 known)..	12,500
☐	266	**2c Washington** watermarked carmine Type II, 5/27/1895, eku	
☐	267	**2c Washington** watermarked carmine Type III,5/31/1895, eku on cover	—
☐	268	**3c Andrew Jackson** watermarked purple, 2/18/1896, eku	
☐	269	**4c Lincoln** watermarked dark brown, 9/25/1895, eku	1,500
☐	270	**5c Grant** watermarked chocolate, 9/14/1895, eku	1,500
☐	271	**6c Garfield** watermarked dull brown, 9/14/1895, eku	1,500
☐	272	**8c Sherman** watermarked violet brown, 12/24/1895, eku	1,500
☐	273	**10c Daniel Webster** watermarked dark green, 7/25/1895 eku	2,500
☐	274	**15c Henry Clay** watermarked dark blue, 5/6/1896, eku	
☐	275	**50c Jefferson** watermarked orange, 2/27/1896, eku....................	3,500
☐	276	**$1 Commodore Perry** watermarked black Type I, 3/1/1898, eku..	—
☐	276A	**$1 Commodore Perry** watermarked black Type II, 4/6/1896, eku .	10,000
☐	277	**$2 James Madison** watermarked bright blue, 7/18/1895, eku.......	12,000
☐	278	**$5 John Marshall** watermarked dark green, 11/3/1896, eku	15,000

1897-98

☐	279	**1c Franklin**, 1/31/1898, eku..	—
☐	279B	**2c Washington (Ty IV)**, 7/6/1899, eku	—
☐	280	**4c Lincoln**, 11/3/1898, eku..	1,500
☐	281	**5c Grant**, 3/19/1898, eku	—
☐	282	**6c Garfield**, 3/13/1899, eku	1,500
☐	282C	**10c Webster (Ty I)**, 12/27/1898, eku..	—
☐	283	**10c Webster (Ty II)**, 3/13/1899, eku	—
☐	284	**15c Clay**, 5/1/1899, eku	3,000
☐	285	**1c Marquette on the Mississippi**, 6/17/1898, First Day Cover, DC, NY..	12,500
☐	286	**2c Farming in the West**, 6/17/1898, First Day Cover, DC, & NY, Baltimore, Omaha, NB	12,000
		Pittsburgh, PA..	7,000
☐	286	6/16/1898, eku, Harrisburg, PA or Camden, NJ............................	13,000

☐	287	4c Indian Hunting Buffalo, 6/17/1898, First Day Cover, DC	25,000
☐	288	5c Fremont on the Rocky Mountains, 6/17/1898, First Day Cover, DC	20,000
☐		Scott 285, 287-288 on 1 cover, 6/17/1898, First Day Cover, DC	30,000
☐	289	8c Troops Guarding Trains, 6/17/1898, First Day Cover, DC, NY ..	25,000
☐	290	10c Hardships of Emigration, 6/17/1898, First Day Cover	25,000
☐		Scott 285-290 on one cover , 6/17/1898 one known..................	50,000
☐	291	50c Western Mining Prospector, 6/17/1898, First Day Cover, 1 known	30,000
☐	292	$1 Western Cattle in a Storm, 6/17/1898, First Day Cover, 1 known	35,000
☐	293	$2 Mississippi River Bridge, 6/24/1898, eku..................................	—

1901

☐	294	1c Fast Lake Navigation, 5/1/1901, First Day Cover (13 known)...	4,800
☐	295	2c "Empire State Express", 5/1/1901, First Day Cover (50-60 known)	2,500
☐	297	5c Bridge at Niagara Falls, 5/1/1901, First Day Cover	15,000
☐		294, 295, 297 on one cover, 5/1/1901, First Day Cover	9,500
☐		294, 296, 297 on one cover, 5/1/1901, First Day Cover	22,500
☐		295, 298 on one cover, 5/1/1901, First Day Cover	9,500
☐		296, 298 on one cover, 5/1/1901, First Day Cover	15,000
☐		297, 298 on one cover, 5/1/1901, First Day Cover	15,000
☐		Scott 294-299, complete set of 6 on one cover, 5/1/01 (9 known)..	30,000

1902-08 (Regular Issue)

☐	300	1c Franklin, 2/3/03, eku..	1,200
☐	301	2c Washington, 1/17/03, First Day Cover	2,750
☐	302	3c Jackson, 3/21/03, eku...	—
☐	303	4c Grant, 3/13/03, eku...	1,200
☐	304	5c Lincoln, 2/10/03, eku..	—
☐	305	6c Garfield, 5/8/03, eku	—
☐	306	8c Martha Washington, 12/27/02, eku	—
☐	307	10c Webster, 3/12/03, eku...	1,500
☐	308	13c Harrison, 11/18/02, eku	7,500
☐	309	15c Clay, 9/11/03, eku	—
☐	310	50c Jefferson, 6/4/03, eku...	—
☐	311	$1 Farragut, 9/30/03, eku..	—
☐	312	$2 Madison, 2/17/04, eku..	—
☐	313	$5 Marshall, 2/17/04, eku..	—
☐	314	1c Franklin (imperf), 2/4/07, eku	—
☐	315	5c Lincoln (imperf pair), 9/15/08, eku	—
☐	319	2c Washington, 11/19/03, eku	—
☐	320	2c Washington (imperf), 10/26/06, eku...	4,000
☐	321	2c Washington (imperf), 10/2/08, eku (2 known on cover)............	170,000

1904

☐	323	1c Livingston, 4/30/04, First Day Cover (6 known)	6,000
☐	324	2c Jefferson, 4/30/04, First Day Cover (10-15 known)..................	5,000
☐		pre-dates exist as early as 4/20/04	
☐	325	3c Monroe, 4/30/04, First Day Cover (5 known)	6,000
☐		323, 324, 325 pre-dates on one cover...	15,000
☐	326	5c McKinley, 4/30/04, First Day Cover (approx. 5 known)	21,000
☐	327	10c Map of Louisiana Purchase, 4/30/04, First Day Cover (2 known)..	22,000
☐		Scott 323-327 on one cover, 4/30/04 (1 known)	90,000

Notice was sent to postmasters that this set was being shipped from Washington on Apr. 21, but could not be sold to the public before Apr. 30, 1904. Because of these instructions, any cover dated before Apr. 30, 1904, is considered a pre-dated cover.

1907

☐	328	1c Capt. John Smith, 4/26/07, First Day Cover (6 known)	6,000
☐	329	2c Founding of Jamestown, 4/26/07, First Day Cover (2 known)..	9,000
☐	330	5c Pocahontas, 5/8/07, eku	15,000

1908-09 (Regular Issue)

☐	331	1c Franklin, 12/1/08, eku..............	—
☐	331a	1c Franklin (booklet single), 12/2/08, First Day Cover (1 known).	18,000
☐	332	2c Washington, 12/3/08, eku	2,000
☐	332a	2c Washington (booklet single), 11/16/08, First Day Cover	
		(1 known)........	35,000
☐	333	3c Washington (Ty I), 1/12/09, eku......	1,000
☐	334	4c Washington, 1/12/09, eku	—
☐	335	5c Washington, 1/12/09, eku........	1,000
☐	336	6c Washington, 1/6/09, eku	1,200
☐	337	8c Washington, 1/8/09, eku..........	1,000
☐	338	10c Washington, 2/1/09, eku (2 known)	1,000
☐	339	13c Washington, 3/5/09, eku	—
☐	340	15c Washington, 3/12/09, eku......	—
☐	341	50c Washington, 10/23/09, eku	2,500
☐	343	1c Franklin (imperf), 1/4/09, eku..	—
☐	344	2c Washington (imperf), 2/1/09, eku........	—
☐	345	3c Washington (Ty I, imperf), 2/13/09, eku........	—
☐	346	4c Washington (imperf), 3/13/09, eku........	—
☐	347	5c Washington (imperf), 3/4/09, eku........	—
☐	348	1c Franklin (coil), 1/25/09, eku ..	—
☐	349	2c Washington (coil), 5/14/09, eku........	—
☐	350	4c Washington (coil), 8/21/12, eku........	—
☐	351	5c Washington (coil), 9/21/09, eku........	1,050
☐	352	1c Franklin (coil), 3/30/09, eku..	1,050
☐	353	2c Washington (coil), 6/14/09, eku........	—
☐	354	4c Washington (coil), 6/9/09, eku........	1,650
☐	355	5c Washington (coil), 10/25/09, eku........	1,650
☐	356	10c Washington (coil), 3/9/09, eku........	1,650
☐	357	1c Franklin (blue paper), 2/22/09, eku........	1,100
☐	358	2c Washington (blue paper), 2/23/09, eku........	750.00
☐	359	3c Washington (blue paper), 12/27/10, eku........	—
☐	361	5c Washington (blue paper), 6/20/10, eku........	—
☐	362	6c Washington (blue paper), 9/14/11, eku........	—
☐	364	10c Washington (blue paper), 2/3/10,eku........	15,000
☐	366	15c Washington (blue paper), 1/15/11, eku........	—

1909

☐	367	2c Lincoln, 2/12/09, any city, First Day Cover (508 known)	500.00
☐		on Lincoln-related post-card........	600.00
☐		pre-dated covers exist as early as 2/8/09 (20 known)	700.00
☐	368	2c Lincoln (imperf), 2/12/09, First Day Cover (6 known).............	13,000
☐	369	2c Lincoln (blue paper), 3/27/09, eku	—

Feb. 12, 1909 was designated as the official First Day of the Lincoln stamp. A total of 277 different cities from 42 states and Puerto Rico are known on Scott 367's FDCs, with Boston, MA and Canton, OH being the most common.

☐	370	**2c Alaska-Yukon**, 5/29/09, First Day Cover (57 known)	3,000
☐		on expo-related post-card (approx. 15 known)	4,000
☐		covers dated 6/1/09,	2,000
☐	371	**2c Alaska-Yukon (imperf)**, 6/7/09, Richmond, VA, (4 known), eku.	—
☐	372	**2c Hudson-Fulton** 9/25/09, any city, First Day Cover	
		(152 known)	800.00
☐		**9/25/09**, Lancaster PA, on 2-part Hudson-Fulton post-card	1,500
		Pre-dates exist as early as 9/23/09 (2 known) and 9/24/09 (33 known).	
		A total of 29 different cities in 10 states are known for this issue.	
☐	373	**2c Hudson-Fulton (imperf)**, 9/25/09, First Day Cover,	
		Poughkeepsie, NY (1 known)	7,500
☐	374	**1c Franklin**, 2/13/11, eku.	—
☐	374a	**1c Franklin** Booklet pane stamp, 4/19/11, eku	700.00

1911-13

☐	390	**1c Franklin (endwise coil)**, 10/18/11, eku	2,000
☐	391	**2c Washington (endwise coil)**, 5/3/11, eku	—
☐	392	**1c Franklin (sidewise coil)**, 12/16/10, eku	1,650
☐	393	**2c Washington (sidewise coil)**, 12/27/10, eku	550.00
☐	394	**3c Washington (sidewise coil)**, 9/18/11, Orangeburg, NY, eku	550.00
☐	395	**4c Washington (sidewise coil)**, 6/21/12, eku	1,650
☐	396	**5c Washington (sidewise coil)**, 5/14/13, eku	950.00

1913-15

☐	397	**1c Balboa (perf 12)**, 1/1/13, First Day Cover .... (10-15 known)	5,000
☐	398	**2c Pedro Miguel Locks (perf 12)**, 1/17/13, eku	425.00
☐	399	**5c Golden Gate (perf 12)**, 1/1/13, First Day Cover (1 known)	19,000
☐	400	**10c San Francisco Bay (perf 12**, orange-yellow), 1/1/13,	
		First Day Cover, (2 known)	10,000
☐		Scott 397, 399 & 400 on one cover, 1/1/13, San Francisco CA	9,000
☐	400A	**10c San Francisco Bay (perf 12**, orange), 11/20/13, eku	3,500
☐	401	**1c Balboa (perf 10)**, 12/21/14, eku	—
☐	402	**2c Pedro Miguel Locks (perf 10)**, 1/13/15, eku	880.00
☐	403	**5c Golden Gate (perf 10)**, 2/6/15, eku	6,250
☐	404	**10c San Francisco Bay (perf 10)**, 8/27/15, eku	5,000

1912-15 (Regular Issue)

☐	405	**1c Washington**, 2/2/12, eku	950.00
☐	405b	**1c Washington (booklet)**, 1/16/12, eku	950.00
☐	406	**2c Washington**, 2/15/12, eku	—
☐	406a	**2c Washington (booklet)**, 5/2/12, eku	—
☐	407	**7c Washington**, 5/1/14, eku (probably a first day cover)	—
		Scott 407, 415, 419, 420 & 421 on one cover, 5/1/14	15,000
☐	408	**1c Washington (imperf)**, 3/27/12, eku	—
☐	408	**1c Washington (Kansas City Roulette perfs)**, 10/22/14, eku	—
☐	409	**2c Washington (imperf)**, 4/15/12, eku	—
☐	409	**2c Washington (w/Schermack III perfs)**, 5/14/12, eku	—
☐	409	**2c Washington (Kansas City Roulette perfs)**, 11/25/14, eku	—
☐	410	**1c Washington (endwise coil)**, 4/17/12, eku	1,500
☐	411	**2c Washington (endwise coil)**, 5/1/12, eku	—
☐	412	**1c Washington (sidewise coil)**, 5/31/12, eku	—
☐	413	**2c Washington (sidewise coil)**, 3/21/12, eku	—
☐	414	**8c Franklin**, 4/20/12, eku	—
☐	415	**9c Franklin**, 5/1/14, eku (probably a first day cover)	—
☐	416	**10c Franklin**, 2/12/12, eku	1,200
☐	417	**12c Franklin**, 5/5/14, eku	—

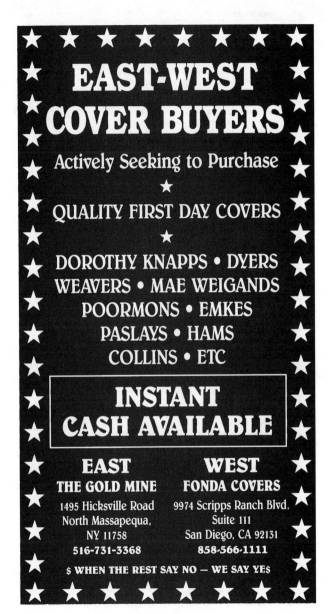

	SCOTT NUMBER	DESCRIPTION	UNCACHETED SINGLE
☐	418	15c Franklin, 4/26/12, eku	1,400
☐	419	20c Franklin, 5/1/14, eku (probably a first day cover)	—
☐	420	30c Franklin, 5/1/14, eku (probably a first day cover)	—
☐	421	50c Franklin (sng line wmrk), 5/1/14, eku (probably a first day cover)	—
☐	422	50c Franklin (dbl line wmrk), 7/15/15, eku	—
☐	423	$1 Franklin (dbl line wmrk), 7/15/15, eku	7,000
☐	424	1c Washington, 10/21/14, eku	—
☐	424a	1c Washington (perf 12x10), 1/8/14, eku	—
☐	424	1c Washington (coil waste), 8/2/15, First Day Cover	5,000
☐	424d	1c Washington (booklet single), 12/20/13, eku	—
☐	425	2c Washington, 11/6/14, eku	—
☐	425e	2c Washington (booklet single), 1/6/14, eku	450.00
☐	426	3c Washington, 10/11/14, eku	—
☐	427	4c Washington, 1/19/15, eku	—
☐	428	5c Washington, 12/2/13, eku	—
☐	428a	5c Washington (perf 12x10), 4/14/15, eku	—
☐	429	6c Washington, 2/6/15, eku	—
☐	430	7c Washington, 6/19/15, eku	—
☐	431	8c Franklin, 1/20/15, eku	—
☐	432	9c Franklin, 2/25/16, eku	—
☐	433	10c Franklin, 11/13/14, eku	—
☐	434	11c Franklin, 10/8/15, eku	—
☐	435	12c Franklin, 2/23/15, eku	—
☐	437	15c Franklin, 11/1/15, eku	—
☐	438	20c Franklin, 11/28/14, eku	—
☐	439	30c Franklin, 2/13/15, eku	—
☐	441	1c Washington (endwise coil), 2/16/15, eku	—
☐	442	2c Washington (endwise coil), 7/22/14, eku	475.00
☐	443	1c Washington (sidewise coil), 6/19/14, eku	1,650
☐	444	2c Washington (sidewise coil), 5/20/14, eku	1,650
☐	445	3c Washington (sidewise coil), 7/1/16, eku	—
☐	446	4c Washington (sidewise coil), 8/4/15, eku	1,600
☐	447	5c Washington (sidewise coil), 5/9/16, eku	—
☐	448	1c Washington (endwise coil), 3/29/16, eku	—
☐	449	2c Washington Ty I (endwise coil), 10/29/15, eku	—
☐	450	2c Washington Ty III (endwise coil), 12/21/15, eku	1,650
☐	452	1c Washington (sidewise coil), 11/25/14, eku	—
☐	453	2c Washington Ty I (sidewise coil), 10/6/14, eku	—
☐	454	2c Washington Ty II (sidewise coil), 7/7/15, eku	—
☐	455	2c Washington Ty III (sidewise coil), 12/15/15, eku	—
☐	456	3c Washington (sidewise coil), 4/13/16, eku	—
☐	457	4c Washington (sidewise coil), 11/5/15, eku	770.00
☐	458	5c Washington (sidewise coil), 4/6/16, eku	1,650
☐	460	$1 Franklin, 5/25/16, eku	—
☐	461	2c Washington (perf 11), 7/14/15, eku	4,000

1916-17

	SCOTT NUMBER	DESCRIPTION	UNCACHETED SINGLE
☐	462	1c Washington, 10/25/16, eku	—
☐	463	2c Washington, 9/12/16, eku	—
☐	464	3c Washington, 3/9/17, eku	800.00
☐	465	4c Washington, 2/18/17, eku	—
☐	466	5c Washington, 12/18/16, eku	—
☐	467	5c Washington carmine (color error), 5/22/17, eku	3,500
☐	468	7c Washington, 11/21/17, eku	—
☐	470	8c Franklin, 10/17/17, eku	—
☐	472	10c Franklin, 12/29/16, eku	—

	473	11c Franklin, 4/13/17, eku	—
	474	12c Franklin, 10/13/16, eku.	—
	475	15c Franklin, 3/2/17, eku.	—
	477	50c Franklin, 8/31/17, eku.	—
	478	$1 Franklin, 11/9/17, eku	—
	479	$2 Madison, 4/6/17, eku.	—
	480	$5 Marshall, 4/6/17, eku.	—
	481	1c Washington (imperf), 11/17/16, eku..........	800.00
	482	2c Washington (imperf), 1/9/17, eku.	—
	482A	2c Washington (Ty Ia, imperf w/Schermack III perfs), 2/17/20, eku.	20,000
	483	3c Washington (Ty I, imperf), 11/2/17, eku	2,000
	484	3c Washington (Ty II, imperf), 4/5/18, eku..........	—

1916-22

	486	1c Washington (endwise coil), 6/30/18, eku	—
	489	3c Washington Ty I (endwise coil), 2/16/17, eku	—
	490	1c Washington (sidewise coil), 3/16/17, eku.	—
	491	2c Washington Ty II (sidewise coil), 1/2/17, eku	1,650
	493	3c Washington Ty I (sidewise coil), 11/2/17, eku.	1,650
	494	3c Washington Ty II (sidewise coil), 4/16/18, eku	—
	495	4c Washington, 1/17/18, eku	—
	496	5c Washington, 9/11/19, eku	—
	497	10c Washington (sidewise coil), 1/31/22, First Day Cover, DC	4,500
		Only seen serviced by Henry Hammelman (7-10 known)	

1917-19

	498	1c Washington, 4/19/17, eku	—
	498e	1c Washington (booklet), 6/22/17, eku..........	—
	498f	1c Washington (AEF booklet single), 8/8/17, eku..........	4,800
	499	2c Washington, 3/27/17, eku	—
	499e	2c Washington (booklet), 7/19/17, eku.	—
	499f	2c Washington (AEF booklet single), 8/7/17, eku..........	8,000
	500	2c Washington Ty Ia, 12/15/19, eku	1,500
	501	3c Washington Ty I, 7/3/17, eku.	—
	501b	3c Washington Ty I (booklet), 2/8/18, eku	—
	502	3c Washington Ty II, 1/30/18, eku.	—
	502c	3c Washington Ty II (imperf between), 5/7/22, eku	—
	503	4c Washington, 7/17/1917, eku	—
	504	5c Washington, 6/9/1917, eku	—
	505	5c Washington error of color, 3/27/17, eku	4,000
	506	6c Washington, 6/26/1917, eku	—
	507	7c Washington, 8/1/1917, eku	—
	508	8c Franklin, 7/7/1917, eku	1,000
	509	9c Franklin, 10/2/1917, eku..........	—
	510	10c Franklin, 3/27/1917, eku	—
	511	11c Franklin, 12/1/1917, eku.	—
	512	12c Franklin, 10/13/1917, eku.	—
	513	13c Franklin, 2/4/19, eku.	—
	514	15c Franklin, 11/15/1917, eku.	2,000
	515	20c Franklin, 5/4/1918, eku.	2,500
	516	30c Franklin, 1/12/18, eku.	—
	517	50c Franklin, 12/28/1917, eku.	—
	518	$1 Franklin, 5/19/17, eku	—
	519	2c Washington, 10/10/1917, eku	—

1918-20

☐ 523	$2 Franklin, 12/17/18, eku	—
☐ 524	$5 Franklin, 7/20/26, eku	—
☐ 525	1c Washington, 12/24/18, eku	—
☐ 526	2c Washington Ty IV, 3/15/20, First Day Cover (50-75 exist).........	1,000
☐ 527	2c Washington Ty V, 4/20/20, eku	—
☐ 528A	2c Washington Ty VI, 7/30/20, eku	—
☐ 528B	2c Washington Ty VII, 11/10/20, eku	—
☐ 529	3c Washington Ty III, 4/8/18, eku.................................	2,200
☐ 530	3c Washington Ty IV, 6./30/18, eku	—
☐ 533	2c Washington Ty V (imperf), 6/30/20, eku	2,500
☐ 534B	2c Washington Ty VII (imperf), 10/20/20, eku, ...	4,000
☐ 535	3c Washington Ty IV (imperf), 10/5/18, eku	1,400

1919

☐ 536	1c Washington, 8/21/19, eku	4,000
☐ 537	3c Victory Issue, 3/3/19, First Day Cover (75-100 known)........	800.00
☐ 538	1c Washington, 6/28/19	—
☐ 539	2c Washington rotary carmine Type II, 6/30/19, eku	30,000
☐ 540	2c Washington, Type II, 6/27/19, eku	1,750
☐ 541	3c Washington, 6/14/19, eku	—

1920

☐ 542	1c Washington, 5/26/20, First Day Cover (40-50 known).............	2,000
☐ 543	1c Washington, 5/29/21, eku	1,000
☐ 544	1c Washington, 12/21/22, eku (2 known)	5,000
☐ 548	1c The Mayflower, 12/21/20, First Day Cover (30-50 exist)	1,000
☐ 549	2c Landing of the Pilgrims, 12/20/20, First Day Cover (3 known).	5,000
	covers dated 12/21/20 (50-75 exist)	750.00
☐ 550	5c Signing the Compact, 12/21/20, First Day Cover (5-10 known)	2,500
	full set of three on one cover, 12/21/20 (15-20 known)	3,500
☐	Scott 548-550 predate 12/18/20, Plymouth, MA	1,600
☐	Pre-dates for 12/20/20 from Plymouth, MA (3 known)	1,200
☐	Blocks of four on 548-550 12/21/20, DC First Day Cover	2,200

1922-26

☐ 551	1/2c Nathan Hale, 4/4/25, DC.................................18.00		
☐	New Haven, CT 25.00		
☐	Unofficial city (20-30 known) 175.00		
☐	Scott 551 & 576 (1/2c Hale & 1 1/2c Harding imperf.)		
	on one cover, DC...150.00		
☐ 552	1c Benjamin Franklin, 1/17/23, DC, pair...............25.00	30.00	
☐	Philadelphia, PA 45.00	60.00	
☐	Norristown, PA 50.00		
☐	Unofficial city (7 known) 175.00		
☐ 553	1 1/2c Warren G. Harding, 3/19/25, DC, pair.............30.00	35.00	
☐	Scott 553, 582, 598 on Scott U482......................175.00		
☐	Scott 553 on Scott U481 Plate Block combination,		
	First Day Cover..500.00		
☐	Unofficial city, (7 known) 150.00		
☐ 554	2c George Washington, 1/15/23, DC.......................40.00	50.00	
☐	Unofficial city Alexandria, VA, Allentown, PA...........300.00		

| 551 | 552, 581, 597, 604 | 553, 576, 582, 598, 605, 631 | 557 | 562 |

| 565 | 567 | 571 | 572 | 573 |

1st George W. Linn cachet   610, 611, 612   614

615   616   617

1st Guy Atwood Jackson cachet   618   619

1st Ernest J. Weschcke cachet   1st Albert C. Roessler cachet

620   621   622   623

14

☐		Scott 554 & 556, Scott 554 & 561, Scott 554 & 562	
		on one cover 250.00	
☐	555	**3c Abraham Lincoln,** 2/12/23, DC 40.00	50.00
☐		Hodgenville, KY 250.00	375.00
☐		Unofficial city (9 known) 200.00	—
☐	556	**4c Martha Washington,** 1/15/23, DC 60.00	100.00
☐		Scott 556 & 561 combination 250.00	
☐		Scott 556 unofficial city (1 known) 300.00	
☐	557	**5c Theodore Roosevelt,** 10/27/22, DC 125.00	175.00
☐		New York, NY 200.00	300.00
☐		Oyster Bay, NY ....2,000.	2,500.
☐	558	**6c James A. Garfield,** 11/20/22, DC 225.00	300.00
☐	559	**7c William McKinley,** 5/1/23, DC 175.00	200.00
☐		Niles, OH 200.00	300.00
☐		Scott 559-560 on one cover 700.00	
☐	560	**8c U.S. Grant,** 5/1/23, DC 175.00	200.00
☐	561	**9c Thomas Jefferson,** 1/15/23, DC 175.00	200.00
☐		Scott 561 on Scott U420 ....300.00	
☐	562	**10c James Monroe,** 1/15/23, DC 175.00	200.00
☐		Scott 554, 556, 561, 562 on one cover ....2,500.	
☐	563	**11c Rutherford B. Hayes,** 10/4/22, DC 600.00	775.00
☐		Fremont, OH (51 known) ....4,000.	
☐	564	**12c Grover Cleveland,** 3/20/23, DC 175.00	200.00
☐		Boston, MA (Philatelic Exhibition) 175.00	200.00
☐		Caldwell, NJ 200.00	225.00
☐		Lynn, MA 400.00	
☐	565	**14c American Indian,** 5/1/23, DC 400.00	600.00
☐		Muskogee, OK ....1,250.	6,500.
☐		Scott 565 and 560 on one cover, DC ....2,200.	
☐	566	**15c Statue of Liberty,** 11/11/22, DC 600.00	
☐	567	**20c Golden Gate,** 5/1/23, DC 600.00	
☐		San Francisco, CA ....1,200.	
☐		Oakland, CA, unofficial city (5 known) ....7,500.	
☐	568	**25c Niagara Falls,** 11/11/22, DC 675.00	1,000.
☐	569	**30c American Buffalo,** 3/20/23, DC 825.00	1,350.
☐		Scott 569 and 564 on one cover, DC (1 known) ....6,000.	
☐	570	**50c Arlington Amphitheater,** 11/11/22, DC ....1,500.	1,650.
☐		Scott 566, 568, 570 on one cover ....7,000.	
☐	571	**$1 Lincoln Memorial,** 2/12/23, DC ....7,000.	
☐		Springfield, IL (17 known) ....6,000.	10,000.
☐		Scott 571,555 on one cover, DC ....10,000.	
		1 exists - legal size	
☐	572	**$2 U.S. Capitol,** 3/20/23, DC ....17,000.	
☐	573	**$5 Head of Freedom Statue,** 3/20/23, DC ....30,000.	
☐	576	**1 1/2c Warren G. Harding,** 4/4/25, DC 45.00	60.00
☐	581	**1c Benjamin Franklin,** unprecanceled 10/17/23, DC (1 known) ....6,500.	
☐	582	**1 1/2c Warren G. Harding,** 3/19/25, DC 50.00	65.00
☐	583	**2c George Washington,** 4/14/24, New York, NY, earliest known use ....—	—
☐	583a	**George Washington,** booklet pane of 6, 8/27/26, DC ....1500.	
☐	584	**3c Abraham Lincoln,** 8/1/25, DC 65.00	90.00
☐	585	**4c Martha Washington,** 4/4/25, DC 65.00	90.00
☐		Unofficial city (3 known) 100.00	
☐	586	**5c Theodore Roosevelt,** 4/4/25, DC 70.00	90.00

☐		Unoffcial city (3 known)	100.00	
☐		585, 586 on one cover	300.00	
☐	587	**6c James A. Garfield**, 4/4/25, DC	70.00	110.00
		Covers exist with Scott 585-587 from DC official), NYC and Philadelphia, RPO (unofficial)		
☐	588	**7c William McKinley**, 5/29/26, DC	75.00	120.00
☐	589	**8c U.S. Grant**, 5/29/26, DC	80.00	125.00
☐	590	**9c Thomas Jefferson**, 5/29/26, DC	80.00	125.00
☐		Scott 588, 589, 590 on one cover	300.00	
☐	591	**10c James Monroe**, 6/8/25, DC	100.00	160.00

1923-29 Coils

☐	597	**1c Benjamin Franklin**, 7/18/23, DC	600.00	750.00
☐	598	**1 1/2c Warren G. Harding**, 3/19/25, DC	60.00	80.00
☐	599	**2c George Washington**, Type I, 1/15/23, DC (37 known)	1,400.	
☐		Lancaster, PA, 1/10/23 (1 known)	3,500.	
☐		South Bend, IN, 1/11/23 (1 known)	1,400.	
☐		**St. Louis**, MO, 1/13/23 (1 known)	1,400.	
		Note: January 10, 1923 is the earliest known use of Scott 599. Philip Ward prepared 37 covers on January 15, 1923, the earliest known use in Washington, DC.		
☐	599A	**2c George Washington**, Type II, 3/29/29, earliest known use	—	
☐	600	**3c Abraham Lincoln**, 5/10/24, DC	90.00	110.00
☐	602	**5c Theodore Roosevelt**, 3/5/24, DC	95.00	125.00
☐	603	**10c James Monroe**, 12/1/24, DC	100.00	150.00
☐	604	**1c Benjamin Franklin**, 7/19/24, DC	90.00	
☐	605	**1 1/2c Warren G. Harding**, 5/9/25, DC	80.00	
☐	606	**2c George Washington**, 12/31/23, DC	140.00	

1923

☐	610	**2c Warren G. Harding**, 9/1/23, DC	30.00	35.00		
☐		Marion, OH (5,000)	20.00	22.50		
☐		Brooklyn, NY; Mt. Rainier, MD; Caledonia, OH (Unofficial cities)	37.50			
☐		**Pre-date**, 8/31/23, DC, (1 known)	250.00			
☐		1st George W. Linn cachet (1st modern cachet)				850.00
☐	611	**2c Warren G. Harding**, imperf. 11/15/23, DC	90.00	110.00		
☐		Pair	100.00			
☐		Pair or Block with line	110.00	160.00		
☐		Center line block		165.00		
☐		Unofficial city	100.00	110.00		
☐	612	**2c Warren G. Harding**, perf 10, 9/12/23, DC	100.00	110.00		

1924

☐	614	**1c Huguenot-Walloon Tercentenary**,				
☐		5/1/24, pair, DC	40.00	45.00		
☐		Albany, NY	40.00	45.00		
☐		Allentown, PA	40.00	45.00		
☐		Charleston, SC	40.00	45.00		
☐		Jacksonville, FL	40.00	45.00		

cover binders

Padded, durable, 3-ring binder will hold up to 100 covers. Features the "D" ring mechanism on the right hand side of album so you don't have to worry about creasing or wrinkling covers when opening or closing binder.

Item	*Description*	*Retail*
CBRD	Cover Binder - Red	$7.95
CBBL	Cover Binder - Blue	$7.95
CBGY	Cover Binder - Gray	$7.95
CBBK	Cover Binder - Black	$7.95

Cover pages sold separately.

T2	Cover Pages Black (25 per pckg)	$4.95
CBBL	Cover Pages Clear (25 per pckg)	$4.95

The cover binders and pages are available from your favorite stamp dealer or direct from:

to order call 1-800-572-6885

17

1st Charles E. Nickles cachet

627

628

1st Herbert H. Griffin cachet

1st James H. Baxter cachet

1st Scott Stamp & Coin Co. cachet

629, 630

643

1st Joshua R. Gerow Jr. cachet

1st Haris R. Hunt cachet

1st Bradie Buchanan cachet

644

645

18

SCOTT NUMBER	DESCRIPTION	UNCACHETED SINGLE	BLOCK	CACHETED SINGLE	BLOCK
	Lancaster, PA	40.00	45.00		
	Mayport, FL	40.00	45.00		
	New Rochelle, NY	40.00	45.00		
	New York, NY	40.00	45.00		
	Philadelphia, PA	40.00	45.00		
	Reading, PA	40.00	45.00		
	Unofficial city	65.00			
615	2c Huguenot-Walloon Tercentenary, 5/1/24, DC	60.00	65.00		
	Albany, NY	60.00	65.00		
	Allentown, PA	60.00	65.00		
	Charleston, SC	60.00	65.00		
	Jacksonville, FL	60.00	65.00		
	Lancaster, PA	60.00	65.00		
	Mayport, FL	60.00	65.00		
	New Rochelle, NY	60.00	65.00		
	New York, NY	60.00	65.00		
	Philadelphia, PA	60.00	65.00		
	Reading, PA	60.00	65.00		
	Unofficial city	80.00			
616	5c Huguenot-Walloon Tercentenary, 5/1/24, DC	80.00	85.00		
	Albany, NY	80.00	85.00		
	Allentown, PA	80.00	85.00		
	Charlestown, SC	80.00	85.00		
	Jacksonville, FL	80.00	85.00		
	Lancaster, PA	80.00	85.00		
	Mayport, FL	80.00	85.00		
	New Rochelle, NY	80.00	85.00		
	New York, NY	80.00	85.00		
	Philadelphia, PA	80.00	85.00		
	Reading, PA	80.00	85.00		
	Unofficial city	125.00			
	Scott 614-616, set of three on one cover, any official city	175.00	350.00		
	Unofficial city	400.00			

Values are for neat, clean covers.

1925

SCOTT NUMBER	DESCRIPTION	UNCACHETED SINGLE	BLOCK	CACHETED SINGLE	BLOCK
617	1c Lexington-Concord, 4/4/25, pair, DC	30.00	40.00		
	Boston, MA	30.00	40.00	125.00	
	Cambridge, MA	25.00	40.00	100.00	
	Concord, MA	27.50	40.00	100.00	
	Concord Junction, MA	30.00	40.00		
	Lexington, MA	30.00	40.00	125.00	
	Unofficial city	45.00			
	1st Guy Atwood Jackson cachet (on any value)			150.00	
618	2c Lexington-Concord, 4/4/25, DC	35.00	40.00		
	Boston, MA	35.00	40.00	125.00	
	Cambridge, MA	35.00	40.00	125.00	
	Concord, MA	35.00	40.00	125.00	
	Concord Junction, MA	35.00	40.00		
	Lexington, MA	45.00	75.00	125.00	
	Unofficial city	50.00			
619	5c Lexington-Concord, 4/4/25, DC	80.00	110.00		

SCOTT NUMBER	DESCRIPTION	UNCACHETED SINGLE BLOCK		CACHETED SINGLE BLOCK	
	Boston, MA 80.00	110.00		150.00	
	Cambridge, MA................................80.00	110.00		150.00	
	Concord, MA...................................80.00	110.00		150.00	
	Concord Junction, MA 80.00	110.00		150.00	
	Lexington, MA.................................80.00	110.00		150.00	
	Unofficial city.................................80.00				
	Scott 617-619 Set on one cover, Concord Junction or Lexington 175.00	250.00			
	Scott 617-619 Set on one cover, any other official city...................140.00	250.00			
	Scott 617-619 Set on one cover, unofficial city...........................200.00	300.00			
	Scott 551,576, 585-587, 617-619 on one cover ....*2,500.*				
	Values are for neat, clean covers.				
620	**2c Norse-American**, 5/18/25, DC 25.00	30.00			
	Algona, IA.......................................25.00	30.00			
	Benson, MN.....................................25.00	30.00			
	Decorah, IA.....................................25.00	30.00			
	Minneapolis, MN.............................25.00	30.00			
	Northfield, MN................................25.00	30.00			
	St.Paul, MN.....................................25.00	30.00			
	Unofficial city.................................55.00				
621	**5c Norse-American**, 5/18/25, DC 40.00	55.00			
	Algona, IA.......................................40.00	55.00			
	Benson, MN.....................................40.00	55.00			
	Decorah, IA.....................................40.00	55.00			
	Minneapolis, MN.............................40.00	55.00			
	Northfield, MN................................40.00	55.00			
	St.Paul, MN.....................................40.00	55.00			
	Unofficial city.................................75.00				
	Scott 620-621 Set on one cover, any city.......55.00	70.00		250.00	
	1st Ernest J.Weschcke cachet................................			300.00	—
	1st Albert C. Roessler cachet................................			300.00	—

1925-26

622	**13c Benjamin Harrison**, 1/11/26, DC 20.00	30.00		—	—
	Indianapolis, IN 30.00	50.00		—	—
	North Bend, OH, unofficial city (500).........175.00	325.00		—	—
	Other unofficial cities 200.00	—		—	—
	Plate blocks, from this period, sell for two to three times the price of singles.				
623	**17c Woodrow Wilson**, 12/28/25, DC 25.00	27.50	300.00	—
	New York, NY 25.00	27.50	300.00	—
	Princeton, NJ..................................25.00	27.50	300.00	—
	Staunton, VA...................................25.00	27.50	300.00	—
	Bellefonte, PA, AMF, unofficial city....................—	—	300.00	—
	Other unofficial cities 30.00	—	—	—
	1st Charles E. Nickles cachet		300.00	—

1926

627	**2c Sesquicentennial Exposition**, 5/10/26, DC 10.00	12.00	70.00	—
	Boston, MA 10.00	12.00	70.00	—
	Philadelphia, PA 10.00	12.00	70.00	—
	Chester, PA, unofficial city ....—	—	60.00	—

SCOTT NUMBER	DESCRIPTION	UNCACHETED SINGLE	BLOCK	CACHETED SINGLE	BLOCK
☐	Valley Forge, PA, unofficial city	15.00	—	70.00	—
☐	Other unofficial cities	18.00	—	55.00	—
☐	1st Herbert H. Griffin cachet			150.00	—
☐	1st James H. Baxter cachet			100.00	

Cacheted Sesquicentennial FDC's are most often found with Chester or Valley Forge, PA, unofficial cancels. Cacheted FDC's on this issue from official FDC cities are worth more than those from most unofficial cities.

☐ 628	5c Ericsson Memorial, 5/29/26, DC	30.00	32.00	450.00	—
☐	Chicago, IL	30.00	32.00	450.00	—
☐	Minneapolis, MN	30.00	32.00	450.00	—
☐	New York, NY	30.00	32.00	450.00	—
☐	Unofficial city	35.00	—	—	—

The cacheted value given above is for a cachet of two crossed gold bars on a blue envelope. Any other cachet sells for one quarter of the value listed.

☐ 629	2c Battle of White Plains, New York, NY,				
☐	10/18/26	6.25	8.50	60.00	—
☐	New York, NY, International Philatelic				
	Exhibition Agency cancellation	6.25	8.50	60.00	—
☐	White Plains, NY (24,830)	6.25	8.50	60.00	—
☐	DC, 10/28/26	3.50	5.00	60.00	—
☐	Unofficial city	3.50	5.00	—	—
☐	10/16/26, pre-date	15.00	30.00	—	—
	1st Scott Stamp & Coin Co. cachet			65.00	—
☐ 630	2c Battle of White Plains, souvenir sheet, single or block identifiably from				
	souvenir sheet	7.00	10.00	65.00	75.00
☐	Imprint strip of 10 (top or bottom)		50.00	—	
☐	Full sheet, 10/18/26	1,800.	—	—	—
☐	Full sheet, official city, 10/18/26	2,000.	—	—	—
☐	Full sheet, 10/28/26	1,000.	—	—	—
☐	Unofficial city, single	50.00	—	—	—

Values for various cachet makers can be determined by using the Cachet Calculator found on pages 32 to 38.

1926-34

☐ 631	1 1/2c Warren G. Harding, imperf, 8/27/26, DC, pair	35.00	40.00	—	—
☐ 632	1c Benjamin Franklin, 6/10/27, DC, pair	45.00	55.00	165.00	—
☐ 632a	Benjamin Franklin, booklet pane of 6, 11/2/27	4,000.	—	—	—
☐ 633	1 1/2c Warren G. Harding, 5/17/27, DC, pair	45.00	55.00	175.00	—
☐ 634	2c George Washington, 12/10/26, DC	50.00	60.00	175.00	—
	Experimental Electric Eye, 3/28/35	—	—	1,000.	—
☐ 634A	2c George Washington, Type 2, 12/20/28, Chicago, IL	775.00	—	—	—
☐ 635	3c Abraham Lincoln, violet, 2/3/27, DC	47.50	57.50	165.00	—
☐ 635a	3c Abraham Lincoln, bright violet, 2/7/34, DC	25.00	38.00	50.00	—
☐ 636	4c Martha Washington, 5/17/27, DC	50.00	55.00	200.00	—
☐ 637	5c Theodore Roosevelt, 3/24/27, DC	50.00	55.00	200.00	—
☐ 638	6c James A. Garfield, 7/27/27, DC	60.00	110.00	200.00	—
☐ 639	7c William McKinley, 3/24/27, DC	60.00	110.00	200.00	—
☐	Scott 637, 639 on one cover	300.00	—	—	—

SCOTT NUMBER	DESCRIPTION	UNCACHETED SINGLE	BLOCK	CACHETED SINGLE	BLOCK
☐ 640	**8c U.S. Grant,** 6/10/27, DC	65.00	120.00	225.00	—
☐	Scott 632, 640 on one cover	300.00	—	—	—
☐ 641	**9c Thomas Jefferson,** 5/17/27, DC	75.00	150.00	225.00	—
☐	Scott 633, 636, 641on one cover	350.00	—	—	—
☐ 642	**10c James Monroe,** 2/3/27, DC	90.00	155.00	225.00	—

1927

SCOTT NUMBER	DESCRIPTION	UNCACHETED SINGLE	BLOCK	CACHETED SINGLE	BLOCK
☐ 643	**2c Vermont Sesquicentennial,** 8/3/27, DC	5.00	6.00	55.00	60.00
☐	Bennington, VT (50,000)	5.00	6.00	55.00	60.00
☐	Unofficial city	7.50	—	65.00	—
☐	1st Joshua R. Gerow Jr. cachet			250.00	—
☐	1st Haris R. Hunt cachet (Scott 643 or 644)			100.00	—
☐	1st Bradie Buchanan cachet			50.00	—
☐	1st S.S. Kurkjian cachet			250.00	—
☐ 644	**2c Burgoyne Campaign,** 8/3/27, DC	12.50	15.00	65.00	70.00
☐	Albany, NY	12.50	15.00	65.00	70.00
☐	Rome, NY	12.50	15.00	65.00	70.00
☐	Syracuse, NY	12.50	15.00	65.00	70.000
☐	Utica, NY	12.50	15.00	65.00	70.00
☐	Oriskany, NY, unofficial city	35.00	—	—	—
☐	Schuylerville, NY, unofficial city	—	—	125.00	—
☐	Other unofficial city	20.00	—	—	—
☐	Scott 643 & 644 on one cover, DC	15.00		100.00	

1928

SCOTT NUMBER	DESCRIPTION	UNCACHETED SINGLE	BLOCK	CACHETED SINGLE	BLOCK
☐ 645	**2c Valley Forge,** 5/26/28, DC	4.00	15.00	50.00	55.00
☐	Cleveland, OH (town cancel)	65.00	85.00	150.00	—
☐	Lancaster, PA	4.00	15.00	60.00	65.00
☐	Norristown, PA (25,000)	4.00	15.00	60.00	65.00
☐	Philadelphia, PA	4.00	15.00	60.00	65.00
☐	Valley Forge, PA (70,000)	4.00	15.00	60.00	65.00
☐	West Chester, PA (15,000)	4.00	15.00	60.00	65.00
☐	Cleveland Midwestern Philatelic Sta. cancel	4.00	15.00	60.00	65.00
☐	Other unofficial city	7.50	—	60.00	—
☐	1st Joseph W. Stoutzenberg cachet			250.00	—
☐	1st Howard Davis Egolf cachet			100.00	—
☐	1st Adam K. Bert cachet			75.00	—
☐	1st Howard W. Weaver cachet			80.00	
☐ 646	**2c Molly Pitcher,** 10/20/28, DC	15.00	20.00	85.00	—
☐	Freehold, NJ (25,000)	15.00	20.00	85.00	—
☐	Red Bank, NJ	15.00	20.00	85.00	—
☐	Unofficial city	15.00	—	90.00	—
☐	1st Ralph Dyer cachet			300.00	—
☐ 647	**2c Hawaii Sesquicentennial,** 8/13/28, DC	15.00	17.50	75.00	80.00
☐	Honolulu, HI	17.50	20.00	75.00	80.00
☐	Unofficial city	20.00	—	85.00	—
☐ 648	**5c Hawaii Sesquicentennial,** 8/13/28, DC	22.50	25.00	75.00	80.00
☐	Honolulu, HI	25.00	28.00	75.00	80.00
☐	Unofficial city	30.00	—	—	—
☐	Scott 647, 648 on one cover	40.00	45.00	250.00	—
☐	1st Reid		—	325.00	—
☐ 649	**2c Aeronautics Conference,** 12/12/28,				
☐	Green International Civil Aeronautic				
	Conference slogan	7.00	9.00	40.00	45.00
☐	DC, Black town cancel	9.00	11.00	40.00	45.00
☐	Unofficial city	15.00	—	—	—

1st Joseph W. Stoutzenberg cachet

1st Howard Davis Egolf cachet

1st Adam K. Bert cachet

646

647

648

649

650

651

1st Floyd D. Shockley cachet

1st Harry C. loor cachet

1st Harry E. Klotzbach cachet

653

654, 655, 656

657

Values for various cachet makers can be determined
by using the Cachet Calculator which begins on page 52A.

SCOTT NUMBER	DESCRIPTION	UNCACHETED SINGLE	BLOCK	CACHETED SINGLE	BLOCK
☐ 650	5c Aeronautics Conference, 12/12/28, Green International Civil Aeronautic				
	Conference slogan	10.00	12.50	50.00	55.00
☐	DC, Black town cancel	13.50	16.00	50.00	55.00
☐	Unofficial city	20.00	—	—	—
☐	Scott 649-650 on one cover, DC	15.00	—	75.00	—

Cacheted values are for covers with printed cachets. Covers with general purpose rubber stamp cachets sell at the uncacheted value. Rubber stamped Chamber of Commerce cachets sell for 1 1/2 to 2 times the uncacheted value.

1929

SCOTT NUMBER	DESCRIPTION	UNCACHETED SINGLE	BLOCK	CACHETED SINGLE	BLOCK
☐ 651	2c George Rogers Clark, Vincennes, IN,				
	2/25/29	6.00	7.50	30.00	32.50
☐	Unofficial city	10.00	—	35.00	—
☐	DC, 2/26/29, first day of sale by				
	Philatelic Agency	3.00	4.00	22.50	32.50
☐	Charlottesville, VA, 2/26/29	7.00	—	30.00	—
☐	1st Floyd D. Shockley cachet			25.00	—
☐	1st Harry C. Ioor cachet			150.00	—
☐ 653	1/2c Nathan Hale, 5/25/29, DC	—	30.00	—	85.00
☐ 654	2c Electric Light Jubilee, 6/5/29, Menlo				
	Park, NJ (77,000)	10.00	12.00	45.00	45.00
☐	Orange, NJ, unofficial	—	—	55.00	—
☐	Other unofficial city	—	—	55.00	60.00
☐	DC, 6/6/29, first day of sale by Philatelic				
	Agency	4.00	5.00	16.50	22.50
☐	1st Harry E. Klotzbach cachet			175.00	—
☐ 655	2c Electric Light Jubilee, 6/11/29, DC	80.00	95.00	200.00	250.00
☐ 656	2c Electric Light Jubilee, coil, 6/11/29, DC	90.00	110.00	200.00	250.00
☐	Line Pair	—	150.00	—	300.00
☐	Scott 655-656 on one cover	175.00	—	400.00	—
☐ 657	2c Sullivan Expedition, Auburn, NY,				
	6/17/29 (5,000)	4.00	5.00	30.00	32.00
☐	Binghamton, NY (50,000)	4.00	5.00	30.00	32.00
☐	Canajoharie, NY (12,000)	4.00	5.00	30.00	32.00
☐	Canandaigua, NY	4.00	5.00	30.00	32.00
☐	Elmira, NY (11,000)	4.00	5.00	30.00	32.00
☐	Geneseo, NY	4.00	5.00	30.00	32.00
☐	Geneva, NY	4.00	5.00	30.00	32.00
☐	Horseheads, NY	4.00	5.00	30.00	32.00
☐	Owego, NY	4.00	5.00	30.00	32.00
☐	Penn Yan, NY	4.00	5.00	30.00	32.00
☐	Perry, NY	4.00	5.00	30.00	32.00
☐	Seneca Falls, NY (8,500)	4.00	5.00	30.00	32.00
☐	Waterloo, NY	4.00	5.00	30.00	32.00
☐	Watkins Glen, NY (6,500)	4.00	5.00	30.00	32.00
☐	Waverly, NY	4.00	5.00	30.00	32.00
☐	Loman, NY, unofficial city	40.00			
☐	Other Unofficial city	6.50	10.00	50.00	55.00
☐	DC, 6/18/29	2.00	3.00	20.00	25.00
☐	1st Robert C. Beazell cachet			450.00	
☐	1st A.C. Elliot cachet			75.00	
☐	1st R. Roscher cachet			80.00	

1st Robert C. Beazell cachet

1st A.C. Elliott cachet

1st Delf Norona cachet

680

681

682

683

684, 686

685, 687

688

689

1st Denys J. Truby cachet

690

**Values for various cachet makers can be determined
by using the Cachet Calculator which begins on page 52A.**

658, 668   669, 679

Kansas and Nebraska Overprints

The first day of sale for the complete series of 22 Kansas-Nebraska overprints, Scott 658 through 679, was May 1, 1929, at the Philatelic Agency in Washington, D.C.

Stamps of that series also are known canceled in April 1929 from 27 Kansas and 28 Nebraska towns. These are relatively scarce and command a price greater than the May 1, 1929, Washington, D.C., cancels.

Listed below are the earliest known cancels of these stamps at Kansas and Nebraska post offices in April 1929. Only a few of each are known to exist.

☐ **658**   **1c Kansas,** 5/1/29, DC, pair............................50.00
☐   Newton, KS, 4/15/29 ....500.00
☐ **659**   **1 1/2c Kansas,** 5/1/29, DC, pair 60.00
☐   Colby, KS, 4/16/29 .... —
☐ **660**   **2c Kansas,** 5/1/29, DC 60.00
☐   Colby, KS, 4/16/29 .... —
☐   Dodge City, KS 4/16/29................................ —
☐   Liberal, KS 4/16/29 .... —
☐ **661**   **3c Kansas,** 5/1/29, DC 75.00
☐   Colby, KS, 4/16/29 .... —
☐ **662**   **4c Kansas,** 5/1/29, DC 70.00
☐   Colby, KS, 4/16/29 .... —
       Plate blocks, from this period, sell for two to
       three times the price of singles.
☐ **663**   **5c Kansas,** 5/1/29, DC 95.00
☐   Colby, KS, 4/16/29 .... —
☐ **664**   **6c Kansas,** 5/1/29, DC 100.00
☐   Newton, KS, 4/15/29 ....900.00
☐ **665**   **7c Kansas,** 5/1/29, DC ....1,250.
☐   Colby, KS, 4/16/29 .... —
☐ **666**   **8c Kansas,** 5/1/29, DC 125.00
☐   Newton, KS, 4/15/29 ....900.00
☐ **667**   **9c Kansas,** 5/1/29, DC 150.00
☐   Colby, KS, 4/16/29 .... —
☐ **668**   **10c Kansas,** 5/1/29, DC 200.00
☐   Colby, KS, 4/16/29 .... —
☐   Scott 658-668 on one cover, DC, 5/1/29......1,300.
☐   Scott 658, 664, 666, 4/15/29 Newton,KS...750.00
       April canceled covers with Kansas overprint stamps are
       also known from Cape Henry, VA; Denver and Pueblo,
       CO; Kansas City, MO, and Waynesboro, PA.
☐ **669**   **1c Nebraska,** 5/1/29, DC, pair.......................50.00
☐   Beatrice, NE, 4/15/29................................400.00
☐ **670**   **1 1/2c Nebraska,** 5/1/29, DC, pair 50.00
☐   Hartington, NE, 4/15/29.............................400.00
☐ **671**   **2c Nebraska,** 5/1/29, DC 60.00

		Auburn, NE, 4/15/29	—	
		Beatrice, NE, 4/15/29	—	
		Hartington, NE, 4/15/29	400.00	
	672	**3c Nebraska,** 5/1/29, DC	75.00	
		Beatrice, NE, 4/15/29	400.00	
		Hartington, NE, 4/15/29	400.00	
	673	**4c Nebraska,** 5/1/29, DC	75.00	
		Beatrice, NE, 4/15/29	500.00	
		Hartington, 4/15/29	500.00	
	674	**5c Nebraska,** 5/1/29, DC	75.00	100.00
		Beatrice, NE, 4/15/29	500.00	
		Hartington, NE, 4/15/29	500.00	
	675	**6c Nebraska,** 5/1/29, DC	100.00	
		Auburn, NE, 4/16/29	400.00	
	676	**7c Nebraska,** 5/1/29, DC	100.00	
		Auburn, NE, 4/17/29	400.00	
	677	**8c Nebraska,** 5/1/29, DC	150.00	
		Humbolt, NE, 4/17/29	250.00	
		Pawnee City, NE, 4/17/29	400.00	
	678	**9c Nebraska,** 5/1/29, DC	150.00	
		Cambridge, NE, 4/17/29	400.00	
	679	**10c Nebraska,** 5/1/29, DC	200.00	
		Tecumseh, NE, 4/18/29	400.00	
		Scott 669-679 on one cover, DC, 5/1/29	1,300.	
		658-679 on one cover (2 known)	5,000	

April canceled covers with Nebraska Overprint stamps are also known from Cleveland, OH; Kansas City, MO; and Washington, DC. There also are 1c and 2c Nebraska overprints canceled April 6, 1929 (pre-date), from Syracuse, NE, known and confirmed genuine by The Philatelic Foundation.

			UNCACHETED SINGLE BLOCK	CACHETED SINGLE BLOCK
	680	**2c Battle of Fallen Timbers,** Erie, PA,			
		9/14/29	3.50 4.00	35.00 40.00
		Maumee, OH	3.50 4.00	35.00 40.00
		Perrysburg OH	3.50 4.00	35.00 40.00
		Toledo, OH	3.50 4.00	35.00 40.00
		Waterville, OH (18,000)	3.50 4.00	35.00 40.00
		Fallen Timbers, PA	7.00	
		Unofficial city	5.00	40.00
		DC, 9/16/29	2.00 3.00	20.00 22.00
		1st Eugene Laird cachet		200.00 —
	681	**2c Ohio River,** Cairo, IL, 10/19/29	3.50 4.00	35.00 40.00
		Cincinnati, OH	3.50 4.00	35.00 40.00
		Evansville, IN (30,000)	3.50 4.00	35.00 40.00
		Homestead, PA (55,000)	3.50 4.00	35.00 40.00
		Louisville, KY	3.50 4.00	35.00 40.00
		Pittsburgh, PA (50,000)	3.50 4.00	35.00 40.00
		Wheeling, WV	3.50 4.00	35.00 40.00
		Unofficial city R.P.O.	7.50	45.00
		R.P.O.10/18/29, pre-date	50.00	
		Other unofficial city		45.00
		DC, 10/21/29	2.00 2.50	20.00 22.00
		1st Delf Norona cachet		70.00

1930

☐	682	2c **Massachusetts Bay Colony,** Boston,			
		MA 4/8/30 (60,000) 3.50	4.00	35.00	40.00
☐		Salem, MA.................................3.50	4.00	35.00	40.00
☐		Unofficial city 6.50		45.00	47.00
☐		DC, 4/11/30................................2.00	2.50	20.00	22.00
☐	683	2c **Carolina-Charleston,** Charleston, SC,			
		4/10/30 (100,000)...........................3.50	4.00	35.00	40.00
☐		Unofficial city 6.00			
☐		DC, 4/11/30................................2.00	1.50	20.00	25.00
☐		**682-683 on one cover,** DC, 4/11/30........4.00		45.00	
☐	684	1 1/2c **Warren G. Harding,** pair, Marion,			
		OH, 12/1/30.................................4.50	5.00	45.00	50.00
☐		DC, 12/2/30................................2.50	3.00	25.00	30.00
☐	685	4c **William H. Taft,** Cincinnati, OH, 6/4/30......6.00	7.50	55.00	60.00
☐		DC, 6/5/30.................................3.00	3.50	25.00	30.00
☐	686	1 1/2c **Warren G. Harding,** coil, Marion,			
		OH, 12/1/30.................................5.00	6.00	50.00	60.00
☐		DC, 12/2/30................................3.00	3.50	25.00	30.00
		Scott 684, 686 on one cover, Marion,			
		OH, 12/1/30.................................7.50		65.00	
☐		Scott 684, 686, DC, 12/2/30 ....3.00		40.00	
☐	687	4c **William H. Taft,** coil 9/18/30, DC........20.00	25.00	75.00	80.00
☐	688	2c **Braddock's Field,** Braddock PA, 7/9/30			
		(50,000)....................................4.00	4.50	30.00	32.00
☐		Unofficial city 7.00		50.00	
☐		DC, 7/10/30................................2.00	2.50	20.00	21.00
☐	689	2c **Von Steuben,** New York, NY, 9/17/30 ....4.00	4.50	30.00	32.00
☐		Unofficial city		50.00	
☐		DC, 9/18/30................................2.00	2.50	20.00	21.00
☐		Scott 687, 689 on one cover, DC.................25.00		75.00	

1931

☐	690	2c **Pulaski,** Brooklyn, NY, 1/16/31 ....4.00	4.50	35.00	38.00
☐		Buffalo, NY................................4.00	4.50	35.00	38.00
☐		Chicago, IL................................4.00	4.50	35.00	38.00
☐		Cleveland, OH.............................4.00	4.50	35.00	38.00
☐		Detroit, MI................................4.00	4.50	35.00	38.00
☐		Gary, IN...................................4.00	4.50	35.00	38.00
☐		Milwaukee, WI.............................4.00	4.50	35.00	38.00
☐		New York, NY..............................4.00	4.50	35.00	38.00
☐		Pittsburgh, PA.............................4.00	4.50	35.00	38.00
☐		Savannah, GA..............................4.00	4.50	35.00	38.00
☐		South Bend, IN.............................4.00	4.50	35.00	38.00
☐		Toledo, OH................................4.00	4.50	35.00	38.00
☐		Unofficial city 8.50		45.00	
☐		DC, 1/17/31................................2.00			
☐		1st Denys J. Truby cachet...........................		90.00	
☐	692	11c **Rutherford B. Hayes,** 9/4/31, DC........115.00	135.00		
☐	693	12c **Grover Cleveland,** 8/25/31, DC.............115.00	135.00		
☐	694	13c **Benjamin Harrison,** 9/4/31, DC.............115.00	135.00		
☐		Woolrich, PA 9/4/31.....................500.00			
☐	695	14c **American Indian,** 9/8/31, DC.................115.00	135.00		

1st Edward G. Hacker cachet

1st Aero Print cachet

1st Covered Wagon cachet

702

703

704

705

706

707

708

709

710

711

712

713

714

715

1st Frederick R. Rice cachet

1st Beverly Hills cachet

1st Linprint cachet

716

717

718

☐	696	15c Statue of Liberty, 8/27/31,DC	125.00 225.00		
☐	697	17c Woodrow Wilson, 7/25/31, Brooklyn,NY 3,000.			
☐		DC, 7/27/31	400.00 725.00		
☐	698	20c Golden Gate, 9/8/31, DC	325.00 650.00		
☐		Woolrich, PA, 9/4/31	500.00		
☐	699	25c Niagara Falls, 7/25/31, Brooklyn, NY.	1,750.		
☐		DC, 7/27/31	400.00 800.00		
☐		Scott 697 and 699 on one cover, Brooklyn, NY	4,000.		
☐	700	30c American Buffalo, 9/8/31, DC	325.00 550.00		
☐		Woolrich, PA, 9/4/31	500.00		
☐	701	50c Arlington Amphitheater, 9/4/31, DC	450.00 875.00		
☐		Woolrich, PA, 9/4/31	700.00		
☐	702	2c Red Cross, 5/21/31, DC	3.00 3.50	35.00 38.00	
☐		Dansville, NY	3.00 3.50	35.00 38.00	
☐		Unofficial city	6.00	45.00	
☐		1st Edward G. Hacker cachet		125.00	
☐		1st August (WSE) cachet		40.00	
☐	703	2c Yorktown, 10/19/31, Wethersfield, CT	3.50 4.00	45.00 50.00	
☐		Yorktown, VA	3.50 4.00	45.00 50.00	
☐		Unofficial city	7.00	55.00	
☐		1st Aero Print cachet		150.00	
☐		1st Walter G. Crosby cachet		450.00	
☐		1st Covered Wagon cachet		75.00	
☐		Washington, DC, 10/20/31	2.00 2.50	20.00 21.00	
☐		10/5/31 pre-date Wenatchee, WA (75) (AAMS #1146)	400.00		
☐		Any pre-date 10/6/31 through 10/18/31.	25.00	80.00	

The Post Office Department experimented with a new stamp distribution method with the Yorktown stamp. This resulted in a number of pre-dates on this issue. FDC's postmarked in unofficial cities sell for 50 percent to 100 percent more than catalogue value.

1932 Washington Bicentennial

☐	704	1/2c olive brown, 1/1/32, DC	—	5.00	— 20.00
☐	705	1c green, pair, 1/1/32, DC	4.00	5.00	18.00 20.00
☐	706	1 1/2c brown, pair, 1/1/32, DC	4.00	5.00	18.00 20.00
☐	707	2c carmine rose, 1/1/32, DC	4.00	5.00	18.00 20.00
☐	708	3c deep violet, 1/1/32, DC	4.00	5.00	18.00 20.00
☐	709	4c light brown, 1/1/32, DC	4.00	5.00	18.00 20.00
☐	710	5c blue, 1/1/32, DC	4.00	5.00	18.00 20.00
☐	711	6c red orange, 1/1/32, DC	4.00	5.00	18.00 20.00
☐	712	7c black, 1/1/32, DC	4.00	5.00	18.00 20.00
☐	713	8c olive bister, 1/1/32, DC	4.50	5.75	18.00 20.00
☐	714	9c pale red, 1/1/32, DC	4.50	5.75	18.00 20.00
☐	715	10c orange yellow, 1/1/32, DC	4.50	5.75	18.00 20.00
☐		Scott 704-715 on one cover, DC	65.00		250.00
☐		1st Plimpton cachet (on any single)			30.00
☐		1st William T. Raley cachet (on any single)			40.00
☐		1st Frederick R. Rice cachet (on any single			25.00

Add 100 percent for unofficial first day cancel on this issue.

☐	716	2c Olympic Winter Games, 1/25/32, Lake Placid, NY	6.00 6.50	35.00 40.00	
☐		Unofficial city		40.00	
☐		DC, 1/26/32	1.50 2.00	10.00 15.00	
☐		1st Beverly Hills cachet		250.00	

719

720, 720b,
721, 722

723

724

725

1st Anderson cachet

1st Henry Grimsland cachet

1st Brookhaven cachet

726

727, 752

728, 730, 766a

729, 731, 767a

733, 735,
753, 768a

732

734

1st Albert B. Parsons cachet

**Values for various cachet makers can be determined
by using the Cachet Calculator which begins on page 52A.**

SCOTT NUMBER	DESCRIPTION	UNCACHETED SINGLE	BLOCK	CACHETED SINGLE	BLOCK
☐ 717	**2c Arbor Day,** 4/22/32, Nebraska City, NE. 4.00	4.50	15.00	18.00	
☐	DC, 4/23/32..1.50	2.00	5.00	6.00	
☐	Adams, NY, 4/23/32..................................6.50		18.00	20.00	
☐	1st Linprint cachet		25.00		
☐ 718	**3c Olympic Games,** 6/15/32, Los Angeles, CA........6.00	6.50	35.00	40.00	
☐	Unofficial..		40.00		
☐	DC, 6/16/32..2.75	3.00	8.00	9.00	
☐ 719	**5c Olympic Games,** 6/15/32, Los Angeles, CA 8.00	8.50	35.00	40.00	
☐	Unofficial..		40.00		
☐	DC, 6/16/32..2.75	3.00	8.00	9.00	
☐	Scott 718-719 on one cover, Los Angeles, CA..10.00	13.50	50.00	55.00	
☐	Scott 718-719 on one cover, DC...................4.50				
☐	Scott 718-719 on one cover, unofficial		65.00		
☐ 720	**3c George Washington,** 6/16/32, DC........7.50	8.50	40.00	45.00	
☐ 720b	**George Washington,** booklet pane of 6,				
	7/25/32, DC..100.00		200.00		
☐ 720b	**George Washington,** booklet single 20.00		60.00		

SCOTT NUMBER	DESCRIPTION	UNCACHETED SINGLE	PAIR	CACHETED SINGLE	PAIR
☐ 721	**3c George Washington,** coil, sideways,				
	6/24/32 ....15.00	20.00	60.00	90.00	
☐ 722	**3c George Washington,** coil, endways,				
	10/12/32 ....15.00	20.00	60.00	90.00	
☐ 723	**6c James A. Garfield,** coil, 8/18/32, Los				
	Angeles, CA...15.00	20.00	60.00	90.00	
☐	DC, 8/19/32...4.00	6.00	30.00	35.00	

SCOTT NUMBER	DESCRIPTION	UNCACHETED SINGLE	BLOCK	CACHETED SINGLE	BLOCK
☐ 724	**3c William Penn,** 10/24/32, New Castle, DE 3.25	4.00	25.00	30.00	
☐	Chester, PA.......................................3.25	4.00	25.00	30.00	
☐	Philadelphia, PA................................3.25	4.00	25.00	30.00	
☐	Unofficial city		30.00		
☐	DC, 10/25/32.....................................1.25	1.50	9.00	10.00	
☐ 725	**3c Daniel Webster,** 10/24/32, Franklin, NH 3.25	4.00	25.00	30.00	
☐	Exeter, NH...3.25	4.00	25.00	30.00	
☐	Hanover, NH (70,000) 3.25	4.00	25.00	30.00	
☐	Marshfield, MA, unofficial............................35.00		37.00		
☐	Webster, MA, unofficial		40.00		
☐	Any other unofficial city.......................		30.00		
☐	DC, 10/25/32.....................................1.25	1.50	9.00	12.00	
☐	Scott 724-725 on one cover 5.00	6.00	50.00		

1933

SCOTT NUMBER	DESCRIPTION	UNCACHETED SINGLE	BLOCK	CACHETED SINGLE	BLOCK
☐ 726	**3c Georgia Bicentennial,** 2/12/33,				
	Savannah, GA (200,000) 3.25	4.00	25.00	30.00	
☐	Any Georgia town, 2/13/33 ....3.25		9.00	12.00	
☐	DC, 2/13/33...1.50	2.50	8.00	9.00	
☐	1st Anderson cachet		150.00		
	Because 2/12/33 was a Sunday, second-day covers for				
	Scott 726 were serviced.				

1st Torkel Gundel cachet

1st Top-Notch cachet

1st Donald Kapner cachet

1st Louis G. Nix cachet

736

737, 738, 754

739, 755

740, 751, 756, 769a

741, 757

742, 750, 758, 770a

743, 759

745, 761

747, 763

744, 760

1st Imperial cachet

746, 762

748, 764

749, 765

34

SCOTT NUMBER	DESCRIPTION	UNCACHETED SINGLE	BLOCK	CACHETED SINGLE	BLOCK
☐ 727	3c Peace of 1783, 4/19/33, Newburgh, NY				
	(349,571).....................................3.50	4.00	25.00	30.00	
☐	Unofficial city			35.00	
☐	DC, 4/20/33.................................1.25	2.00	8.00	9.00	
☐	1st Henry Grimsland cachet			300.00	
☐	1st Brookhaven cachet			90.00	
☐	1st Eagle Cover Service cachet........................			75.00	
☐	1st Newburgh Chamber of Commerce.................			50.00	
☐ 728	1c Century of Progress, 5/25/33, strip of 3,				
	Chicago, IL...................................3.00	3.50	20.00	25.00	
☐	Unofficial city			20.00	
☐	DC, 5/26/33.................................1.00	2.00	9.00	12.00	
☐ 729	3c Century of Progress, 5/25/33, Chicago,IL ...3.00	3.50	20.00	25.00	
☐	Chicago Ridge fancy cancel 10.00	12.00	40.00	50.00	
☐	Any other unofficial city.................................			20.00	
☐	DC, 5/26/33.................................1.00	2.00	9.00	12.00	
☐	Scott 728-729 on one cover 5.00	6.00	25.00	30.00	
☐	1st Lan W. Kreicker cachet..............................			40.00	
	Total FDC's mailed May 25: 232,251.				
☐ 730	3c American Philatelic Society, imperf.				
	pane of 25, 8/25/33, Chicago, IL 100.00			200.00	
☐ 730a	American Philatelic Society, strip of 3 ....3.25	4.00	20.00	25.00	
☐	DC, 8/28/33.................................1.25	2.00	9.00	12.00	
	Values for various cachet makers can be determined by				
	using the Cachet Calculator found on pages 32 to 38.				
☐ 731	3c American Philatelic Society, imperf.				
	pane of 25, 8/25/33, Chicago, IL 100.00			200.00	
☐ 731a	American Philatelic Society, single 3.25	4.00	20.00	25.00	
☐	DC, 8/28/33.................................1.25	2.00	9.00	12.00	
☐	Scott 730a, 731a on one cover 5.50	6.50	20.00	22.00	
	Total FDC's mailed Aug. 25: 65,218.				
☐ 732	3c National Recovery Act, 8/15/33, DC				
	(65,000)......................................3.25	4.00	20.00	25.00	
☐	Nira, IA, 8/17/33 unofficial 2.50	5.00	20.00	22.00	
☐ 733	3c Byrd Antarctic, 10/9/33, DC 9.00	11.00	20.00	22.50	
☐	1st Albert B. Parsons cachet.............................			75.00	
☐ 734	5c Kosciuszko, 10/13/33, Boston, MA				
	(23,025)......................................4.50	6.00	20.00	25.00	
☐	Buffalo, NY (14,981) 5.50	7.00	20.00	25.00	
☐	Chicago, IL (26,306)....................................4.50	6.00	20.00	25.00	
☐	Detroit, MI (17,792) 5.25	6.00	20.00	25.00	
☐	Pittsburgh, PA (6,282)................................32.50	37.50	60.00	70.00	
☐	Kosciuszko, MS (27,093) 5.25	6.00	20.00	25.00	
☐	St. Louis, MO (17,872) 5.25	6.00	20.00	25.00	
☐	DC, 10/14/33...............................1.60	2.00	20.00	25.00	
☐	Unofficial city 10.00	12.00	40.00	50.00	

1934

SCOTT NUMBER	DESCRIPTION	UNCACHETED SINGLE	BLOCK	CACHETED SINGLE	BLOCK
☐ 735	3c National Stamp Exhibition, imperf. pane				
	of 6, 2/10/34, New York, NY 40.00			75.00	
☐	DC, 2/19/34.................................27.50				
☐	1st Minkus cachet...			60.00	
☐ 735a	National Stamp Exhibition, single				
	(450,715)..5.00	6.00	20.00	25.00	
☐	DC, 2/19/34.................................2.75	3.50	10.00	12.00	

772

774

773

1st Winfred Milton Grandy cachet

1st William H. Espenshade cachet

1st Norwood B. Scatchard cachet

775

776

777

778

1st John C. Sidenius cachet

1st Walter Czubay cachet

1st J. W. Clifford cachet

1st House of Farnam cachet

☐	**736** **3c Maryland Tercentenary,** 3/23/34, St. Mary's City, MD (148,785).............1.60		2.00	20.00	25.00
☐	DC, 3/24/34..1.00		1.00	6.00	7.00
☐	1st Torkel Gundel cachet			300.00	
☐	1st Top-Notch cachet			40.00	
☐	1st Donald Kapner cachet			40.00	
☐	1st Louis G. Nix cachet			200.00	
☐	**737** **3c Mothers of America,** perf. 11x10 1/2, 5/2/34, any city......................................1.60		2.00	15.00	20.00
☐	**738** **3c Mothers of America,** perf 11, 5/2/34, any city..1.60		2.00	15.00	20.00
☐	Scott 737-738 on one cover 4.00		5.00	30.00	
	FDC's mailed at Washington May 2: 183,359.				
☐	**739** **3c Wisconsin Tercentenary,** 7/7/34, Green Bay, WI (130,000) 1.10		1.65	20.00	25.00
☐	DC, 7/9/34..1.00		1.10	5.75	9.50

National Parks Issue

☐	**740** **1c Yosemite,** strip of 3, 7/16/34, Yosemite, CA (60,000) 2.75		3.25	10.00	12.00
☐	DC, (26,219) 2.25		2.75	7.00	8.00
☐	**741** **2c Grand Canyon,** pair, 7/24/34, Grand Canyon, AZ (75,000) 2.75		3.25	10.00	12.00
☐	DC, (30,080) 2.25		2.75	7.00	8.00
☐	**742** **3c Mt. Rainier,** 8/3/34, Longmire, WA (64,500)...3.00		3.50	10.00	12.00
☐	DC, (30,114) 2.50		3.00	7.00	8.00
☐	**743** **4c Mesa Verde,** 9/25/34, Mesa Verde, CO (51,882)...2.75		3.25	10.00	12.00
☐	DC, (21,729) 2.25		2.75	7.00	8.00
☐	**744** **5c Yellowstone,** 7/30/34, Yellowstone, WY (87,000)...2.50		3.00	10.00	12.00
☐	DC (32,150) 2.25		2.75	7.00	8.00
☐	**745** **6c Crater Lake,** 9/5/34, Crater Lake, OR (45,282)...3.25		3.75	10.00	12.00
☐	DC (19,161) 3.00		3.50	7.00	8.00
☐	**746** **7c Acadia,** 10/2/34, Bar Harbor, ME (51,312)..3.25		3.75	10.00	12.00
☐	DC, (20,163) 3.00		3.50	7.00	8.00
☐	**747** **8c Zion,** 9/18/34, Zion, UT (43,650) 3.75		4.25	10.00	12.00
☐	DC (19,001) 3.25		3.75	7.00	8.00
☐	**748** **9c Glacier Park** 8/27/34, Glacier Park, MT (52,626)...3.75		4.00	10.00	12.00
☐	1st Imperial cachet			60.00	
☐	DC (16,250) 3.50		4.00	7.00	8.00
☐	**749** **10c Smoky Mountains,** 10/8/34, Sevierville, TN (39,000) 7.50		8.50	12.50	14.00
☐	DC (18,368) 6.00		7.00	10.00	12.50
☐	Smokemont, TN, unofficial			25.00	
☐	Scott 740-749 with park cancels on one cover.....			150.00	
☐	**750** **3c American Philatelic Society,** imperf. pane of 6, 8/28/34, Atlantic City, NJ 40.00			75.00	
☐	**750a** **American Philatelic Society,** single (40,000)...3.25		4.25	10.00	12.00
☐	DC, 9/4/34..2.00		2.50	8.00	10.00

782

783

784

1st Historic Art cachet

785

786

787

788

789

790

791

792

793

794

Values for various cachet makers can be determined by using the Cachet Calculator which begins on page 52A.

	751	1c Trans-Mississippi Philatelic Exposition, imperf. pane of 6, 10/10/34, Omaha, NE 35.00		65.00	
	751a	Trans-Mississippi Philatelic Exposition, strip of 3 (125,000) 3.25	4.25	10.00	—
		DC, 10/15/34 ....2.00	2.50	6.00	—

1934 Special Printing

Nos. 752-771 issued 3/15/35.

	752	3c Peace of 1783, DC 5.00	7.50	35.00	40.00
	753	3c Byrd Antarctic, DC 6.00	7.50	35.00	40.00
	754	3c Mothers of America, DC...........6.00	7.50	35.00	40.00
	755	3c Wisconsin Tercentenary, DC 6.00	7.50	35.00	40.00
	756	1c Yosemite, strip of 3, DC...........6.00	7.50	35.00	40.00
	757	2c Grand Canyon, pair, DC 6.00	7.50	35.00	40.00
	758	3c Mount Rainier, DC 6.00	7.50	35.00	40.00
	759	4c Mesa Verde, DC 6.50	7.50	35.00	40.00
	760	5c Yellowstone, DC...........6.50	7.50	35.00	40.00
	761	6c Crater Lake, DC...........6.50	7.50	35.00	40.00
	762	7c Acadia, DC 6.50	7.50	35.00	40.00
	763	8c Zion, DC 7.50	8.00	35.00	40.00
	764	9c Glacier Park, DC...........7.50	8.00	35.00	40.00
	765	10c Smoky Mountains, DC...........7.50	8.00	35.00	40.00
	766	1c Century of Progress, imperf. pane of 25, imperf, DC...........		350.00	
	766a	Century of Progress, strip of 3 ....5.50	7.50	40.00	45.00
	767	3c Century of Progress, imperf. pane of 25, DC...........		350.00	
	767a	Century of Progress, single...........5.50	7.50	40.00	45.00
	768	3c Byrd, imperf. pane of 6, DC...........		350.00	
	768a	Byrd, single...........6.50	8.50	40.00	45.00
	769	1c Yosemite, imperf. pane of 6, DC...........		350.00	
	769a	Yosemite, strip of 3 ....4.00	6.00	40.00	45.00
	770	3c Mount Rainier, imperf. pane of 6, DC		350.00	
	770a	Mount Rainier, single...........5.00	7.00	40.00	45.00
	771	16c Air Mail Special Delivery, DC...........12.50	16.00	40.00	60.00

Uncacheted covers, from this period, sell for about 20% that of cacheted covers.

	772	3c Connecticut Tercentenary, 4/26/35, Hartford, CT.			
		(217,800) 12.50	20.00	25.00	
		DC, 4/27/35 ....2.00	2.50	3.25	
		1st Winfred Milton Grandy cachet 30.00			
	773	3c California-Pacific Exposition, 5/29/35, San Diego, CA (214,042) 12.50	20.00	25.00	
		DC, 5/31/35 ....1.25	1.75	2.75	
		1st William H. Espenshade cachet 35.00			
	774	3c Boulder Dam, 9/30/35, Boulder City, NV (166,180) 12.50	20.00	25.00	
		DC, 10/1/35 ....2.00	2.75	3.75	
		1st Norwood B. Scatchard cachet 75.00			
	775	3c Michigan Centenary, 11/1/35, Lansing, MI (176,962) 12.50	20.00	25.00	

1st Cachet Craft cachet

1st Pilgrim cachet

1st Fidelity Stamp Co. cachet

795

796

798

797

799

800

801

802

804, 839, 848

815, 847

HOW TO USE THIS BOOK

The number in the first column is its Scott number or
identifying number. Following that is the denomination
of the stamp, description, date of issue, and the value.

SCOTT NUMBER	DESCRIPTION	SINGLE	BLOCK	PLATE BLOCK
☐	DC, 11/2/35 .... 1.25		1.75	2.00
☐	1st Risko Art Studio cachet 200.00			

1936

SCOTT NUMBER	DESCRIPTION	SINGLE	BLOCK	PLATE BLOCK
☐	**776** **3c Texas Centennial**, 3/2/36, Gonzales, TX			
	(319,150) 20.00		25.00	30.00
☐	DC, 3/3/36 .... 2.00		2.50	3.50
☐	1st John C. Sidenius cachet 75.00			
☐	1st Walter Czubay cachet 75.00			
☐	**777** **3c Rhode Island Tercentenary**, 5/4/36, Providence,			
	RI (245,400) 12.50		20.00	25.00
☐	DC, 5/5/36 .... 2.00		2.50	3.25
☐	1st J.W. Clifford cachet 35.00			
☐	**778** **3c TIPEX**, souvenir sheet, 5/9/36, New York, NY			
	(297,194) (TIPEX cancellation) 16.00			
☐	DC, 5/11/36 .... 3.50			
☐	1st House of Farnam cachet 500.00			
☐	**778a-778d** Single from sheet 5.00			
☐	**782** **3c Arkansas Centennial**, 6/15/36, Little Rock, AR			
	(376,693) 12.50		18.00	20.00
☐	DC, 6/16/36 .... 1.00		1.75	2.75
☐	**783** **3c Oregon Territory**, 7/14/36, Astoria, OR (91,110)... 8.50		9.50	15.00
☐	Daniel, WY (67,013) 8.50		9.50	15.00
☐	Lewiston, ID (86,100) 8.00		9.00	15.00
☐	Missoula, MT (59,883) 8.50		9.50	15.00
☐	Walla Walla, WA (106,150) 8.00		9.00	15.00
☐	DC, 7/15/36 .... 1.25		1.75	2.75
☐	1st Whitman Centennial Inc. cachet 35.00			
☐	**784** **3c Susan B. Anthony**, 8/26/36 DC (178,500) 12.50		20.00	25.00
☐	1st Historic Art cachet 35.00			
☐	1st Dean Aubry cachet 30.00			

1936-37

SCOTT NUMBER	DESCRIPTION	SINGLE	BLOCK	PLATE BLOCK
☐	**785** **1c Army**, strip of 3, 12/15/36, DC 7.50		9.00	12.00
☐	**786** **2c Army**, pair, 1/15/37 .... 7.50		9.00	12.00
☐	**787** **3c Army**, 2/18/37, DC 7.50		9.00	12.00
☐	1st William J. Von Ohlen cachet 60.00			
☐	**788** **4c Army**, 3/23/37, DC 7.50		9.00	12.00
☐	**789** **5c Army**, 5/26/37, West Point, NY (160,000) 7.50		9.00	12.00
☐	DC, 5/27/37 .... 1.25		1.75	2.75
☐	Scott 785-789 on one cover 40.00			
☐	1st Pavois cachet 20.00			
☐	**790** **1c Navy**, strip of 3, 12/15/36, DC 7.50		9.00	12.00
☐	**791** **2c Navy**, pair, 1/15/37, DC 7.50		9.00	12.00
☐	**792** **3c Navy**, 2/18/37, DC 7.50		9.00	12.00
☐	**793** **4c Navy**, 3/23/37, DC 7.50		9.00	12.00
☐	**794** **5c Navy**, 5/26/37, Annapolis, MD (202,806) 7.50		9.00	12.00
☐	DC, 5/27/37 .... 1.25		1.75	2.75
☐	Scott 790-794 on one cover 40.00			
☐	Scott 785-794 on one cover 80.00			

Covers for both 1c values total 390,749; 2c values total
292,570; 3c values total 320,888; 4c values total 331,000.
Uncacheted covers from this period sell for about 20% that of cacheted covers.

1937

SCOTT NUMBER	DESCRIPTION	SINGLE	BLOCK	PLATE BLOCK
☐	**795** **3c Northwest Ordinance Centennial**, 7/13/37,			
	Marietta, OH (130,531) 9.00		10.00	13.00

835

836

837

838

1st Artcraft cachet

852

853

854

855

856

858

857

859

864

869

874

879

884

889

HOW TO USE THIS BOOK

The number in the first column is its Scott number or identifying number. Following that is the denomination of the stamp, description, date of issue, and the value.

42

		DESCRIPTION	SINGLE	BLOCK	PLATE BLOCK
☐		New York, NY (125,134) 9.00		10.00	13.00
☐		DC, 7/14/37 ....1.20		1.75	2.75
☐		1st William S. Linto cachet 125.00			
☐		1st Cachet Craft cachet 100.00			
☐	796	5c Virginia Dare, 8/18/37, Manteo, NC (226,730)....12.50		20.00	25.00
☐		Dare, VA, unofficial 12.50			
☐		DC, 8/27/37 ....1.50		2.50	3.50
☐	797	10c Society of Philatelic Americans, souvenir sheet,			
		8/26/37, Asheville, NC (164,215)............................10.00			
☐		DC, 8/27/37 ....1.50			
☐	798	3c Constitution Sesquicentennial, 9/17/37,			
		Philadelphia, PA (281,478)...................12.50		18.00	20.00
☐		DC, 9/18/37 ....1.00		1.50	2.50
☐		1st Pilgrim cachet 100.00			
☐		1st Fidelity Stamp Co. cachet.................20.00			
☐	799	3c Hawaii, 10/18/37, Honolulu, HI (320,334) 10.00		12.00	14.00
☐		DC, 10/19/37...1.00		1.50	2.50
☐	800	3c Alaska, 11/12/37, Juneau, AK (230,370) 10.00		12.00	14.00
☐		DC, 11/13/37...1.00		1.50	2.50
☐	801	3c Puerto Rico, 11/25/37, San Juan, PR (244,054) ..10.00		12.00	14.00
☐		DC, 11/26/37...1.00		1.50	2.50
☐	802	3c Virgin Islands, 12/15/37, Charlotte Amalie, VI			
		(225,469)..10.00		12.00	14.00
☐		DC, 12/16/37...1.00		1.50	2.50
☐		799-802 Set of 4 on one cover 40.00		—	—

1938-54 Presidential Issue

		DESCRIPTION	SINGLE	BLOCK	PLATE BLOCK
☐	803	1/2c Benjamin Franklin, block of 6, 5/19/38,			
		Philadelphia, PA (224,901)...............................		3.00	3.50
☐		DC, 5/20/38..		1.00	1.25
☐	804	1c George Washington, strip of 3, 4/25/38, DC			
		(124,037)..3.00		3.50	6.00
☐	804b	George Washington, booklet pane of 6, 1/27/39,DC 15.00			
☐	805	1 1/2c Martha Washington, pair, 5/5/38, DC			
		(138,339)..3.00		3.50	4.00
☐	806	2c John Adams, pair, 6/3/38, DC (127,806)....2.00		2.50	4.00
☐	806b	John Adams, booklet pane of 6, 1/27/39, DC 15.00			
☐	807	3c ThomasJefferson, 6/16/38, DC (118,097)..............3.00		3.50	4.00
☐	807a	Thomas Jefferson, booklet pane of 6, 1/27/39, DC..18.00			
☐		Scott 804b, 806b, 807a on one cover, 1/27/39, DC..60.00			
☐	808	4c James Madison, 7/1/38 (118,765), DC..................3.00		4.00	5.00
☐	809	4 1/2c White House, 7/11/38, DC (115,820)...............3.00		4.00	5.00
☐	810	5c James Monroe, 7/21/38, DC (98,282) 3.00		4.00	5.00
☐	811	6c John Q. Adams, 7/28/38, DC (97,428) 3.00		4.00	5.00
☐	812	7c Andrew Jackson, 8/4/38, DC (98,414)..................3.00		4.00	5.00
☐	813	8c Martin Van Buren, 8/11/38, DC (94,857) 3.00		4.00	5.00
☐	814	9c William H. Harrison, 8/18/38, DC (91,229) 3.00		4.00	5.00
☐	815	10c John Tyler, 9/2/38, DC (84,707)..........................3.00		4.00	5.00
☐	816	11c James K. Polk. 9/8/38, DC (63,966)....................3.00		4.00	5.00
☐	817	12c Zachary Taylor, 9/14/38, DC (62,935)..................3.00		4.00	5.00
☐	818	13c Millard Fillmore, 9/22/38, (58,965).....................3.00		4.00	5.00
☐	819	14c Franklin Pierce, 10/6/38, DC (49,819)..................3.00		4.00	5.00
☐	820	15c James Buchanan, 10/13/38, DC (52,209) 3.00		4.00	5.00
☐	821	16c Abraham Lincoln, 10/20/38, DC (59,566)............5.00		6.00	8.00

			SINGLE	BLOCK	PLATE BLOCK
☐	822	**17c Andrew Johnson,** 10/27/38, DC (55,024).............5.00		6.00	8.00
☐	823	**18c U.S. Grant,** 11/3/38, DC(53,124) 5.00		6.00	8.00
☐	824	**19c Rutherford B. Hayes,** 11/10/38, DC (54,124) 5.00		6.00	8.00
☐	825	**20c James A. Garfield,** 11/10/38, DC (51,971)...........5.00		6.00	8.00
☐		Scott 824,825 on one cover...................................40.00			
☐	826	**21c Chester A. Arthur,** 11/22/38, DC (44,367) 5.00		6.00	8.00
☐		1st Union College cachet......................................40.00			
☐	827	**22c Grover Cleveland,** 11/22/38, DC (44,358).............5.00		6.00	8.00
☐		Scott 826,827 on one cover...................................40.00			
☐	828	**24c Benjamin Harrison,** 12/2/38, DC (46,592)...........5.00		6.00	8.00
☐	829	**25c William McKinley,** 12/2/38, DC (45,691)..............6.00		7.50	10.00
☐		Scott 828, 829 on one cover 40.00			
☐	830	**30c Theodore Roosevelt,** 12/8/38, DC (43,528)..........7.50		9.00	14.00
☐	831	**50c William Howard Taft,** 12/8/38, DC (41,984)......10.00		12.50	20.00
☐		Scott 830, 831 on one cover			40.00
☐	832	**$1 Woodrow Wilson,** 8/29/38, DC (24,618) 60.00		70.00	80.00
☐	832c	**$1 Woodrow Wilson,** dry-printed, 8/31/54, DC			
		(20,202)..30.00		40.00	45.00
☐	833	**$2 Warren G. Harding,** 9/29/38, DC(19,895)..........125.00		175.00	250.00
☐	834	**$5 Calvin Coolidge,** 11/17/38, DC (15,615).............180.00		275.00	450.00
☐		**803-834 Set of 32 covers,** matched cachets......................550.00		650.00	800.00

1938-42 Presidential Electric Eye Issues

			SINGLE	BLOCK	PLATE BLOCK
☐	803	**1/2c Benjamin Franklin,** block of 6, 9/8/41, DC		11.00	13.00
☐	804	**1c George Washington,** strip of 3, 9/8/41, DC............7.00		11.00	13.00
☐		Scott 803, 804, E 15 on one cover 25.00		40.00	
		Total for Scott 803, 804, and E15 Electric Eye is 22,000.			
☐	805	**1 1/2c Martha Washington,** pair, 1/16/41 ....10.00		11.00	13.00
		Total for Scott 805 Electric Eye is less than 10,000.			
☐	806	**2c John Adams,** pair, 6/3/38, DC, Type I 10.00		11.00	13.00
☐	806	**2c John Adams,** pair, 4/5/39, DC, Type II.................10.00		11.00	13.00
☐	807	**3c Thomas Jefferson,** 4/5/39, DC 10.00		11.00	13.00
☐		Scott 806, 807 on one cover 12.00		20.00	
		Total for Scott 806 and 807 Electric Eye is 28,500.			
☐	808	**4c James Madison,** 10/28/41, DC 15.00		16.00	20.00
☐	809	**4 1/2c White House,** 10/28/41, DC 15.00		16.00	20.00
☐	810	**5c James Monroe,** 10/28/41, DC...............................15.00		16.00	20.00
☐	811	**6c John Q. Adams,** 9/25/41, DC................................15.00		16.00	20.00
☐	812	**7c Andrew Jackson,** 10/28/41, DC 15.00		16.00	20.00
☐	813	**8c Martin Van Buren,** 10/28/41, DC.........................15.00		16.00	20.00
☐	814	**9c William H. Harrison,** 10/28/41, DC......................15.00		16.00	20.00
☐	815	**10c John Tyler,** 9/25/41, DC 15.00		16.00	20.00
☐		Scott 811,815 on one cover....................................25.00		35.00	
		Total for Scott 811 and 815 Electric Eye is 7,300.			
☐	816	**11c James K. Polk,** 10/8/41, DC 20.00		22.00	25.00
☐	817	**12c Zachary Taylor,** 10/8/41, DC..............................20.00		22.00	25.00
☐	818	**13c Millard Fillmore,** 10/8/41, DC............................20.00		22.00	25.00
☐	819	**14c Franklin Pierce,** 10/8/41, DC.............................20.00		22.00	25.00
☐	820	**15c James Buchanan,** 10/8/41, DC 20.00		22.00	25.00
☐		Scott 816-820 on one cover 30.00		47.50	
☐	821	**16c Abraham Lincoln,** 1/7/42, DC.............................25.00		28.00	30.00
☐	822	**17c Andrew Johnson,** 10/28/41, DC...........................25.00		28.00	30.00
☐		Scott 808-810, 812-814, 822 on one cover............35.00		55.00	
		Total for Scott 808-810 and 812-814, 822 Electric Eye is 16,200.			

☐	823	**18c U.S. Grant**, 1/7/42, DC................................25.00	28.00	30.00
☐	824	**19c Rutherford B. Hayes**, 1/7/42, DC.....................25.00	28.00	30.00
☐	825	**20c James A. Garfield**, 1/7/42, DC 25.00	28.00	30.00
☐		Scott 824-825 on one cover 30.00	55.00	
☐	826	**21c Chester Arthur**, 1/7/42, DC..............................25.00	28.00	30.00
☐		Scott 821,823-826 on one cover 35.00	55.00	
☐	827	**22c Grover Cleveland**, 1/28/42, DC 35.00	40.00	45.00
☐	828	**24c Benjamin H. Harrison**, 1/28/42, DC 35.00	40.00	45.00
☐	829	**25c William McKinley**, 1/28/42, DC..........................45.00	50.00	55.00
☐	830	**30c Theodore Roosevelt**, 1/28/42, DC........................45.00	50.00	55.00
☐	831	**50c William Howard Taft**, 1/28/42, DC...................50.00	55.00	60.00
☐		Scott 827-831 on one cover 100.00	150.00	

Total for Scott 827-831 Electric Eye is 6,700. These covers must have sheet selvage electric eye markings attached to stamps.

1938

☐	835	**3c Constitution Ratification**, 6/21/38, Philadelphia, PA (232,873)...12.50	20.00	22.00
☐		DC, 6/16/38...1.00	1.50	2.50
☐	836	**3c Swedish-Finnish Tercentenary**, 6/27/38, Wilmington, DE (225,617).....................................12.50	20.00	22.00
☐		DC, 6/28/38...1.00	1.50	2.50
☐		1st Staehle cachet 50.00		
☐	837	**3c Northwest Territory**, 7/15/38, Marietta, OH (180,170)...12.50	20.00	22.00
☐		DC, 7/16/38...1.00	1.50	2.50
☐	838	**3c Iowa Territory**, 8/24/38, Des Moines, IA (209,860)...12.50	20.00	22.00
☐		DC, 8/25/38...1.00	1.50	2.50
☐		1st G.S. Purcell cachet 30.00		

Perf. 10 Vertically   1939 Presidential Coils

☐	839	**1c George Washington**, strip of 3, 1/20/39, DC................	5.00	10.00
☐	840	**1 1/2c Martha Washington**, pair, 1/20/39, DC	5.00	10.00
☐	841	**2c John Adams**, pair, 1/20/39, DC	5.00	10.00
☐	842	**3c Thomas Jefferson**, 1/20/39, DC 5.00	7.00	10.00
☐	843	**4c James Madison**, 1/20/39, DC 5.00	7.00	10.00
☐	844	**4 1/2c White House**, 1/20/39, DC 5.00	7.00	10.00
☐	845	**5c James Monroe**, 1/20/39, DC...................................5.00	7.00	10.00
☐	846	**6c John Q. Adams**, 1/20/39, DC...................................7.00	8.00	12.50
☐	847	**10c John Tyler**, 1/20/39, DC 9.00	12.50	15.00
☐		Scott 839-847 set of 9 on one cover, 1/20/39.........50.00	75.00	125.00

Perf. 10 Horizontally

☐	848	**1c George Washington**, strip of 3, 1/27/39, DC................	5.00	10.00
☐	849	**1 1/2c Martha Washington**, pair, 1/27/39, DC	5.00	10.00
☐	850	**2c John Adams**, pair, 1/27/39, DC....................................	5.00	10.00
☐	851	**3c Thomas Jefferson**, 1/27/39, DC 6.00	8.00	12.50
☐		Scott 848-851 set of 4 on one cover 30.00	40.00	60.00

1939

☐ 852 **3c Golden Gate International Exposition,** 2/18/39,
San Francisco, CA (352,165) 15.00 20.00 22.00

☐ 853 **3c New York World's Fair,** 4/1/39, New York, NY
(585,565) 17.50 20.00 22.00
☐ 1st Artcraft cachet..175.00 250.00 350.00
☐ 1st Artcraft cachet, Unofficial city 600.00

☐ 854 **3c Washington Inauguration,** 4/30/39, New York,
NY (395,644) 10.00 15.00 20.00

☐ 855 **3c Baseball Centennial,** 6/12/39, Cooperstown, NY
(398,199) 40.00 50.00 65.00
☐ 1st Leatherstocking Stamp Club cachet 45.00

☐ 856 **3c Panama Canal,** 8/15/39, USS Charleston, Canal
Zone (230,974) 10.00 15.00 20.00

☐ 857 **3c Printing Tercentenary,** 9/25/39, New York, NY
(295,270) 9.00 12.00 15.00
☐ 1st Ross Engraving Co. cachet 35.00
☐ 1st George Newmann cachet...............................35.00

☐ 858 **3c 50th Anniversary of Statehood**
11/2/39, Bismarck, ND, (142,106) 10.00 12.00 15.00
☐ Pierre, SD, 11/2/39 (150,429)............................10.00 12.00 15.00
☐ Helena, MT, 11/8/39 (130,273) 10.00 12.00 15.00
☐ Olympia, WA, 11/11/39 (150,429)........................10.00 12.00 15.00

1940 Famous Americans

☐ 859 **1c Washington Irving,** strip of 3, 1/29/40,
Tarrytown, NY (170,969).....................................3.00 3.50 4.00

☐ 860 **2c James Fenimore Cooper,** pair, 1/29/40,
Cooperstown, NY (154,836)..................................3.00 3.50 4.00

☐ 861 **3c Ralph Waldo Emerson,** 2/5/40, Boston, MA
(185,148) 3.00 3.50 4.00

☐ 862 **5c Louisa May Alcott,** 2/5/40, Concord, MA
(134,325) 3.00 3.50 4.25

☐ 863 **10c Samuel L. Clemens,** 2/13/40, Hannibal, MO
(150,492) 4.00 5.00 6.50 225.00

☐ 864 **1c Henry W. Longfellow,** strip of 3, 2/16/40,
Portland, ME (160,508) 3.00 3.50 4.00

☐ 865 **2c John Greenleaf Whittier,** pair, 2/16/40,
Haverhill, MA (148,423) 3.00 3.50 4.00

☐ 866 **3c James Russell Lowell,** 2/20/40, Cambridge, MA ...3.00 3.50 4.00
☐ 867 **5c Walt Whitman,** 2/20/40, Camden, NJ (134,185) ...4.00 5.00 7.00
☐ 868 **10c James Whitcomb Riley,** 2/24/40, Greenfield, IN
(131,760) 6.00 7.00 9.00

☐ 869 **1c Horace Mann,** strip of 3, 3/14/40, Boston, MA
(186,854) 3.00 3.50 4.00

☐ 870 **2c Mark Hopkins,** pair, 3/14/40, Williamstown,
MA (140,286) 3.00 3.50 4.00

☐ 871 **3c Charles W. Eliot** 3/28/40, Cambridge, MA
(155,708) 3.00 3.50 4.00

☐ 872 **5c Frances E. Willard,** 3/28/40, Evanston, IL
(140,483) 4.00 5.00 7.00

☐ 873 **10c Booker T. Washington,** 4/7/40, Tuskegee
Institute, AL (163,507) 6.00 7.00 9.00 150.00

☐ 874 **1c John James Audubon,** strip of 3, 4/8/40, St.
Francisville, LA (144, 123).................................3.00 3.50 4.00

1st Aristocrats cachet

1st Spartan cachet

895

894

896

897

898

899

900

901

1st Fleetwood cachet

903

902

904

905

906

907

908

909

910

Values for various cachet makers can be determined by using the Cachet Calculator which begins on page 52A.

		SINGLE	BLOCK	PLATE BLOCK	CERM PROG
☐ 875	2c Dr. Crawford W. Long, pair, 4/8/40, Jefferson, GA (158,128)................3.00	3.00	3.50	4.00	150.00
☐ 876	3c Luther Burbank, 4/17/40, Santa Rosa, CA (147,003)................3.00	3.00	3.50	4.00	
☐ 877	5c Dr. Walter Reed, 4/17/40, DC (154,464).................2.50	2.50	3.50	5.00	
☐ 878	10c Jane Addams, 4/26/40, Chicago, IL (132,375)................5.00	5.00	6.00	8.00	
☐ 879	1c Stephen Collins Foster, strip of 3, 5/3/40, Bardstown, KY (183,461)................3.00	3.00	3.50	4.00	
☐	1st Foster Assembly of Bardstown cachet......20.00				
☐	1st Bardstown Distillery cachet......................20.00				
☐ 880	2c John Philip Sousa, pair, 5/3/40, DC (131,422) 3.00	3.00	3.50	4.00	
☐	1st Fifth Battalion Marine Corps Reserve cachet.20.00				
☐ 881	3c Victor Herbert, 5/13/40, New York, NY (168,200)................3.00	3.00	3.50	4.00	
☐ 882	5c Edward A. MacDowell, 5/13/40, Peterborough, NH (135,155)................3.00	3.00	3.50	4.00	150.00
☐ 883	10c Ethelbert Nevin, 6/10/40, Pittsburgh, PA (121,951)................5.00	5.00	6.00	8.00	
☐ 884	1c Gilbert Charles Stuart, strip of 3, 9/5/40, Narragansett, RI 131,965)................3.00	3.00	3.50	4.00	
☐ 885	2c James A. McNeill Whistler, pair, 9/5/40, Lowell, MA (130,962)................3.00	3.00	3.50	4.00	
☐ 886	3c Augustus Saint-Gaudens, 9/16/40, New York, NY (138,200)................3.00	3.00	3.50	4.00	150.00
☐ 887	5c Daniel Chester French, 9/16/40, Stockbridge, MA (124,608) 3.00	3.00	3.50	4.00	
☐ 888	10c Frederic Remington, 9/30/40, Canton, NY (116,219)................5.00	5.00	6.00	8.00	
☐ 889	1c Eli Whitney, strip of 3, 10/7/40, Savannah, GA (140,868)................3.00	3.00	3.50	4.00	
☐ 890	2c Samuel F.B. Morse, pair, 10/7/40, New York, NY (135,388)................3.00	3.00	3.50	4.00	150.00
☐ 891	3c Cyrus Hall McCormick, 10/14/40, Lexington, VA (137,415) 3.00	3.00	3.50	4.00	
☐	1st International Harvester cachet................20.00				
☐ 892	5c Elias Howe, 10/14/40, Spencer, MA (126,334) 5.00	5.00	6.00	8.00	150.00
☐ 893	10c Alexander Graham Bell, 10/28/40, Boston, MA (125,372)................7.50	7.50	8.50	10.00	
☐	859-893 Set of 35 covers, matched cachets ....125.	125.	175.	250.	
☐	859-893 Set on 1 cover, 10/28/40................200.	200.			

1940

		SINGLE	BLOCK	PLATE BLOCK	CERM PROG
☐ 894	3c Pony Express, 4/3/40, St. Joseph, MO (194,589)....9.00	9.00	10.00	11.00	
☐	Sacramento, CA (160,849)................9.00	9.00	10.00	11.00	
☐	1st Aristocrats cachet 25.00	25.00			
☐ 895	3c Pan American Union, 4/14/40, DC (182,401).........8.00	8.00	9.00	10.00	
☐ 896	3c Idaho Statehood, 7/3/40, Boise, ID (156,429) 8.00	8.00	9.00	10.00	
☐	1st Papercraft Corp. cachet 30.00	30.00			
☐	1st Scenic Craft cachet 30.00	30.00			
☐ 897	3c Wyoming Statehood, 7/10/40, Cheyenne, WY (156,709)................8.00	8.00	9.00	10.00	
☐	1st Spartan cachet 30.00	30.00			

1st Smartcraft cachet   1st Pent Arts cachet

916   921   922

923   924   925

926   927   928

930

929   1st Bi-Color Craft cachet

934   937

1st Fluegel Cover cachet

☐ 898　**3c Coronado Expedition,** 9/7/40, Albuquerque, NM
　　　　(161,012)..8.00　9.00　10.00
☐　　　1st Albuquerque Philatelic Society cachet......20.00
☐ 899　**1c Defense,** strip of 3, 10/16/40, DC...........................6.00　9.00　10.00
☐ 900　**2c Defense,** pair, 10/16/40, DC ....6.00　9.00　10.00
☐ 901　**3c Defense,** 10/16/40, DC...6.00　9.00　10.00
☐　　　Scott 899-901 on one cover (450,083)............10.00　12.00　15.00
☐ 902　**3c Thirteenth Amendment,** 10/20/40, World's Fair,
　　　　NY (156,146)...8.00　9.00　10.00　150.00

1941

☐ 903　**3c Vermont Statehood,** 3/4/41, Montpelier, VT
　　　　(182,423)..9.00　10.00　11.00
☐　　　1st Dorothy Knapp cachet ....1500.
☐　　　1st Fleetwood cachet 90.00

1942

☐ 904　**3c Kentucky Statehood,** 6/1/42, Frankfort, KY
　　　　(155,730)..7.00　8.00　9.00
☐　　　1st Signed Fleetwood cachet 75.00
☐ 905　**3c "Win the War,"** 7/4/42, DC (191,168)......................7.00　8.00　8.00
☐ 906　**5c Chinese Commemorative,** 7/7/42, Denver, CO
　　　　(168,746)..10.00　12.00　14.00

1943

☐ 907　**2c Allied Nations,** pair, 1/14/43, DC (178,865)............5.00　5.25　7.00
☐ 908　**1c Four Freedoms,** strip of 3, 2/12/43, DC (193,800)..4.00　5.25　7.00

1943-44 Overrun Countries

☐ 909　**5c Poland,** 6/22/43, Chicago, IL (88, 170)...................5.00　6.00　15.00　110.00
☐　　　Washington, DC (136,002) ....4.00　5.00　15.00
☐　　　1st Smartcraft cachet 20.00
☐　　　1st Pent Arts cachet..30.00
☐　　　1st Polonus Philatelic Society cachet..............25.00
☐ 910　**5c Czechoslovakia,** 7/12/43, DC (145,112) ....4.00　5.00　15.00
☐ 911　**5c Norway,** 7/27/43, DC (130,054)..............................4.00　5.00　15.00
☐ 912　**5c Luxemboarg,** 8/10/43, DC (166,367) ....4.00　5.00　15.00
☐ 913　**5c Netherlands,** 8/24/43, DC (148,763) ....4.00　5.00　15.00
☐ 914　**5c Belgium,** 9/14/43, DC (154,220)..............................4.00　5.00　15.00
☐ 915　**5c France,** 9/28/43, DC (163,478)...............................4.00　5.00　15.00
☐ 916　**5c Greece,** 10/12/43, DC (166,553)............................4.00　5.00　15.00
☐ 917　**5c Yugoslavia,** 10/26/43, DC (161,835)........................4.00　5.00　15.00
☐ 918　**5c Albania,** 11/9/43, DC (162,275)..............................4.00　5.00　15.00
☐ 919　**5c Austria,** 11/23/43, DC (172,285) ....4.00　5.00　15.00
☐ 920　**5c Denmark,** 12/7/43, DC (173,784) ....4.00　5.00　15.00
☐　　　Scott 909-920 on one cover 65.00
☐ 921　**5c Korea,** 11/2/44, DC (192,860) ....5.00　6.00　11.00
☐　　　Scott 909-921 on one cover 85.00

935

936

938

939

940

941

942

1st Artmaster cachet

1st WCO cachet

943

944

946

945

947

948

949

950

951

**Values for various cachet makers can be determined
by using the Cachet Calculator which begins on page 52A.**

cover binders

Padded, durable, 3-ring binder will hold up to 100 covers. Features the "D" ring mechanism on the right hand side of album so you don't have to worry about creasing or wrinkling covers when opening or closing binder.

Item	Description	Retail
CBRD	Cover Binder - Red	$7.95
CBBL	Cover Binder - Blue	$7.95
CBGY	Cover Binder - Gray	$7.95
CBBK	Cover Binder - Black	$7.95

Cover pages sold separately.

T2	Cover Pages Black (25 per pckg)	$4.95
CBBL	Cover Pages Clear (25 per pckg)	$4.95

The cover binders and pages are available from your favorite stamp dealer or direct from:

SCOTT

P.O. Box 828 Sidney OH 45365-0828

to order call 1-800-572-6885

1st Fulton cachet

1st C. W. George cachet

952

953

1st Jackson cachet

954

955

956

957

958

959

960

961

962

963

964

965

966

**Values for various cachet makers can be determined
by using the Cachet Calculator which begins on page 52A.**

1944

☐ 922	3c **Transcontinental Railroad**, 5/10/44, Ogden, UT				
	(151,324)..9.00		9.50	10.00	
☐	Omaha, NE (171,000) 9.00		9.50	10.00	
☐	San Francisco,CA (125,000)...................9.00		9.50	10.00	
☐ 923	3c **Steamship**, 5/22/44, Kings Point, NY (152,324) . 9.00		9.50	10.00	
☐	Savannah, GA (181,472) 9.00		9.50	10.00	
☐ 924	3c **Telegraph**, 5/24/44, DC (141,907) 9.00		9.50	10.00	
☐	Baltimore, MD (136,480) 9.00		9.50	10.00	
☐ 925	3c **Philippines**, 9/27/44 (214,865), DC........9.00		9.50	10.00	
☐	1st Hobby Life cachet 35.00				
☐ 926	3c **Motion Picture**, 10/31/44, Los Angeles,				
	Hollywood Sta., CA (190,660) 9.00		9.50	10.00	
☐	New York, NY (176,473) 9.00		9.50	10.00	

1945

☐ 927	3c **Florida Statehood**, 3/3/45, Tallahassee, FL				
	(228,435)..9.00		9.50	10.00	
☐ 928	5c **United Nations Conference**, 4/25/45, San				
	Francisco, CA (417,450) 9.00		12.50	17.50	
☐ 929	3c **Iwo Jima (Marines)**, 7/11/45, DC (391,650) 15.00		16.00	18.00	
☐	1st Nu-Art cachet................................30.00				

1945-46

☐ 930	1c **Franklin D. Roosevelt**, strip of 3, 7/26/45, Hyde				
	Park, NY (390,219) 3.50		4.50	6.50	
☐	1st Bi-Color Croft cachet.....................25.00				
☐ 931	2c **Franklin D. Roosevelt** pair, 8/24/45, Warm				
	Springs, GA (426,142)..........................3.50		4.50	6.50	
☐ 932	3c **Franklin D. Roosevelt**, 6/27/45, DC (391,650) 3.50		4.50	6.50	
☐	1st Fluegel Covers cachet 75.00				
☐ 933	5c **Franklin D. Roosevelt**, 1/30/46, DC (466,766) . .3.50		4.50	6.50	
☐	Scott 930-933 on one cover 8.00				
☐ 934	3c **Army**, 9/28/45, DC (392,300) 10.00		12.00	15.00	
☐	1st R. Lee Southworth cachet....................40.00				
☐ 935	3c **Navy**, 10/27/45, Annapolis, MD (460,352) 10.00		12.00	15.00	
☐ 936	3c **Coast Guard**, 11/10/45, New York, NY				
	(405,280)...10.00		12.00	15.00	110.00
☐ 937	3c **Alfred E. Smith**, 11/26/45, New York, NY				
	(424,950)...3.00		3.50	6.00	100.00
☐ 938	3c **Texas Statehood**, 12/29/45, Austin, TX (397,860) .9.00		10.00	12.00	

1946

☐ 939	3c **Merchant Marine**, 2/26/46, DC (432,141) 10.00		12.00	15.00	
☐	Scott 929, 934-936, 939 on one cover, 2/26/46.30.00				
☐ 940	3c **Veterans of World War II**, 5/9/46, DC (492,786).10.00		12.00	15.00	
☐	1st Artmaster cachet 20.00				
☐	1st WCO cachet................................30.00				
☐	Scott 929, 934-936, 939-940 on one cover, ...35.00				
☐ 941	3c **Tennessee Statehood**, 6/1/46, Nashville, TN				
	(463,512)..4.00		5.00	6.00	
☐ 942	3c **Iowa Statehood**, 8/3/46, Iowa City, IA (517,505).4.00		5.00	6.00	90.00
	1st Iowa City Stamp Club cachet 25.00				

☐ 943 **3c Smithsonian Institution,** 8/10/46, DC (402,448) .4.25   5.50   6.75
☐   1st Z-Special cachet...30.00
☐ 944 **3c Kearny Expedition,** 10/16/46, Santa Fe, NM
    (384,300)...4.25   5.50   6.75   90.00

1947

☐ 945 **3c Thomas A. Edison,** 2/11/47, Milan, OH
    (632,473)...4.25   5.50   6.75   75.00
☐   1st Dorn's Wines cachet.................................20.00
☐ 946 **3c Joseph Pulitzer,** 4/10/47, New York, NY
    (580,870)...4.25   5.50   6.75   85.00
☐ 947 **3c Postage Stamp Centenary,** 5/17/47, New York,
    NY (712,873)...4.25   5.50   6.75
☐   1st Fulton cachet 30.00
☐ 948 **5c & 10c CIPEX,** souvenir sheet, 5/19/47, New
    York, NY (502,175)...6.00
☐ 949 **3c Doctors,** 6/9/47, Atlantic City, NJ (508,016) 10.00   12.00   15.00
☐ 950 **3c Utah,** 7/24/47, Salt Lake City, UT (456,416) 3.00   3.50   4.00   75.00
☐ 951 **3c U.S. Frigate Constitution,** 10/21/47, Boston,
    MA (683,416)..8.00   9.00   10.00   85.00
☐   1st C.W. George cachet 75.00
☐   1st Sun Craft cachet 25.00
☐ 952 **3c Everglades National Park,** 12/5/47, Florida
    City, FL.. 4.25   5.50   6.75   75.00
☐   1st Artist Craft cachet....................................20.00
☐   1st Miami Philatelic Society cachet 20.00
☐   1st Velvatone cachet 100.00

1948

☐ 953 **3c George Washington Carver,** 1/5/48, Tuskegee
    Institute, AL (402,179)......................................4.25   5.50   6.75   80.00
☐   1st Ira Bennett cachet 60.00
☐   1st Jackson cachet..40.00
☐ 954 **3c California Gold Centennial,** 1/24/48, Coloma,
    CA (526,154) 4.25   5.50   6.75
☐ 955 **3c Mississippi Territory,** 4/7/48, Natchez, MS
    (434,804)...4.25   5.50   6.75
☐ 956 **3c Four Chaplains,** 5/28/48, DC (459,070) 4.25   5.50   6.75
☐ 957 **3c Wisconsin Statehood,** 5/29/48, Madison, WI
    (470,280)...4.25   5.50   6.75   70.00
☐   1st Halpert cachet...20.00
☐   1st Pearson cachet...20.00
☐ 958 **5c Swedish Pioneers,** 6/4/48, Chicago, IL (364,318)4.25   5.50   6.75   65.00
☐   1st American Institute of Swedish Arts,
    Literature & Science cachet............................20.00
☐ 959 **3c Progress of Women,** 7/19/48, Seneca Falls, NY
    (401,923)...4.25   5.50   6.75
☐ 960 **3c William Allen White,** 7/31/48, Emporia, KS
    (385,648)...4.25   5.50   6.75
☐ 961 **3c U.S.-Canada Friendship,** 8/2/48, Niagara
    Falls, NY (406,467)...4.25   5.50   6.75   70.00
☐ 962 **3c Francis Scott Key,** 8/9/48, Frederick, MD, (505,930)4.25   5.50   6.75   50.00
☐ 963 **3c Salute to Youth,** 8/11/48, DC (347,070)...............4.25   5.50   6.75
☐ 964 **3c Oregon Territory,** 8/14/48, Oregon City, OR
    (365,898)...4.25   5.50   6.75   65.00

SCOTT NUMBER	DESCRIPTION	SINGLE	PLATE BLOCK	CERM PROG	
☐ 965	3c Harlan Fiske Stone, 8/25/48, Chesterfield, NH (362,170)..........4.25		5.50	6.75	
☐ 966	3c Palomar Mountain Observatory, 8/30/48, Palomar Mountain,CA (401,365) 4.25		5.50	6.75	75.00
☐ 967	3c Clara Barton, 9/7/48, Oxford, MA (362,000)...... 4.25		5.50	6.75	50.00
☐ 968	3c Poultry Industry, 9/9/48, New Haven, CT (475,000)..........................4.25		5.50	6.75	60.00
☐ 969	3c Gold Star Mothers, 9/21/48, DC (386,064)..........4.25		5.50	6.75	
☐ 970	3c Fort Kearny, 9/22/48, Minden, NE (429,633) 4.25		5.50	6.75	45.00
☐ 971	3c Volunteer Firemen, 10/4/48, Dover, DE (399,630) (2 types)* 8.00		9.00	12.00	70.00*
☐	1st Mack (Mack Trucks) cachet 25.00				
☐ 972	3c Indian Centennial, 10/15/48, Muskogee, OK (459,528)..........................4.25		5.50	6.75	
☐ 973	3c Rough Riders, 10/27/48, Prescott, AZ (399,198).4.25		5.50	6.75	
☐ 974	3c Juliette Low, 10/29/48, Savannah, GA (476,573).4.25		5.50	6.75	
☐ 975	3c Will Rogers, 11/4/48, Claremore, OK (450,350) ..4.25		5.50	6.75	
☐	1st Kolor Kover cachet 100.00				
☐ 976	3c Fort Bliss, 11/5/48, El Paso, TX (421,000) 4.25		5.50	6.75	75.00
☐	1st El Paso Stamp Club cachet 20.00				
☐ 977	3c Moina Michael, 11/9/48, Athens, GA (374,090)...4.25		5.50	6.75	
☐ 978	3c Gettysburg Address, 11/19/48, Gettysburg, PA (511,990)..........................4.25		5.50	6.75	65.00
☐ 979	3c American Turners, 11/20/48, Cincinnati, OH (434,090)..........................4.25		5.50	6.75	60.00
☐	1st AmericanTurners cachet,11/21/48,Wash.DC15.00				
☐ 980	3c Joel Chandler Harris, 12/9/48, Eatonton, GA (426,199) 4.25		5.50	6.75	

1949

SCOTT NUMBER	DESCRIPTION	SINGLE	PLATE BLOCK	CERM PROG	
☐ 981	3c Minnesota Territory, 3/3/49, St. Paul, MN (458,750)..........................2.50		3.50	4.50	50.00
☐ 982	3c Washington and Lee University, 4/12/49, Lexington, VA (447,910) 2.50		3.50	4.50	50.00
☐ 983	3c Puerto Rico Election, 4/27/49, San Juan, PR (390,416)..........................2.50		3.50	4.50	
☐ 984	3c Annapolis Tercentenary, 5/23/49, Annapolis, MD (441,802) 2.50		3.50	4.50	50.00
☐ 985	3c G.A.R., 8/29/49, Indianapolis, IN (471,696) 2.50		3.50	4.50	50.00
☐ 986	3c Edgar Allan Poe, 10/7/49, Richmond, VA (371,020)..........................2.50		3.50	4.50	55.00

1950

SCOTT NUMBER	DESCRIPTION	SINGLE	PLATE BLOCK	CERM PROG	
☐ 987	3c Bankers, 1/3/50, Saratoga Springs, NY (388,622)..2.00		2.25	3.00	50.00
☐ 988	3c Samuel Gompers, 1/27/50, DC (332,023) 2.00		2.25	3.00	
☐ 989	3c National Capital Sesquicentennial (Freedom), 4/20/50, DC (371,743) 2.00		2.25	2.75	
☐ 990	3c National Capital Sesquicentennial (Executive), 6/12/50, DC (376,789) 2.00		2.25	2.75	55.00
☐ 991	3c National Capital Sesquicentennial (Judicial), 8/2/50, DC (324,007) 2.00		2.25	2.75	
☐ 992	3c National Capital Sesquicentennial (Legislative), 11/22/50, DC (352,215) 2.00		2.25	2.75	
☐	989-992 on one cover 6.00				

967

968

969

970

971

972

973

974

975

976

977

978

979

980

981

982

983

984

986

985

987

988

989

58

SCOTT NUMBER	DESCRIPTION	SINGLE	PLATE BLOCK	CERM BLOCK	PROG
☐ 993	3c Railroad Engineers, 4/29/50, Jackson, TN (420,830)......6.00		7.00	8.00	55.00
☐ 994	3c Kansas City Centenary, 6/3/50, Kansas City, MO (405,390)......2.00		2.25	2.75	40.00
☐ 995	3c Boy Scouts, 6/30/50, Valley Forge, PA (622,972).8.00		9.00	12.00	45.00
☐	1st Boy Scouts of America cachet...................25.00				
☐ 996	3c Indiana Territory, 7/4/50, Vincennes, IN (359,643)......2.00		2.25	2.75	40.00
☐ 997	3c California Statehood, 9/9/50, Sacramento, CA (391,919)......2.00		2.25	2.75	

1951

SCOTT NUMBER	DESCRIPTION	SINGLE	PLATE BLOCK	CERM BLOCK	PROG
☐ 998	3c United Confederate Veterans, 5/30/51, Norfolk, VA (374,235) 2.00		2.25	2.75	40.00
☐	1st Dietz Printing Co. cachet 30.00				
☐ 999	3c Nevada Centennial, 7/14/51, Genoa, NV (336,890) (2 types)* 2.00		2.25	2.75	30.00*
☐ 1000	3c Landing of Cadillac, 7/24/51, Detroit, MI (323,094)......2.00		2.25	2.75	35.00
☐ 1001	3c Colorado Statehood, 8/1/51, Minturn, CO (311,568) 2.00		2.25	2.75	30.00
☐ 1002	3c American Chemical Society, 9/4/51, New York, NY (436,419)......2.00		2.25	2.75	30.00
☐ 1003	3c Battle of Brooklyn, 12/10/51, Brooklyn, NY (420,000)......2.00		2.25	2.75	35.00

1952

SCOTT NUMBER	DESCRIPTION	SINGLE	PLATE BLOCK	CERM BLOCK	PROG
☐ 1004	3c Betsy Ross, 1/2/52, Philadelphia, PA (314,312)...2.00		2.25	2.75	30.00
☐	1st Knoble/Bogert cachet...............................75.00				
☐	1st Steelcraft cachet 30.00				
☐ 1005	3c 4-H Clubs, 1/15/52, Springfield, OH (383,290) ...2.00		2.25	2.75	20.00
☐ 1006	3c B. & O. Railroad, 2/28/52, Baltimore, MD (441,600)......4.00		4.25	4.50	35.00
☐	1st M.W. Beck cachet......................................20.00				
☐	1st T. Raquere cachet 20.00				
☐ 1007	3c American Automobile Association, 3/4/52, Chicago, IL (520, 123)......2.00		2.25	2.75	30.00
☐	1st American Automobile Association cachet 15.00				
☐ 1008	3c NATO, 4/4/52, DC (313,518)......2.00		2.25	2.75	
☐ 1009	3c Grand Coulee Dam, 5/15/52, Grand Coulee, WA (341,680)......2.00		2.25	2.75	30.00
☐ 1010	3c Lafayette, 6/13/52, Georgetown, SC (349,102)....2.00		2.25	2.75	30.00
☐ 1011	3c Mt. Rushmore Memorial, 8/11/52, Keystone, SD (337,027) 2.00		2.25	2.75	30.00
☐ 1012	3c Engineering Centennial, 9/6/52, Chicago, IL (318,483)......2.00		2.25	2.75	30.00
☐ 1013	3c Service Women, 9/11/52, DC (308,062)...............2.00		2.25	2.75	
☐ 1014	3c Gutenberg Bible, 9/30/52, DC (387,078) 2.00		2.25	2.75	45.00
☐ 1015	3c Newspaper Boys, 10/4/52, Philadelphia, PA (626,000) (2 types)* 2.00		2.25	2.75	30.00*
☐ 1016	3c Red Cross, 11/21/52, New York, NY (439,252) ...4.00		5.00	8.00	25.00

990

991

992

993

994

995

996

997

998

999

1000

1001

1002

1003

1004

**Values for various cachet makers can be determined
by using the Cachet Calculator which begins on page 52A.**

1953

		SINGLE	BLOCK	PLATE BLOCK	CERM PROG
☐ 1017	3c National Guard, 2/23/53, DC (387,618)...............2.00		2.25	2.75	30.00
☐ 1018	3c Ohio Sesquicentennial, 3/2/53, Chillicothe, OH				
	(407,983)..2.00		2.25	2.75	25.00
☐	1st Boerger cachet..25.00				
☐ 1019	3c Washington Territory, 3/2/53, Olympia, WA				
	(344,047)..2.00		2.25	2.75	40.00
☐	1st Tacoma Stamp Club cachet.....................20.00				
	1st Washington Territorial Centennial				
☐	Commission cachet 15.00				
☐ 1020	3c Louisiana Purchase, 4/30/53, St. Louis, MO				
	(425,600)..2.00		2.25	2.75	30.00
☐ 1021	5c Opening of Japan Centennial, 7/14/53, DC				
	(320,541)..2.00		2.25	2.75	30.00
☐	1st Overseas Mailers cachet 70.00				
☐ 1022	3c American Bar Association, 8/24/53, Boston,				
	MA (410,036) 5.00		6.00	8.00	25.00
☐ 1023	3c Sagamore Hill, 9/14/53, Oyster Bay, NY				
	(379,750)..2.00		2.25	2.75	30.00
☐ 1024	3c Future Farmers, 10/13/53, Kansas City, MO				
	(424,193)..2.00		2.25	2.75	25.00
☐ 1025	3c Trucking Industry, 10/27/53, Los Angeles, CA				
	(875,021)..2.00		2.25	2.75	25.00
☐ 1026	3c General Patton, 11/11/53, Fort Knox, KY				
	(342,600)..2.00		2.25	2.75	100.00
☐	1st World Wars Tank Corps Assoc. cachet 15.00				
☐ 1027	3c New York City, 11/20/53, New York, NY				
	(387,914)..2.00		2.25	2.75	25.00
☐ 1028	3c Gadsden Purchase, 12/30/53, Tucson, AZ				
	(363,250)..2.00		2.25	2.75	25.00

1954

		SINGLE	BLOCK	PLATE BLOCK	CERM PROG
☐ 1029	3c Columbia University, 1/4/54, New York, NY				
	(550,745)..2.00		2.25	2.75	35.00

1954-68 Liberty Issue

		SINGLE	BLOCK	PLATE BLOCK	CERM PROG
☐ 1030a	1/2c Benjamin Franklin, block of 6, 10/20/55, DC				
	(223,122).......................................		1.00	1.25	30.00
☐ 1031b	1c George Washington, strip of 3, 8/26/54,				
	Chicago, IL (272,581)................................1.00		1.00	1.50	30.00
☐ 1031A	1 1/4c Palace of the Governors, strip of 3,				
	6/17/60, Santa Fe, NM 1.00		1.00	1.50	15.00
☐	1031A and 1054A on one cover 1.50				
	Total for Scott 1031A and 1054A is 501,848.				
☐ 1032	1 1/2c Mount Vernon, pair, 2/22/56, Mount				
	Vernon, VA (270,109)................................1.00		1.25	1.50	40.00
☐ 1033	2c Thomas Jefferson, pair, 9/15/54, San				
	Francisco, CA (307,300) 1.00		1.25	1.50	30.00
☐ 1034	2 1/2c Bunker Hill Monument, pair, 6/17/59,				
	Boston, MA (315,060) 1.00		1.25	1.50	20.00
☐ 1035e	3c Statue of Liberty, 6/24/54, Albany, NY (340,001)1.00		1.25	1.50	
	(2 types)*..				35.00*
☐ 1035a	Statue of Liberty, booklet pane of 6, 6/30/54, DC				
	(131,839)..5.00				

1st Velvatone cachet

1005

1006 1007 1008 1009

1010 1012

1011

1013 1016

1015 1016 1017

HOW TO USE THIS BOOK
The number in the first column is its Scott number or identifying number. Following that is the denomination of the stamp, description, date of issue, and the value.

SCOTT NUMBER	DESCRIPTION	SINGLE	PLATE BLOCK	BLOCK	CERM PROG
☐ 1035b	Statue of Liberty, tagged, 7/6/66, DC 55.00				
☐ 1036c	4c Abraham Lincoln, 11/19/54, New York, NY				
	(374,064) (2 types)* 1.00		1.25	1.50	35.00*
☐ 1036a	Abraham Lincoln, booklet pane of 6, 7/31/58,				
	Wheeling, WV (135,825) 4.00				
☐ 1036b	Abraham Lincoln, tagged, DC (500)...................100.00				
☐ 1037	4 1/2c The Hermitage, 3/16/59, Hermitage, TN				
	(320,000)................................1.00		1.25	1.50	35.00
☐ 1038	5c James Monroe, 12/2/54, Fredericksburg, VA				
	(255,650)................................1.00		1.25	1.50	25.00
☐ 1039a	6c Theodore Roosevelt 11/18/55, New York, NY				
	(257,551) (3 types)* 1.00		1.25	1.50	25.00*
☐ 1040	7c Woodrow Wilson, 1/10/56, Staunton, VA				
	(200,111) (2 types)* 1.00		1.25	1.50	20.00*
☐ 1041	8c Statue of Liberty, (flat plate),4/9/54, DC (340,077)1.00		1.25	1.50	20.00
☐ 1041B	8c Statue of Liberty (rotary), 4/9/54, DC 1.00		1.25	1.50	
☐ 1042	8c Statue of Liberty, (Giori press), 3/22/58,				
	Cleveland, OH, (223,899) (4 types)*..................1.00		1.25	2.00	15.00*
	1st Cascade cachet............................35.00				
☐ 1042A	8c John J. Pershing, 11/17/61, New York, NY				
	(321,031)................................1.00		1.25	2.00	15.00
☐ 1043	9c The Alamo, 6/14/56, San Antonio, TX				
	(207,086)................................1.50		2.00	3.00	50.00
☐ 1044	10c Independence Hall, 7/4/56, Philadelphia, PA				
	(220,930)................................1.00		1.25	2.00	25.00
☐ 1044b	Independence Hall, tagged, 7/6/66, DC.................50.00				
☐ 1044A	11c Statue of Liberty, 6/15/61, DC (238,905)...........1.00		1.25	2.00	22.00
☐ 1044Ac	Statue of Liberty, tagged, 1/11/67, DC 50.00				
☐ 1045	12c Benjamin Harrison, 6/6/59, Oxford, OH				
	(225,869)................................1.00		1.25	2.00	25.00
☐ 1045a	Benjamin Harrison, tagged, 5/6/68.....................50.00				
☐ 1046	15c John Jay, 12/12/58, DC (205,680)...................1.00		1.50	2.00	
☐ 1046a	John Jay, tagged, 7/6/66, DC 50.00				
☐ 1047	20c Monticello, 4/13/56, Charlottesville, VA				
	(147,860) (2 types)* 1.20		1.75	2.50	25.00*
☐ 1048	25c Paul Revere, 4/18/58, Boston, MA (196,530)				
	(2 types)*................................1.30		2.00	2.50	40.00*
☐ 1049a	30c Robert E. Lee, 9/21/55, Norfolk, VA				
	(120, 166) (2 types)* 2.00		2.50	3.00	35.00*
☐ 1050a	40c John Marshall, 9/24/55, Richmond, VA				
	(113,972)................................2.00		2.50	3.00	55.00
☐ 1051a	50c Susan B. Anthony, 8/25/55, Louisville, KY				
	(110,220)................................6.00		10.00	12.50	45.00
☐ 1052a	$1 Patrick Henry, 10/7/55, Joplin, MO (80,191) ...10.00		15.00	25.00	70.00
☐ 1053	$5 Alexander Hamilton, 3/19/56, Paterson, NJ				
	(34,272)................................50.00		90.00	125.00	100.00

SCOTT NUMBER	DESCRIPTION	SINGLE	PAIR	LINE PAIR	CERM PROG

1954-73 Liberty Coils

☐ 1054	1c George Washington, strip of 3, 10/8/54,				
	Baltimore, MD (196,318) (2 types)*		1.00	1.50	25.00*
☐ 1054A	1 1/4c Palace of the Governors, strip of 3,				
	6/17/60, Santa Fe, NM		1.00	1.75	15.00

1st Overseas Mailers cachet

1018

1019

1020

1021

1022

1023

1024

1025

1026

1027

1028

1029

1031, 1054

1033, 1055

1036, 1058

1060

**Values for various cachet makers can be determined
by using the Cachet Calculator which begins on page 52A.**

SCOTT NUMBER	DESCRIPTION	SINGLE	BLOCK	PLATE BLOCK	CERM PROG
☐ 1055	2c Thomas Jefferson, 10/22/54, St. Louis, MO (162,050)		1.00	1.50	45.00
☐ 1055a	Thomas Jefferson, tagged, pair, 5/6/68, DC	40.00			
☐ 1056	2 1/2c Bunker Hill, 9/9/59, Los Angeles, CA (198,680)		2.00	3.00	35.00
☐ 1057	3c Statue of Liberty, 7/20/54, DC (137,139)	1.00	1.00	1.75	
☐ 1058	4c Abraham Lincoln, 7/31/58, Mandan, ND (184,079)	1.00	1.00	1.75	
☐ 1059	4 1/2c The Hermitage, 5/1/59, Denver, CO (202,454)	1.75	2.00	3.00	
☐ 1059A	25c Paul Revere, 2/25/65, Wheaton, MD (184,954)	1.75	2.00	3.00	
☐ 1059Ab	Paul Revere, tagged, 4/3/73, New York, NY	40.00			

SCOTT NUMBER	DESCRIPTION	SINGLE	BLOCK	PLATE BLOCK	CERM PROG

1954

☐ 1060	3c Nebraska Territory, 5/7/54, Nebraska City, (401,015)	1.75	1.85	2.00	25.00
☐ 1061	3e Kansas Territory, 5/31/54, Fort Leavenworth, KS (349,145)	1.75	1.85	2.00	25.00
☐ 1062	3c George Eastman, 7/12/54, Rochester, NY (630,448)	1.75	1.85	2.00	30.00
☐ 1063	3c Lewis & Clark Expedition, 7/28/54, Sioux City, IA (371,557)	1.75	1.85	2.00	25.00

1955

☐ 1064	3c Pennsylvania Academy of Fine Arts, 1/15/55 Philadelphia, PA (307,040)	1.75	1.85	2.00	20.00
☐ 1065	3c Land Grant Colleges, 2/12/55, East Lansing, (419,241)	1.75	1.85	2.00	15.00
☐ 1066	8c Rotary International, 2/23/55, Chicago, IL (350,625)	1.75	2.00	3.00	50.00
☐ 1067	3c Armed Forces Reserve, 5/21/55, DC (300,436)	2.00	2.25	3.00	20.00
☐ 1068	3c New Hampshire, 6/21/55, Franconia, NH (330,630)	1.00	1.10	1.50	18.00
☐	1st Texture Craft cachet	35.00			
☐ 1069	3c Soo Locks, 6/28/55, Sault Sainte Marie, MI (316,616)	1.75	1.85	2.00	55.00
☐ 1070	3c Atoms for Peace, 7/28/55, DC (351,940)	1.75	1.85	2.00	
☐ 1071	3c Fort Ticonderoga, 9/18/55, Fort Ticonderoga, NY (342,946)	1.75	1.85	2.00	20.00
☐ 1072	3c Andrew Mellon, 12/20/55, DC (278,897)	1.75	1.85	2.00	18.00

1956

☐ 1073	3c Benjamin Franklin, 1/17/56, Philadelphia, PA (351,260)	1.75	1.85	2.00	30.00
☐	Poor Richard Station	1.75	1.85	2.00	
☐ 1074	3c Booker T. Washington, 4/5/56, Booker T. Washington Birthplace, VA (272,659)	1.75	1.85	2.00	35.00
☐ 1075	3c & 8c FIPEX, Souvenir Sheet, 4/28/56, New York, NY (429,327)	5.00			35.00
☐ 1076	3c FIPEX, 4/30/56, New York, NY, (526,090)	1.75	1.85	2.00	35.00
☐ 1077	3c Wildlife Conservation (Turkey), 5/5/56, Fond du Lac, WI (292,121)	1.75	1.85	2.00	25.00

1st Cascade cachet

1061

1062

1063

1065

1066

1064

1067

1068

1069

1070

1071

1072

1073

1074

1076

1077

1078

1080

1082

Values for various cachet makers can be determined by using the Cachet Calculator which begins on page 52A.

SCOTT NUMBER	DESCRIPTION	SINGLE	PAIR	LINE PAIR	CERM PROG
☐ 1078	3c Wildlife Conservation (Antelope), 6/22/56, Gunnison, CO (294,731)	1.75	1.85	2.00	25.00
☐ 1079	3c Wildlife Conservation (Salmon), 11/9/56, Seattle, WA (346,800)	1.75	1.85	2.00	25.00
☐ 1080	3c Pure Food and Drug Laws, 6/27/56, DC (411,761)	1.75	1.85	2.00	18.00
☐ 1081	3c Wheatland, 8/5/56, Lancaster, PA (340,142)	1.75	1.85	2.00	18.00
☐ 1082	3c Labor Day, 9/3/56, Camden, NJ (338,450)	1.75	1.85	2.00	25.00
☐ 1083	3c Nassau Hall, 9/22/56, Princeton, NJ (350,756)	1.75	1.85	2.00	22.00
☐ 1084	3c Devils Tower, 9/24/56, Devils Tower, WY (285,090)	1.75	1.85	2.00	30.00
☐ 1085	3c Children, 12/15/56, DC (305,125)	1.75	1.85	2.00	22.00

1957

SCOTT NUMBER	DESCRIPTION	SINGLE	PAIR	LINE PAIR	CERM PROG
☐ 1086	3c Alexander Hamilton, 1/11/57, New York, NY (305,117)	1.75	1.85	2.00	40.00
☐ 1087	3c Polio, 1/15/57, DC (307,630)	2.00	2.25	2.75	20.00
☐ 1088	3c Coast & Geodetic Survey, 2/11/57, Seattle, WA (309,931)	1.75	1.85	2.00	15.00
☐ 1089	3c Architects, 2/23/57, New York, NY (368,840)	1.75	1.85	2.00	15.00
☐ 1090	3c Steel Industry, 5/22/57, New York, NY (473,284)	1.75	1.85	2.00	30.00
☐ 1091	3c International Naval Review, 6/10/57, U.S.S. Saratoga, Norfolk, VA (365,933) (2 types)*	1.75	1.85	2.00	15.00*
☐ 1092	3c Oklahoma Statehood, 6/14/57, Oklahoma City, OK (327,172)	1.75	1.85	2.00	18.00
☐ 1093	3c School Teachers, 7/1/57, Philadelphia, PA (375,986)	1.75	1.85	2.00	30.00
	"Philadelpia" error cancel	8.00	10.00		
☐ 1094	4c Flag, 7/4/57, DC (523,879)	1.75	1.85	2.00	
☐ 1095	3c Shipbuilding, 8/15/57, Bath, ME (347,432)	1.75	1.85	2.00	10.00
☐ 1096	8c Ramon Magsaysay, 8/31/57, DC (334,558)	1.75	1.85	2.00	20.00
☐ 1097	3c Lafayette Bicentenary, 9/6/57, Easton, PA (260,421) (3 types)*	1.75	1.85	2.00	25.00*
	Fayetteville, NC (230,000)	1.75	1.85	2.00	
	Louisville, KY (207,856)	1.75	1.85	2.00	
☐ 1098	3c Wildlife Conservation (Whooping Cranes), 11/22/57, New York, NY (342,970) (2 types)*	1.75	1.85	2.00	20.00*
	New Orleans, LA (154,327)	1.75	1.85	2.00	
	Corpus Christi, TX (280,990)	1.75	1.85	2.00	
☐ 1099	3c Religious Freedom, 12/27/57, Flushing NY (357,770)	1.75	1.85	2.00	12.00

1958

SCOTT NUMBER	DESCRIPTION	SINGLE	PAIR	LINE PAIR	CERM PROG
☐ 1100	3c Gardening-Horticulture, 3/15/58, Ithaca, NY (451,292)	1.75	1.85	2.00	25.00
☐ 1104	3c Brussels Fair, 4/17/58, Detroit, MI (428,073)	1.75	1.85	2.00	22.00
☐ 1105	3c James Monroe, 4/28/58, Montross, VA (326,988)	1.75	1.85	2.00	20.00
☐ 1106	3c Minnesota Statehood, 5/11/58, Saint Paul, MN (475,522)	1.75	1.85	2.00	25.00
☐ 1107	3c International Geophysical Year, 5/31/58, Chicago, IL (397,000)	1.75	1.85	2.00	18.00
☐ 1108	3c Gunston Hall, 6/12/58, Lorton, VA (349,801)	1.75	1.85	2.00	
☐ 1109	3c Mackinac Bridge, 6/25/58, Mackinac Bridge, MI (445,605), no cancel	1.75	1.85	2.00	45.00

		SINGLE	BLOCK	PLATE BLOCK	CERM PROG
☐ 1110	**4c Simon Bolivar,** 7/24/58, DC 1.75		1.85	2.00	
☐ 1111	**8c Simon Bolivar,** 7/24/58, DC 1.75		1.85	2.00	
☐	Scott 1110-1111 on one cover 2.00				50.00
	Total for Scott 1110-1111 is 708,777.				
☐ 1112	**4c Atlantic Cable,** 8/15/58, New York, NY (365,072)1.75		1.85	2.00	25.00

1958-59

		SINGLE	BLOCK	PLATE BLOCK	CERM PROG
☐ 1113	**1c Lincoln Sesquicentennial,** 2/12/59, Hodgenville, KY (379,862)		1.00	1.50	20.00
☐ 1114	**3c Lincoln Sesquicentennial,** pair, 2/27/59, New York, NY (437,737) 1.75		1.85	2.00	20.00
☐ 1115	**4c Lincoln-Douglas Debates,** 8/27/58, Freeport, IL (373,063)...1.75		1.85	2.00	20.00
☐	1st Western Cachets cachet 25.00				
☐ 1116	**4c Lincoln Sesquicentennial,** 5/30/59, DC (894,887).......................................1.75		1.85	2.00	20.00
☐	Scott 1113-16 on one cover 5.00				

1958

		SINGLE	BLOCK	PLATE BLOCK	CERM PROG
☐ 1117	**4c Lajos Kossnth,** 9/19/58, DC 1.75		1.85	2.00	
☐ 1118	**8c Lajos Kossuth,** 9/19/58, DC 1.75		1.85	2.00	
☐	Scott 1117-1118 on one cover 2.00				45.00
	Total for Scott 1117 and 1118 is 722,188.				
☐ 1119	**4c Freedom of Press,** 9/22/58, Columbia, MO (411,752) (2 types)* 1.75		1.85	2.00	25.00*
☐ 1120	**4c Overland Mail,** 10/10/58, San Francisco, CA (352,760)...1.75		1.85	2.00	40.00
☐ 1121	**4c Noah Webster,** 10/16/58, West Hartford, CT (364,608)...1.75		1.85	2.00	30.00
☐ 1122	**4c Forest Conservation,** 10/27/58, Tucson, AZ (405,959)...1.75		1.85	2.00	30.00
☐ 1123	**4c Fort Duquesne,** 11/25/58, Pittsburgh, PA (421,764)...1.75		1.85	2.00	60.00

1959

		SINGLE	BLOCK	PLATE BLOCK	CERM PROG
☐ 1124	**4c Oregon Statehood,** 2/14/59, Astoria, OR (452,764) (2 types)* 1.75		1.85	2.00	20.00*
☐ 1125	**4c Jose de San Martin,** 2/25/ 59, DC 1.75		1.85	2.00	
☐ 1126	**8c Jose de San Martin,** 2/25/59, DC 1.75		1.85	2.00	
☐	Scott 1125-1126 on one cover 2.00				30.00
	Total for Scott 1125 and 1126 is 910,208.				
☐ 1127	**4c NATO,** 4/1/59, DC (361,040)...................1.75		1.85	2.00	20.00
☐	1st Gold Craft cachet 35.00				
☐ 1128	**4c Arctic Explorations,** 4/6/59, Cresson, PA (397,770)...1.75		1.85	2.00	25.00
☐ 1129	**8c World Peace through World Trade,** 4/20/59, DC (503,618) 1.75		1.85	2.00	
☐ 1130	**4c Silver Centennial,** 6/8/59, Virginia City, NV (337,233)...1.75		1.85	2.00	50.00
☐ 1131	**4c St. Lawrence Seaway,** 6/26/59, Massena, NY (543,211)...1.75		1.85	2.00	38.00
	Joint issue with Canada 10.00				
	Joint issue with Canada dual cancel 200.00				30.0
☐ 1132	**4c Flag (49 stars),** 7/4/59, Auburn, NY (523,773)....1.75		1.85	2.00	40.00
☐ 1133	**4c Soil Conservation,** 8/26/59, Rapid City, SD (400,613) (2 types)* 1.75		1.85	2.00	25.00*

		SINGLE	BLOCK	PLATE BLOCK	CERM PROG
☐ 1134	**4c Petroleum Industry,** 8/27/59, Titusville, PA				
	(801,859)............................1.75	1.75	1.85	2.00	25.00
☐	1st Col. Drake Philatelic Society cachet..........15.00	15.00			
☐ 1135	**4c Dental Health,** 9/14/59, New York, NY				
	(649,813)............................5.00	5.00	5.25	5.50	25.00
☐ 1136	**4c Ernst Reuter,** 9/29/59 DC......................1.75	1.75	1.85	2.00	
☐ 1137	**8c Ernst Reuter,** 9/29/59 DC......................1.75	1.75	1.85	2.00	
☐	Scott 1136-1137 on one cover..........................2.00	2.00			20.00
	Total for Scott 1136 and 1137 is 1,207,933.				
☐ 1138	**4c Dr. Ephraim McDowell,** 12/3/59, Danville, KY				
	(344,603)............................1.75	1.75	1.85	2.00	35.00

1960-61

		SINGLE	BLOCK	PLATE BLOCK	CERM PROG
☐ 1139	**4c American Credo,** George Washington, 1/20/60,				
	Mount Vernon, VA (438,335) 1.00	1.00	1.15	2.00	20.00
☐ 1140	**4c American Credo,** Benjamin Franklin, 3/31/60,				
	Philadelphia, PA (497,913) 1.00	1.00	1.15	2.00	12.00
☐ 1141	**4c American Credo,** Thomas Jefferson, 5/18/60,				
	Charlottesville, VA (454,903) 1.00	1.00	1.15	2.00	15.00
☐ 1142	**4c American Credo,** Francis Scott Key, 9/14/60,				
	Baltimore, MD (501,129) (4 types)*..........1.00	1.00	1.15	2.00	15.00*
☐ 1143	**4c American Credo,** Abraham Lincoln, 11/19/60,				
	New York, NY (467,780) (3 types)*..................1.00	1.00	1.15	2.00	15.00*
☐	1st Ritz cachet 20.00	20.00			
☐	1st National Urban League cachet 20.00	20.00			
☐	1st Springfield, (IL) Philatelic Society cachet .15.00	15.00			
☐ 1144	**4c American Credo,** Patrick Henry, 1/11/61,				
	Richmond, VA (415,252) (3 types)*..................1.00	1.00	1.15	2.00	15.00*

1960

		SINGLE	BLOCK	PLATE BLOCK	CERM PROG
☐ 1145	**4c Boy Scouts,** 2/8/60, DC (1,419,955) 4.00	4.00	4.25	4.75	85.00
☐ 1146	**4c Olympic Winter Games,** 2/18/60, Olympic				
	Valley, CA (516,456)........................1.00	1.00	1.10	1.50	
☐ 1147	**4c Thomas G. Masaryk,** 3/7/60, DC..........1.00	1.00	1.10	1.50	
☐ 1148	**8c Thomas G. Masaryk,** 3/7/60, DC..........1.00	1.00	1.25	1.50	
☐	Scott 1147-1148 on one cover 2.00	2.00			15.00
	Total for Scott 1147 and 1148 is 1,710,726.				
☐ 1149	**4c World Refugee Year,** 4/7/60, DC (413,298)..........1.00	1.00	1.10	1.50	20.00
☐ 1150	**4c Water Conservation,** 4/18/60, DC				
	(648,988)............................1.00	1.00	1.10	1.50	25.00
☐ 1151	**4c SEATO,** 5/31/60, DC (514,926) 1.10	1.10	1.00	1.50	20.00
☐ 1152	**4c American Woman,** 6/2/60, DC (830,385)..........1.00	1.00	1.10	1.50	50.00
☐ 1153	**4c 50-Star Flag,** 7/4/60, Honolulu, HI (820,900)......1.00	1.00	1.10	1.50	20.00
☐ 1154	**4c Pony Express Centennial,** 7/19/60,				
	Sacramento, CA (520,223) 1.00	1.00	1.10	1.50	35.00
☐ 1155	**4c Employ the Handicapped,** 8/28/60, New York,				
	NY (439,638)............................1.00	1.00	1.10	1.50	15.00
☐ 1156	**4c World Forestry Congress,** 8/29/60, Seattle, WA				
	(350,848)............................1.00	1.00	1.10	1.50	35.00
☐ 1157	**4c Mexican Independence,** 9/16/60, Los Angeles,				
	CA (360,297) 1.00	1.00	1.10	1.50	40.00
☐	Dual US and Mexico stamp with US cancel..........25.00	25.00			
☐	Dual US and Mexico with Mexican cancel..........300.00	300.00			
☐ 1158	**4c U.S.-Japan Treaty,** 9/28/60, DC (545,150)..........1.00	1.00	1.10	1.50	20.00

1079   1081   1083

1084   1085   1086   1087

1088   1089

1090   1091   1092   1096

1093   1094   1095

1097   1098   1099   1100

**Values for various cachet makers can be determined
by using the Cachet Calculator which begins on page 52A.**

☐ 1159	4c Ignacy Jan Paderewski, 10/8/60, DC	1.00	1.00	1.50	
☐ 1160	8c Ignacy Jan Paderewski, 10/8/60, DC	1.00	1.25	1.50	
☐	Scott 1159-1160 on one cover	2.00			15.00
	Total for Scott 1159 and 1160 is 1,057,438.				
☐ 1161	4c Robert A. Taft 10/10/60, Cincinnati, OH (312,116)	1.00	1.10	1.50	25.00
☐ 1162	4c Wheels of Freedom, 10/15/60, Detroit, MI				
	(380,551)	1.00	1.10	1.50	18.00
☐ 1163	4c Boys' Clubs of America, 10/18/60, New York,				
	NY (435,009)	1.00	1.10	1.50	20.00
☐ 1164	4c Automated Post Office, 10/20/60, Providence,				
	RI (458,237)	1.00	1.10	1.50	12.00
☐ 1165	4c Gustaf Emil Mannerheim, 10/26/60, DC	1.00	1.10	1.50	
☐ 1166	8c Gustaf Emil Mannerheim, 10/26/60, DC	1.00	1.25	1.50	
☐	Scott 1165-1166 on one cover	2.00			15.00
	Total for Scott 1165 and 1166 is 1,168, 770.				
☐ 1167	4c Camp Fire Girls, 11/1/60, New York, NY				
	(324,944)	1.00	1.10	1.50	45.00
☐ 1168	4c Giuseppe Garibaldi, 11/2/60, DC	1.10	1.10	1.50	
☐ 1169	8c Giuseppe Garibaldi, 11/2/60, DC	1.00	1.25	1.50	
☐	Scott 1168-1169 on one cover	2.00			15.00
	Total for Scott 1168 and 1169 is 1,001,490.				
☐ 1170	4c Walter F. George, 11/5/60, Vienna, GA				
	(278,890)	1.00	1.10	1.50	12.00
☐ 1171	4c Andrew Carnegie, 11/25/60, New York, NY				
	(318,180)	1.00	1.10	1.50	25.00
☐ 1172	4c John Foster Dulles, 12/6/60, DC (400,055)	1.00	1.10	1.50	15.00
☐ 1173	4c Echo I, 12/15/60, DC (583,747)	3.00	3.50	4.00	25.00

1961

☐ 1174	4c Mahatma Gandhi, 1/26/61, DC	1.00	1.10	1.50	
☐ 1175	8c Mahatma Gandhi, 1/26/61, DC	1.00	1.25	1.50	
☐	Scott 1174-1175 on one cover	2.00			15.00
	Total for Scott 1174 and 1175 is 1,013,315.				
☐ 1176	4c Range Conservation, 2/2/61, Salt Lake City, UT				
	(357,101)	1.00	1.10	1.50	30.00
☐ 1177	4c Horace Greeley, 2/3/61, Chappaqua, NY				
	(359,205)	1.00	1.10	1.50	20.00

1961-65 Civil War Centennial

☐ 1178	4c Fort Sumter, 4/12/61, Charleston, SC (602,599)	3.00	3.25	4.00	25.00
☐ 1179	4c Battle of Shiloh, 4/7/62, Shiloh, TN (526,062)	3.00	3.25	4.00	20.00
☐ 1180	5c Battle of Gettysburg, 7/1/63, Gettysburg, PA				
	(600,205)	3.00	3.25	4.00	20.00
☐ 1181	5c Battle of Wilderness, 5/5/64, Fredericksburg,				
	VA (450,904)	3.00	3.25	4.00	20.00
☐ 1182	5c Appomattox, 4/9/65, Appomattox, VA				
	(653,121) (3 types)*	3.00	3.25	4.00	20.00*
☐ 1178-82	Civil War on one 4/9/65	12.00			

1961

☐ 1183	4c Kansas Statehood, 5/10/61, Council Grove, KS				
	(480,561)	1.00	1.10	1.50	15.00
☐ 1184	4c George W. Norris, 7/11/61, DC (482,875)	1.00	1.10	1.50	15.00
☐ 1185	4c Naval Aviation, 8/20/61, San Diego, CA				
	(416,391)	1.00	1.50	2.50	30.00

1104   1105   1106

1107   1108

1109

1110-11

1112   1115

1113

1114

1st Western Cachets cachet

1116   1117-18

**Values for various cachet makers can be determined
by using the Cachet Calculator which begins on page 52A.**

		SINGLE	BLOCK	PLATE BLOCK	CERM PROG
☐ 1186	4c Workmen's Compensation, 9/4/61, Milwaukee, WI (410,236) (2 types)*............1.00		1.10	1.50	15.00*
☐ 1187	4c Frederic Remington, 10/4/61, DC (723,443) 1.00		1.10	1.50	15.00
☐ 1188	4c Republic of China, 10/10/61, DC (463,900).........1.00		1.10	1.50	18.00
☐ 1189	4c Naismith-Basketball, 11/6/61, Springfield, MA (479,917)................8.00		9.00	10.00	18.00
☐ 1190	4c Nursing, 12/28/61, DC (964,005) (2 types)*.......14.00		15.00	20.00	15.00*
☐	1st American Hospital Supply Corp. cachet ...20.00				

1962

		SINGLE	BLOCK	PLATE BLOCK	CERM PROG
☐ 1191	4c New Mexico Statehood, 1/6/62, Santa Fe, NM (365,330).............1.00		1.10	1.50	15.00
☐	1st Glory cachet 25.00				
☐ 1192	4c Arizona Statehood, 2/14/62, Phoenix, AZ (508,216).............1.00		1.10	1.50	15.00
☐	1st Vivid cachet................25.00				
☐	1st Tucson Chamber of Commerce cachet 15.00				
☐ 1193	4c Project Mercury, 2/20/62, Cape Canaveral, FL (3,000,000)...............3.00		4.00	6.00	
☐	Any other city 5.00		6.00	7.00	
☐	1st Marg cachet 25.00				
☐ 1194	4c Malaria Eradication, 3/30/62, DC (554, 175).......1.00		1.10	1.50	15.00
☐ 1195	4c Charles Evans Hughes, 4/11/62, DC (554,424) ..1.00		1.10	1.50	15.00
☐ 1196	4c Seattle World's Fair, 4/25/62, Seattle, WA (771,856)................1.00		1.10	1.50	15.00
☐	1st Top of the Needle, Inc. cachet 10.00				
☐	1st Boeing Employee's Stamp Club cachet 12.00				
☐ 1197	4c Louisiana Statehood, 4/30/62, New Orleans, LA (436,681)................1.00		1.10	1.50	18.00
☐ 1198	4c Homestead Act, 5/20/62, Beatrice, NE (487,450)1.00		1.10	1.50	15.00
☐ 1199	4c Girl Scout Jubilee, 7/24/62, Burlington, VT (634,347)................3.50		3.75	4.00	22.00
☐ 1200	4c Brien McMahon, 7/28/62, Norwalk, CT (384,419) (2 types)* 1.00		1.10	1.50	18.00*
☐ 1201	4c Apprenticeship, 8/31/62, DC, 1,003,548).......1.00		1.10	1.50	15.00
☐ 1202	4c Sam Rayburn, 9/16/62, Bonham, TX (401,042). .1.00		1.10	1.50	15.00
☐ 1203	4c Dag Hammarskjold, 10/23/62, New York, NY (500,683)................1.00		1.10	1.50	18.00
☐	1st Dag Hammarskjold Foundation cachet 15.00				
☐	Inverted yellow, 10/26/62, Vanderveer Sta.,				
☐	Brooklyn, NY earliest known use ....2,000.				
☐ 1204	4c Hanmarskjold Special Printing, yellow inverted, 11/16/62, DC (c. 75,000)................6.00		7.50	10.00	
☐ 1205	4c Christmas, 11/1/62, Pittsburgh, PA (491,312) 1.10		1.50		20.00
☐ 1206	4c Higher Education, 11/14/62, DC (627,347).........1.00		1.10	1.50	15.00
☐ 1207	4c Winslow Homer, 12/15/62, Gloucester, MA (498,866)................1.00		1.10	1.50	18.00

1963-66

		SINGLE	BLOCK	PLATE BLOCK	CERM PROG
☐ 1208	5c Flag, 1/9/63, DC (696,185) 1.00		1.10	1.50	12.00
☐ 1208a	Flag, tagged, 8/25/66, DC 40.00				

1962-66

		SINGLE	BLOCK	PLATE BLOCK	CERM PROG
☐ 1209	1c Andrew Jackson, 3/22/63, block of 5 or 6, New York, NY (392,363)		1.00	1.50	15.00

1119   1122

1120   1121   1125-26

1123   1124

1127

1128   1129

1130   1131   1132

1134

SOIL CONSERVATION

1133   1135   1136-37

1138

1139-44   1145

1146

1st Ritz cachet

1147-48   1151

74

SCOTT NUMBER	DESCRIPTION	SINGLE	BLOCK	PLATE BLOCK	CERM PROG
☐ 1209a	**Andrew Jackson,** block of 5 or 6, tagged, 7/6/66, DC...40.00				
☐ 1213	**5c George Washington,** 11/23/62, New York, NY				
	(360,531)...1.00				15.00
☐ 1213a	**George Washington,** booklet pane of 5, 11/23/62,				
	New York, NY (111,452) 4.00				
☐ 1213b	**George Washington,** tagged, 10/28/63, Dayton, OH				
	& DC..40.00				
☐ 1213c	**George Washington,** booklet pane of 5, tagged,				
	10/28/63, Dayton, OH...................................100.00				
☐	DC (750) 115.00				

SCOTT NUMBER	DESCRIPTION	SINGLE	PAIR	LINE PAIR	CERM PROG
☐ 1225	**1c Andrew Jackson. coil,** pair & strip of 3,				
	5/31/63, Chicago, IL (238,952)..........................		1.00	1.00	15.00
☐ 1225a	**Andrew Jackson,** coil, pair & strip of 3, tagged,				
	7/6/66, DC		5.00		
☐ 1229	**5c George Washington,** coil, 11/23/62, New York,				
	NY (184,627)...1.00		1.00	1.00	
☐ 1229a	**George Washington,** coil, tagged, 10/28/63,				
	Dayton, OH & DC		40.00		
☐	Scott 1213b, 1213c, 1229a on one cover,				
	Dayton, OH 70.00				

SCOTT NUMBER	DESCRIPTION	SINGLE	BLOCK	PLATE BLOCK	CERM PROG

1963

☐ 1230	**5c Carolina Charter,** 4/6/63, Edenton, NC				
	(426,200) (2 types)* 1.00	1.10		1.50	15.00*
☐ 1231	**5c Food for Peace,** 6/4/63, DC.................................1.00	1.10		1.50	15.00
☐ 1232	**5c West Virginia Statehood,** 6/20/63, Wheeling,				
	WV (413,389)..1.00	1.10		1.50	20.00
☐ 1233	**5c Emancipation Proclamation,** 8/16/63, Chicago,				
	IL (494,886) 1.00	1.10		1.50	15.00
☐ 1234	**5c Alliance for Progress,** 8/17/63, DC (528,095) 1.00	1.10		1.50	15.00
☐ 1235	**5c Cordell Hull,** 10/5/63, Carthage, TN (391,631) ..1.00	1.10		1.50	15.00
☐ 1236	**5c Eleanor Roosevelt,** 10/11/63, DC (860,155) 1.00	1.10		1.50	15.00
☐ 1237	**5c Science,** 10/14/63, DC (504,503).........................1.00	1.10		1.50	18.00
☐ 1238	**5c City Mail Delivery,** 10/26/63, DC (544,806).........1.00	1.10		1.50	22.00
☐ 1239	**5c Red Cross Centenary,** 10/29/63, DC (557,678).....1.00	1.10		1.50	15.00
☐ 1240	**5c Christmas,** 11/1/63, Santa Claus, IN (458,619) ..1.00	1.10		1.50	20.00
	1st Lily Spandorf cachet 20.00				
☐ 1240a	**Christmas,** tagged, 11/2/63, DC (500)....................60.00				
☐ 1241	**5c John James Audubon,** 12/7/63, Henderson, KY				
	(518,855)...1.00	1.10		1.50	15.00

1964

☐ 1242	**5c Sam Houston,** 1/10/64, Houston, TX (487,986)...1.00	1.10		1.50	20.00
☐	Mr. Zip Imprint 10.00	15.00			
	Scott 1242 was the first stamp to have Mr. Zip imprints.				
☐ 1243	**5c Charles M. Russell,** 3/19/64, Great Falls, MT				
	(658,745)...1.00	1.10		1.50	40.00

1149

1150

1151

1153

1152

1154

1155

1156

1157

1158

1159-60

1161

1162

1164

1163

1165-66

1168-69

1170

1167

1171

1172

1173

1174-75

1176

1177

1178-82

☐ 1244	5c N.Y. World's Fair, 4/22/64, World's Fair, NY				
	(1,656,346) (2 types)*..1.00	1.10		1.50	18.00*
☐	1st Sarzin Metallic cachet.................................30.00				
☐	On Scott U546 ....5.00				
☐ 1245	5c John Muir, 4/29/64, Martinez, CA (446,925) 1.00	1.10		1.50	15.00
☐ 1246	5c Kennedy Memorial, 5/29/64, Boston, MA				
	(2,003,096)..2.50	3.50	5.00	25.00
☐	Any city 2.50	3.50	5.00	
☐	1st Cover Craft cachet.....................................40.00				
☐ 1247	5c New Jersey Tercentenary, 6/15/64, Elizabeth,				
	NJ (526,879)..1.00	1.00		1.50	15.00
☐ 1248	5c Nevada Statehood, 7/22/64, Carson City, NV				
	(584,973)...1.00	1.00		1.50	15.00
☐ 1249	5c Register & Vote, 8/1/64, DC (533,439) 1.00	1.00		1.50	15.00
☐ 1250	5c Shakespeare, 8/14/64, Stratford, CT (524,053) ..1.75	2.25		2.50	50.00
☐ 1251	5c Drs. Mayo, 9/11/64, Rochester, MN (674,846) 5.00	5.50	8.00	25.00
☐ 1252	5c American Music, 10/15/64, New York, NY				
	(466,107) (2 types)*...1.00	1.10		1.50	15.00*
☐ 1253	5c Homemakers, 10/26/64, Honolulu, HI				
	(435,392)...1.00	1.10		1.50	15.00
☐ 1254	5c Holly, 11/9/64, Bethlehem, PA............................1.00				
☐ 1254a	Holly, tagged, 11/10/64, Dayton, OH.....................40.00				
☐ 1255	5c Mistletoe, 11/9/64, Bethlehem, PA......................1.00				
☐ 1255a	Mistletoe, tagged, 11/10/64, Dayton, OH...............40.00				
☐ 1256	5c Poinsettia, 11/9/64, Bethlehem, PA 1.00				
☐ 1256a	Poinsettia, tagged, 11/10/64, Dayton, OH..............40.00				
☐ 1257	5c Sprig of Conifer, 11/9/64, Bethlehem, PA............1.00				
☐ 1257a	Sprig of Conifer, 11/10/64, Dayton, OH 40.00				
☐ 1257b	Christmas, se-tenant (794,900)	3.00	4.00	80.00
☐ 1257b	Christmas, tagged, se-tenant............................	80.00			
☐ 1254-1257	5c Christmas, ...				80.00
☐ 1258	5c Verrazano-Narrows Bridge, 11/21/64, Staten				
	Island, NY (619,780) 1.00	1.10		1.50	15.00
☐ 1259	5c Fine Arts, 12/2/64, DC (558,046) 1.00	1.10		1.50	20.00
☐ 1260	5c Amateur Radio, 12/15/64, Anchorage, AK...........1.00	1.10		1.50	28.00

1965

☐ 1261	5c Battle of New Orleans, 1/8/65, New Orleans, LA				
	(466,029) (4 types)* 1.00	1.10		1.50	25.00*
☐ 1262	5c Physical Fitness-Sokol, 2/15/65, DC (864,848) ..1.00	1.10		1.50	10.00
☐ 1263	5c Crusade Against Cancer, 4/1/65, DC (744,485)...1.00	1.10		1.50	20.00
☐ 1264	5c Churchill Memorial, 5/13/65, Fulton, MO				
	(733,580)...1.00	1.10		1.50	12.00
☐ 1265	5c Magna Carta, 6/15/65, Jamestown, VA				
	(479,065)...1.00	1.10		1.50	40.00
☐ 1266	5c International Cooperation Year, 6/26/65, San				
	Francisco, CA (402,925).....................................1.00	1.10		1.50	35.00
☐ 1267	5c Salvation Army, 7/2/65, New York, NY (634,228)1.00	1.10		1.50	15.00
☐ 1268	5c Dante Alighieri, 7/17/65, San Francisco, CA				
	(424,893)...1.00	1.10		1.50	15.00
☐ 1269	5c Herbert Hoover, 8/10/65, West Branch, IA				
	(698,182)...1.00	1.10		1.50	15.00
☐ 1270	5c Robert Fulton, 8/19/65, Clermont, NY (550,330) ..1.00	1.10		1.50	15.00
☐ 1271	5c Settlement of Florida, 8/28/65, St. Augustine,				
	FL (465,000)..1.00	1.10		1.50	15.00

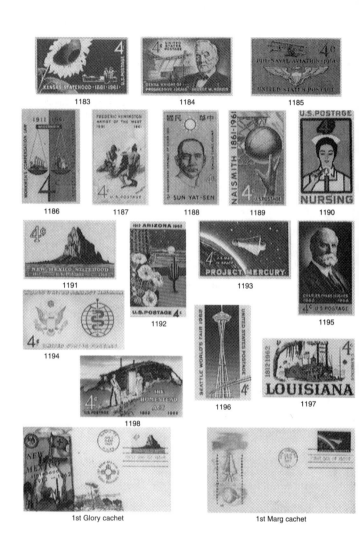

1183

1184

1185

1186

1187

1188

1189

1190

1191

1192

1193

1194

1195

1196

1197

1198

1st Glory cachet

1st Marg cachet

**Values for various cachet makers can be determined
by using the Cachet Calculator which begins on page 52A.**

cover box

10.5"
4.25"
7.5"

Keep your collection organized in this handsome
and durable cover box. Box will hold hundreds
of covers. Available in classic marble styling.

Item	Description	Retail
CVBOX	Marble Cover Box	$6.95

1199

1200

1201

1202

1203

1204

1205

1206

1207

1209, 1225

1231

1208

1213, 1229

1230

1232

1233

1234

1235

1236

1237

1238

1239

1240

**Values for various cachet makers can be determined
by using the Cachet Calculator which begins on page 52A.**

SCOTT NUMBER	DESCRIPTION	SINGLE	PLATE BLOCK	PLATE BLOCK	CERM PROG
☐	Scott 1271 with Spain stamp 100.00				
☐	Scott 1271 with Spain stamp dual cancel.........400.00				
☐ 1272	5c Traffic Safety, 9/3/65, Baltimore, MD				
	(527,075)...............................1.00		1.10	1.50	15.00
☐ 1273	5c John Singleton Copley, 9/17/65, DC (613,484) ...1.00		1.10	1.50	15.00
☐ 1274	11c International Telecommunication Union,				
	10/6/65, DC (332,818) 1.00		1.10	1.50	20.00
☐ 1275	5c Adlai E. Stevenson, 10/23/65, Bloomington, IL				
	(755,656).......................................1.00		1.10	1.50	15.00
☐ 1276	5c Christmas, 11/2/65, Silver Bell, AZ (705,039)				
	(2 types)* 1.00		1.10	1.50	25.00*
☐ 1276a	Christmas, tagged, 11/15/65, DC (300c) 55.00				

1965-68 Prominent Americans

SCOTT NUMBER	DESCRIPTION	SINGLE	PLATE BLOCK	PLATE BLOCK	CERM PROG
☐ 1278	1c Thomas Jefferson, block of 5 or 6, 1/12/68,				
	Jeffersonville, IN......................................		1.00	1.00	25.00
☐ 1278a	Thomas Jefferson, booklet pane of 8, 1/12/68,				
	Jeffersonville, IN................................2.50				25.00
☐	Dull gum, 3/1/71, DC............................100.00				
	Total for Scott 1278, 1278a and 1299 is 655,680.				
☐ 1278b	Thomas Jefferson, booklet pane of 4 plus 2 labels,				
	5/10/71, DC.......................................15.00				
☐ 1279	1 1/4c Albert Gallatin, 1/30/67, Gallatin, MO				
	(439,010)..		1.00	1.00	20.00
☐ 1280	2c Frank Lloyd Wright, strip of 3, 6/8/66, Spring				
	Green, WI (460,427).............................1.00				18.00
☐ 1280a	Frank Lloyd Wright, booklet pane of 5 plus label,				
	1/8/68, Buffalo, NY (147,244)....................4.00				20.00
☐ 1280c	Frank Lloyd Wright, booklet pane of 6, 5/7/71,				
	Spokane, WA......................................15.00				50.00
☐	Dull gum, 10/31/75, Cleveland, OH...............100.00				
☐ 1281	3c Francis Parkman, 9/16/67, Boston, MA				
	(518,355)..		1.25	1.60	15.00
☐ 1282	4c Abraham Lincoln, 11/19/65, New York, NY				
	(445,629) (2 types).............................		1.10	1.50	15.00
☐ 1282a	Abraham Lincoln, tagged, 12/1/65, Dayton, OH 40.00				
☐	DC..45.00				
☐ 1283	5c George Washington, 2/22/66, DC (525,372) 1.00		1.10	1.50	50.00
	1st B'nai B'rith Philatelic Service cachet 20.00				
☐ 1283a	George Washington, tagged, 2/23/66, Dayton,				
	OH (c. 200) 100.00				
☐	DC..30.00				
☐ 1283B	5c George Washington, Redrawn, 11/17/67,				
	New York, NY (328,983) (2 types)* 1.00		1.10	1.50	15.00*
☐ 1284	6c Franklin D. Roosevelt, 1/29/66, Hyde Park, NY				
	(448,631)...1.00		1.10	1.50	15.00
☐ 1284a	Franklin D. Roosevelt, tagged, 12/29/66, DC 40.00				
☐ 1284b	Franklin D. Roosevelt, booklet pane of 8,				
	12/28/67, DC......................................3.00				
	Total for Scott 1284b and 1298 is 312,330.				
☐ 1284c	Franklin D. Roosevelt, booklet pane of 5, 1/9/68,				
	DC...125.00				
☐ 1285	8c Albert Einstein, 3/14/66, Princeton, NJ				
	(366,803)..1.50		2.00	2.75	20.00
☐ 1285a	Albert Einstein, tagged, 7/6/66, DC.................40.00				

1245

1st Cover Craft cachet

1241

1242

1243

1244

1246

1248

1247

1249

1250

1251

1254-57

1252

1253

1258

1259

1261

1260

HOW TO USE THIS BOOK

The number in the first column is its Scott number or identifying number. Following that is the denomination of the stamp, description, date of issue, and the value.

SCOTT NUMBER	DESCRIPTION	SINGLE	BLOCK	PLATE BLOCK	CERM PROG
☐ 1286	10c Andrew Jackson, 3/15/67, Hermitage, TN				
	(255,945) 1.00		1.25	1.50	20.00
☐ 1286A	12c Henry Ford, 7/30/68, Greenfield Village,				
	MI (342,850) 1.25		1.50	1.75	22.00
☐ 1287	13c John F. Kennedy, 5/29/67, Brookline, MA				
	(391,195) 1.50		2.00	2.75	28.00
☐ 1288	15c Oliver Wendell Holmes, 3/8/68, DC (322,970). .1.00		1.25	1.50	28.00
☐ 1288B	15c Oliver Wendell Holmes, Redrawn, booklet				
	single, 6/14/78, Boston, MA (387, 119) 1.00		1.25	1.50	
☐ 1288Bc	Oliver Wendell Holmes, booklet pane of 8 ....3.00				
☐ 1289	20c George C. Marshall, 10/24/67, Lexington, VA				
	(221,206) 1.00		1.25	1.50	25.00
☐ 1289a	George C. Marshall, tagged, 4/3/73, New York, NY 40.00				
☐ 1290	25c Frederick Douglass, 2/14/67, DC (213,730) 1.25		1.25	1.75	32.00
☐ 1290a	Frederick Douglass, tagged, 4/3/73, New York, NY 40.00				
☐ 1291	30c John Dewey, 10/21/68, Burlington, VT				
	(162,790) 1.25		2.00	3.00	35.00
☐ 1291a	John Dewey, tagged, 4/3/73, New York, NY 40.00				
☐ 1292	40c Thomas Paine, 1/29/68, Philadelphia, PA				
	(157,947) 1.60		2.50	4.00	40.00
☐ 1292a	Thomas Paine, tagged, 4/3/73, New York, NY 40.00				
☐ 1293	50c Lucy Stone, 8/13/68, Dorchester, MA				
	(140,410) 3.25		4.00	7.50	45.00
☐ 1293a	Lucy Stone, tagged, 4/3/73, New York, NY 40.00				
☐ 1294	$1 Eugene O'Neill, 10/16/67, New London, CT				
	(103,102) (2 types)* 7.50		10.00	15.00	50.00*
☐ 1294a	Eugene O'Neill, tagged, 4/3/73, New York, NY 65.00				
☐ 1295	$5 John Bassett Moore, 12/3/66, Smyrna, DE				
	(41,130) 40.00		55.00	95.00	75.00
☐ 1295a	John Bassett Moore, tagged, 4/3/73, New York, NY 125.00				
	Scott 1295 &1295a on one cover 250.00				
	Total for 1059b, 1289a, 1290a, 1291a, 1292a,				
	1293a, 1294a, 1295a is 17,533.				

SCOTT NUMBER	DESCRIPTION	SINGLE	PAIR	LINE PAIR	CERM PROG

1966-68 Prominent Americans Coils
Perf. 10 Horizontally

☐ 1297	3c Francis Parkman, 11/4/75, Pendleton, OR				
	(166,798)		1.00	1.50	15.00
☐ 1298	6c Franklin D. Roosevelt, 12/28/67, DC 1.00		1.10	1.50	

Perf. 10 Vertically

☐ 1299	1c Thomas Jefferson, pair & strip of 3, 1/12/68,				
	Jeffersonville, IN		1.00	1.50	25.00
☐ 1303	4c Abraham Lincoln, pair, 5/28/66, Springfield, IL				
	(322,563)		1.00	1.50	25.00
	1st A Hartford Cover cachet 20.00				
☐ 1304	5c George Washington, 9/8/66, Cincinnati, OH				
	(245,400) 1.00		1.00	1.50	15.00
☐ 1304C	5c George Washington, Redrawn, strip of 4,				
	3/31/81, earliest known use, DC 25.00				
☐ 1305	6c Franklin D. Roosevelt, 2/28/68, DC (317,199).....1.00		1.10	1.50	

1267

1262

1263

1264

1268

1265

1266

1269

1270

1272

1271

1273

1274

1276

1278, 1299

1287

1275

HOW TO USE THIS BOOK
The number in the first column is its Scott number or
identifying number. Following that is the denomination
of the stamp, description, date of issue, and the value.

SCOTT NUMBER	DESCRIPTION	SINGLE	BLOCK	PLATE BLOCK	CERM PROG
☐ 1305E	15c Oliver Wendell Holmes 6/14/78, Boston, MA				
	(387,119)..................................1.00		1.25	1.50	
☐	Scott 1288c, 1305E on one cover 6.50				
☐ 1305C	$1 Eugene O'Neill 1/12/73, Hempstead, NY				
	(121,217)..................................5.00		7.00	9.00	50.00

SCOTT NUMBER	DESCRIPTION	SINGLE	BLOCK	PLATE BLOCK	CERM PROG

1966

☐ 1306	5c Migratory Bird Treaty, 3/16/66, Pittsburgh, PA				
	(555,485)..................................1.00		1.10	1.50	18.00
☐ 1307	5c Humane Treatment of Animals, 4/9/66, New				
	York, NY (524,420) (2 types)* 1.00		1.10	1.50	12.00*
☐ 1308	5c Indiana Statehood, 4/16/66, Corydon, IN				
	(575,557)..................................1.00		1.10	1.50	15.00
☐ 1309	5c American Circus, 5/2/66, Delavan, WI				
	(754,076) (2 types)*...........................2.50		3.00	4.50	25.00*
	1st Cliff's Covers cachet 20.00				
☐ 1310	5c SIPEX, 5/21/66, DC (637,802) 1.00		1.10	1.50	20.00
☐ 1311	5c SIPEX, Souvenir Sheet, 5/23/66, DC (700,882). ...1.00				25.00
☐ 1312	5c Bill of Rights, 7/1/66, Miami Beach, FL				
	(562,920)..................................1.00		1.10	1.50	25.00
☐ 1313	5c Polish Millennium, 7/30/66, DC (712,603)...........1.00		1.10	1.50	
☐ 1313	5c Polish Millennium. 7/30/66 DC...............................				15.00
☐ 1314	5c National Park Service, 8/25/66, Yellowstone				
	National Park, WY (528,170) (2 types)*...........1.00		1.10	1.50	15.00
☐ 1314a	National Park Service, tagged, 8/26/66, DC............50.00				
☐ 1315	5c Marine Corps Reserve, 8/29/66, DC (585,923)....1.00		1.10	1.50	18.00
☐ 1315a	Marine Corps Reserve, tagged, 8/29/66, DC 50.00				
☐ 1316	5c General Federation of Women's Clubs, 9/12/66,				
	New York, NY (383,334) (2 types)*...........1.00		1.10	1.50	20.00*
☐ 1316a	General Federation of Women's Clubs, tagged,				
	9/13/66, DC.......................................50.00				
☐ 1317	5c Johnny Appleseed, 9/24/66, Leominster, MA				
	(794,610)..................................1.50		1.75	2.00	20.00
☐ 1317a	Johnny Appleseed, tagged, 9/26/66, DC............50.00				
☐ 1318	5c Beautification of America, 10/5/66, DC				
	(564,440)..................................1.00		1.10	1.50	25.00
☐ 1318a	Beautification of America, tagged, 10/5/66, DC 50.00				
☐ 1319	5c Great River Road, 10/21/66, Baton Rouge, LA				
	(330,933)..................................1.00		1.10	1.50	20.00
☐ 1319a	Great River Road, tagged, 10/22/66, DC 50.00				
☐ 1320	5c Savings Bonds-Servicemen, 10/26/66, Sioux				
	City, IA (444,421) 1.00		1.10	1.50	15.00
	1st Border Croft cachet....................25.00				
☐ 1320a	Savings Bonds-Servicemen, tagged, 10/27/66, DC 50.00				
☐ 1321	5c Christmas, 11/1/66, Christmas, MI (537,650)......1.00		1.10	1.50	25.00
☐ 1321a	Christmas, tagged, 11/2/66, DC 50.00				
☐	Dayton, OH, 11/2/66 ....50.00				
☐ 1322	5c Mary Cassatt, 11/17/66, DC (593,389)..................1.00		1.10	1.50	22.00
☐ 1322a	Mary Cassatt, tagged, 11/17/66, DC 50.00				

1967

☐ 1323	5c National Grange, 4/17/67, DC (603,460) 1.00		1.10	1.50	25.00

1306

1307

1308

1309

1310-11

1312

1313

1315

1314

1316

1318

1317

SCOTT NUMBER	DESCRIPTION	SINGLE	PAIR	LINE PAIR	CERM PROG
☐ 1324	5c Canada Centenary, 5/25/67, Montreal, Quebec (711,795)	1.00	1.10	1.50	18.00
☐ 1325	5c Erie Canal, 7/4/67, Rome, NY (784,611)	1.00	1.10	1.50	18.00
☐ 1326	5c "Peace"-Lions, 7/5/67, Chicago, IL (393, 197)	1.00	1.10	1.50	15.00
☐ 1327	5c Henry David Thoreau, 7/12/67, Concord, MA (696,789)	1.00	1.10	1.50	15.00
☐ 1328	5c Nebraska Statehood, 7/29/67, Lincoln, NE (1,146,957)	1.00	1.10	1.50	15.00
☐ 1329	5c Voice of America, 8/1/67, DC (445,190)	1.00	1.10	1.50	20.00
☐ 1330	5c Davy Crockett, 8/17/67, San Antonio, TX (462,291)	1.25	1.50	1.75	18.00
☐ 1331	5c Space-walking astronaut, 9/29/67, Kennedy Space Center, FL	4.00			
☐ 1331a	Space Accomplishments, se-tenant pair, FL (667,267)	10.00	12.50	15.00	20.00
☐ 1332	5c Gemini 4 capsule, 9/29/67, Kennedy Space Center, FL	4.00			
☐ 1333	5c Urban Planning, 10/2/67, DC (389,009)	1.00	1.10	1.50	20.00
☐ 1334	5c Finland Independence, 10/6/67, Finland, MN (408,532)	1.00	1.10	1.50	18.00
☐ 1335	5c Thomas Eakins, 11/2/67, DC (648,054)	1.00	1.10	1.50	18.00
☐ 1336	5c Christmas, 11/6/67, Bethlehem, GA (462,118)	1.00	1.10	1.50	20.00
☐ 1337	5c Mississippi Statehood, 12/11/67, Natchez, MS (379,612)	1.00	1.10	1.50	18.00

1968-69

☐ 1338	6c Flag, Giori Press, 1/24/68, DC (412,120)	1.00	1.10	1.50	15.00
☐ 1338A	6c Flag, coil, 5/30/69, Chicago, IL (248,434)	1.00pr	1.10	lp1.50	15.00
☐ 1338D	6c Flag, 8/7/70, Huck Press, DC (356,280). "Plate Block" value is for block of 4 with plate numbers	1.00	1.10	1.50	
☐ 1338F	8c Flag, 5/10/71, DC. "Plate Block" value is for block of 4 with plate numbers	1.00	1.10	1.50	
☐ 1338G	6c Flag, coil, 5/10/71, DC	1.00pr	1.00	lp1.50	
	Total for Scott 1338F-1338G is 235,543.				

1968

☐ 1339	6c Illinois Statehood, 2/12/68, Shawneetown, IL (761,640)	1.00	1.10	1.50	18.00
☐ 1340	6c Hemis Fair '68, 3/30/68, San Antonio, TX (469,909)	1.00	1.10	1.50	18.00
☐ 1341	$1 Airlift, 4/4/68, Seattle, WA (105,088)	8.00	9.50	15.00	70.00
☐ 1342	6c Youth-Elks, 5/1/68, Chicago, IL (354,711)	1.00	1.10	1.50	15.00
☐ 1343	6c Law and Order, 5/17/68, DC (407,081)	1.00	1.10	1.50	20.00
☐ 1344	6c Register and Vote, 6/27/68, DC (355,685)	1.00	1.10	1.50	20.00
☐ 1345	6c Ft. Moultrie, 7/4/68, Pittsburgh, PA	3.00			
☐ 1346	6c Ft. McHenry, 7/4/68, Pittsburgh, PA	3.00			
☐ 1347	6c Washington's Cruisers, 7/4/68, Pittsburgh, PA	3.00			
☐ 1348	6c Bennington, 7/4/68, Pittsburgh, PA	3.00			
☐ 1349	6c Rhode Island, 7/4/68, Pittsburgh, PA	3.00			
☐ 1350	6c First Stars & Stripes, 7/4/68, Pittsburgh, PA	3.00			
☐ 1351	6c Bunker Hill, 7/4/68, Pittsburgh, PA	3.00			
☐ 1352	6c Grand Union, 7/4/68, Pittsburgh, PA	3.00			
☐ 1353	6c Philadelphia Light Horse, 7/4/68, Pittsburgh, PA	3.00			
☐ 1354	6c First Navy Jack, 7/4/68, Pittsburgh, PA	3.00			

1319

1320

1321

1322

1323

1324

1325

1326

1327

1328

1330

1329

1331-32

**Values for various cachet makers can be determined
by using the Cachet Calculator which begins on page 52A.**

		SINGLE	BLOCK	PLATE BLOCK	CERM PROG
☐ 1354a	Se-tenant strip Historic Flags (2 types)* 12.00				20.00
	Total for Scott 1345-1354 is 2,924,962.				
☐ 1355	6c Walt Disney, 9/11/68, Marceline, MO				
	(499,505) (2 types)*.....................................15.00	16.00		20.00	45.00*
☐ 1356	6c Father Marquette, 9/20/68, Sault Sainte Marie				
	MI (379,710).......................................1.00	1.10		1.50	15.00
☐ 1357	6c Daniel Boone, 9/26/68, Frankfort, KY				
	(333,440)...1.25	1.50		1.75	15.00
☐ 1358	6c Arkansas River Navigation, 10/1/68, Little				
	Rock, AR (358,025) 1.00	1.10		1.50	50.00
☐ 1359	6c Leif Erikson, 10/9/68, Seattle, WA (376,565) 1.00	1.10		1.50	30.00
☐ 1360	6c Cherokee Strip, 10/15/68, Ponca, OK (339,330)..1.00	1.10		1.50	18.00
☐ 1361	6c John Trumbull, 10/18/68, New Haven, CT				
	(378,285)...1.00	1.10		1.50	20.00
☐ 1362	6c Waterfowl Conservation, 10/24/68, Cleveland,				
	OH (349,719).....................................1.00	1.10		1.50	25.00
☐	1st Ducks Unlimited, Inc. cachet 30.00				
☐ 1363	6c Christmas, tagged, 11/1/68, DC (739,055).				
	"Plate Block" value is for block of 4 with plate				
	numbers...1.00	1.10		1.50	25.00
☐ 1363a	6c Christmas, untagged, 11/2/68, DC 15.00				
☐ 1364	6c American Indian, 11/4/68, DC (415,964)..............1.25	1.50		1.75	20.00

1969

		SINGLE	BLOCK	PLATE BLOCK	CERM PROG
☐ 1365	6c Capitol, Azaleas & Tulips, 1/16/69, DC 1.00				
☐ 1366	6c Washington Monument & Daffodils, 1/16/69,DC.1.00				
☐ 1367	6c Poppies & Lupines along Highway, 1/16/69, DC 1.00				
☐ 1368	6c Blooming Crabapples, 1/16/69, DC 1.00				
☐ 1368a	Se-tenant blocks, Beautification of America				
	(1,094,184)	4.00		5.00	25.00
☐ 1369	6c American Legion, 3/15/69, DC (632,035) 1.00	1.25		2.00	15.00
☐ 1370	6c Grandma Moses, 5/1/69, DC (367,880)................1.00	1.25		2.00	20.00
☐ 1371	6c Apollo 8, 5/5/69, Houston, TX (908,634) 4.00	6.00		9.00	25.00
☐ 1372	6c W.C. Handy, 5/17/69, Memphis, TN (398,216). 1.00	1.25		2.00	16.00
☐ 1373	6c California Settlement, 7/16/69, San Diego, CA				
	(530,210)...1.00	1.25		1.25	25.00
☐ 1374	6c John Wesley Powell, 8/1/69, Page, AZ (434,433) 1.00	1.25		2.00	18.00
☐ 1375	6c Alabama Statehood, 8/2/69, Huntsville, AL				
	(485,801) (2 types)*..........................1.00	1.25		2.00	18.00*
☐ 1376	6c Douglas Fir, 8/23/69, Seattle, WA 1.50				
☐ 1377	6c Lady's-slipper, 8/23/69, Seattle, WA 1.50				
☐ 1378	6c Ocotillo, 8/23/69, Seattle, WA 1.50				
☐ 1379	6c Franklinia, 8/23/69, Seattle, WA........................1.50				
☐ 1379a	Se-tenant, (737,935) Botanical Congress	5.00		6.00	30.00
☐ 1380	6c Dartmouth College Case, 9/22/69, Hanover,				
	NH (416,327).....................................1.00	1.00		1.50	10.00
☐ 1381	6c Professional Baseball, 9/24/69, Cincinnati, OH				
	(414,942) 15.00	16.00		20.00	70.00
☐ 1382	6c Intercollegiate Football, 9/26/69, New				
	Brunswick, NJ (414,860)....................7.00	8.00		10.00	50.00
☐ 1383	6c Dwight D. Eisenhower, 10/14/69, Abilene, KS				
	(1,009,560)..1.00	1.10		1.50	15.00
☐ 1384	6c Christmas, 11/3/69, Christmas, FL (555,550).				
	"Plate Block" value is for block of 4 with plate				
	number...1.00	1.10		1.50	25.00

1333

1334

1335

1336

1337

1338

1339

1340

1341

1342

1343

1344

1345-54

1355

1356

Values for various cachet makers can be determined by using the Cachet Calculator which begins on page 52A.

		SINGLE	BLOCK	PLATE BLOCK	CERM PROG
☐ 1384a	**Christmas,** Precancel, New Haven, Memphis, Baltimore, Atlanta 11/4/69 (250) 200.00				
☐ 1385	**6c Hope for Crippled,** 11/20/69, Columbus, OH (342,676)...2.00	2.00	2.25	2.50	15.00
☐ 1386	**6c William M. Harnett,** 12/3/69, Boston, MA (408,860)...1.00	1.00	1.10	1.50	18.00

1970

☐ 1387	**6c American Bald Eagle,** 5/6/70, New York, NY (2 types)*..1.50				
☐ 1388	**6c African Elephant Herd,** 5/6/70, New York, NY (2 types)*..1.50				
☐ 1389	**6c Tlingit Chief,** Ceremonial Canoe, 5/6/70, New York, NY (2 types)*............................1.50				
☐ 1390	**6c Brontosaurus, Stegosaurus & Allosaurus** 5/6/70, New York, NY...1.50				
☐ 1390a	**Se-tenant,** Natural History, (834,260)(2 types)*		4.00	5.00	20.00*
☐ 1391	**6c Maine Statehood,** 7/9/90, Portland, ME (472,165)...1.00	1.00	1.10	1.50	20.00
☐ 1392	**6c Wildlife Conservation,** 7/20/70, Custer, SD (309,418)...1.00	1.00	1.25	2.00	20.00

1970-74

☐ 1393	**6c Dwight D. Eisenhower,** 8/6/70, DC 1.00	1.00	1.10	1.50	15.00
☐ 1393a	**Dwight D. Eisenhower,** booklet pane of 8, 8/6/70, DC...3.00				
☐ 1393a	**Dwight D. Eisenhower,** booklet pane of 8, dull gum, 3/1/71, DC...75.00				
☐ 1393b	**Dwight D. Eisenhower,** booklet pane of 5 plus labels, 8/6/70, DC 1.50				
☐	Scott 1393a, 1393b (two different slogans in label) 3 panes on one FDC, 8/6/70, DC 11.50				
	Total for Scott 1393-1393b, 1401 is 823,540.				
☐ 1393D	**7c Benjamin Franklin,** 10/20/72, Philadelphia, PA (309,276)...1.00	1.00	1.10	1.50	18.00
☐ 1394	**8c Dwight D. Eisenhower,** 5/10/71, DC.....................1.00	1.00	1.10	1.50	
☐ 1395	**8c Dwight D. Eisenhower,** 5/10/71, DC 1.00	1.00	1.10	1.50	
☐ 1395a	**Dwight D. Eisenhower,** booklet pane of 8, 5/10/71, DC...3.00				
☐ 1395b	**Dwight D. Eisenhower,** booklet pane of 6, 5/10/71, DC...3.00				
☐	Scott 1395a, 1395b on one cover, 5/10/72, DC .5.00				
	Total for Scott 1394-1395b, 1402 is 813,947.				
☐ 1395c	**Dwight D. Eisenhower,** booklet pane of 4 plus labels, 1/28/72, Casa Grande, AZ.....................2.25				32.00
☐ 1395d	**Dwight D. Eisenhower,** booklet pane of 7 plus label, 1/28/72, Casa Grande, AZ 2.00				50.00
☐	Scott 1395c, 1395d on one cover.....................3.00				
☐ 1396	**8c USPS Emblem,** 7/1/71, DC 1.00	1.00	1.10	1.50	25.00
☐	Unofficial city...—				
	Washington, D. C post office had "First Day of Issue" postmark, but Scott 1396 was available at every post office on 7/1/71. More than 18,000 different cities are known with first day postmarks out of 39,521 possible. Values of the individual covers range from $1.				
☐ 1397	**14c Fiorello H. LaGuardia,** 4/24/72, New York, NY (180,114) 1.00	1.00	1.25	1.75	18.00

1357

1358

1360

1359

1361

1362

1363

1365-68

1364

1369

1370

1371

1372

1373

1374

1375

1380

1376-79

1381

1382

Values for various cachet makers can be determined by using the Cachet Calculator which begins on page 52A.

		SINGLE	BLOCK	PLATE BLOCK	CERM PROG
☐ 1398	16c Ernie Pyle, 5/7/71, DC (444,410)	1.25	1.50	1.75	10.00
☐ 1399	18c Elizabeth Blackwell, 1/23/74, Geneva, NY				
	(217,938) (2 types)*	1.00	1.50	2.50	10.00*
☐ 1400	21c Amadeo Giannini, 6/27/73, San Mateo, CA				
	(282,520)	1.00	1.50	2.50	12.00

1970-71 Coils

		SINGLE	BLOCK	PLATE BLOCK	
☐ 1401	6c Dwight D. Eisenhower, 8/6/70, DC	1.00pr	1.25	lp2.00	
☐ 1402	8c Dwight D. Eisenhower, 5/10/71, DC	1.00pr	1.25	lp2.00	

1970

		SINGLE	BLOCK	PLATE BLOCK	CERM PROG
☐ 1405	6c Edgar Lee Masters, 8/22/70, Petersburg, IL				
	(372,804)	1.00	1.10	1.50	22.00
☐ 1405	6c Edgar Lee Masters, 2nd Day. 8/23/70, Garnett, KS ...				38.00
☐ 1406	6c Woman Suffrage, 8/26/70, Adams, MA				
	(508,142)	1.00	1.10	1.50	25.00
☐ 1407	6c South Carolina, 9/12/70, Charleston, SC				
	(533,000)	1.00	1.10	1.50	20.00
☐ 1408	6c Stone Mountain Memorial, 9/19/70, Stone				
	Mountain, GA (558,546)	1.00	1.10	1.50	10.00
☐ 1409	6c Fort Snelling, 10/17/70, Fort Snelling, MN				
	(497,611)	1.00	1.10	1.50	12.00
☐ 1410	6c Globe & Wheat, 10/28/70, San Clemente, CA	1.25			
☐ 1411	6c Globe & City, 10/28/70, San Clemente, CA	1.25			
☐ 1412	6c Globe & Bluegill, 10/28/70, San Clemente, CA	1.25			
☐ 1413	6c Globe & Seagull, 10/28/70, San Clemente, CA	1.25			
☐ 1413a	Se-tenant, Anti-Pollution, (1,033,147). "Plate Block"				
	value is for block of 4 with plate numbers		4.00	5.00	30.00
☐ 1414	6c Christmas, 11/5/70, DC. "Plate Block" value				
	is for block of 4 with plate numbers	1.40	1.75	3.00	
☐ 1414a	Christmas, precanceled, 11/5/70, DC	10.00			
☐ 1414 & 1414a	11/5/70 on one cover	15.00			
☐ 1415	6c Tin & Cast-iron Locomotive, 11/5/70, DC	1.40			
☐ 1415a	Tin & Cast-iron Locomotive, precanceled	7.50			
☐ 1416	6c Toy Horse on Wheels, 11/5/70, DC	1.40			
☐ 1416a	Toy Horse on Wheels, precanceled	7.50			
☐ 1417	6c Mechanical Tricycle, 11/5/70, DC	1.40			
☐ 1417a	Mechanical Tricycle, precanceled	7.50			
☐ 1418	6c Doll Carriage, 11/5/70, DC	1.40			
☐ 1418a	Doll Carriage, precanceled	7.50			
☐ 1418b	Se-tenant, "Plate Block" value is for block of 4				
	with plate numbers		3.50	5.00	22.00
☐ 1418c	Se-tenant, precanceled		30.00		
☐	Scott 1414a-1418a set of 5 on one cover	35.00			55.00
	Total for Scott 1414-1418 or 1414a-1418a is 2,014,450.				
☐ 1419	6c United Nations, 11/20/70, New York, NY				
	(474,070)	1.50	1.75	2.00	12.00
☐ 1420	6c Landing of the Pilgrims, 11/21/70, Plymouth,				
	MA (629,850)	1.00	1.10	1.50	15.00
☐ 1421	6c Disabled Veterans, 11/24/70, Cincinnati, OH,				
	or Montgomery, AL	1.00	1.10	1.50	15.00
☐ 1422	6c U.S. Servicemen, 11/24/70, Cincinnati, OH, or				
	Montgomery, AL	1.00	1.10	1.50	12.00
☐	Scott 1421-1422 on one cover	1.75	1.85	2.00	
	476,610 covers were postmarked in Cincinnati; 336,417 in Montgomery.				

U.S. 6¢ POSTAGE

DWIGHT D.
EISENHOWER

1383

Christmas

1384

HOPE
FOR THE CRIPPLED

6¢

1385

SIX CENTS

UNITED STATES POSTAGE

AMERICAN PAINTING

WILLIAM M. HARNETT

1386

EISENHOWER·USA

1393

U.S 6¢

AMERICAN BALD EAGLE

1387-90

MAINE STATEHOOD

1820-1970

1391

EISENHOWER USA

1394, 1395, 1402

6¢

1392

U.S. MAIL

6 cents

1396

ELIZABETH BLACKWELL FIRST WOMAN PHYSICIAN

US POSTAGE 18¢

1399

GIANNINI
AMADEO P.
BANKER

USA 21¢

1400

EDGAR LEE
MASTERS
AMERICA'S POET

UNITED STATES 6¢

1405

WOMAN SUFFRAGE

50ᵀᴴ ANNIVERSARY 6¢

1406

SOUTH CAROLINA
1670
1970

6¢

1407

Stone Mountain Memorial

UNITED STATES 6 CENTS

1408

GREAT NORTHWEST
1820 FORT SNELLING 1970

US 6¢

1409

SAVE OUR WATER

UNITED STATES · SIX CENTS

1410-13

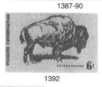

Christmas
6 U.S.

1415-18

Christmas 6¢

1414

UNITED STATES POSTAGE 6 CENTS

UN

United Nations 25ᵗʰ Anniversary

1419

U.S. POSTAGE 6 CENTS

1420

cover binders

Padded, durable, 3-ring binder will hold up to 100 covers. Features the "D" ring mechanism on the right hand side of album so you don't have to worry about creasing or wrinkling covers when opening or closing binder.

Item	Description	Retail
CBRD	Cover Binder - Red	$7.95
CBBL	Cover Binder - Blue	$7.95
CBGY	Cover Binder - Gray	$7.95
CBBK	Cover Binder - Black	$7.95
	Cover pages sold separately.	
T2	Cover Pages Black (25 per pckg)	$4.95
CBBL	Cover Pages Clear (25 per pckg)	$4.95

The cover binders and pages are available from your favorite stamp dealer or direct from:

SCOTT

P.O. Box 828 Sidney OH 45365-0828

to order call 1-800-572-6885

1421   1422   1423   1424

1425

1st Bazaar cachet   1st Colorano Silk cachet

1426

1427-30

1433

1431

1434-35

1432   1436   1437   1438   1439

1440-43

1444   1445   1446   1447

1971

☐ 1423	6c **American Wool Industry**, 1/19/71, Las Vegas, NV (379,911)..1.00	1.10		1.50	18.00
☐	1st Bazaar cachet 25.00				
☐	1st Colorono Silk cachet...............................250.00				
☐ 1424	6c **Gen. Douglas MacArthur**, 1/26/71, Norfolk, VA (720,035)..1.00	1.10		1.50	15.00
☐ 1425	6c **Blood Donor**, 3/12/71, New York, NY (644,497)..1.25	1.50		1.75	18.00
☐ 1426	8c **Missouri Sesquicentennial**, 5/8/71, Independence, MO (551,000). "Plate Block" value is for block of 4 with plate numbers 1.00	1.25		1.50	18.00
☐ 1427	8c **Trout**, 6/12/71, Avery Island, LA..........................1.25				
☐ 1428	8c **Alligator**, 6/12/71, Avery Island, LA.....................1.25				
☐ 1429	8c **Polar Bear & Cubs**, 6/12/71, Avery Island, LA ...1.25				
☐ 1430	8c **California Condor**, 6/12/71, Avery Island, LA 1.25				
☐ 1430a	**Se-tenant** (679,483)..	3.00		5.00	25.00
☐ 1431	8c **Antarctic Treaty**, 6/23/71, DC (419,200) 1.00	1.25		1.50	12.00
☐ 1432	8c **American Revolution Bicentennial**, 7/4/71, DC (434,930)..1.00	1.25		1.50	
☐	1st Medallion cachet 25.00				
☐ 1433	8c **John Sloan**, 8/2/71, Lock Haven, PA (482,265)....1.00	1.25		1.50	12.00
☐ 1434a	8c **Space Achievement Decade**, se-tenant pair, 8/2/71, Kennedy Space Center, FL (1,403,644).2.50	3.25		4.00	
☐	Houston, TX (811,560), pair 2.50	3.25		4.00	
☐	Huntsville, AL (524,000), pair (3 papers)*........3.00	4.00		5.00	35.00*
☐	1st Manned Space Flight Covers cachet 15.00				
☐	1st Swanson cachet.......................................15.00				
☐ 1436	8c **Emily Dickinson**, 8/28/71, Amherst, MA (498,180)..1.00	1.25		1.50	12.00
☐ 1437	8c **San Juan**, 9/12/71, San Juan, PR (501,688) 1.00	1.25		1.50	18.00
☐ 1438	8c **Prevent Drug Abuse**, 10/4/71, Dallas, TX (425,330). "Plate Block" value is for block of 4 with plate numbers...1.00	1.25		1.50	15.00
☐ 1439	8c **CARE**, 10/27/71, New York, NY (402,121). "Plate Block" value is for block of 4 with plate numbers...1.00	1.25		1.50	18.00
☐ 1440	8c **Decatur House**, 10/29/71, DC 1.25				
☐ 1441	8c **Whaling Ship Charles W. Morgan**, 10/29/71, DC...1.25				
☐ 1442	8c **Cable Car**, 10/29/71, San Diego, CA....................1.25				
☐ 1443	8c **San Xavier del Bac Mission**, 10/29/71, DC..........1.25				
☐ 1443a	**Se-tenant**, (783,242)..	3.00		4.00	75.00
☐ 1444	8c **Christmas**, 11/10/71, DC (348,038).....................1.00	1.25		1.50	10.00
☐ 1445	8c **Christmas**, 11/10/71, DC (580,062).......................1.00	1.25		1.50	10.00
☐	Scott 1444-1445 on one cover 1.75				

1972

☐ 1446	8c **Sidney Lanier**, 2/3/72, Macon, GA (394,800) 1.00	1.25		1.50	12.00
☐ 1447	8c **Peace Corps**, 2/11/72, DC (453,660), "Plate Block" value is for block of 4 with plate numbers 1.00	1.25		1.50	12.00

1453

1448-51

1452

1455

1456-59

1460-62

1454

1464-67

1468

1463

1469

1470

1471

1472

1474

1st Coulson cachet

1473

1484-87

1475

1476-79

1480-83

98

National Parks Centennial

☐ 1451a 2c Cape Hatteras National Seashore, se-tenant,
4/5/72, Hatteras, NC (505,697) 1.25 2.00

☐ 1448-1451 2c National Parks Centennial. 4/5/72. Hatteras, NC
(without insert) 15.00

☐ 1452 6c Wolf Trap Farm, 6/26/72, Vienna, VA (403,396) .1.00 1.25 1.50 35.00
☐ 1453 8c Old Faithful, 3/1/72, Yellowstone National
Park, WY 1.00 1.25 1.50 25.00

☐ DC (847,500) 1.00 1.25 1.50

☐ 1454 15c Mt. McKinley, 7/28/72, Mt. McKinley
National Park, AK (491,456) 1.00 1.25 2.00 45.00

☐ 1455 8c Family Planning, 3/18/72, New York, NY
(691,385) 1.00 1.25 1.50 15.00

☐ 1456 8c Glass Blower, 7/4/72, Williamsburg, VA 1.00
☐ 1457 8c Silversmith, 7/4/72, Williamsburg, VA 1.00
☐ 1458 8c Wigmaker, 7/4/72, Williamsburg, VA 1.00
☐ 1459 8c Hatter, 7/4/72, Williamsburg, VA 1.00
☐ 1459a Se-tenant, Colonial American Craftsmen(1,914,976)...... 2.50 3.50 15.00

☐ 1460 6c Olympics, 8/17/72, DC. "Plate Block" value is
for block of 4 with plate numbers 1.00 1.25 1.50

☐ 1461 8c Winter Olympics, 8/17/72, DC. "Plate Block"
value is for block of 4 with plate numbers 1.00 1.25 1.50

☐ 1462 15c Olympics, 8/17/72, DC. "Plate Block" value is
for block of 4 with plate numbers 1.00 1.50 2.00
Scott 1460-1462 and C85 on one cover............2.00
Total for Scott 1460-1462 and C85 is 971,536.

☐ 1460-1462, C85 6c-15c Olympic Games, (2 types)*.................... 10.00*

☐ 1463 8c Parent Teacher Association, 9/15/72, San
Francisco, CA (523,454)................................1.00 1.25 1.50 10.00

☐ 1464 8c Fur Seals, 9/20/72 Warm Springs, OR 1.50
☐ 1465 8c Cardinal, 9/20/72 Warm Springs, OR.................1.50
☐ 1466 8c Brown Pelican, 9/20/72 Warm Springs, OR.........1.50
☐ 1467 8c Bighorn Sheep, 9/20/72 Warm Springs, OR 1.50
☐ 1467a Se-tenant, (733,778)...1.50 3.00 5.00 12.00

☐ 1468 8c Mall Order, 9/27/72, Chicago, IL (759,666).
"Plate Block" value is for block of 4 with plate
numbers 1.00 1.25 2.00 30.00

☐ 1469 8c Osteopathic Medicine, 10/9/72, Miami, FL
(607, 160). "Plate Block" value is for block of 4
with plate numbers...1.00 1.25 2.00 10.00

☐ 1470 8c Tom Sawyer, 10/13/72, Hannibal, MO (459,013).1.00 1.25 2.00 20.00
1st Coulson cachet 15.00

☐ 1471-1472 8c Christmas, 11/9/72, DC, either stamp 1.00 1.25 2.00 12.00
Scott 1471-1472 on one cover
(718,821 total for both)....................................2.00

☐ 1473 8c Pharmacy, 11/10/72, Cincinnati, OH (804,320). 10.00 11.00 20.00 10.00
☐ 1474 8c Stamp Collecting, 11/17/72, New York, NY
(434,680)...1.50 1.75 2.00 12.00

1973

☐ 1475 8c Love, 1/26/73, Philadelphia, PA (422,294).
"Plate Block" value is for block of 4 with plate
numbers 1.00 1.25 1.50 12.00

1500-02

1488

1489-98

1499

1503

1504-06

1509, 1519

1510, 1520

1507

1508

1526

1511

1518

1525

1528

1529

1527

1530-37

1538-41

1542

1547

Communications in Colonial Times

☐ 1476　8c Pamphleteer, 2/16/73, Portland, OR (431,784) ...1.00　1.25　　1.50　12.00
☐ 1477　8c Broadside, 4/13/73, Atlantic City, NJ (423,437) ..1.00　1.25　　1.50　12.00
☐ 1478　8c Postrider, 6/22/73, Rochester, NY (586,850)........1.00　1.25　　1.50　12.00
☐ 1479　8c Drummer, 9/28/73, New Orleans, LA (522,427). .1.00　1.25　　1.50　12.00
☐ 1480　8c British merchantman, 7/4/73, Boston, MA 1.00
☐ 1481　8c British three-master, 7/4/73, Boston, MA 1.00
☐ 1482　8c Boats & ship's hulk 7/4/73, Boston, MA 1.00
☐ 1483　8c Boat & dock, 7/4/73, Boston, MA 1.00
☐ 1483a　**Se-tenant,** Boston Tea Party, (897,870)........................　3.00　　4.00　25.00

American Arts

☐ 1484　8c George Gershwin, 2/28/73, Beverly Hills, CA
　　　　(448,814). "Plate Block" value is for block of 4
　　　　with plate numbers..1.00　1.25　　1.50　45.00
☐ 1485　8c Robinson Jeffers, 8/13/73, Carmel, CA
　　　　(394,261). "Plate Block" value is for block of 4
　　　　with plate numbers..1.00　1.25　　1.50　12.00
☐ 1486　8c Henry O. Tanner, 9/10/73, Pittsburgh, PA
　　　　(424,065). "Plate Block" value is for block of 4
　　　　with plate numbers..1.00　1.25　　1.50　12.00
☐ 1487　8c Willa Cather, 9/20/73, Red Cloud, NE
　　　　(435,784). "Plate Block" value is for block of 4
　　　　with plate numbers..1.00　1.25　　2.00　　8.00
☐ 1488　8c Nicolaus Copernicus, 4/23/73, DC (734,190).......1.75　2.00　　2.25　10.00
☐ 1489　8c Stamp Counter, 4/30/73, any city 1.00
☐ 1490　8c Mail Collection, 4/30/73, any city 1.00
☐ 1491　8c Letter Facing on Conveyor Belt, 4/30/73, any city1.00
☐ 1492　8c Parcel Post Sorting, 4/30/73, any city.................1.00
☐ 1493　8c Mail Canceling, 4/30/73, any city 1.00
☐ 1494　8c Manual Letter Routing, 4/30/73, any city 1.00
☐ 1495　8c Electronic Letter Routing, 4/30/73, any city.......1.00
☐ 1496　8c Loading Mail on Truck, 4/30/73, any city 1.00
☐ 1497　8c Mailman, 4/30/73, any city 1.00
☐ 1498　8c Rural Mail Delivery, 4/30/73, any city................1.00
　　　　Any block of 4/block of 4 with plate number...........　1.25　　2.00
　　　　Strip of 10 on one cover....................................9.00
☐ 1498a　Postal Service Employees (4 cities)..............................　　　　　　　　　　15.00
☐ 1499　8c Harry S. Truman, 5/8/73, Independence, MO
　　　　(938,636)..1.00　1.25　　1.50　15.00
☐ 1500　6c Electronics, 7/10/73, New York, NY ....1.00　1.25　　1.50
☐ 1501　8c Electronics, 7/10/73, New York, NY ....1.00　1.25　　1.50
☐ 1502　15c Electronics, 7/10/73, New York, NY ....1.00　1.25　　1.75
　　　　Scott 1500-1502 and C86 on one cover..................　3.00　　5.00　30.00
　　　　Total for Scott 1500-1502 and C86 is 1,197,700.
☐ 1503　8c Lyndon B. Johnson, 8/27/73, Austin, TX
　　　　(701,490)..1.00　1.25　　1.50　15.00

1973-74 Rural America

☐ 1504　8c Angus Cattle, 10/5/73, St. Joseph, MO
　　　　(521,427)..1.00　1.25　　1.50　15.00
☐ 1505　10c Chautauqua, 8/6/74, Chautauqua, NY
　　　　(411,105) (2 types)*...1.00　1.25　　1.50 15.00*
☐ 1506　10c Wheat, 8/16/74, Hillsboro, KS (468,280) ....1.00　1.25　　1.50　15.00

1543-46

1548

Retarded Children
Can Be Helped
1549

1551

1552

1550

1553

1555

1556

Paul Laurence
Dunbar
1554

1557

1558

US Bicentennial 10c
1564

Sybil Ludington
1559-62

US Bicentennial 10cents
1563

1565-68

1569-70

1st Gothic Covers cachet

1571

102

1973

		SINGLE	BLOCK	PLATE BLOCK	CERM PROG
☐ 1507	8c Christmas, 11/7/73, DC	1.00	1.25	1.50	
☐ 1508	8c Christmas, 11/7/73, DC	1.00	1.25	1.50	
	Scott 1507-1508 on one cover				
	(807,468 total for both)		1.75		15.00

1973-74

☐ 1509	10c Crossed Flags, 12/8/73, San Francisco, CA.				
	"Plate Block" value is for block of 4 with plate				
	numbers	1.00	1.25	1.50	18.00
	Total for Scott 1509 and 1519 is 341,528.				
☐ 1510	10c Jefferson Memorial, 12/14/73, DC	1.00	1.25	1.50	
☐ 1510b	Jefferson Memorial, booklet pane of 5 plus labels,				
	12/14/73, DC	2.25			
☐ 1510c	Jefferson Memorial, booklet pane of 8, 12/14/73, DC	2.50			
☐ 1510d	Jefferson Memorial, booklet pane of 6, 8/5/74,				
	Oakland, CA	5.00			25.00
	Total for Scott 1510, 1510b, 1510c, and 1520 is 686,300.				
☐ 1511	10c Zip Code, 1/4/74, DC (335,220). "Plate Block"				
	value is for block of 4 with plate numbers	1.00	1.00	1.50	
☐ 1518	6.3c Liberty Bell, coil, 10/1/74, DC (221,141) (2 types)*	pr1.00		lp1.50	10.00*
☐ 1519	10c Crossed Flags, coil, 12/8/73, San Francisco, CA	1.00	pr1.00	lp1.50	60.00
☐ 1520	10c Jefferson Memorial, coil, 12/14/73, DC	1.00	pr1.25	lp1.50	

1974

☐ 1525	10c Veterans of Foreign Wars, 3/11/74, DC				
	(543,598)	1.00	1.25	1.50	15.00
☐ 1526	10c Robert Frost, 3/26/74, Derry, NH (500,425)	1.00	1.25	1.50	12.00
☐ 1527	10c EXPO '74, 4/18/74, Spokane, WA (565,548).				
	"Plate Block" value is for block of 4 with plate				
	numbers	1.00	1.25	1.50	15.00
☐ 1528	10c Horse Racing, 5/4/74, Louisville, KY				
	(623,983)	2.00	2.50	3.50	22.00
☐	1st Henry Koehler cachet	15.00			
☐ 1529	10c Skylab, 5/14/74, Houston, TX (972,326)	2.00	2.50	3.50	20.00
☐ 1530	10c Michelangelo, 6/6/74, DC	1.00			20.00
☐ 1531	10c Five Feminine Virtues, 6/6/74, DC	1.00			20.00
☐ 1532	10c Old Scraps, 6/6/74, DC	1.00			20.00
☐ 1533	10c The Lovely Reader, 6/6/74, DC	1.00			20.00
☐ 1534	10c Lady Writing Letter, 6/6/74, DC	1.00			20.00
☐ 1535	10c Inkwell & Quill, 6/6/74, DC	1.00			20.00
☐ 1536	10c Mrs. John Douglas, 6/6/74, DC	1.00			20.00
☐ 1537	10c Don Antonio Noriega, 6/6/74, DC	1.00			20.00
	Any block of 4/block of 4 with plate numbers		1.75	2.00	
	Strip of 8 on one cover	4.00			
	Total for Scott 1530-1537 is 1,374,765.				
☐ 1538	10c Petrified Wood, 6/13/74, Lincoln, NE	1.00			22.00
☐ 1539	10c Tourmaline, 6/13/74, Lincoln, NE	1.00			22.00
☐ 1540	10c Anethyst 6/13/74, Lincoln, NE	1.00			22.00
☐ 1541	10c Rhodochrosite, 6/13/74, Lincoln, NE	1.00			22.00
☐ 1541a	Se-tenant (865,368)		2.50	4.00	
☐ 1542	10c Kentucky Settlement, 6/15/74, Harrodsburg,				
	KY (478,239)	1.00	1.25	1.50	10.00

1572-75

1576

1579-80

1577-78

1584

1592, 1617

1593

1596

1599, 1619

1608

1622, 1625

HOW TO USE THIS BOOK
The number in the first column is its Scott number or
identifying number. Following that is the denomination
of the stamp, description, date of issue, and the value.

		SINGLE	BLOCK	PLATE BLOCK	CERM PROG
☐ 1543	10c **Carpenter's Hall,** 7/4/74, Philadelphia, PA 1.00				
☐ 1544	10c **"We ask but for peace,"** 7/4/74, Philadelphia, PA 1.00				
☐ 1545	10c **"Deriving their just powers,"** 7/4/74, Philadelphia, PA 1.00				
☐ 1546	10c **Independence Hall,** 7/4/74, Philadelphia, PA 1.00				
☐ 1546a	**Se-tenant** First Continental Congress **(2,124,957)**	2.75	3.50	22.00	
☐ 1547	10c **Energy Conservation,** 9/23/74, Detroit, MI (587,210) (2 types)★..............................1.00	1.25	1.50	10.00★	
☐ 1548	10c **Legend of Sleepy Hollow,** 10/10/74, North Tarrytown, NY (514,836) 1.00	1.25	1.50	20.00	
☐ 1549	10c **Retarded Children,** 10/12/74, Arlington, TX (412,882)..1.00	1.25	1.50	20.00	
☐ 1550	10c **Christmas,** 10/23/74, New York, NY. "Plate Block" value is for block of 4 with plate numbers. 1.00	1.25	1.50		
☐ 1551	10c **Christmas,** 10/23/74, New York, NY. "Plate Block" value is for block of 4 with plate numbers. 1.00	1.25	1.50		
☐	Scott 1550-1551 on one 1.75			25.00	
☐ 1552	10c **Christmas,** self-adhesive, 11/15/74, New York, NY (477,410). 1.00				
☐	1st Glen cachet..............................20.00				
☐ 1550-1552	**Christmas** 1552 was added to the 1550-1551 program			85.00	

1975 American Arts

		SINGLE	BLOCK	PLATE BLOCK	CERM PROG
☐ 1553	10c **Benjamin West,** 2/10/75, Swarthmore, PA (465,017). "Plate Block" value is for block of 4 with plate numbers.............................1.00	1.25	1.50	20.00	
☐ 1554	10c **Paul Laurence Dunbar,** 5/1/75, Dayton, OH (397,347). "Plate Block" value is for block of 4 with plate numbers.............................1.00	1.25	1.50	12.00	
☐ 1555	10c **D.W. Griffith,** 5/27/75, Beverly Hills, CA (424,167)...1.00	1.25	1.50	12.00	
☐ 1556	10c **Pioneer-Jupiter,** 2/28/75, Mountain View, CA (594,896)...2.00	2.50	4.00	20.00	
☐ 1557	10c **Mariner 10,** 4/4/75, Pasadena, CA (563,636).....2.00	2.50	4.00	20.00	
☐ 1558	10c **Collective Bargaining,** 3/13/75, DC (412,329). "Plate Block" value is for block of 4 with plate numbers....................................1.00	1.25	1.50	15.00	
☐ 1559	8c **Sybil Ludington,** 3/25/75, Carmel, NY (394,550). "Plate Block" value is for block of 4 with plate numbers.............................1.00	1.25	1.50	12.00	
☐ 1560	10c **Salem Poor,** 3/25/75, Cambridge, MA (415,565). "Plate Block" value is for block of 4 with plate numbers.............................1.00	1.25	1.50	15.00	
☐ 1561	10c **Haym Salomon,** 3/25/75, Chicago, IL (447,630). "Plate Block" value is for block of 4 with plate numbers.............................1.00	1.25	1.50	18.00	
☐ 1562	18c **Peter Francisco,** 3/25/75, Greensboro, NC (415,000). "Plate Block" value is for block of 4 with plate numbers.............................1.00	1.25	1.50	15.00	
☐	Scott 1559-1562 set on one cover, any city 5.00				
☐ 1563	10c **Lexington-Concord Battle,** 4/19/75, Lexington, MA, or Concord, MA (975,020). "Plate Block" value is for block of 4 with plate numbers 1.00	1.25	1.50	15.00	
☐	Dual cancel.......................................2.00				

		SINGLE	BLOCK	PLATE BLOCK	CERM PROG
☐ 1564	**10c Battle of Bunker Hill,** 6/17/75, Charlestown, MA, (557,130). "Plate Block" value is for block of 4 with plate numbers (2 types)*........................1.00		1.25	1.50	15.00*
☐ 1565	**10c Soldier with Flintlock Musket,** 7/4/75, DC 1.00				
☐ 1566	**10c Sailor with Grappling Hook,** 7/4/75, DC............1.00				
☐ 1567	**10c Marine with Musket,** 7/4/75, DC.......................1.00				
☐ 1568	**10c Militiaman,** 7/4/75, DC 1.00				
☐ 1568a	**Se-tenant,** Military uniforms(1,134, 831). "Plate Block" value is for block of 4 with plate numbers		2.50	3.50	18.00
☐ 1569	**10c Apollo,** Soyuz before link-up, 7/15/75, Kennedy Space Center, FL 3.00				
☐ 1569a	**Se-tenant,** (1,427,046) 4.00		5.00	6.00	
☐ 1570	**10c Apollo,** Soyuz after link-up, 7/15/75, Kennedy Space Center, FL 3.00				
☐	Scott 1569-1570 with Russian stamps, dual cancel450.00				
☐ 1571	**10c International Women's Year,** 8/26/75, Seneca Falls, NY (476,769). "Plate Block" value is for block of 4 plate numbers 1.00		1.25	1.50	18.00
☐	1st Gothic Covers cachet................................20.00				
☐ 1572	**10c Stagecoach & Trailer Truck,** 9/3/75, Philadelphia, PA 1.00				
☐ 1573	**10c Locomotives,** 9/3/75, Philadelphia, PA..............1.00				
☐ 1574	**10c Early Mail Plane,** Jet, 9/3/75, Philadelphia, PA.1.00				
☐ 1575	**10c Satellite, Dishes,** 9/3/75, Philadelphia, PA.........1.00				
☐ 1575a	**Se-tenant,** Postal Service Bicentennial(969,999), "Plate Block" value is for block of 4 with plate numbers...		1.25	1.50	18.00
☐ 1576	**10c World Peace through Law,** 9/29/75, DC (386,736) 1.00		1.25	1.50	
☐ 1577	**10c "Banking,"** coins, 10/6/75, New York, NY..........1.00				
☐ 1577a	**Se-tenant,** Banking & Commerce (555,580) "Plate Block" value is for block of 4 with plate numbers 1.10		1.00	1.50	12.00
☐ 1578	**10c "Commerce,"** coins, 10/6/75, New York, NY......1.00				
☐ 1579	**10c Christmas,** 10/14/75, DC, "Plate Block" value is for block of 4 with plate numbers 1.00		1.25	1.50	
☐ 1580	**10c Christmas,** 10/14/75, DC, "Plate Block" value is for block of 4 with plate numbers 1.00		1.25	1.50	
☐	Scott 1579-1580 on one cover (730,079) 2.00				
☐	(2 types)*				20.00

1975-81 Americana Issue

		SINGLE	BLOCK	PLATE BLOCK	CERM PROG
☐ 1581	**1c Inkwell & Quill,** multiple for First Class rate, 12/8/77, St. Louis, MO 1.00		1.25		
☐ 1582	**2c Speaker's Stand,** multiple for First Class rate, 12/8/77, St. Louis, MO 1.00		1.25		
☐ 1584	**3c Early Ballot Box,** multiple for First Class rate, 12/8/77, St. Louis, MO 1.00		1.25		
☐ 1585	**4c Books, Bookmark & Eyeglasses,** multiple for First Class rate, 12/8/77, St. Louis, MO...................1.00		1.25		
☐ 1581-1585	**1c-4c American Series**				12.00
	Total for Scott 1581-1585 is 530,033.				
☐ 1590	**9c Dome of the Capitol,** booklet single plus postage for First Class rate, 3/11/77, New York, NY....10.00				
☐ 1591	**9c Dome of the Capitol,** perf. 11 x 10 1/2, multiple for First Class rate, 11/24/75, DC (190,117) 1.00		1.25	1.50	

☐ 1592	**10c Contemplation of Justice,** multiple for First Class rate, 11/17/77, New York, NY (359,050)..1.00	1.25		1.75	10.00
☐ 1593	**11c Early American Printing Press,** multiple for First Class rate, 11/13/75, Philadelphia, PA (217,755)...1.00	1.25		1.75	12.00
☐ 1594	**12c Torch,** multiple for First Class rate, 4/8/81, Dallas, TX..1.00	1.25		1.75	12.00
	Total for Scott 1594 and 1816 is 280,930.				
☐ 1595	**13c Liberty Bell,** booklet single, 10/31/75, Cleveland, OH...1.00				
☐ 1595a	**Liberty Bell,** booklet pane of 6, 10/31/75, Cleveland, OH...2.00				
☐ 1595b	**Liberty Bell,** booklet pane of 7 + label, 10/31/75, Cleveland, OH................................2.75				
☐ 1595c	**Liberty Bell,** booklet pane of 8, 10/31/75, Cleveland, OH...2.50				
☐ 1595a-1595c	**Liberty Bell,** booklet panes....................................				20.00
	Total for Scott 1595a-1595c is 256, 734.				
☐ 1595d	**Liberty Bell,** booklet pane of 5 + label, 4/2/76, Liberty, MO (92,223) 2.25				15.00
☐ 1596	**13c Eagle & Shield,** 12/1/75, Juneau, AK (418,272). "Plate Block" value is for block of 4 with plate numbers...1.00	1.25		1.75	12.00
☐ 1597	**15c Ft. McHenry Flag,** 6/30/78, Baltimore, MD. "Plate Block" value is for block of 4 with plate numbers 1.00	1.25		1.75	12.00
☐ 1598	**15c Ft. McHenry Flag,** booklet single, 6/30/78, Baltimore, MD...1.00				
☐ 1598a	**Ft. McHenry Flag** booklet pane of 8.........................2.50				50.00
	Total for Scott 1597-1598 and 1618C is 315,359.				
☐ 1599	**16c Head,** Statue of Liberty, 3/31/78, New York, NY 1.00	1.25		1.75	
	Total for Scott 1599 and 1619 is 376,338.				
☐ 1603	**24c Old North Church,** 11/14/75, Boston, MA (208,973) 1.00	1.25		1.75	12.00
☐ 1604	**28c Ft. Nisqually,** 8/11/78, Tacoma, WA (159,639)...1.25	1.75		3.00	10.00
☐ 1605	**29c Sandy Hook Lighthouse,** 4/14/78, Atlantic City, NJ (193,476).......................................1.50	1.75		2.75	12.00
☐ 1606	**30c Morris Township School No. 2,** 8/27/79, Devils Lake, ND (186,882)................................1.25	1.50		2.50	15.00
☐ 1608	**50c Iron "Betty" Lamp,** 9/11/79, San Juan, PR (159,540)..1.50	2.00		3.00	22.00
☐ 1610	**$1 Rush Lamp & Candle Holder,** 7/2/79, San Francisco, CA (255,575)....................................3.00	4.50		7.50	
☐ 1611	**$2 Kerosene Table Lamp,** 11/16/78, New York, NY (173,596) 7.00	8.50		10.00	18.00
☐ 1612	**$5 Railroad Lantern,** 8/23/79, Boston, MA (129,192) 15.00	20.00		25.00	30.00

1975-79 Americana Coils

☐ 1613	**3.1c Guitar,** 10/25/79, Shreveport, LA (230,403).............	1.00	1.50	
☐ 1614	**7.7c Saxhorns,** 11/20/76, New York, NY (285,298)	1.00	1.50	12.00
☐ 1615	**7.9c Drum,** 4/23/76, Miami, FL (193,270)	1.00	1.50	12.00
☐ 1615C	**8.4c Piano,** 7/13/78, Interlochen, MI (200,392)..............	1.00	1.50	35.00
☐ 1616	**9c Dome of the Capitol,** 3/5/76, Milwaukee, WI (128,171)...	1.00	1.50	15.00

SCOTT NUMBER	DESCRIPTION	SINGLE	PAIR	LINE PAIR	CERM PROG
☐ 1617	10c Contemplation of Justice, 11/4/77, Tampa, FL (184,954)		1.00	1.50	12.00
☐	1st Bill Ressl cachet	15.00			
☐	1st Sandra's Cachets cachet	15.00			
☐ 1618	13c Liberty Bell, 11/25/75, Allentown, PA (320,387)	1.00	1.10	1.50	12.00
☐ 1618C	15c Ft. McHenry Flag, 6/30/78, Baltimore, MD	1.00	1.00	1.10	50.00
☐ 1597, 1618C on one cover		3.00			
☐ 1619	16c Statue of Liberty Head, 3/31/78, New York, NY	1.00	1.10	1.50	

SCOTT NUMBER	DESCRIPTION	SINGLE	PLATE BLOCK	CERM BLOCK	PROG

1975-77

SCOTT NUMBER	DESCRIPTION	SINGLE	PLATE BLOCK	CERM BLOCK	PROG
☐ 1622	13c Flag over Independence Hall, 11/15/75, Philadelphia, PA, "Plate Block" value is for block of 4 with plate numbers	1.00	1.25	1.75	12.00
☐ 1623	13c Flag over Capitol, booklet single, perf. 11x10 1/2, 3/11/77, New York, NY	1.00			
☐ 1623a	Flag over Capitol, booklet pane of 7 + 1 Scott 1590, 3/11/77, New York, NY	30.00			
☐ 1623B	Flag over Capitol, booklet single, perf. 10, 3/11/77, New York, NY	1.50			
☐ 1623Bc	Flag over Capitol, booklet pane of 7 + 1 Scott 1590a, 3/11/77, New York, NY	15.00			20.00
☐ 1623Bc-1623d Flag over Capitol, booklet pane of 8 with perf. 10 1/2x11 stamps added.					60.00
	Total for all versions of Scott 1623 is 242,208.				
☐	Scott 1622 & 1625 on one cover	5.00			

SCOTT NUMBER	DESCRIPTION	SINGLE	PAIR	LINE PAIR	CERM PROG
☐ 1625	13c Flag over Independence Hall, coil, 11/15/75, Philadelphia, PA		1.00	1.50	50.00
	Total for Scott 1622 and 1625 is 362,959.				

SCOTT NUMBER	DESCRIPTION	SINGLE	PLATE BLOCK	CERM BLOCK	PROG

1976

SCOTT NUMBER	DESCRIPTION	SINGLE	PLATE BLOCK	CERM BLOCK	PROG
☐ 1629	13c Drummer boy, 1/1/76, Pasadena, CA	1.75			
☐ 1630	13c Old Drummer, 1/1/76, Pasadena, CA	1.75			
☐ 1631	13c Fifer, 1/1/76, Pasadena, CA	1.75			
☐ 1631a	Se-tenant, (1,013,067). "Block"value is for block of 6. "Plate Block" value is for block of 6 with plate numbers		2.00	2.25	
☐	1st Postmasters of America cachet	30.00			
☐ 1632	13c Interphil '76, 1/17/76, Philadelphia, PA (519,902)	1.00	1.25	1.75	15.00
☐ 1633	13c Delaware, 2/23/76, DC	1.50			
☐ 1634	13c Pennsylvania, 2/23/76, DC	1.50			
☐ 1635	13c New Jersey, 2/23/76, DC	1.50			
☐ 1636	13c Georgia, 2/23/76, DC	1.50			
☐ 1637	13c Connecticut, 2/23/76, DC	1.50			
☐ 1638	13c Massachusetts, 2/23/76, DC	1.50			
☐ 1639	13c Maryland, 2/23/76, DC	1.50			
☐ 1640	13c South Carolina, 2/23/76, DC	1.50			
☐ 1641	13c New Hampshire, 2/23/76, DC	1.50			
☐ 1642	13c Virginia, 2/23/76, DC	1.50			
☐ 1643	13c New York, 2/23/76, DC	1.50			
☐ 1644	13c North Carolina, 2/23/76, DC	1.50			

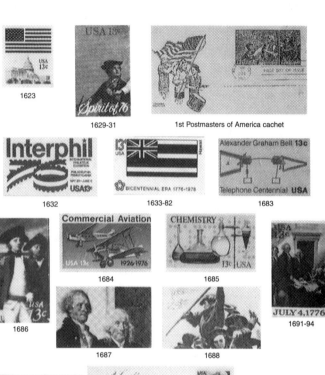

1623

1629-31

1st Postmasters of America cachet

1632

1633-82

1683

Commercial Aviation

1684

CHEMISTRY

1685

1686

1687

1688

1691-94

1689

1st Metropolitan FDC Society cachet

1690

**Values for various cachet makers can be determined
by using the Cachet Calculator which begins on page 52A.**

☐ 1645	13c **Rhode Island**, 2/23/76, DC 1.50				
☐ 1646	13c **Vermont**, 2/23/76, DC...................................1.50				
☐ 1647	13c **Kentucky**, 2/23/76, DC.................................1.50				
☐ 1648	13c **Tennessee**, 2/23/76, DC................................1.50				
☐ 1649	13c **Ohio**, 2/23/76, DC 1.50				
☐ 1650	13c **Louisiana**, 2/23/76, DC.................................1.50				
☐ 1651	13c **Indiana**, 2/23/76, DC....................................1.50				
☐ 1652	13c **Mississippi**, 2/23/76, DC...............................1.50				
☐ 1653	13c **Illinois**, 2/23/76, DC....................................1.50				
☐ 1654	13c **Alabama**, 2/23/76, DC...................................1.50				
☐ 1655	13c **Maine**, 2/23/76, DC......................................1.50				
☐ 1656	13c **Missouri**, 2/23/76, DC..................................1.50				
☐ 1657	13c **Arkansas**, 2/23/76, DC..................................1.50				
☐ 1658	13c **Michigan**, 2/23/76, DC..................................1.50				
☐ 1659	13c **Florida**, 2/23/76, DC....................................1.50				
☐ 1660	13c **Texas**, 2/23/76, DC 1.50				
☐ 1661	13c **Iowa**, 2/23/76, DC..1.50				
☐ 1662	13c **Wisconsin**, 2/23/76, DC................................1.50				
☐ 1663	13c **California**, 2/23/76, DC.................................1.50				
☐ 1664	13c **Minnesota**, 2/23/76, DC................................1.50				
☐ 1665	13c **Oregon**, 2/23/76, DC.....................................1.50				
☐ 1666	13c **Kansas**, 2/23/76, DC.....................................1.50				
☐ 1667	13c **West Virginia**, 2/23/76, DC...........................1.50				
☐ 1668	13c **Nevada**, 2/23/76, DC.....................................1.50				
☐ 1669	13c **Nebraska**, 2/23/76, DC..................................1.50				
☐ 1670	13c **Colorado**, 2/23/76, DC 1.50				
☐ 1671	13c **North Dakota**, 2/23/76, DC............................1.50				
☐ 1672	13c **South Dakota**, 2/23/76, DC............................1.50				
☐ 1673	13c **Montana**, 2/23/76, DC 1.50				
☐ 1674	13c **Washington**, 2/23/76, DC...............................1.50				
☐ 1675	13c **Idaho**, 2/23/76, DC.......................................1.50				
☐ 1676	13c **Wyoming**, 2/23/76, DC...................................1.50				
☐ 1677	13c **Utah**, 2/23/76, DC...1.50				
☐ 1678	13c **Oklahoma**, 2/23/76, DC.................................1.50				
☐ 1679	13c **New Mexico**, 2/23/76, DC...............................1.50				
☐ 1680	13c **Arizona**, 2/23/76, DC....................................1.50				
☐ 1681	13c **Alaska**, 2/23/76, DC......................................1.50				
☐ 1682	13c **Hawaii**, 2/23/76, DC 1.50				
	Complete set of 50..75.00				
☐ 1682a	**Se-tenant,** State Flags complete pane on one (4 cities)...				60.00
☐	Canceled at state capitals, each................................2.00				
☐	Canceled at state capitals, complete set of 50 ......100.00				
☐	2/23/76, dual cancels (State & DC)........................150.00				
	Total for Scott 1633-1682 is 3,514,070.				
☐ 1683	13c **Telephone Centenary**, 3/10/76, Boston, MA (662,515)..1.00		1.25	1.50	15.00
☐ 1684	13c **Commercial Aviation**, 3/19/76, Chicago, IL (631,555). "Plate Block" value is for block of 4 with plate numbers..1.00		1.25	1.50	15.00
☐	1st hfb cachet...15.00				
☐ 1685	13c **Chemistry**, 4/6/76, New York, NY (557,600). "Plate Block" value is for block of 4 with plate numbers..1.00		1.25	1.50	15.00
☐ 1686	13c **Surrender of Cornwallis**, souvenir sheet, 5/29/76, Philadelphia, PA 6.00				

1695-98

1699

1700

1701

1702

1st Carrollton cachet

1705

1704

US Bicentennial 13c

1st Doris Gold cachet

1710

Pueblo Art USA 13c

1706-09

1st GAMM cachet

1st Spectrum cachet

HOW TO USE THIS BOOK
The number in the first column is its Scott number or
identifying number. Following that is the denomination
of the stamp, description, date of issue, and the value.

☐ 1687   **18c Declaration of Independence,** souvenir sheet, 5/29/76, Philadelphia, PA 7.50

☐ 1688   **24c Washington Crossing the Delaware,** souvenir sheet, 5/29/76, Philadelphia, PA........................9.00

☐ 1689   **31c Washington at Valley Forge,** souvenir sheet, 5/29/76, Philadelphia, PA................................10.00

    Scott 1686a-1689e, any single from sheets 1.00

    Total for Scott 1686-1689 is 879,890.

☐ 1686-1689 **13c-31c Bicentennial Souvenir Sheets**
(any single stamp)(2 types)*....................................   25.00*

☐ 1690   **13c Benjamin Franklin,** 6/1/76, Philadelphia, PA ...1.00   1.25   1.50 15.00

    In Combo with Canadian issue, dual cancels....1.75

    1st Metropolitan FDC Society cachet 15.00

☐ 1691   **13c Declaration of Independence,** 7/4/76, Philadelphia, PA 1.00

☐ 1692   **13c Declaration of Independence,** 7/4/76, Philadelphia, PA 1.00

☐ 1693   **13c Declaration of Independence,** 7/4/76, Philadelphia, PA 1.00

☐ 1694   **13c Declaration of Independence,** 7/4/76, Philadelphia, PA 1.00

☐ 1694a **Se-tenant,** "Plate Block" value is for block of 8 with plate numbers 2.00   2.50 40.00

    Total for Scott 1691-1694 is 2,093,880.

☐ 1695   **13c Diving,** 7/16/76, Lake Placid, NY......................1.00

☐ 1696   **13c Skiing,** 7/16/76, Lake Placid, NY.......................1.00

☐ 1697   **13c Running,** 7/16/76, Lake Placid, NY 1.00

☐ 1698   **13c Skating,** 7/16/76, Lake Placid, NY.....................1.00

☐ 1698a **Se-tenant,** Olympic Games, (1,140,189). "Plate Block" value is for block of 4 with plate numbers 2.00   2.50 22.00

☐ 1699   **13c Clara Maass,** 8/18/76, Belleville, NJ (646,506). "Plate Block" value is for block of 4 with plate numbers 2.00   2.25   2.75 15.00

☐ 1700   **13c Adolph S. Ochs,** 9/18/76, New York, NY (582,580) 1.00   1.25   1.50

☐ 1701   **13c Christmas (Nativity),** 10/27/76, Boston, MA. "Plate Block" value is for block of 4 with plate numbers 1.00   1.25   1.50

☐ 1702   **13c Christmas ("Winter Pastime"),** 10/27/76, Boston, MA. "Plate Block" value is for block of 4 with plate numbers 1.00   1.25   1.50

    Scott 1701-1702 set on one cover...............1.75

☐ 1703   **13c Christmas ("Winter Pastime"),** 10/27/76, Boston, MA. "Plate Block" value is for block of 4 with plate numbers 1.00   1.25

☐ 1701-1702 **Christmas** (Copley & Currier) 20.00

☐ 1701-1703 **Christmas** (Copley & Currier), Photogravure 45.00

    Total for Scott 1701-1703 is 330,450.

1977

☐ 1704   **13c Washington at Princeton,** 1/3/77, Princeton, NJ (695,335). "Plate Block" value is for block of 4 with plate numbers 1.00   1.25   1.50 18.00

    1st Carrollton cachet.....................................20.00

☐ 1705   **13c Sound Recording,** 3/23/77, DC (632,216) 1.00   1.25   1.50 18.00

    1st Weddle cachet 100.00

1st Tudor House cachet

1711

1716

1st Comic Cachets

1st Ham cachet

1712-15

1717-20

1721

1722

1723-24

1725

HOW TO USE THIS BOOK
The number in the first column is its Scott number or identifying number. Following that is the denomination of the stamp, description, date of issue, and the value.

	SCOTT NUMBER	DESCRIPTION	SINGLE	BLOCK	PLATE BLOCK	CERM PROG
☐	1706	**13c Zia Pot,** 4/13/77, Santa Fe, NM............1.00				
☐	1707	**13c San Ildefonso Pot,** 4/13/77, Santa Fe, NM..........1.00				
☐	1708	**13c Hopi Pot,** 4/13/77, Santa Fe, NM............1.00				
☐	1709	**13c Acoma Pot,** 4/13/77, Santa Fe, NM............1.00				
☐	1709a	**Se-tenant,** Pueblo Pottery (1,194,554). "Plate Block" value for block of 4 with plate numbers		2.00	3.00	12.00
☐		1st Jack Davis Covers cachet.................30.00				
☐		"Sante Fe" error in cancel........................10.00	12.00			
☐	1710	**13c Lindbergh Flight,** 5/20/77, Roosevelt Field Sta., NY (3,985,989). "Plate Block" value is for block of 4 with plate numbers.................3.00		3.25	3.50	25.00
☐		1st Doris Gold cachet 60.00				
☐		1st GAMM cachet 50.00				
☐		1st Spectrum cachet 25.00				
☐		1st Tudor House cachet 20.00				
☐		1st Global Cachets........................20.00				
☐		1st Z-Silk cachet........................20.00				
☐	1711	**13c Colorado Statehood,** 5/21/77, Denver, CO (510, 880). "Plate Block" value is for block of 4 with plate numbers............1.00		1.25	1.50	12.00
☐	1712	**13c Swallowtail,** 6/6/77, Indianapolis, IN............1.00				
☐	1713	**13c Checkerspot,** 6/6/77, Indianapolis, IN............1.00				
☐	1714	**13c Dogface,** 6/6/77, Indianapolis, IN............1.00				
☐	1715	**13c Orange-tip,** 6/6/77, Indianapolis, IN............1.00				
☐	1715a	**Se-tenant,** Butterflies(1,218,278). "Plate Block" value is for block of 4 with plate numbers............		2.00	3.00	18.00
☐		1st Comic cachet........................20.00				
☐		1st Ham cachet........................450.00				
☐	1716	**13c Lafayette,** 6/13/77, Charleston, SC (514,506)....1.00		1.25	1.50	15.00
☐	1717	**13c Seamstress,** 7/4/77, Cincinnati, OH............1.00				
☐	1718	**13c Blacksmith,** 7/4/77, Cincinnati, OH............1.00				
☐	1719	**13c Wheelwright,** 7/4/77, Cincinnati, OH............1.00				
☐	1720	**13c Leatherworker,** 7/4/77, Cincinnati, OH............1.00				
☐	1720a	**Se-tenant,** Skilled Hands for Independence (1,263,568). "Plate Block" value is for block of 4 with plate numbers............		1.75	2.50	18.00
☐	1721	**13c Peace Bridge,** 8/4/77, Buffalo, NY (512,995)....1.00		1.25	1.50	15.00
☐		**U.S. and Canadian** stamps on one cover, U.S. cancel........................2.00				
☐		Dual U.S. and Canadian cancels 3.00				
☐	1722	**13c Battle of Oriskany,** 8/6/77, Herkimer, NY (605,906). "Plate Block" value is for block of 4 with plate numbers............1.00		1.25	1.50	22.00
☐	1723	**13c Energy Conservation,** 10/20/77, DC 1.00				
☐	1723a	**Se-tenant,** "Plate Block" value is for block of 4 with plate numbers............1.25		1.25	1.50	
☐	1724	**13c Energy Development,** 10/20/77, DC 1.00				
		Total for Scott 1723-1724 is 410,299.				
☐	1725	**13c Alta California,** 9/9/77, San Jose, CA (709,457)........................1.00		1.25	1.50	10.00
☐	1726	**13c Articles of Confederation,** 9/30/77, York, PA (605,455)........................1.00		1.25	1.50	16.00
☐	1727	**13c Talking Pictures,** 10/6/77, Hollywood, CA (570,195)........................2.00		2.25	3.00	25.00

1726

1727

US Bicentennial 13cents

1728

1729

1730

USA 13c

1734

1731

1732

1st Calhoun Collector's Society Gold Foil Cachet

1733

1735

1st Rob Cuscaden cachet

1st Western Silk Cachets

HOW TO USE THIS BOOK
The number in the first column is its Scott number or identifying number. Following that is the denomination of the stamp, description, date of issue, and the value.

SCOTT NUMBER	DESCRIPTION	SINGLE	BLOCK	PLATE BLOCK	CERM PROG
☐ 1728	13c **Surrender at Saratoga,** 10/7/77, Schuylerville, NY (557,529). "Plate Block" value is for block of 4 with plate numbers.................1.00	1.25	1.50	15.00	
☐ 1729	13c **Christmas (Valley Forge),** 10/21/77, Valley Forge, PA (583,139). "Plate Block" value is for block of 4 with plate numbers..........................1.00	1.25	1.50	25.00	
☐	1st HJS cachet.................................15.00				
☐ 1730	13c **Christmas (mailbox),** 10/21/77, Omaha, NE (675,786). "Plate Block" value is for block of 4 with plate numbers.....................................1.00	1.25	1.50	20.00	
☐	Scott 1729-1730 on one cover 3.00				
☐	Scott 1729-1730 on one cover with dual cancels .4.00				

1978

SCOTT NUMBER	DESCRIPTION	SINGLE	BLOCK	PLATE BLOCK	CERM PROG
☐ 1731	13c **Carl Sandburg,** 1/6/78, Galesburg, IL (493,826)...1.00	1.25	1.50	15.00	
☐	1st Calhoun Collector's Society Gold Foil Cachet 20.00				
☐	1st Rob Cuscaden cachet 15.00				
☐	1st Western Silk cachet....................................35.00				
☐	1st Nova cachet..15.00				
☐	1st Susan Richardson cachet 15.00				
☐ 1732	13c **Captain Cook,** 1/20/78, Honolulu, HI, or Anchorage, AK..1.00	1.25	1.50		
☐ 1732a	**Se-tenant,** Captain Cook 1.75	1.85	2.00		
☐ 1733	13c **Resolution & Discovery,** 1/20/78, Honolulu, HI, or Anchorage, AK..................................1.00	1.25	1.50	18.00	
☐	Scott 1732-1733 on one cover with dual cancel .2.00				
☐	1st K.M.C. Venture cachet...............................70.00				
	Total for Scott 1732-33 is 1,496,659.				
☐ 1734	13c **Indian Head Penny,** 1/11/78, Kansas City, MO (512,426) (2 types)*................................1.00	1.25	2.00	15.00*	

1978-80 Regular Issues

SCOTT NUMBER	DESCRIPTION	SINGLE	BLOCK	PLATE BLOCK	CERM PROG
☐ 1735	(15c) **"A" & Eagle,** non-denominated, 5/22/78, Memphis, TN.......................................1.00	1.25	1.50		
☐	1st G. Peltin cachet 30.00				
☐ 1736	(15c) **"A" & Eagle,** non-denominated, booklet single, 5/22/78, Memphis, TN...........1.00	1.25	1.50		
☐ 1736a	**"A" & Eagle,** booklet pane of 8 ....2.50				
☐ 1737	15c **Roses,** booklet single, 7/11/78, Shreveport, LA, (445,003)...1.00				
☐ 1737a	**Roses,** booklet pane of 8 ....2.50			20.00	
☐ 1738	15c **Windmills,** 2/7/80, Lubbock, TX, booklet single...1.00				
☐ 1739	15c **Windmills,** 2/7/80, Lubbock, TX, booklet single...1.00				
☐ 1740	15c **Windmills,** 2/7/80, Lubbock, TX, booklet single...1.00				
☐ 1741	15c **Windmills,** 2/7/80, Lubbock, TX, booklet single...1.00				
☐ 1742	15c **Windmills,** 2/7/80, Lubbock, TX, booklet single...1.00				
☐ 1742a	**Booklet** pane of 10....................................3.50			48.00	
	Total for Scott 1738-1742 is 708,411.				
☐ 1743	(15c) **"A" & Eagle,** coil, 5/22/78, Memphis, TX........1.00 pr l.00 lp l.50				
☐	1st Kribbs Kover cachet...................................40.00				
	Total for Scott 1735, 1736 and 1743 is 689,049.				

☐ 1744	**13c Harriet Tubman**, 2/1/78, DC (493,495) "Plate Block" value is for block of 4 with plate numbers. ...1.00		1.25	2.00	25.00
☐ 1745	**13c Quilt design**, 3/8/78, Charleston, WV.................1.00				
☐ 1746	**13c Quilt design**, 3/8/78, Charleston, WV.................1.00				
☐ 1747	**13c Quilt design**, 3/8/78, Charleston, WV.................1.00				
☐ 1748	**13c Quilt design**, 3/8/78, Charleston, WV.................1.00				
☐ 1748a	**Se-tenant,** American Quilts (1,081,827), "Plate Block" value is for block of 4 with numbers		2.00	3.00	20.00
☐	1st F. Collins cachet..500.00				
☐ 1749	**13c Ballet**, 4/26/78, New York, NY 1.00				
☐ 1750	**13c Theatre Dance**, 4/26/78, New York, NY.............1.00				
☐ 1751	**13c Folk Dance**, 4/26/78, New York, NY...................1.00				
☐ 1752	**13c Modern Dance**, 4/26/78, New York, NY...............1.00				
☐ 1752a	**Se-tenant,** American Dance (1,626,493) "Plate Block" value is for block of 4 with plate numbers		1.75	2.50	10.00
☐	Ist Andrews cachet...30.00				
☐	1st Annable cachet...15.00				
☐	1st Great Picture Covers cachet....................20.00				
☐ 1753	**13c French Alliance**, 5/4/78, York, PA (705,240) 1.00		1.25	1.50	12.00
☐ 1754	**13c Early Cancer Detection (Papanicolaou)**, 5/18/78, DC (535,584) 1.00		1.25	1.50	25.00
☐ 1755	**13c Jimmie Rodgers**, 5/24/78, Meridian, MS (599,287). "Plate Block" value is for block of 4 with plate numbers...1.50		1.75	2.00	22.00
☐ 1756	**15c George M. Cohan**, 7/3/78, Providence, RI (740,750). "Plate Block" value is for block of 4 with plate numbers...1.50		1.75	2.00	18.00
☐	1st Richard S. Byron cachet............................15.00				
☐ 1757	**13c CAPEX Souvenir Sheet**, 6/10/78, Toronto, Ontario (1,994,067)..3.50				
☐ 1757a	**13c Cardinal** 1.00				
☐ 1757b	**13c Mallard**...1.00				
☐ 1757c	**13c Canada Goose** 1.00				
☐ 1757d	**13c Blue Jay**..1.00				
☐ 1757e	**13c Moose** 1.00				
☐ 1757f	**13c Chipmunk**...1.00				
☐ 1757g	**13c Red Fox** 1.00				
☐ 1757h	**13c Raccoon**...1.00				
☐ 1758	**15c Photography**, 6/26/78, Las Vegas, NV (684,987). "Plate Block" value is for block of 4 with plate numbers...1.50		1.75	2.00	15.00
☐ 1759	**15c Viking Missions to Mars**, 7/20/78, Hampton, VA (805,051)..2.00		2.50	3.00	25.00
☐	1st Softones cachet 20.00				
☐ 1760	**15c Great gray Owl**, 8/26/78, Fairbanks, AK 1.00				
☐ 1761	**15c Saw-whet Owl**, 8/26/78, Fairbanks, AK.............1.00				
☐ 1762	**15c Barred Owl**, 8/26/78, Fairbanks, AK 1.00				
☐ 1763	**15c Great Horned Owl**, 8/26/78, Fairbanks, AK 1.00				
☐ 1763a	**Se-tenant,** American Owls, (1,690,474)...........................		2.00	2.50	18.00
☐ 1764	**15c Giant Sequoia**, 10/9/78, Hot Springs National Park, AR..1.00				
☐ 1765	**15c White Pine**, 10/9/78, Hot Springs National Park, AR..1.00				

1st F. Collins Cachet

1744

1749-52

1st Andrews Cachet cachet

US Bicentennial 13c
1753

1754

1755

1756

Photography USA 15c
1758

Viking missions to Mars
1759

1st Softones cachet

1764-67

1760-63

**Values for various cachet makers can be determined
by using the Cachet Calculator which begins on page 52A.**

SCOTT NUMBER	DESCRIPTION	SINGLE	BLOCK	PLATE BLOCK	CERM PROG
☐ 1766	15c White Oak, 10/9/78, Hot Springs National Park, AR 1.00				
☐ 1767	15c Gray Birch, 10/9/78, Hot Springs National Park, AR 1.00				
☐ 1767a	Se-tenant, American Trees (1,139,100)		2.00	2.50	18.00
☐ 1768	15c Christmas (Madonna), 10/18/78, DC (553,064) 1.00		1.25	1.50	32.00
☐ 1769	15c Christmas (Hobby Horse), 10/18/78, Holly, MI (603,008). "Plate Block" value is for block of 4 with plate numbers (2 types)*........1.00		1.25	1.50	22.00*
☐	Scott 1768-1769 on one cover 3.00				
☐	Scott 1768-1769 dual cancels.................4.00				

1979

SCOTT NUMBER	DESCRIPTION	SINGLE	BLOCK	PLATE BLOCK	CERM PROG
☐ 1770	15c Robert F. Kennedy, 1/12/79, DC (624,582) 2.00		2.50	3.50	30.00
☐	1st Bittings cachet................20.00				
☐	1st DRC cachet 50.00				
☐ 1771	15c Martin Luther King, Jr. 1/13/79, Atlanta, GA (726, 149). "Plate Block" value is for block of 4 with plate numbers 1.00		1.25	1.50	30.00
☐ 1772	15c International Year of the Child, 2/15/79, Philadelphia, PA (716,782)....................1.00		1.25	1.50	10.00
☐ 1773	15c John Steinbeck, 2/27/79, Salinas, CA (709,073) 1.25		1.50	1.75	15.00
☐ 1774	15c Albert Einstein, 3/4/79, Princeton, NJ (641,423) 1.50		2.00	3.00	18.00
☐ 1775	15c Coffeepot, 4/19/79, Lancaster, PA 1.00				
☐ 1776	15c Tea Caddy, 4/19/79, Lancaster, PA....1.00				
☐ 1777	15c Sugar Bowl, 4/19/79, Lancaster, PA....1.00				
☐ 1778	15c Coffeepot, 4/19/79, Lancaster, PA 1.00				
☐ 1778a	Se-tenant, Pennsylvania Toleware(1,581,963). "Plate Block" value is for block of 4 with plate numbers...		2.00	2.50	12.00
☐ 1779	15c Virginia Rotunda, 6/4/79, Kansas City, MO 1.00				
☐ 1780	15c Baltimore Cathedral, 6/4/79, Kansas City,MO ...1.00				
☐ 1781	15c Boston State House, 6/4/79, Kansas City, MO. ..1.00				
☐ 1782	15c Philadelphia Exchange, 6/4/79, Kansas City,MO....................1.00				
☐ 1782a	Se-tenant, American Architecture, (1,219,258)		2.00	2.50	20.00
☐ 1783	15c Persistent Trillium, 6/7/79, Milwaukee, WI 1.00				
☐ 1784	15c Hawaiian Wild Broadbean, 6/7/79, Milwaukee, WI 1.00				
☐ 1785	15c Contra Costa Wallflower, 6/7/79, Milwaukee, WI 1.00				
☐ 1786	15c Antioch Dunes Evening Primrose, 6/7/79, Milwaukee, WI 1.00				
☐ 1786a	Se-tenant, Endangered Flora(1,436,268). "Plate Block" value is for block of 4 with plate numbers		2.00	2.50	15.00
☐ 1787	15c Seeing Eye Dogs, 6/15/79, Morristown, NJ (588,826). "Plate Block" value is for block of 4 with plate numbers 1.00		1.25	1.50	28.00
☐ 1788	15c Special Olympics, 8/9/79, Brockport, NY (651,344). "Plate Block" value is for block of 4 with plate numbers 1.00		1.25	1.50	18.00
☐ 1789	15c John Paul Jones, 9/23/79, Annapolis, MD, perf. 11x12. "Plate Block" value is for block of 4 with plate numbers 1.00		1.25	1.50	15.00

1770

1768

1769

1772

1771

1773

1st Bittings cachet

Einstein
USA 15c
1774

1775-8

1st DRC cachet

Architecture USA 15c
1779-82

1783-6

Seeing For Me
1787

Special Olympics
Skill-Sharing-Joy
USA 15c
1788

I have not yet begun to fight
John Paul Jones
US Bicentennial 15c
1789

1790

1795-8

Christmas USA 15c
1799

Christmas
1800

HONORING VIETNAM VETERANS
NOV 11 1979
1802

**Values for various cachet makers can be determined
by using the Cachet Calculator which begins on page 52A.**

☐ 1789A **John Paul Jones,** perf. 11. "Plate Block" value is
for block of 4 with plate numbers....................1.00   1.25   1.50

☐   1st D. Cunningham cachet 8.00
Total for Scott 1789 and 1789A is 587,018.

☐ 1790 **10c Olympic Games,** 9/5/79, Olympia, WA
(305, 122). "Plate Block" value is for block of 4
with plate numbers 1.00   1.50   2.00   15.00

☐ 1791 **15c Running,** 9/28/79, Los Angeles, CA....................1.00
☐ 1792 **15c Swimming,** 9/28/79, Los Angeles, CA 1.00
☐ 1793 **15c Rowing,** 9/28/79, Los Angeles, CA.....................1.00
☐ 1794 **15c Equestrian,** 9/28/79, Los Angeles, CA................1.00
☐ 1794a **Se-tenant,** Olympic Games(1,561,366). "Plate Block"
value is for block of 4 with plate numbers 2.00   2.50   15.00

☐ 1795 **15c Speed Skating,** 2/1/80, Lake Placid, NY...........1.00
☐ 1796 **15c Downhill Skiing,** 2/1/80, Lake Placid, NY..........1.00
☐ 1797 **15c Ski Jump,** 2/1/80, Lake Placid, NY....................1.00
☐ 1798 **15c Hockey,** 2/1/80, Lake Placid, NY 1.00
☐ 1798b **Se-tenant,** Winter Olympic Games (1,166,302). "Plate
Block" value is for block of 4 with plate numbers...   2.00   2.50

☐ 1795-1798 15¢ Winter Olympic Games 15.00

☐ 1799 **15c Christmas (Madonna & Child),** 10/18/79, DC
(686,990). "Plate Block" value is for block of 4
with plate numbers 1.00   1.25   1.50   12.00

☐ 1800 **15c Christmas (Santa Claus),** 10/18/79, North
Pole, AK (511,829). "Plate Block" value is for
block of 4 with plate numbers 1.00   1.25   2.00   15.00

☐   Scott 1799-1800 on one cover 2.00
☐   Scott 1799-1800 on one cover, dual cancels.....3.00

☐ 1801 **15c Will Rogers,** 11/4/79, Claremore, OK
(1,643,151). "Plate Block" value is for block of 4
with plate numbers (2 types)*.........................1.00   1.25   1.50   23.00*

☐   1st Jemm Covers cachet................................25.00

☐ 1802 **15c Vietnam Veterans,** 11/11/79, Arlington, VA,
(445,934). "Plate Block" value is for block of 4
with plate numbers 2.50   3.00   4.00   25.00

☐   1st Brennan cachet 15.00

☐ 1803 **15c W.C. Fields,** 1/29/80, Beverly Hills, CA
(633,303). "Plate Block" value is for block of 4
with plate numbers 1.75   2.00   3.00   25.00

☐   1st Gill Craft cachet......................................30.00
☐   1st Kover Kids cachet 20.00

☐ 1804 **15c Benjamin Banneker,** 2/15/80, Annapolis, MD
(647,126). "Plate Block" value is for block of 4
with plate numbers 1.00   1.25   1.50   25.00

☐   1st Queensbury cachet..................................20.00

☐ 1805 **15c "Letters Preserve Memories,"** 2/25/80, DC.......1.00
☐ 1806 **15c "P.S. Write Soon,"** 2/25/80, DC 1.00
☐ 1807 **15c "Letters Lift Spirits,"** 2/25/80, DC 1.00
☐ 1808 **15c "P.S. Write Soon,"** 2/25/80, DC 1.00
☐ 1809 **15c "Letters Shape Opinions,"** 2/25/80, DC.............1.00
☐ 1810 **15c "P.S. Write Soon,"** 2/25/80, DC 1.00
☐ 1810a **Se-tenant,** National Letter Writing Week, (1,083,360)
on one 2.50   12.00

Note: Marginal markings require 12 stamps, plate blocks 36.

1801

1803

1804

1805-10

1811

1st Brennan cachet

1st Gill Craft cachet

1818-20

1821

1823

1824

1825

1822

1st American Postal Arts Society Cachet (Post/Art)

1st D.J. Graf Cachet

HOW TO USE THIS BOOK

The number in the first column is its Scott number or identifying number. Following that is the denomination of the stamp, description, date of issue, and the value.

1980-81 Americana Coils

	SCOTT NUMBER	DESCRIPTION	PAIR	LINE PAIR	CERM PROG
☐	1811	1c Inkwell & Quill, 3/6/80, New York, NY (262,921).......	1.00	1.25	
☐	1813	3.5c Weaver Violins, 6/23/80, Williamsburg, PA	1.00	1.25	
		Total for Scott 1813 and U590 is 716,988.			
☐	1816	12c Torch, 4/8/81, Dallas, TX	1.00	1.25	
		Total for Scott 1594 and 1816 is 280,930.			

	SCOTT NUMBER	DESCRIPTION	SINGLE	BLOCK	PLATE BLOCK	CERM PROG
☐	1818	(18c) "B" & Eagle, 3/15/81, San Francisco, CA........1.00		1.25	1.65	
☐	1819	(18c) "B" & Eagle, booklet single, 3/15/81, San Francisco, CA 1.00				
☐	1819a	"B" & Eagle, booklet pane of 8 ....3.00				
☐	1820	(18c) "B" & Eagle coil, 3/15/81, San Francisco, CA 1.00		1.25	1.65	
		Total for Scott 1818-1820, U592 and UX88 is 511,688.				

1980

☐	1821	15c Frances Perkins, 4/10/80, DC (678,966)............1.00		1.25	1.50	10.00
		1st Samuel Gompers Stamp Club cachet 12.00				
☐	1822	15c Dolley Madison, 5/20/80, DC (331,048) 1.00		1.25	1.50	10.00
		1st American Postal Arts Society cachet (Post/Art) 30.00				
☐		1st D.J. Graf cachet..25.00				
☐	1823	15c Emily Bissell, 5/31/80, Wilmington, DE (649,509) 1.00		1.25	2.00	8.00
☐	1824	15c Helen Keller, 6/27/80, Tuscumbia, AL (713,061) 1.00		1.25	1.65	18.00
☐	1825	15c Veterans Administration, 7/21/80, DC (634,101) 1.00		1.25	1.50	10.00
☐	1826	15c Bernardo de Galvez, 7/23/80, New Orleans, LA (658,061) 1.00		1.25	1.50	10.00
☐	1827	15c Brain Coral, Beaugregory Fish, 8/26/80, Charlotte Amalie, VI..1.00				
☐	1828	15c Elkhorn Coral, Porkfish, 8/26/80, Charlotte Amalie, VI 1.00				
☐	1829	15c Chalice Coral, Moorish Idol 8/26/80, Charlotte Amalie, VI..1.00				
☐	1830	15c Finger Coral, Sabertooth Blenny, 8/26/80, Charlotte Amalie, VI..1.00				
☐	1830a	Se-tenant, Coral Reefs (1,195,126) "Plate Block" value is for block of 4 with plate numbers		2.00	2.50	28.00
☐	1831	15c Organized Labor, 9/1/80, DC (759,973). "Plate Block" value is for block of 4 with plate numbers. 1.00		1.25	1.50	

Coral Reefs USA 15c

Organized Labor Proud and Free USA 15c

Edith Wharton

Learning never ends

| 1826 | 1827-30 | 1831 | 1832 | 1833 |

Indian Art USA 15c

Architecture USA 15c

Christmas USA 15c

Season's Greetings USA 15c

| 1834-7 | 1838-41 | 1842 | 1843 |

Igor Stravinsky

Ralph Bunche

Robert Millikan

USA 15c Everett Dirksen

Whitney Moore Young
Black Heritage USA 15c

| 1845 | 1860 | 1866 | 1874 | 1875 |

**Values for various cachet makers can be determined
by using the Cachet Calculator which begins on page 52A.**

SCOTT NUMBER	DESCRIPTION	SINGLE	PLATE BLOCK	PLATE BLOCK	CERM PROG
☐ 1832	15c Edith Wharton, 9/5/80, New Haven, CT (633,917) 1.00		1.25	1.50	12.00
☐ 1833	15c American Education, 9/12/80, DC (672,592). "Plate Block" value is for block of 4 with plate numbers 1.00		1.25	1.50	10.00
☐ 1834	15c Bella Bella Tribe, 9/25/80, Spokane, WA 1.00				
☐ 1835	15c Chilkat Tlingit Tribe, 9/25/80, Spokane, WA 1.00				
☐ 1836	15c Tlingit Tribe, 9/25/80, Spokane, WA 1.00				
☐ 1837	15c Bella Coola Tribe, 9/25/80, Spokane, WA..........1.00				
☐ 1837a	Se-tenant, Pacific Northwest Indian Masks, (2,195,136) "Plate Block" value is for block of 4 with plate numbers		2.00	2.50	20.00
☐ 1838	15c Smithsonian, 10/9/80, New York, NY 1.00				
☐ 1839	15c Trinity Church, 10/9/80, New York, NY............1.00				
☐ 1840	15c Penn Academy, 10/9/80, New York, NY............1.00				
☐ 1841	15c Lyndhurst, 10/9/80, New York, NY 1.00				
☐ 1841a	Se-tenant American Architecture, (2,164,721)		2.00	2.50	10.00
☐ 1842	15c Christmas (Madonna & Child), 10/31/80, DC (718,614). "Plate Block" value is for block of 4 with plate numbers 1.00		1.25	1.50	14.00
☐ 1843	15c Christmas (Wreath & Toys), 10/31/80, Christmas, MI (755,108). "Plate Block" value is for block of 4 with plate numbers 1.00		1.25	1.50	20.00
☐	Scott 1842-1843 on one cover 3.00				
☐	Scott 1842-1843 on one cover, dual cancels.....4.00				

1980-85 Great Americans

☐ 1844	1c Dorothea Dix, 9/23/83, Hampden, ME (164,140)		1.00	1.00	8.00
☐ 1845	2c Igor Stravinsky, 11/18/82, New York, NY (501,719).................................		1.00	1.00	6.00
☐	1st Phil-Mart cachet....................................15.00				
☐ 1846	3c Henry Clay, 7/13/83, DC (204,320)		1.00	1.00	8.00
☐ 1847	4c Carl Schurz, 6/3/83, Watertown, WI (165,010)		1.00	1.00	8.00
☐ 1848	5c Pearl Buck, 6/25/83, Hillsboro, WV (231,852)...........		1.00	1.00	15.00
☐ 1849	6c Walter Lippmann, 9/19/85, Minneapolis, MN (371,990)..1.00		1.00	1.50	8.00
☐ 1850	7c Abraham Baldwin, 1/25/85, Athens, GA (402,285)..1.00		1.25	1.50	8.00
☐	1st RTI cachet................................20.00				
☐ 1851	8c Henry Knox, 7/25/85, Thomaston, ME (315,937)..1.00		1.25	1.50	8.00
☐ 1852	9c Sylvanus Thayer, 6/7/85, Braintree, MA (345,649)..1.00		1.25	1.50	8.00
☐ 1853	10c Richard Russell, 5/31/84, Winder, GA (183,581)..1.00		1.25	1.65	8.00
☐ 1854	11c Alden Partridge, 2/12/85, Northfield, VT (442,311)..1.00		1.25	1.65	8.00
☐ 1855	13c Crazy Horse, 1/15/82, Crazy Horse, SD 1.50		1.75	2.25	28.00
☐ 1856	14c Sinclair Lewis, 3/21/85, Sauk Centre, MN (308,612)..1.00		1.25	1.65	8.00
☐ 1857	17c Rachel Carson, 5/28/81, Springdale, PA (273,686)..1.00		1.25	1.75	16.00
☐ 1858	18c George Mason, 5/7/81, Gunston Hall, VA (461,937)..1.00		1.25	1.75	8.00
☐ 1859	19c Sequoyah, 12/27/80, Tahlequah, OK (241,325) .1.50		1.75	2.25	14.00

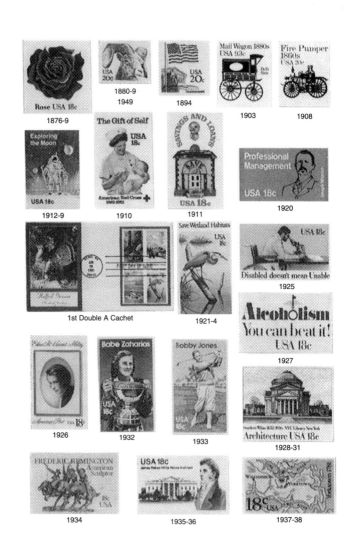

Rose USA 18c

1876-9

1880-9
1949

1894

Mail Wagon 1880s USA 9.3c

1903

Fire Pumper 1860s USA 20c

1908

Exploring the Moon
USA 18c

1912-9

The Gift of Self
USA 18c
American Red Cross

1910

SAVINGS AND LOANS
USA 18c

1911

Professional Management
USA 18c

1920

1st Double A Cachet

Save Wetland Habitats
USA 18c

1921-4

USA 18c

Disabled doesn't mean Unable

1925

Alcoholism
You can beat it!
USA 18c

1927

1926

Babe Zaharias
USA 18c

1932

Bobby Jones
USA 18c

1933

Architecture USA 18c

1928-31

FREDERIC REMINGTON
American Sculptor
18c USA

1934

USA 18c

1935-36

18c USA

1937-38

**Values for various cachet makers can be determined
by using the Cachet Calculator which begins on page 52A.**

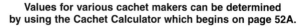

SCOTT NUMBER	DESCRIPTION	SINGLE	PLATE BLOCK	BLOCK	CERM PROG
☐ 1860	20c Ralph Bunche, 1/12/82, New York, NY	1.00	1.25	1.75	12.00
☐ 1861	20c Thomas Gallaudet, 6/10/83, West Hartford, CT (261,336)	1.00	1.25	1.75	12.00
☐ 1862	20c Harry S Truman, 1/26/84, DC (267,631)	1.25	1.50	2.50	8.00
☐	1st Caricature cachet	25.00			
☐ 1863	22c John J. Audubon, 4/23/85, New York, NY (516,249)	1.00	1.35	2.00	6.00
☐ 1864	30c Frank Laubach, 9/2/84, Benton, PA (118,974) (2 types)*	1.25	1.35	2.00	8.00*
☐ 1865	35c Charles Drew, 6/3/81, DC (383,882)	1.25	2.00	3.00	16.00
☐ 1866	37c Robert Millikan, 1/26/82, Pasadena, CA	1.25	2.00	3.00	10.00
☐ 1867	39c Grenville Clark, 3/20/85, Hanover, NH (297,797)	1.25	2.00	3.00	10.00
☐ 1868	40c Lillian Gilbreth, 2/24/84, Montclair, NJ (110,588)	1.25	2.00	3.00	10.00
☐ 1869	50c Chester W. Nimitz, 2/22/85, Fredericksburg, TX (376,166)	2.00	3.00	3.50	15.00
☐	1st Gulf Coast FDC Group cachet	15.00			

1981

SCOTT NUMBER	DESCRIPTION	SINGLE	PLATE BLOCK	BLOCK	CERM PROG
☐ 1874	15c Everett Dirksen, 1/4/81, Pekin, IL (665,755)	1.00	1.25	1.50	18.00
☐ 1875	15c Whitney Moore Young, Jr., 1/30/81, New York, NY (963,870)	1.00	1.25	1.50	12.00
☐ 1876	18c Rose, 4/23/81, Ft. Valley, GA	1.00			
☐ 1877	18c Camellia, 4/23/81, Ft. Valley, GA	1.00			
☐ 1878	18c Dahlia, 4/23/81, Ft. Valley, GA	1.00			
☐ 1879	18c Lily, 4/23/81, Ft. Valley, GA	1.00			
☐ 1879a	Se-tenant Flowers, (1,966,599)		2.50	3.00	18.00
☐ 1880	18c Bighorn, 5/14/81, Boise, ID	1.00			
☐ 1881	18c Puma, 5/14/81, Boise, ID	1.00			
☐ 1882	18c Harbor seal, 5/14/81, Boise, ID	1.00			
☐ 1883	18c Bison, 5/14/81, Boise, ID	1.00			
☐ 1884	18c Brown bear, 5/14/81, Boise, ID	1.00			
☐ 1885	18c Polar bear, 5/14/81, Boise, ID	1.00			
☐ 1886	18c Elk, 5/14/81, Boise, ID	1.00			
☐ 1887	18c Moose, 5/14/81, Boise, ID	1.00			
☐ 1888	18c White-tailed deer, 5/14/81, Boise, ID	1.00			
☐ 1889	18c Pronghorn, 5/14/81, Boise, ID	1.00			
☐ 1889a	Booket pane of 10 (1,641,749)	5.00			18.00
☐ 1890	18c Flag and Anthem, 4/24/81, Portland,ME. "Plate Block" value is for block of 4 with plate numbers	1.00	1.25	1.50	
☐ 1891	18c Flag and Anthem, coil, 4/24/81, Portland, ME	1.00	pr1.25		
☐ 1892	6c Field of Stars, booklet single, 4/24/81, Portland, ME	1.00			
☐ 1893	18c Flag and Anthem, booklet single, 4/24/81, Portland, ME	1.00			
☐	Scott 1890, 1891 and 1893 on one cover	4.00			
☐ 1893a	Flag and Anthem, booklet pane of 8 (6 Scott 1893 + 2 Scott 1892)	2.50			20.00
	Total for all versions Scott 1890-1893 is 691,526.				
☐ 1894	20c Flag over Supreme Court, 12/17/81, DC. "Plate Block" value is for block of 4 with plate numbers	1.00	1.25	1.50	

SCOTT NUMBER	DESCRIPTION	SINGLE	BLOCK	PLATE BLOCK	CERM PROG
☐ 1895	20c **Flag over Supreme Court**, coil, 12/17/81, DC	...1.00	pr1.25		
☐ 1896	20c **Flag over Supreme Court**, booklet single, 12/17/81, DC	...1.00	1.25	1.50	
☐ 1896a	**Flag over Surpeme Court**, booklet pane of 6	...6.00			
☐	Scott 1894, 1895, 1896a on one cover	...7.00			
☐ 1896b	**Flag over Supreme Court**, booklet pane of 10, 6/1/82	...10.00			10.00

SCOTT NUMBER	DESCRIPTION	SINGLE	PAIR	LINE PAIR	CERM PROG

1981-84 Transportation Coils

SCOTT NUMBER	DESCRIPTION	SINGLE	PAIR	LINE PAIR	CERM PROG
☐ 1897	1c **Omnibus**, 8/19/83, Arlington, VA (109,436)		1.00	12.50	12.00
☐ 1897A	2c **Locomotive**, 5/20/82, Chicago, IL (290,020)		1.00	12.50	15.00
☐ 1898	3c **Handcar**, 3/25/83, Rochester, NY (77,900)		1.00	12.50	15.00
☐ 1898A	4c **Stagecoach**, 8/19/82, Milwaukee, WI (152,940)		1.00	10.00	15.00
☐ 1899	5c **Motorcycle**, 10/10/83, San Francisco, CA (188,240)		1.00	12.50	22.00
☐ 1900	5.2c **Sleigh**, 3/21/83, Memphis, TN (141,979)		1.00	25.00	
☐	Combination with Scott U604		1.00	25.00	
☐ 1900a	**Sleigh**, untagged (Bureau precanceled), 3/21/83		200.00	800.00	
☐ 1901	5.9c **Bicycle**, 2/17/82, Wheeling, WV (814,419)		1.00	20.00	
☐ 1901a	**Bicycle**, untagged (Bureau precanceled), 2/17/82		300.00	*2,000*	
☐ 1902	7.4c **Baby Buggy**, 4/7/84, San Diego, CA (187,797)		1.00		
☐ 1902a	**Baby Buggy**, untagged (Bureau precanceled), 4/7/84		500.00		
☐ 1903	9.3c **Mail Wagon**, 12/15/81, Shreveport, LA (199,645)		1.00	20.00	
☐ 1903a	**Mail Wagon**, untagged (Bureau precanceled), 12/15/81		500.00	*2,000*	
☐ 1904	10.9c **Hansom Cab**, 3/26/82, Chattanooga, TN		1.00	25.00	20.00
☐ 1904a	**Hansom Cab**, untagged (Bureau precanceled), 3/26/82		500.00	*2,000*	
☐ 1905	11c **Railroad Caboose**, 2/3/84, Chicago, IL (172,753)	...1.00	1.00		
☐ 1906	17c **Electric Auto**, 6/25/81, Greenfield Village, MI (239,458)	...1.00	1.25	17.50	
☐	1st Four Flags Cover Group cachet	...12.00			
☐ 1907	18c **Surrey**, 5/18/81, Notch, MO (207,801)	...1.00	1.25	30.00	18.00
☐ 1908	20c **Fire Pumper**, 12/10/81, Alexandria, VA (304,668)	...1.00	1.25	30.00	

SCOTT NUMBER	DESCRIPTION	SINGLE	BLOCK	PLATE BLOCK	CERM PROG

1983

SCOTT NUMBER	DESCRIPTION	SINGLE	BLOCK	PLATE BLOCK	CERM PROG
☐ 1909	$9.35 **Eagle and Moon**, 8/12/83, booklet single, Kennedy Space Center, FL (77,858)	...70.00			
☐	Flown on Space Shuttle, (not FDC)	...30.00			
☐ 1909a	**Eagle and Moon**, booklet pane of 3	...175.00			

1981

SCOTT NUMBER	DESCRIPTION	SINGLE	BLOCK	PLATE BLOCK	CERM PROG
☐ 1910	18c **American Red Cross**, 5/1/81, DC (874,972)	...1.00	1.25	1.50	10.00
☐ 1911	18c **Savings Loans Sesquicentennial**, 5/8/81, Chicago, IL. (740,910)	...1.00	1.25	1.50	10.00

		SINGLE	BLOCK	PLATE BLOCK	CERM PROG
☐ 1912	18c **Moon Walk**, 5/21/81, Kennedy Space Center,FL	1.00			
☐ 1913	18c **Columbia Launch**, 5/21/81, Kennedy Space Center, FL	1.00			
☐ 1914	18c **Columbia Releasing Satellite**, 5/21/81, Kennedy Space Center, FL	1.00			
☐ 1915	18c **Skylab**, 5/21/81, Kennedy Space Center, FL	1.00			
☐ 1916	18c **Pioneer II**, 5/21/81, Kennedy Space Center, FL.	1.00			
☐ 1917	18c **Columbia & Booster**, 5/21/81, Kennedy Space Center, FL	1.00			
☐ 1918	18c **Columbia in Orbit**, 5/21/81, Kennedy Space Center, FL	1.00			
☐ 1919	18c **Space Telescope**, 5/21/81, Kennedy Space Center, FL	1.00			
☐ 1919a	**Se-tenant**, Space Achievement, (7,027,549)		1.25	4.00	22.00
☐ 1920	18c **Professional Management**, 6/18/81, Philadelphia, PA (713,096)	1.00	1.00	1.50	8.00
☐	1st Garik Covers cachet	30.00			
☐ 1921	18c **Great Blue Heron**, 6/26/81, Reno, NV	1.00			
☐ 1922	18c **Badger**, 6/26/81, Reno, NV	1.00			
☐ 1923	18c **Grizzly Bear**, 6/26/81, Reno, NV	1.00			
☐ 1924	18c **Ruffed Grouse**, 6/26/81, Reno, NV	1.00			
☐ 1924a	**Se-tenant**, Preservation of Wildlife Habitats (2,327,609)		2.50	3.00	10.00
☐	1st Double A cachet	20.00			
☐ 1925	18c **International Year of the Disabled**, 6/29/81, Milford, MI (714,244)	1.00	1.25	1.50	8.00
☐ 1926	18c **Edna St. Vincent Millay**, 7/10/81, Austerlitz, NY (725,978)	1.00	1.25	1.50	10.00
☐ 1927	18c **Alcoholism**, 8/19/81, DC. "Plate Block" value is for block of 4 with plate numbers	1.00	1.25	1.50	8.00
☐	1st Uncovers cachet	25.00			
☐ 1928	18c **New York University Library**, 8/28/81, New York, NY	1.00			
☐ 1929	18c **Biltmore House**, 8/28/81, New York, NY	1.00			
☐ 1930	18c **Palace of the Arts**, 8/28/81, New York, NY	1.00			
☐ 1931	18c **National Farmer's Bank**, 8/28/81, New York, NY.	1.00			
☐ 1931a	**Se-tenant**, American Architecture, (1,998,208)		2.50	3.00	8.00
☐ 1932	18c **Mildred Didrikson Zaharias**, 9/22/81, Pinehurst, NC	5.00	5.50	6.00	
☐ 1933	18c **Robert Tyre Jones**, 9/22/81, Pinehurst, NC	8.00	8.50	9.00	
☐	Scott 1932-1933 on one cover	9.00			30.00
	Total for Scott 1932-1933 is 1,231,543.				
☐ 1934	18c **Frederic Remington**, 10/9/81, Oklahoma City, OK (1,367,009)	1.00	1.25	1.50	12.00
☐ 1935	18c **James Hoban**, 10/13/81, DC	1.00	1.25	1.50	
☐ 1936	20c **James Hoban**, 10/13/81, DC	1.00	1.25	1.50	
☐	Scott 1935-1936 on one cover	3.00			30.00
☐	Scott 1935-1936 on one cover with Irish Hoban stamp	9.00			
	Total for Scott 1935-1936 is 635,012.				
☐ 1937	18c **Battle of Yorktown**, 10/16/81, Yorktown, VA	1.00			
☐ 1938	18c **Battle of Virginia Capes**, 10/16/81, Yorktown,VA.	1.00			
☐ 1938a	**Se-tenant**, Battles of Yorktown & Virginia Capes		1.50	2.00	12.00
	Total for Scott 1937-1938 is 1,098,278.				

1st Court of Honor cachet

John Hanson
President Continental Congress
USA 20c

1941

1939

1st Pugh Cachet

1950

Domestic Mail

US Postage

1946-48

1st M.J. Phiilatelics cachet

1952

South Carolina
USA 20c

1953-2002

1940

1951

2003

**Values for various cachet makers can be determined
by using the Cachet Calculator which begins on page 52A.**

☐ 1939 **(20c) Christmas (Botticelli)**, 10/28/81, Chicago, IL
(481,395)..1.00   1.25   1.50   12.00
☐   1st Court of Honor cachet..............................15.00
☐ 1940 **(20c) Christmas (Bear & Sleigh)**, 10/28/81,
Christmas Valley, OR (517,989)......................1.00   1.25   1.50   18.00
☐   Scott 1939-1940 on one cover, one cancel 2.00   3.00   4.00
☐   Scott 1939-1940 on one cover, dual cancels.....3.00   4.00
☐ 1941 **20c John Hanson**, 11/5/81, Frederick, MD
(605,616)..1.00   1.25   1.50   10.00
☐ 1942 **20c Barrel Cactus**, 12/11/81, Tucson, AZ.................1.00
☐ 1943 **20c Agave**, 12/11/81, Tucson, AZ 1.00
☐ 1944 **20c Beavertail Cactas**, 12/11/81, Tucson, AZ 1.00
☐ 1945 **20c Saguaro**, 12/11/81, Tucson, AZ...........................1.00
☐ 1945a **Se-tenant**, Desert Plants, (1,770,187) (2 types)* 2.50   3.00 18.00*
☐   1st Pugh cachet..75.00
☐ 1946 **(20c) "C" and Eagle**, 10/11/81, Memphis, TN..........1.00   1.25   1.50
☐ 1947 **(20c) "C" and Eagle**, coil, 10/11/81, Memphis, TN ..1.00 pr1.25   lp1.50
☐ 1948 **(20c) "C" and Eagle**, booklet single, 10/11/81,
Memphis, TN..1.00
☐ 1948a **"C" and Eagle**, booklet pane of 10...........................3.50
       Total for Scott 1946-1948, U594 and UX92 is 304,404.

1982

☐ 1949 **20c Bighorn Sheep**, booklet single, 1/8/82,
Bighorn, MT..1.00
☐   1st New Direxions cachet 15.00
☐ 1949a **Bighorn Sheep**, booklet pane of 10...........................6.00   18.00
☐ 1950 **20c Franklin D. Roosevelt**, 1/30/82, Hyde Park, NY 1.00   1.25   1.50   12.00
☐   1st Aurora Covers cachet................................15.00
☐ 1951 **20c Love**, 2/1/82, Boston, MA (325,727)....................1.00   1.25   1.50   10.00
☐   1st Chaczyk Cachets & Covers cachet.............30.00
☐ 1952 **20c George Washington**, 2/22/82, Mount Vernon,
VA..1.00   1.25   1.50   10.00
☐   1st M.J. Philatelic cachet 15.00
☐   1st Ricale cachet..15.00
☐ 1953 **20c Alabama**, 4/14/82, DC..1.25
☐ 1954 **20c Alaska**, 4/14/82, DC..1.25
☐ 1955 **20c Arizona**, 4/14/82, DC..1.25
☐ 1956 **20c Arkansas**, 4/14/82, DC 1.25
☐ 1957 **20c California**, 4/14/82, DC 1.25
☐ 1958 **20c Colorado**, 4/14/82, DC..1.25
☐ 1959 **20c Connecticut**, 4/14/82, DC.....................................1.25
☐ 1960 **20c Delaware**, 4/14/82, DC..1.25
☐ 1961 **20c Florida**, 4/14/82, DC...1.25
☐ 1962 **20c Georgia**, 4/14/82, DC..1.25
☐ 1963 **20c Hawaii**, 4/14/82, DC 1.25
☐ 1964 **20c Idaho**, 4/14/82, DC 1.25
☐ 1965 **20c Illinois**, 4/14/82, DC 1.25
☐ 1966 **20c Indiana**, 4/14/82, DC..1.25
☐ 1967 **20c Iowa**, 4/14/82, DC..1.25
☐ 1968 **20c Kansas**, 4/14/82, DC...1.25
☐ 1969 **20c Kentucky**, 4/14/82, DC 1.25
☐ 1970 **20c Louisiana**, 4/14/82, DC...1.25
☐ 1971 **20c Maine**, 4/14/82, DC...1.25
☐ 1972 **20c Maryland**, 4/14/82, DC..1.25

	Scott Number	Description	Single	Plate Block	Cerm Block	Prog
☐	1973	20c Massachusetts, 4/14/82, DC................................1.25				
☐	1974	20c Michigan, 4/14/82, DC 1.25				
☐	1975	20c Minnesota, 4/14/82, DC.....................................1.25				
☐	1976	20c Mississippi, 4/14/82, DC....................................1.25				
☐	1977	20c Missouri, 4/14/82, DC..1.25				
☐	1978	20c Montana, 4/14/82, DC..1.25				
☐	1979	20c Nebraska, 4/14/82, DC.......................................1.25				
☐	1980	20c Nevada, 4/14/82, DC 1.25				
☐	1981	20c New Hampshire, 4/14/82, DC 1.25				
☐	1982	20c New Jersey, 4/14/82, DC....................................1.25				
☐	1983	20c New Mexico, 4/14/82, DC...................................1.25				
☐	1984	20c New York, 4/14/82, DC.......................................1.25				
☐	1985	20c North Carolina, 4/14/82, DC 1.25				
☐	1986	20c North Dakota, 4/14/82, DC 1.25				
☐	1987	20c Ohio, 4/14/82, DC...1.25				
☐	1988	20c Oklahoma, 4/14/82, DC.......................................1.25				
☐	1989	20c Oregon, 4/14/82, DC..1.25				
☐	1990	20c Pennsylvania, 4/14/82, DC..................................1.25				
☐	1991	20c Rhode Island, 4/14/82, DC..................................1.25				
☐	1992	20c South Carolina, 4/14/82, DC 1.25				
☐	1993	20c South Dakota, 4/14/82, DC 1.25				
☐	1994	20c Tennessee, 4/14/82, DC.......................................1.25				
☐	1995	20c Texas, 4/14/82, DC..1.25				
☐	1996	20c Utah, 4/14/82, DC..1.25				
☐	1997	20c Vermont, 4/14/82, DC..1.25				
☐	1998	20c Virginia, 4/14/82, DC 1.25				
☐	1999	20c Washington, 4/14/82, DC 1.25				
☐	2000	20c West Virginia, 4/14/82, DC 1.25				
☐	2001	20c Wisconsin, 4/14/82, DC.......................................1.25				
☐	2002	20c Wyoming, 4/14/82, DC 1.25				
☐		Complete set of 50 ....75.00				
☐		Cancels of state capitals, any single 1.75				
☐		Complete set of 50 state capitals 90.00				
☐	2002b	Complete pane State Birds & Flowers (4 cities) perf.10 1/2x11 1/4				30.00
☐	2003	20c U.S.-Netherlands, 4/20/82, DC. "Plate Block"				
		value is for block of 4 with plate numbers.......1.00	1.25	1.50	22.00
☐		Combination with Netherlands stamp 7.50				
☐	2004	20c Library of Congress, 4/21/82, DC 1.00	1.25	1.50	8.00
☐	2005	20c Consumer Education, coil, 4/27/82, DC.............1.00	pr1.25lp25.00		8.00
☐	2006	20c Solar Energy, 4/29/82, Knoxville, TN 1.00				
☐	2007	20c Synthetic Fuels, 4/29/82, Knoxville, TN 1.00				
☐	2008	20c Breeder Reactor, 4/29/82, Knoxville, TN...........1.00				
☐	2009	20c Fossil Fuels, 4/29/82, Knoxville, TN 1.00				
☐	2009a	Se-tenant Knoxville World's Fair....................................	2.50	3.00	10.00
☐	2010	20c Horatio Alger, 4/30/82, Willow Grove, PA 1.00	1.25	1.50	12.00
☐	2011	20c Aging Together, 5/21/82, Sun City, AZ				
		(510,677)..1.00	1.25	1.50	10.00
☐	2012	20c The Barrymores, 6/8/82, New York, NY...........1.00	1.25	1.50	6.00
☐	2013	20c Dr. Mary E. Walker, 6/10/82, Oswego, NY........1.00	1.25	1.50	10.00
☐	2014	20c International Peace Gardens, 6/30/82,				
		Dunseith, ND...1.00	1.25	1.50	10.00
☐	2015	20c America's Libraries, 7/13/82, Philadelphia, PA.1.00	1.25	1.50	8.00
☐		1st WSC cachet 15.00				
☐	2016	20c Jackie Robinson, 8/2/82, Cooperstown, NY........8.00	9.00	10.00	35.00
☐		1st Armadillo Covers cachet 15.00				

cover box

10.5"

4.25" 7.5"

Keep your collection organized in this handsome
and durable cover box. Box will hold hundreds
of covers. Available in classic marble styling.

Item	Description	Retail
CVBOX	Marble Cover Box	$6.95

2004

2005

2006-9

Horatio Alger
2010

THE BARRYMORES

Aging together

2011

International Peace Garden

2014

Dr. Mary Walker
Army Surgeon
2013

Performing Arts USA 20c
2012

Touro USA 20c

2017

USA 20c
Wolf Trap Farm Park
for the performing arts
2018

Medal of Honor
USA 20c
2013

America's
A B O
Libraries
X Y Z
USA 20c
Legacies to Mankind
2015

Architecture USA 20c
2019-22

FRANCIS OF ASISI 1182-1982 · USA 20c
2023

Jackie Robinson

USA 20c
Black Heritage
2016

HOW TO USE THIS BOOK
The number in the first column is its Scott number or identifying number. Following that is the denomination of the stamp, description, date of issue, and the value.

Scott	Description	Single	Block	Plate Block	Cerm Prog
☐ 2017	20c Touro Synagogue, 8/22/82, Newport, RI (517,264). "Plate Block" value is for block of 4 with plate numbers 1.00		1.25	1.65	10.00
☐ 2018	20c Wolf Trap Farm Park, 9/1/82, Vienna, VA (764,361)...1.00		1.25	1.50	8.00
☐ 2019	20c Fallingwater, 9/30/82, DC 1.00				
☐ 2020	20c Illinois Institute of Technology, 9/30/82, DC.....1.00				
☐ 2021	20c Gropius House, 9/30/82, DC.......................1.00				
☐ 2022	20c Dulles Airport, 9/30/82, DC 1.00				
☐ 2022a	Se-tenant, American Architecture, (1,552,567)...........		2.50	3.00	8.00
☐ 2023	20c St. Francis of Assisi, 10/7/82, San Francisco, CA (530,275) 1.00		1.25	1.50	18.00
☐ 2024	20c Ponce de Leon, 10/12/82, San Juan, PR (530,275). "Plate Block" value is for block of 4 with plate numbers 1.00		1.25	1.50	10.00
☐ 2025	13c Christmas (Kitten & Puppy), 11/3/82, Danvers, MA (239,219) 1.00		1.25	1.50	20.00
☐ 2026	20c Christmas (Madonna & Child), 10/28/82, DC (462,982). "Plate Block" value is for block of 4 with plate numbers 1.00		1.25	1.50	10.00
☐ 2027	20c Children & Sleds, 10/28/82, Snow, OK 1.00				
☐ 2028	20c Children & Snowman, 10/28/82, Snow, OK....1.00				
☐ 2029	20c Children Playing, 10/28/82, Snow, OK............1.00				
☐ 2030	20c Children Decorating Tree, 10/28/82, Snow, OK.1.00				
☐ 2030a	Se-tenant, Christmas (Children) (676,950)...................		2.50	3.00	18.00
☐	Scott 2026-2030, either city.............................1.50				
☐	Scott 2026-3030 dual cancels............................2.50				

1983

Scott	Description	Single	Block	Plate Block	Cerm Prog
☐ 2031	20c Science & Industry, 1/19/83, Chicago, IL (526,693)...1.00		1.25	1.50	10.00
☐ 2032	20c Intrepid, Albuquerque, NM, & DC 1.00				
☐ 2033	20c Balloons Ascending, Albuquerque, NM, & DC. ...1.00				
☐ 2034	20c Balloons Ascending, Albuquerque, NM, & DC. .1.00				
☐ 2035	20c Explorer II, Albuquerque, NM, & DC................1.00				
☐ 2035a	Se-tenant, Balloons, 3/31/83, (989,305)		2.50	3.00	18.00
☐ 2036	20c U.S.-Sweden, 3/24/83, Philadelphia, PA (526,373)..1.00		1.25	1.50	14.00
☐	1st Panda cachet..25.00				
☐	Combination cover with Swedish issue.............6.00				
☐ 2037	20c Civilian Conservation Corps, 4/5/83, Luray, VA (483,824) 1.00		1.25	1.50	8.00
☐ 2038	20c Joseph Priestley, 4/13/83, Northumberland, PA (673,266)...1.00		1.25	1.50	8.00
☐ 2039	20c Voluntarism, 4/20/83, DC (574,708). "Plate Block" value is for block of 4 with plate numbers.......1.00		1.25	1.50	8.00
☐ 2040	20c U.S.-Germany, 4/29/83, Germantown, PA (611,109)...1.00		1.25	1.50	15.00
☐	Combination cover with German issue 6.00				
☐ 2041	20c Brooklyn Bridge, 5/17/83, Brooklyn, NY (815,085)..1.00		1.25	1.50	6.00
☐ 2042	20c T.V.A., 5/18/83, Knoxville, TN (837,588). "Plate Block" value is for block of 4 with plate numbers...1.00		1.25	1.50	8.00

2026

2024

2025

2031

2027-30

2036

2032-5

2037

2039

2038

2041

2042

2040

2043

2044

2046

2047

HOW TO USE THIS BOOK

The number in the first column is its Scott number or
identifying number. Following that is the denomination
of the stamp, description, date of issue, and the value.

SCOTT NUMBER	DESCRIPTION	SINGLE	PLATE BLOCK	CERM PROG

		SINGLE	BLOCK	BLOCK	PROG
☐ 2043	20c Physical Fitness, 5/14/83, Houston, TX (501,336). "Plate Block" value is for block of 4 with plate numbers 1.00	1.25	1.50	10.00
☐ 2044	20c Scott Joplin, 6/9/83, Sedalia, MO (472,667) 1.00	1.25	1.50	32.00
☐ 2045	20c Medal of Honor, 6/7/83, DC (1,623,995)............3.75	4.00	4.50	14.00
☐ 2046	20c Babe Ruth, 7/6/83, Chicago, IL (1,277,907) (2 types)*..6.00	6.50	8.00	40.00*
☐	1st Eastern Covers, Inc., cachet....................15.00			
☐	1st Dome cachet..25.00			
☐ 2047	20c Nathaniel Hawthorne, 7/8/83, Salem, MA (442,793)...1.00	1.25	1.50	10.00
☐ 2048	13c Discus, 7/28/83, South Bend, IN 1.00			
☐ 2049	13c High Jump, 7/28/83, South Bend, IN 1.00			
☐ 2050	13c Archery, 7/28/83, South Bend, IN 1.00			
☐ 2051	13c Boxing, 7/28/83, South Bend, IN.......................1.00			
☐ 2051a	Se-tenant, 1984 Los Angeles Olympics, (909,332)..........	2.50	3.00	12.00
☐ 2052	20c Signing of Treaty of Paris, 9/2/83, DC (651,208)...1.00	1.25	1.50	10.00
☐	1st TF cachet 30.00			
☐	Combo with French stamp.............................10.00			
☐ 2053	20c Civil Service, 9/9/83, DC (422,206)....................1.00	1.25	1.50	8.00
☐ 2054	20c Metropolitan Opera, 9/14/83, New York, NY (807,609)...1.00	1.25	1.50	6.00
☐	1st Desert Sun cachet 15.00			
☐ 2055	20c Charles Steinmetz, 9/21/83, DC........................1.00			
☐ 2056	20c Edwin Armstrong, 9/21/83, DC 1.00			
☐ 2057	20c Nikola Tesla, 9/21/83, DC 1.00			
☐ 2058	20c Philo T. Farnsworth, 9/21/83, DC......................1.00			
☐ 2058a	Se-tenant, American Inventors, (1,006,516)	2.50	3.00	8.00
☐ 2059	20c First American streetcar, 10/8/83, Kennebunkport, ME...............................1.00			
☐ 2060	20c Electric Streetcar, 10/8/83, Kennebunkport, ME1.00			
☐ 2061	20c "Bobtail" Horsecar, 10/8/83, Kennebunkport, ME...1.00			
☐ 2062	20c St. Charles Streetcar, 10/8/83, Kennebunkport, ME...1.00			
☐ 2062a	Se-tenant, Streetcars, (1,116,909)	2.50	3.00	12.00
☐ 2063	20c Christmas (Madonna & Child), 10/28/83, DC (361,874)...1.00	1.25	1.50	10.00
☐ 2064	20c Christmas (Santa Claus), 10/28/83, Santa Claus, IN (388,749). "Plate Block" value is for block of 4 with plate numbers.........................1.00	1.25	1.50	10.00
☐ 2065	20c Martin Luther, 11/11/83, DC (463,777) 3.00	2.50	4.00	10.00

1984

		SINGLE	BLOCK	BLOCK	PROG
☐ 2066	20c Alaska Statehood, 1/3/84, Fairbanks, AK (816,591)...1.00	1.25	1.50	8.00
☐ 2067	20c Ice Dancing, 1/6/84, Lake Placid, NY 1.00			
☐ 2068	20c Alpine Skiing, 1/6/84, Lake Placid, NY..............1.00			
☐ 2069	20c Nordic Skiing, 1/6/84, Lake Placid, NY..............1.00			
☐ 2070	20c Hockey, 1/6/84, Lake Placid, NY 1.00			
☐ 2070a	Se-tenant, Winter Olympic Games, (1,245,807).............	2.50	3.00	12.00
☐ 2071	20c Federal Deposit Insurance Corporation, 1/12/84, DC (536,329) 1.00	1.25	1.50	8.00

Medal of Honor
USA 20c
2045

2048-51

Treaty of Paris 1783
US Bicentennial 20 cents
2052

CIVIL SERVICE
1883
1983
USA 20c
2053

METROPOLITAN OPERA
1883 1983 USA 20c
2054

USA
20c
Charles Steinmetz
2055-58

USA 20c
First American streetcar, New York City 1832
2059-62

Season's Greetings USA 20c
2064

Christmas USA 20c
Raphael, 1480-1520, National Gallery
2063

Martin Luther
1483-1983 USA 20c
2065

USA 20c
1959 1984
Alaska Statehood
2066

Olympics
USA
20c
2067-70

FEDERAL DEPOSIT INSURANCE CORPORATION
$
2071

LO♥E
LO♥E
LO♥E
LO♥E
LO♥E
USA 20c
2072

Carter G. Woodson
Black Heritage USA 20c
2073

SOIL AND WATER CONSERVATION
USA 20c
2074

ACT OF 1934
USA 20c
2075

NATIONAL ARCHIVES
USA
2081

**Values for various cachet makers can be determined
by using the Cachet Calculator which begins on page 52A.**

SCOTT NUMBER	DESCRIPTION	SINGLE	PLATE BLOCK	CERM PROG
☐ 2072	20c Love, 1/31/84, DC (327,727). "Plate Block" value is for block of 4 with plate numbers 1.00	1.25	1.50	8.00
☐ 2073	20c Carter Woodson, 2/1/84, DC (387,583)..............1.00	1.25	1.50	10.00
☐ 2074	20c Soil & Water Conservation, 2/6/84, Denver, CO (426,101) 1.00	1.25	1.50	8.00
☐ 2075	20c Credit Union Act, 2/10/84, Salem, MA (523,583)..1.00	1.25	1.50	8.00
☐ 2076	20c Wild Pink Orchid, 3/5/84, Miami, FL.................1.00			
☐ 2077	20c Yellow Lady's Slipper Orchid, 3/5/84, Miami, FL 1.00			
☐ 2078	20c Spreading Pogonia Orchid, 3/5/84, Miami, FL..1.00			
☐ 2079	20c Pacific Calypso Orchid, 3/5/84, Miami, FL........1.00			
☐ 2079a	Se-tenant, Orchids, (1,063,237)	2.50	3.00	14.00
☐ 2080	20c Hawaii Statehood, 3/12/84, Honolulu, HI (546,930)..1.00	1.25	1.50	8.00
☐ 2081	20c National Archives, 4/16/84, DC (414,415).........1.00	1.25	1.50	8.00
☐ 2082	20c Diving, 5/4/84, Los Angeles, CA 1.00			
☐ 2083	20c Long Jump, 5/4/84, Los Angeles, CA 1.00			
☐ 2084	20c Wrestling, 5/4/84, Los Angeles, CA...................1.00			
☐ 2085	20c Kayak, 5/4/84, Los Angeles, CA 1.00			
☐ 2085a	Se-tenant, 1984 Los Angeles Olympics (1,172,313).1.00	2.50	3.00	12.00
☐ 2086	20c New Orleans World Exposition, 5/11/84, New Orleans, LA (467,408).......................................1.00	1.25	1.50	8.00
☐ 2087	20c Health Research, 5/17/84, New York, NY (845,007)..1.00	1.25	1.50	6.00
☐ 2088	20c Douglas Fairbanks, 5/23/84, Denver, CO (547, 134). "Plate Block" value is for block of 4 with plate numbers..1.00	1.25	1.50	8.00
☐ 2089	20c Jim Thorpe, 5/24/84, Shawnee, OK (568,544)...6.00	7.00	9.00	25.00
☐	(2nd Day), 5/25/84, Yale, OK......................................			35.00
☐ 2090	20c John McCormack, 6/6/84, Boston, MA (464,117)..1.00	1.25	1.50	10.00
☐	Scott 2090 with Ireland stamp, dual cancel 20.00			
☐ 2091	20c St. Lawrence Seaway, 6/26/84, Massena, NY (550,173)..1.00	1.25	1.50	10.00
☐	Scott 2091 with Canada stamp........................5.00			
☐	Joint Issue with Canada dual cancels.............25.00			
☐ 2092	20c Waterfowl Preservation Act, 7/2/84, Des Moines, IA (549,388)......................................1.00	1.25	1.50	12.00
☐	1st George Van Natta cachet 40.00			
☐ 2093	20c Roanoke Voyages, 7/13/84, Manteo, NC (443,725)..1.00	1.25	1.50	25.00
☐ 2094	20c Herman Melville, 8/1/84, New Bedford, MA (379,293)..1.75	2.00	2.25	12.00
☐ 2095	20c Horace A. Moses, 8/6/84, Bloomington, IN (459,386). "Plate Block" value is for block of 4 with plate numbers..1.00	1.25	1.50	8.00
☐ 2096	20c Smokey the Bear, 8/13/84, Capitan, NM (506,833)..2.00	3.00	4.00	15.00
☐	1st Long Island Cover Society cachet 15.00			
☐ 2097	20c Roberto Clemente, 8/17/84, Carolina, PR (547,387)..15.00	16.00	17.00	35.00
☐ 2098	20c Beagle & Boston Terrier, 9/7/84, New York, NY 1.00			
☐ 2099	20c Chesapeake Bay Retriever & Cocker Spaniel, 9/7/84, New York, NY 1.00			
☐ 2100	20c Alaskan Malamute & Collie, 9/7/84, New York, NY 1.00			

2080 — Hawaii Statehood 1959-1984

2076-79 — Ωkipuk andwa bebw

2082-85

2086 — Louisiana World Exposition / Fresh water as a source of Life

2087 — Health Research USA 20c

2091

2092 — Preserving Wetlands 1984

2088 — DOUGLAS FAIRBANKS / Performing Arts USA 20c

2089 — Jim Thorpe

2090 — JOHN McCORMACK / Performing Arts USA 20c

2093 — Roanoke Voyages North Carolina 1584

2094 — Herman Melville

2095 — Horace Moses

2096 — SMOKEY

2097 — Roberto Clemente

Values for various cachet makers can be determined by using the Cachet Calculator which begins on page 52A.

142

☐ 2101	20c Black & Tan Coonhound & American Foxhound, 9/7/84, New York, NY......1.00				
☐ 2101a ☐	Se-tenant, Dogs, (1,157,373)........... 1st Heartland FDC cachet....................20.00		2.50	3.00	10.00
☐ 2102	20c Crime Prevention, 9/26/84, DC (427,564) 1.00		1.25	1.50	8.00
☐ 2103	20c Hispanic Americans, 10/31/84, DC (416,796) ..1.00		1.25	1.50	10.00
☐ 2104	20c Family Unity, 10/1/84, Shaker Heights, OH (400,659). "Plate Block" value is for block of 4 with plate numbers...........1.00		1.25	1.50	8.00
☐ 2105	20c Eleanor Roosevelt, 10/11/84, Hyde Park, NY (479,919)...........1.00		1.25	1.50	8.00
☐ 2106	20c Nation of Readers, 10/16/84, DC (437,559) 1.00		1.25	1.50	8.00
☐ 2107	20c Christmas (Madonna), 10/30/84, DC (386,385)...........1.00		1.25	1.50	10.00
☐ 2108	20c Christmas (Santa Claus), 10/30/84, Jamaica, NY (430,843)...........1.00		1.25	1.50	10.00
☐ 2109	20c Vietnam Veterans' Memorial, 11/10/84, DC (434,489)...........4.50		5.00	5.50	18.00

1985

☐ 2110	22c Jerome Kern, 1/23/85, New York, NY (503,855)...........1.00		1.25	1.50	6.00
☐ 2111	(22c) "D" & Eagle, 2/1/85, Los Angeles, CA.............1.00		1.25	1.50	
☐ 2112	(22c) "D" & Eagle, coil, 2/1/85, Los Angeles, CA 1.00 pr1.25				
☐ 2113	(22c) "D" & Eagle, booklet single, 2/1/85, Los Angeles, CA...........1.00				
☐ 2113a	"D" & Eagle, booklet pane of 10 ....7.50				
	Total for Scott 2111-2113a is 513,027.				
☐ 2114	22c Flag over Capitol Dome, 3/29/85, DC...........1.00		1.25	1.50	
☐ 2115	22c Flag over Capitol Dome, coil, 3/29/85 DC...........1.00 pr1.25				
☐ 2114-2115	Flag, sheet and coil...........				10.00
	Total for Scott 2114-2115 is 268,161.				
☐ 2115b	22c Flag over Capitol Dome, pre-phosphored, coil, 5/23/87, Secaucus, NJ 1.00 pr5.00				8.00
☐ 2116	22c Flag over Capitol Dome, booklet single, 3/29/85, Waubeka, WI (234,318) 1.00				
☐ 2116a	Flag over Capitol Dome, booklet pane of 5...............3.50				
☐ 2117	22c Frilled Dogwinkle, 4/4/85, Boston, MA 1.00				
☐ 2118	22c Reticulated Helmet, 4/4/85, Boston, MA...........1.00				
☐ 2119	22c New England Neptune, 4/4/85, Boston, MA......1.00				
☐ 2120	22c Calico Scallop, 4/4/85, Boston, MA...........1.00				
☐ 2121	22c Lightning Whelk, 4/4/85, Boston, MA 1.00				
☐ 2121a	Booklet pane of 10 ....7.50				15.00
	Total for Nos. 2117-2121 is 426,290.				
☐ 2122	$10.75 Eagle & Half Moon, 4/29/85, San Francisco, CA (93,154)...........60.00				
☐ 2122a	Eagle & Half Moon, booklet pane of 3 ....150.00				
☐ 2122b	Reissue, bk sgl, 6/19/89 ....250.00				
☐ 2122c	Reissue, booklet pane of 3...........700.00				

HOW TO USE THIS BOOK
The number in the first column is its Scott number or identifying number. Following that is the denomination of the stamp, description, date of issue, and the value.

2098-01

TAKE A BITE OUT OF
CRIME

2102

Hispanic Americans
A Proud Heritage USA 20

2103

2104

2105

A Nation of
Readers
USA 20c

2106

Christmas USA 20c

2107

Season's Greetings

2108

Domestic Mail
D
US Postage

2111

JEROME KERN

Performing Arts USA

2110

Vietnam Veterans Memorial USA 20c

2109

New England Neptune

2117-21

USA 22

2114

Tricycle 1880s
6 USA

2126

USA $10.75

2122

Mary McLeod Bethune

Black Heritage USA 22

2137

Iceboat 1880s
USA 14

2134

Mallard Decoy

Folk Art USA 22

2138-41

Winter Special Olympics

2142

22 USA
Rural
Electrification
Administration

2144

**Values for various cachet makers can be determined
by using the Cachet Calculator which begins on page 52A.**

1985-88 Transportation Coils

			SINGLE	PAIR	LINE PAIR	CERM PROG
☐	2123	3.4c School Bus, 6/8/85, Arlington, VA (131,480) ....—		1.00	12.50	12.00
☐	2123a	School Bus, untagged (Bureau precanceled), 6/8/85, Arlington, VA, earliest known use............—	250.00		—	
☐	2124	4.9c Buckboard, 6/21/85, Reno, NV............................—		1.00	13.50	
☐	2124a	Buckboard, untagged (Bureau precanceled), 6/21/85, DC, earliest known use...........................—	250.00		—	
☐	2125	5.5c Star Route Truck, 11/1/86, Ft. Worth, TX (136,021) ....—		1.00		20.00
☐	2125a	Star Route Truck, untagged (Bureau precanceled), 11/1/86, DC ....—		5.00		
☐	2126	6c Tricycle, untagged (Bureau precanceled), 5/6/85, Childs, MD (151,494) ....—		1.00		12.00
☐	2127	7.1c Tractor, 2/6/87, Sarasota, FL (167,555) ....—		1.00		12.00
☐	2127a	Tractor, untagged (Bureau precancel "Nonprofit Org." in black), 2/6/87, Sarasota, FL........................		5.00		8.00
☐	2127a	Tractor, untagged (Bureau precancel "Nonprofit 5-Digit Zip+4" in black), 5/26/89, Rosemont, IL		1.00		
☐	2128	8.3c Ambulance, 6/21/85, Reno, NV ....—		1.00	10.00	
☐	2128a	Ambulance, untagged (Bureau precanceled), 6/21/85, DC, earliest known use...........................—	250.00		—	
☐	2129	8.5c Tow Truck, 1/24/87, Tucson, AZ (224,285) ....—		1.00		12.00
☐	2129a	Tow Truck, untagged (Bureau precanceled), 1/24/87, DC ....—		5.00		
☐	2130	10.1c Oil Wagon, 4/18/85, Oil Center, NM...................—		1.00		12.00
☐	2130a	Oil Wagon, untagged (black Bureau precancel), 4/18/85, DC, earliest known use..........................—	250.00			
☐	2130a	Oil Wagon, untagged (red Bureau precancel), 6/27/88, DC ....—		1.00		
☐	2131	11c Stutz Super Bearcat, 6/11/85, Baton Rouge, LA (135,037) ....—		1.00	15.00	12.00
☐	2132	12c Stanley Steamer, 4/2/85, Kingfield, ME, (173,998) ....—		1.00	12.50	
☐	2132a	Stanley Steamer, untagged (Bureau precanceled), 4/2/85, DC ....—	60.00		—	
☐	2133	12.5c Pushcart, 4/18/85, Oil Center, NM.....................—	1.25			
		Total for Scott 2130 and 2133 is 319,953.				
☐	2133a	Pushcart, untagged (Bureau precanceled), 4/18/85, DC ....—	60.00			
☐	2134	14c Ice Boat, 3/23/85, Rochester, NY (324,710)..........—		1.25	15.00	12.00
		1st C.L. cachets 15.00				
☐	2135	17c Dog Sled, 8/20/86, Anchorage, AK (112,009).......—		1.25		12.00
☐	2136	25c Bread Wagon, 11/22/86, Virginia Beach, VA (151,950)..1.25		1.25		12.00

2143

2146

F.A. Bartholdi, Statue of Liberty Sculptor
2147

2152

Social Security Act 1935-1985 USA 22
2153

AMERIPEX86
2145

18
2149

USA 21.1
2150

Veterans World War I
2154

USA 22
Morgan
2155-58

22
USA
Public Education
2159

22
YMCA Youth Camping — USA
2160-63

Help End Hunger — USA 22
2164

CHRISTMAS
USA 22
2165

Season's Greetings — USA 22
2166

**Values for various cachet makers can be determined
by using the Cachet Calculator which begins on page 52A.**

SCOTT NUMBER	DESCRIPTION	SINGLE	PLATE BLOCK	CERM BLOCK	PROG

1985-86

SCOTT NUMBER	DESCRIPTION	SINGLE	PLATE BLOCK	CERM BLOCK	PROG
☐ 2137	22c Mary McLeod Bethune, 3/5/85, DC (413,244)...1.00		1.25	1.50	12.00
☐ 2138	22c Broadbill Decoy, 3/22/85, Shelburne, VT..........1.00				
☐ 2139	22c Mallard Decoy, 3/22/85, Shelburne, VT............1.00				
☐ 2140	22c Canvasback Decoy, 3/22/85, Shelburne, VT......1.00				
☐ 2141	22c Redhead Decoy, 3/22/85, Shelburne, VT...........1.00				
☐ 2141a	Se-tenant, Duck Decoys, (923,249)		2.75	3.50	14.00
☐ 2142	22c Winter Special Olympics, 3/25/85, Park City, UT (253,074)..1.00		1.25	1.50	10.00
☐ 2143	22c Love, 4/17/85, Hollywood, CA (283,072)............1.00		1.25	1.50	10.00
☐ 2144	22c Rural Electrificafion Administration, 5/11/85, Madison, SD (472,895). "Plate Block" value is for block of 4 with plate numbers (2 types)*....1.00		1.25	1.50	10.00*
☐ 2145	22c Ameripex '86, 5/25/85, Rosemont, IL (457,038)1.00		1.25	1.50	10.00
☐ 2146	22c Abigail Adams, 6/14/85, Quincy, MA (491,026).1.00		1.25	1.50	10.00
☐ 2147	22c Frederic Auguste Bartholdi, 7/18/85, New York, NY (594,896) 1.00		1.25	1.50	12.00

SCOTT NUMBER	DESCRIPTION	SINGLE	PAIR	CERM PROG
☐ 2149	18c George Washington & Monument, 11/6/85, ... (376,238)..	1.25		12.00
☐ 2149a	George Washington & Monument, untagged (Bureau precanceled), 11/6/85		5.00	
☐ 2150	21.1c Envelopes, 10/22/85, DC (119,941)......................	1.25		12.00
☐ 2150a	Envelopes, untagged (Bureau precanceled), 10/22/85, DC..		5.00	

SCOTT NUMBER	DESCRIPTION	SINGLE	PLATE BLOCK	CERM BLOCK	PROG
☐ 2152	22c Korean War Veterans, 7/26/85, DC (391,754)...1.00		1.25	1.50	12.00
☐ 2153	22c Social Security Act, 8/14/85, Baltimore, MD (265,143)...1.00		1.25	1.50	15.00
☐ 2154	22c World War I Veterans, 8/26/85, Milwaukee,WI.1.00		1.25	1.50	10.00
☐ 2155	22c Quarter Horse, 9/25/85, Lexington, KY.............1.25				
☐ 2156	22c Morgan, 9/25/85, Lexington, KY........................1.25				
☐ 2157	22c Saddlebred, 9/25/85, Lexington, KY..................1.25				
☐ 2158	22c Appaloosa, 9/25/85, Lexington, KY 1.25				
☐ 2158a	Se-tenant, Horses. (1,135,368)......................................		5.00	6.00	14.00
☐ 2159	22c Public Education in America, 10/1/85, Boston, MA (356,030) 1.00		1.25	1.50	6.00
☐ 2160	22c YMCA Youth Camping, 10/7/85, Chicago, IL.....1.00				
☐ 2161	22c Boy Scouts, 10/7/85, Chicago, IL 1.00				
☐ 2162	22c Big Brothers/Big Sisters, 10/7/85, Chicago, IL .1.00				
☐ 2163	22c Camp Fire, Inc., 10/7/85, Chicago, IL................1.00				
☐ 2163a	Se-tenant, International Youth Year, (1,202,541)		2.50	3.00	8.00
☐ 2164	22c Help End Hunger, 10/15/85, DC (299,485)........1.00		1.25	1.50	8.00
☐ 2165	22c Christmas (Madonna & Child), 10/30/85, Detroit, MI...1.00		1.25	1.50	10.00
☐ 2166	22c Christmas (Poinsettia), 10/30/85, Nazareth, MI (524,929) 1.00		1.25	1.50	10.00

2167

2168

2170

2171

2172

2177

2179

2183

2191

2194

2195

2198-2201

2202

2203

2204

2205-09

2210

2220-23

2216a

2217a

2211

2224

2218a

2219a

1986

☐ 2167 22c Arkansas Statehood, 1/3/86, Little Rock, AR
(364,729)..1.00 1.25 1.50 8.00
☐   1st LMG cachets...30.00

1986-94 Great Americans

☐ 2168 1c Margaret Mitchell, 6/30/86, Atlanta, GA
(316,764)..1.50 1.75 2.00 8.00
☐ 2169 2c Mary Lyon, 2/28/87, S. Hadley, MA (349,831) 1.00 1.25 1.50 12.00
☐ 2170 3c Dr. Paul Dudley White, 9/15/86, Washington,DC 1.00 1.25 1.50 8.00
☐ 2171 4c Father Flanagan, 7/14/86, Boys Town, NE
(367,883)..1.00 1.25 1.50 8.00
☐ 2172 5c Hugo Black, 2/27/86, DC (303,012) 1.00 1.25 1.50 8.00
☐   1st Key Kachets cachet.................................20.00
☐ 2173 5c Luiz Munoz Marin, 2/18/90, San Juan, PR..........1.00 1.25 1.00 6.00
☐ 2175 10c Red Cloud, 8/15/87, Red Cloud, NE (300,472)...1.50 1.75 2.00 10.00
☐ 2176 14c Julia Ward Howe, 2/12/87, Boston, MA
(454,829)..1.00 1.25 1.50 8.00
☐ 2177 15c Buffalo Bill Cody, 6/6/88, Cody, WY
(356,395)..1.00 1.25 1.50 18.00
☐ 2178 17c Belva Ann Lockwood, 6/18/86, Middleport, NY
(249,215)..1.00 1.25 1.65 6.00
☐ 2179 20c Virginia Apgar, 10/24/94, Dallas. TX 1.00 1.25 1.65 6.00
☐ 2180 21c Chester Carlson, 10/21/88, Rochester, NY
(288,073)..1.00 1.25 1.65 20.00
☐ 2181 23c Mary Cassatt, 11/4/88, Philadelphia, PA
(322,537)..1.00 1.25 1.65 10.00
☐ 2182 25c Jack London, 1/11/86, Glen Ellen, CA
(358,686)..1.25 1.25 1.65 8.00
☐ 2182a Jack London, booklet pane of 10, 5/3/88,
San Francisco, CA...6.00
☐ 2183 28c Sitting Bull, 9/14/89, Rapid City, SD
(126,777)..1.50 1.75 2.00 6.00
☐ 2184 29c Earl Warren, 3/9/92, DC (175,517)....................1.25   6.00
☐ 2185 29c Thomas Jefferson, 4/13/93
Charlottesville, VA 1.25   8.00
☐ 2186 35c Dennis Chavez, 4/3/91, Albuquerque, NM
(285,570)... 1.25   8.00
☐ 2187 40c Claire Chennault, 9/6/90, Monroe, LA
(186,761)..1.50   6.00
☐ 2188 45c Harvey Cushing, 6/17/88, Cleveland, OH
(135,140)..1.25   10.00
☐ 2189 52c Hubert Humphrey, 6/3/91, Minneapolis, MN
(93,391)..1.35   10.00
☐ 2190 56c John Harvard, 9/3/86, Cambridge, MA 1.25 2.50 3.00 10.00
☐ 2191 65c Hap Arnold, 11/5/88, Gladwyne, PA (129,829)..1.50 3.00 3.50 10.00
☐ 2192 75c Wendell Wilkie, 2/18/92, Bloomington, IN
47,086)..1.50 3.00 3.50
☐ 2193 $1 Dr. Bernard Revel, 9/23/86, New York, NY.........3.00 5.50 6.00 8.00
☐ 2194 $1 Johns Hopkins, 6/7/89, Baltimore, MD
(159,049)..3.00 4.50 6.00 15.00
☐ 2195 $2 William Jennings Bryan, 3/19/86, Salem, IL
(123,430)..5.00 10.00 15.00 15.00
☐ 2196 $5 Bret Harte, 8/25/87, Twain Harte, CA
(111,431)..20.00 25.00 30.00 25.00

☐ 2197	25c **Jack London,** booklet single, 5/3/88, San Francisco, CA 1.25				
☐ 2197a	**Jack London,** booklet pane of 6 ....4.00				
	Total for Scott 2183a, 2197, and 2197a is 94,655.				

1986

☐ 2198	22c **Handstamped Cover, Memorabilia,** 1/23/86 State College, PA 1.00				
☐ 2199	22c **Boy & Stamp Collection,** 1/23/86 State College, PA 1.00				
☐ 2200	22c **Scott U.S. 836, Sweden 268 & 271,** 1/23/86 State College, PA 1.00				
☐ 2201	22c **Scott U.S. 2216,** 1/23/86 State College, PA 1.00				
☐ 2201a	**Booklet pane of 4** 5.00				12.00
☐ 2201b	**Booklet pane of 4,** black omitted on 2198, 2201...350.00				
	Total for Scott 2198-2201 is 675,924.				
☐ 2202	22c **Love,** 1/30/86, New York, NY 1.00	1.25	1.50	12.00	
	1st Cat-Chet cachet 20.00				
☐ 2203	22c **Sojourner Truth,** 2/4/86, New Paltz, NY (342,985) 1.00	1.25	1.50	12.00	
☐ 2204	22c **Republic of Texas,** 3/2/86, San Antonio, TX (380,450) 1.00	1.25	1.50	10.00	
☐ 2205	22c **Muskellunge,** 3/21/86, Seattle, WA 1.00				
☐ 2206	22c **Atlantic Cod,** 3/21/86, Seattle, WA 1.00				
☐ 2207	22c **Largemouth Bass,** 3/21/86, Seattle, WA 1.00				
☐ 2208	22c **Bluefin Tuna,** 3/21/86, Seattle, WA 1.00				
☐ 2209	22c **Catfish,** 3/21/86, Seattle, WA 1.00				
☐ 2209a	**Booklet pane of 5** (2 types)* 2.50				12.00*
☐	1st Ohio Cachetmakers Association cachet 15.00				
	Total for Scott 2205-2209 is 988,184.				
☐ 2210	22c **Public Hospitals,** 4/11/86, New York, NY (403,665) 1.00	1.25	1.50	6.00	
☐ 2211	22c **Duke Ellington,** 4/29/86, New York, NY (397,894) 1.00	1.25	1.50	8.00	
☐ 2216	**Sheet of 9,** 5/22/86, Chicago, IL 4.00				15.00
☐ 2216a	22c **George Washington** 1.50				
☐ 2216b	22c **John Adams** 1.50				
☐ 2216c	22c **Thomas Jefferson** 1.50				
☐ 2216d	22c **James Madison** 1.50				
☐ 2216e	22c **James Monroe** 1.50				
☐ 2216f	22c **John Quincy Adams** 1.50				
☐ 2216g	22c **Andrew Jackson** 1.50				
☐ 2216h	22c **Martin Van Buren** 1.50				
☐ 2216i	22c **William H. Harrison** 1.50				
☐ 2217	**Sheet of 9,** 5/22/86, Chicago, IL 5.00				
☐ 2217a	22c **John Tyler** 1.50				
☐ 2217b	22c **James Knox Polk** 1.50				
☐ 2217c	22c **Zachary Taylor** 1.50				
☐ 2217d	22c **Millard Fillmore** 1.50				
☐ 2217e	22c **Franklin Pierce** 1.50				
☐ 2217f	22c **James Buchanan** 1.50				
☐ 2217g	22c **Abraham Lincoln** 1.50				
☐ 2217h	22c **Andrew Johnson** 1.50				
☐ 2217i	22c **Ulysses S. Grant** 1.50				

SCOTT NUMBER	DESCRIPTION	SINGLE	PLATE BLOCK	CERM PROG
☐ 2218	Sheet of 9, 5/22/86, Chicago, IL	25.00		
☐ 2218a	22c Rutherford B. Hayes	1.50		
☐ 2218b	22c James A. Garfield	1.50		
☐ 2218c	22c Chester A. Arthur	1.50		
☐ 2218d	22c Grover Cleveland	1.50		
☐ 2218e	22c Benjamin Harrison	1.50		
☐ 2218f	22c William McKinley	1.50		
☐ 2218g	22c Theodore Roosevelt	1.50		
☐ 2218h	22c William H. Taft	1.50		
☐ 2218i	22c Woodrow Wilson	1.50		
☐ 2219	Sheet of 9, 5/22/86, Chicago, IL	5.00		
☐ 2219a	22c Warren G. Harding	1.50		
☐ 2219b	22c Calvin Coolidge	1.50		
☐ 2219c	22c Herbert Hoover	1.50		
☐ 2219d	22c Franklin Delano Roosevelt	1.50		
☐ 2219e	22c White House	1.50		
☐ 2219f	22c Harry S. Truman	1.50		
☐ 2219g	22c Dwight D. Eisenhower	1.50		
☐ 2219h	22c John F. Kennedy	1.50		
☐ 2219i	22c Lyndon B. Johnson	1.50		
	Total for Scott 2216-2219 and 2216a-2219i is 9,009,599.			
☐ 2220	22c Elisha Kent Kane, 5/28/86, North Pole, AK	1.00		
☐ 2221	22c Adolphus W. Greely, 5/28/86, North Pole, AK	1.00		
☐ 2222	22c Vilhjalmur Stefansson, 5/28/86, North Pole, AK	1.00		
☐ 2223	22c Robert E. Peary & Matthew Henson, 5/28/86, North Pole, AK	1.00		
☐ 2223a	Se-tenant, Polar Exploreres, (760,999)	4.00	5.00	8.00
☐ 2224	22c Statue of Liberty, 7/4/86, New York, NY (1,540,308)	2.00	2.50 3.50	30.00

SCOTT NUMBER	DESCRIPTION	SINGLE	PAIR	CERM PROG

1986-87 Transportation Coils

☐ 2225	1c Omnibus, re-engraved, 11/26,86, DC (57,845)	—	1.00	
☐ 2226	2c Locomotive, re-engraved, 3/6/87, Milwaukee, WI (169,484)	_	1.00	12.00
☐ 2228	4c Stagecoach, re-engraved, 8/15/86, DC, earliest known use	150.00		
☐ 2231	8.3c Ambulance, re-engraved, 8/24/86, DC, earliest known use	150.00		

SCOTT NUMBER	DESCRIPTION	SINGLE	PLATE BLOCK	CERM PROG

1986

☐ 2235	22c Navajo Art, 9/4/86, Window Rock, AZ	1.00		
☐ 2236	22c Navajo Art, 9/4/86, Window Rock, AZ	1.00		
☐ 2237	22c Navajo Art, 9/4/86, Window Rock, AZ	1.00		
☐ 2238	22c Navajo Art, 9/4/86, Window Rock, AZ	1.00		
☐ 2238a	Se-tenant, Navajo Art, (1,102,520)	2.50	3.00	10.00
☐ 2239	22c T.S. Eliot, 9/26/86, St. Louis, MO (304,764)	1.00	1.25 1.50	8.00
☐ 2240	22c Highlander Figure, 10/1/86, DC	1.00		
☐ 2241	22c Ship Figurehead, 10/1/86, DC	1.00		
☐ 2242	22c Nautical Figure, 10/1/86, DC	1.00		
☐ 2243	22c Cigar-store Figure, 10/1/86, DC	1.00		
☐ 2243a	Se-tenant, Woodcarved Figurines, (629,399)	2.50	3.00	12.00

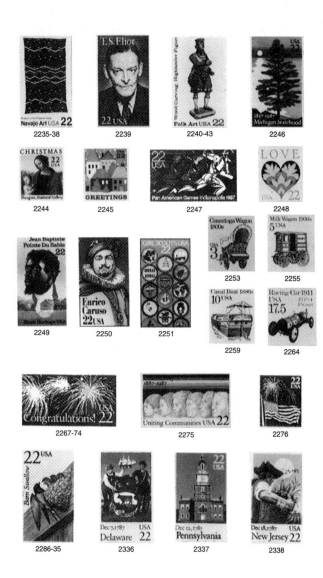

Navajo Art USA **22**
2235-38

T. S. Eliot
22 USA
2239

Wood Carving; Highlander Figure
Folk Art USA **22**
2240-43

USA 22
1837-1987 Michigan Statehood
2246

CHRISTMAS
22 USA
Perugino, National Gallery
2244

22
USA
GREETINGS
2245

22 USA
Pan American Games Indianapolis 1987
2247

LOVE
USA 22
2248

Jean Baptiste
Pointe Du Sable
22
Black Heritage USA
2249

Enrico
Caruso
22 USA
2250

GIRL SCOUTS USA
22
2251

Conestoga Wagon 1800s
USA 3
2253

Milk Wagon 1900s
5 USA
2255

Canal Boat 1880s
10 USA
2259

Racing Car 1911
USA 17.5
ZIP+4 Presort
2264

Congratulations! USA 22
2267-74

1837-1987
Uniting Communities USA 22
2275

22 USA
2276

22 USA
Barn Swallow
2286-35

Dec 7,1787 USA
Delaware 22
2336

22 USA
Dec 12, 1787
Pennsylvania
2337

Dec 18,1787 USA
New Jersey 22
2338

**Values for various cachet makers can be determined
by using the Cachet Calculator which begins on page 52A.**

SCOTT NUMBER	DESCRIPTION	SINGLE	BLOCK	PLATE BLOCK	CERM PROG
☐ 2244	22c Christmas (Madonna & Child), 10/24/86, DC (467,999)..	1.00	1.25	1.50	12.00
☐ 2245	22c Christmas (Winter Village), 10/24/86 Snow Hill, MD (504,851)...	1.00	1.25	1.50	12.00

1987

SCOTT NUMBER	DESCRIPTION	SINGLE	BLOCK	PLATE BLOCK	CERM PROG
☐ 2246	22c Michigan Statehood, 1/26/87, Lansing, MI (379,117)...	1.00	1.25	1.50	8.00
☐ 2247	22c Pan American Games, 1/29/87, Indianapolis, IN (344,731)	1.00	1.25	1.50	8.00
☐ 2248	22c Love, 1/30/87, San Francisco, CA (333,329)	1.00	1.25	1.50	8.00
☐ 2249	22c Jean Baptiste Pointe du Sable, 2/20/87, Chicago, IL (313,054)..	2.00	2.50	3.00	14.00
☐ 2250	22c Enrico Caruso, 2/27/87, New York, NY (389,834)...	1.00	1.25	1.50	6.00
☐ 2251	22c Girl Scouts, 3/12/87, DC (556,391)	1.00	1.25	1.50	10.00

SCOTT NUMBER	DESCRIPTION	SINGLE	PAIR	CERM PROG

1987-88 Transportation Coils

SCOTT NUMBER	DESCRIPTION	SINGLE	PAIR	CERM PROG
☐ 2252	3c Conestoga Wagon, 2/29/88, Conestoga, PA (155,203)	—	1.00	12.00
☐	1st Gil Lewis cachet..		15.00	
☐ 2253	5c Milk Wagon, 9/25/87, Indianapolis, IN	—	1.00	12.00
☐ 2254	5.3c Elevator, 9/16/88, New York, NY (142,705).............	—	1.00	10.00
☐ 2255	7.6c Carreta, 8/30/88, San Jose, CA (140,024)................	—	1.00	12.00
☐ 2256	8.4c Wheel Chair, 8/12/88, Tucson, AZ (136,337)...........	—	1.00	12.00
☐ 2257	10c Canal Boat, 4/11/87, Buffalo, NY (171,952)	—	1.00	10.00
☐ 2258	13c Patrol Wagon, 10/29/88, Anaheim, CA (132,928)	—	1.25	10.00
☐ 2259	13.2c Coal Car, 7/19/88, Pittsburgh, PA (123,965)..........	—	1.25	12.00
☐ 2260	15c Tugboat, 7/12/88, Long Beach, CA (134,926)...........	—	1.25	12.00
☐	1st One Fifty-Five Co. cachet.................................		20.00	
☐ 2261	16.7c Popcorn Wagon, 7/7/88, Chicago, IL (117,908).....	—	1.25	14.00
☐ 2262	17.5c Racing Car, 9/25/87, Indianapolis, IN	—	1.25	
☐ 2262a	Racing Car, untagged (Bureau precanceled)..................	—	5.00	
☐ 2263	20c Cable Car, 10/28/88, San Francisco, CA (150,068)...	—	1.25	12.00
☐ 2264	20.5c Fire Engine, 9/28/88, San Angelo, TX (123,043)...	—	1.25	12.00
☐ 2265	21c Railroad Mail Car, 8/16/88, Santa Fe, NM (124,430)		1.25	12.00
☐ 2266	24.1c Tandem Bicycle, 10/26/88, Redmond, WA (136,593)..	—	1.25	12.00

SCOTT NUMBER	DESCRIPTION	SINGLE	BLOCK	PLATE BLOCK	CERM PROG

1987

SCOTT NUMBER	DESCRIPTION	SINGLE
☐ 2267	22c "Congratulations," 4/20/87, Atlanta, GA 1.75	
☐ 2268	22c "Get Well," 4/20/87, Atlanta, GA.....................1.75	
☐ 2269	22c "Thank You," 4/20/87, Atlanta, GA..................1.75	
☐ 2270	22c "Love You, Dad," 4/20/87, Atlanta, GA 1.75	
☐ 2271	22c "Best Wishes," 4/20/87, Atlanta, GA.................1.75	
☐ 2272	22c "Happy Birthday," 4/20/87, Atlanta, GA...........1.75	
☐ 2273	22c "Love You, Mother," 4/20/87, Atlanta, GA 1.75	
☐ 2274	22c "Keep In Touch," 4/20/87, Atlanta, GA.............1.75	
☐ 2274a	Booklet pane of 10..7.00	15.00

Total for Scott 2267-2274 is 1,588,129.

☐ 2275	22c United Way Centenary, 4/28/87, DC				
	(556,391) (2 types)* 1.00	1.25	2.00	8.00*
☐ 2276	22c Flag & Fireworks, booklet single, 5/9/87,				
	Denver, CO (398,855) (2 types)*.....................1.00	1.25	2.00	8.00*
☐ 2276a	Flag & Fireworks, booklet pane of 20, 11/30/87 ...12.00				
☐ 2277	(25c) "E" & Earth, 3/22/88, DC................................1.25	1.25	2.00	
☐ 2278	25c Flag and Clouds, 5/6/88, Boxborough, MA				
	(131,265)..1.25	1.25	2.00	10.00
☐ 2279	(25c) "E" and Earth, coil, 3/22/88, DC....................1.25			
☐ 2280	25c Flag Over Yosemite, coil, 5/20/88,				
	Yosemite, CA (144,339)................................1.25			10.00
☐ 2281	25c Honeybee, coil, 9/2/88, Omaha, NE				
	(122,853)..1.25			12.00
☐	1st Ralph J. Pohl cachet 15.00			
☐ 2282	(25c) "E" & Earth, booklet single, 3/22/88, DC 1.25			
☐ 2282a	"E" & Earth, booklet pane of 10....................6.00			
	Total for Scott 2277, 2279 and 2282 is 363,639.			
☐	Scott 2277, 2279 and 2282 on one cover...........4.00			
☐ 2283	25c Pheasant, booklet single, 4/29/88, Rapid				
	City, SD (167,053) 1.25			
☐ 2283a	Pheasant, booklet pane of 10.................................6.00			15.00
☐ 2284	25c Owl, booklet single, 5/28/88, Arlington, VA. 1.25			
☐ 2285	25c Grosbeak, booklet single, 5/28/88,				
	Arlington, VA 1.25			
☐ 2285b	Booklet pane of 10..6.00			10.00
	Total for Scott 2284-2285 is 272,359.			
☐ 2285A	25c Flag and Clouds, booklet single, 7/5/88, DC				
	(117,303)..1.25			
☐ 2285c	Flag and Clouds, booklet pane of 6.........................4.00			
☐ 2286	22c Barn Swallow, 6/13/87, Toronto, ONT..............1.00			
☐ 2287	22c Monarch Butterfly, 6/13/87, Toronto, ONT 1.00			
☐ 2288	22c Bighorn Sheep, 6/13/87, Toronto, ONT 1.00			
☐ 2289	22c Broad-tailed Hummingbird, 6/13/87,				
	Toronto, ONT 1.00			
☐ 2290	22c Cottontail, 6/13/87, Toronto, ONT 1.00			
☐ 2291	22c Osprey, 6/13/87, Toronto, ONT 1.00			
☐ 2292	22c Mountain Lion, 6/13/87, Toronto, ONT 1.00			
☐ 2293	22c Luna Moth, 6/13/87, Toronto, ONT....................1.00			
☐ 2294	22c Mule Deer, 6/13/87, Toronto, ONT.....................1.00			
☐ 2295	22c Gray Squirrel, 6/13/87, Toronto, ONT 1.00			
☐ 2296	22c Armadillo, 6/13/87, Toronto, ONT 1.00			
☐ 2297	22c Eastern Chipmunk, 6/13/87, Toronto, ONT 1.00			
☐ 2298	22c Moose, 6/13/87, Toronto, ONT 1.00			
☐ 2299	22c Black Bear, 6/13/87, Toronto, ONT....................1.00			
☐ 2300	22c Tiger Swallowtail, 6/13/87, Toronto, ONT 1.00			
☐ 2301	22c Bobwhite, 6/13/87, Toronto, ONT......................1.00			
☐ 2302	22c Ringtail, 6/13/87, Toronto, ONT 1.00			
☐ 2303	22c Red-winged Blackbird, 6/13/87, Toronto,ONT..1.00			
☐ 2304	22c American Lobster, 6/13/87, Toronto, ONT 1.00			
☐ 2305	22c Black-tailed Jack Rabbit, 6/13/87, Toronto, ONT 1.00			
☐ 2306	22c Scarlet Tanager, 6/13/87, Toronto, ONT 1.00			
☐ 2307	22c Woodchuck, 6/13/87, Toronto, ONT...................1.00			
☐ 2308	22c Roseate Spoonbill, 6/13/87, Toronto, ONT 1.00			

	Scott Number	Description	Single	Plate Block	Cerm Block	Prog
☐	2309	22c Bald Eagle, 6/13/87, Toronto, ONT	1.00			
☐	2310	22c Alaskan Brown Bear, 6/13/87, Toronto, ONT	1.00			
☐	2311	22c Iiwi, 6/13/87, Toronto, ONT	1.00			
☐	2312	22c Badger, 6/13/87, Toronto, ONT	1.00			
☐	2313	22c Pronghorn, 6/13/87, Toronto, ONT	1.00			
☐	2314	22c River Otter, 6/13/87, Toronto, ONT	1.00			
☐	2315	22c Ladybug, 6/13/87, Toronto, ONT	1.00			
☐	2316	22c Beaver, 6/13/87, Toronto, ONT	1.00			
☐	2317	22c White-tailed Deer, 6/13/87, Toronto, ONT	1.00			
☐	2318	22c Blue Jay, 6/13/87, Toronto, ONT	1.00			
☐	2319	22c Pika, 6/13/87, Toronto, ONT	1.00			
☐	2320	22c Bison, 6/13/87, Toronto, ONT	1.00			
☐	2321	22c Snowy Egret, 6/13/87, Toronto, ONT	1.00			
☐	2322	22c Gray Wolf, 6/13/87, Toronto, ONT	1.00			
☐	2323	22c Mountain Goat, 6/13/87, Toronto, ONT	1.00			
☐	2324	22c Deer Mouse, 6/13/87, Toronto, ONT	1.00			
☐	2325	22c Black-tailed Prairie Dog, 6/13/87, Toronto, ONT	1.00			
☐	2326	22c Box Turtle, 6/13/87, Toronto, ONT	1.00			
☐	2327	22c Wolverine, 6/13/87, Toronto, ONT	1.00			
☐	2328	22c American Elk, 6/13/87, Toronto, ONT	1.00			
☐	2329	22c California Sea Lion, 6/13/87, Toronto, ONT	1.00			
☐	2330	22c Mockingbird, 6/13/87, Toronto, ONT	1.00			
☐	2331	22c Raccoon, 6/13/87, Toronto, ONT	1.00			
☐	2332	22c Bobcat, 6/13/87, Toronto, ONT	1.00			
☐	2333	22c Black-footed Ferret, 6/13/87, Toronto, ONT.	1.00			
☐	2334	22c Canada Goose, 6/13/87, Toronto, ONT	1.00			
☐	2335	22c Red Fox, 6/13/87, Toronto, ONT	1.00			
☐		1st Bennett Cachetoon cachet	30.00			
☐		Complete Set	75.00			
☐	2335a	Pane of 50	30.00		35.00	

1987-90 Ratification of the Constitution

	Scott Number	Description	Single	Plate Block	Cerm Block	Prog
☐	2336	22c Delaware, 7/4/87, Dover, DE (505,770)	1.75	2.00	2.50	12.00
☐	2337	22c Pennsylvania, 8/26/87, Harrisburg, PA (367,184)	1.75	2.00	2.50	12.00
☐	2338	22c New Jersey, 9/11/87, Trenton, NJ (432,899)	1.75	2.00	2.50	12.00
☐	2339	22c Georgia, 1/6/88, Atlanta, GA (467,804)	1.75	2.00	2.50	12.00
		1st 7-1-71 Chapter 50 cachet	15.00			
☐	2340	22c Connecticut, 1/9/88, Hartford, CT (379,706)	1.75	2.00	2.50	12.00
☐	2341	22c Massachusetts, 2/6/88, Boston, MA (412,616)	1.75	2.00	2.50	12.00
☐	2342	22c Maryland, 2/15/88, Annapolis, MD (376,403)	1.75	2.00	2.50	12.00
☐	2343	25c South Carolina, 5/23/88, Columbia, SC (322,938)	1.75	2.00	2.50	12.00
☐	2344	25c New Hampshire, 6/21/88, Concord, NH (374,402) (2 types)*	1.75	2.00	2.50	12.00*
☐	2345	25c Virginia, 6/25/88, Williamsburg, VA(474,079)	1.75	2.00	2.50	12.00
☐	2346	25c New York, 7/26/88, Albany, NY (385,793)	1.75	2.00	2.50	12.00
☐	2347	25c North Carolina, 8/22/89, Fayetteville, NC (392,953)	1.75	2.00	2.50	10.00
☐	2348	25c Rhode Island, 5/29/90, Pawtucket, RI (305,566) (2 types)*	1.75	2.00	2.50	14.00*

1987

	Scott Number	Description	Single	Plate Block	Cerm Block	Prog
☐	2349	22c U.S.-Morocco Diplomatic Relations, 7/17/87, DC (372,814)	1.00	1.25	1.50	10.00
☐		1st Anagram cachet	20.00			

January 2, 1788
Georgia

2339

January 9, 1788
Connecticut

2340

Feb 6, 1788
Massachusetts

2341

April 28, 1788 USA
Maryland 22

2342

Friendship
with Morocco
1787-1987

USA 22

2349

William Faulkner

2350

Lacemaking USA 22

2351-54

U.S. Constitution

2360

CPA

22 USA

2361

The Bicentennial
of the Constitution of
the United States
of America
1787-1987   USA 22

2355-59

Stourbridge Lion USA 22

2362-66

CHRISTMAS
22 USA

Morant, National Gallery

2367

USA 22 GREETINGS

2368

22 USA

2369

Happy Bicentennial
Australia!

1788
1988 USA 22

2370

James Weldon
Johnson
22

Black Heritage USA

2371

USA 22

Siamese Cat, Exotic Shorthair Cat

2372-75

22 USA

KNUTE ROCKNE

2376

156

Scott Number	Description	Single	Block	Plate Block	Cerm Prog
☐ 2349	with Morocco stamp........................75.00				
☐	1st Anagram Cachet with joint issue 75.00				
☐ 2350	22c William Faulkner, 8/3/87, Oxford, MS				
	(480,024)..1.00		1.25	1.50	8.00
☐ 2351	22c Lacemaking, 8/14/87 Ypsilanti, MI.............1.00				
☐ 2352	22c Lacemaking, 8/14/87 Ypsilanti, MI.............1.00				
☐ 2353	22c Lacemaking, 8/14/87 Ypsilanti, MI.............1.00				
☐ 2354	22c Lacemaking, 8/14/87 Ypsilanti, MI.............1.00				
☐ 2354a	Se-tenant, Lacemaking		2.75	3.50	8.00
☐ 2355	22c "The Bicentennial," 8/28/87, DC.................1.50				
☐ 2356	22c "We the People," 8/28/87, DC....................1.50				
☐ 2357	22c "Establish Justice," 8/28/87, DC 1.50				
☐ 2358	22c "And Secure," 8/28/87, DC 1.50				
☐ 2359	22c "Do Ordain," 8/28/87, DC 1.50				
☐ 2359a	Booklet pane of 5, Constitution Bicentennial..........9.00				10.00
	Total for Scott 2355-2359 is (1,008,799).				
☐ 2360	22c Signing of the Constitution, 9/17/87,				
	Philadelphia, PA (719,975) 1.00		1.25	1.50	
☐	1st Alexia cachet..25.00				
☐	1st Olde Well cachet 35.00				
☐ 2361	22c Certified Public Accounting, 9/21/87,				
	New York, NY (362,099) 10.00		11.00	15.00	30.00
☐ 2362	22c Stourbridge Lion, 10/1/87, Baltimore, MD........1.00				
☐ 2363	22c Best Friend of Charleston, 10/1/87,				
	Baltimore, MD..1.00				
☐ 2364	22c John Bull, 10/1/87, Baltimore, MD 1.00				
☐ 2365	22c Brother Jonathan, 10/1/87, Baltimore, MD 1.00				
☐ 2366	22c Gowan & Marx, 10/1/87, Baltimore, MD...........1.00				
☐ 2366a	Booklet pane of 5, Locomotives 3.00				15.00
	Total for Scott 2362-2366 is 976,694.				
☐ 2367	22c Christmas (Madonna & Child), 10/23/87,				
	DC (320,406)..1.00		1.25	1.50	8.00
☐ 2368	22c Christmas (Ornaments), 10/23/87,				
	Anaheim, CA (375,858)..............................1.00		1.25	1.50	16.00

1988

Scott Number	Description	Single	Block	Plate Block	Cerm Prog
☐ 2369	22c 1988 Winter Olympics, 1/10/88, Anchorage, AK				
	(395, 198)..1.00		1.25	1.50	10.00
☐ 2370	22c Australia Bicentennial, 1/26/88, DC				
	(523,465)..1.00		1.25	1.50	10.00
☐ 2370	with Australia stamp, dual cancels.................15.00				
☐ 2371	22c James Weldon Johnson, 2/2/88, Nashville, TN				
	(465,282)..1.00		1.25	1.50	10.00
☐ 2372	22c Siamese & Exotic Shorthair, 2/5/88,				
	New York, NY..2.50				
☐ 2373	22c Abyssinian & Himalayan, 2/5/88, New York, NY2.50				
☐ 2374	22c Maine Coon & Burmese, 2/5/88, New York, NY2.50				
☐ 2375	22c American Shorthair & Persian, 2/5/88,				
	New York, NY..2.50				
☐ 2375a	Se-tenant Cats, (872,734).............................		6.00	8.00	12.00
☐ 2376	22c Knute Rockne, 3/9/88, Notre Dame, IN				
	(404,311)..4.00		4.50	5.00	15.00
☐ 2377	25c Francis Ouimet, 6/13/88, Brookline, MA				
	(383,168)..4.00		4.50	5.00	15.00
☐ 2378	25c Love, 7/4/88, Pasadena, CA (399,038) 1.25		1.50	1.75	

2377

2390-93

2379

2378

2380

2386-89

2394

2395-98

2399

2400

	Scott Number	Description	Single	Block	Plate Block	Cerm Prog
☐	2379	45c Love, 8/8/88, Shreveport, LA (121,808) 1.25		2.00	2.50	10.00
☐	2380	25c Summer Olympics, 8/19/88, Colorado Springs, CO				
		(402,616)..1.25		1.50	1.75	10.00
☐	2381	25c 1928 Locomobile, 8/25/88, Detroit, MI.........1.25				
☐	2382	25c 1929 Pierce-Arrow, 8/25/88, Detroit, MI..........1.25				
☐	2383	25c 1931 Cord, 8/25/88, Detroit, MI......................1.25				
☐	2384	25c 1932 Packard, 8/25/88, Detroit, MI 1.25				
☐	2385	25c 1935 Duesenberg, 8/25/88, Detroit, MI.............1.25				
☐	2385a	Booklet pane of 5...3.00				12.00
		Total for Scott 2381-2385 is 875,801.				
☐	2386	25c Nathaniel Palmer, 9/14/88, DC........................1.25				
☐	2387	25c Lt. Charles Wilkes, 9/14/88, DC.....................1.25				
☐	2388	25c Richard E. Byrd, 9/14/88, DC 1.25				
☐	2389	25c Lincoln Ellsworth, 9/14/88, DC 1.25				
☐	2389a	Se-tenant, Antarctic Explorers, (720,537)		3.00	3.50	10.00
☐	2390	25c Deer, 10/1/88, Sandusky, OH..........................1.50				
☐	2391	25c Horse, 10/1/88, Sandusky, OH 1.50				
☐	2392	25c Camel, 10/1/88, Sandusky, OH 1.50				
☐	2393	25c Goat, 10/1/88, Sandusky, OH 1.50				
☐	2393a	Se-tenant, Carousel Animals, (856,380)...................		3.50	4.00	30.00
☐	2394	$8.75 Eagle in Flight, 10/4/88, Terre Haute, IN				
		(66,558)...30.00		40.00	50.00	25.00
☐		Sheet of 20 ....350.00				
☐	2395	25c "Happy Birthday," 10/22/88,				
		King of Prussia, PA...1.25				
☐	2396	25c "Best Wishes," 10/22/88, King of Prussia, PA...1.25				
☐	2396a	Booklet pane of 6 (3 No. 2395 +3 No. 2396) 4.00				18.00
☐	2397	25c "Thinking of You," 10/22/88, King of				
		Prussia, PA..1.25				
☐	2398	25c "Love You," 10/22/88, King of Prussia, PA........1.25				
☐	2398a	Booklet pane of 6 (3 No. 2397 + 3 No. 2398) 4.00				
		Total for Scott 2395-2398 is 126, 767.				
☐	2399	25c Christmas (Madonna), 10/20/88, DC (247,291).1.25		1.50	1.75	10.00
☐	2400	25c Christmas (Sleigh & Village), 10/20/88,				
		Berlin, NH (412,213)..1.25		1.50	1.75	10.00

1989

	Scott Number	Description	Single	Block	Plate Block	Cerm Prog
☐	2401	25c Montana Statehood, 1/15/89, Helena, MT				
		(353,319)..1.25		1.50	1.75	8.00
☐		1st Steve Wilson cachet 30.00				
☐	2402	25c A. Philip Randolph, 2/3/89, New York, NY				
		(363,174)...1.25		1.50	1.75	10.00
☐	2403	25c North Dakota Statehood, 2/21/89, Bismarck, ND				
		(306,003)...1.25		1.50	1.75	6.00
☐	2404	25c Washington Statehood, 2/22/89, Olympia,WA				
		(445,174)...1.25		1.50	1.75	6.00
☐	2405	25c Experiment, 3/3/89, New Orleans, LA...............1.25				
☐	2406	25c Phoenix, 3/3/89, New Orleans, LA...................1.25				
☐	2407	25c New Orleans, 3/3/89, New Orleans, LA 1.25				
☐	2408	25c Washington, 3/3/89, New Orleans, LA...............1.25				
☐	2409	25c Walk in the Water, 3/3/89, New Orleans,LA......1.25				
☐	2409a	Booklet pane of 5...4.00				10.00
		Total for Scott 2405-2409 is 981,674.				
☐	2410	25c World Stamp Expo '89, 3/16/89, New York,NY				
		(296,310)..1.25		1.50	1.75	6.00

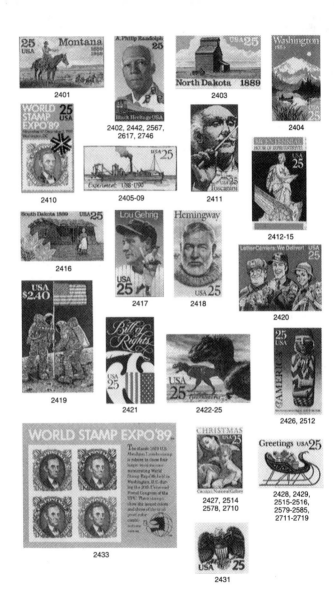

2401

2402, 2442, 2567,
2617, 2746

2403

2404

2410

2405-09

2411

2412-15

2416

2417

2418

2420

2419

2421

2422-25

2426, 2512

2433

2427, 2514
2578, 2710

2428, 2429,
2515-2516,
2579-2585,
2711-2719

2431

160

SCOTT NUMBER	DESCRIPTION	SINGLE	BLOCK	PLATE BLOCK	CERM PROG
☐ 2411	25c Arturo Toscanini, 3/25/89, New York, NY (309,441)......................1.25		1.50	1.75	6.00

1989-90

SCOTT NUMBER	DESCRIPTION	SINGLE	BLOCK	PLATE BLOCK	CERM PROG
☐ 2412	25c House of Representatives, 4/4/89, DC (327,755)1.25		1.50	1.75	6.00
☐ 2413	25c Senate, 4/6/89, DC (341,288)............................1.25		1.50	1.75	100.00
☐ 2414	25c Executive Branch, 4/16/89, Mount Vernon, VA 1.25		1.50	1.75	6.00
☐ 2415	25c Supreme Court, 2/2/90, DC................................1.25		1.50	1.75	6.00

1989

SCOTT NUMBER	DESCRIPTION	SINGLE	BLOCK	PLATE BLOCK	CERM PROG
☐ 2416	25c South Dakota Statehood, 5/3/89, Pierre, SD (348,370)......................1.25		1.50	1.75	6.00
☐ 2417	25c Lou Gehrig, 6/10/89, Cooperstown, NY (694,227)......................6.00		7.00	9.00	15.00
☐	1st Edken cachet............................25.00				
☐ 2418	25c Ernest Hemingway, 7/17/89, Key West, FL (345,436)......................1.25		1.50	1.75	8.00
☐ 2419	$2.40 Moon Landing, 7/20/89, DC (208,982) 7.00		12.00	17.50	8.00
	(with NASA program)				60.00
☐ 2420	25c Letter Carriers, 8/30/89, Milwaukee, WI (372,241)......................1.25		1.50	1.75	6.00
☐ 2421	25c Bill of Rights, 9/25/89, Philadelphia, PA (900,384)......................1.25		1.50	1.75	6.00
☐ 2422	25c Tyrannosaurus Rex, 10/1/89, Orlando, FL.......1.25				
☐ 2423	25c Pteranodon, 10/1/89, Orlando, FL....................1.25				
☐ 2424	25c Stegosaurus, 10/1/89, Orlando, FL....................1.25				
☐ 2425	25c Brontosaurus, 10/1/89, Orlando, FL..................1.25				
☐ 2425a	Se-tenant, Dinosaurs, (871,634)..............		3.00	3.50	20.00
☐ 2426	25c America, 10/12/89, San Juan, PR (215,285)......1.25		1.50	1.75	
☐ 2427	25c Christmas (Madonna & Child), 10/19/89,DC (395,321)......................1.25		1.50	1.75	
☐ 2427a	Booklet pane of 10......................6.00				8.00
☐ 2427, 2427a	Traditional Christmas, sheet stamp & booklet pane (10/19/89), DC				8.00
☐ 2428	25c Christmas (Sleigh), 10/19/89, Westport, CT......1.25		1.50	1.75	
☐ 2428, 2429a	Contemporary Christmas sheet stamp & booklet pane (10/19/89), Westport, CT				8.00
☐ 2429	25c Christmas (Sleigh), booklet single, 10/19/89, Westport, CT 1.25				
☐ 2429a	Booklet pane of 10......................6.00				
	Total for Scott 2428-2429a was 345,931.				
☐ 2431	25c Eagle & Shield, self-adhesive, booklet single, 11/10/89, Virginia Beach, VA......................1.25				6.00
☐ 2433	90c World Stamp Expo, souvenir sheet of 4, 11/17/89, DC 15.00				20.00
☐ 2434	25c Stagecoach, 11/19/89, DC................................1.25				
☐ 2435	25c Paddlewheel Steamer, 11/19/89, DC.................1.25				
☐ 2436	25c Biplane, 11/19/89, DC......................................1.25				
☐ 2437	25c Depot-hack type Automobile, 11/19/89, DC 1.25				
☐ 2437a	Se-tenant, Traditional Mail Delivery, (916,389).............		3.00	3.50	10.00
☐ 2438	25c Traditional Mail Delivery, souvenir sheet of 4, 11/28/89, DC (241,634)......................2.00				10.00

1990

SCOTT NUMBER	DESCRIPTION	SINGLE	BLOCK	PLATE BLOCK	CERM PROG
☐ 2439	25c Idaho Statehood, 1/6/90, Boise, ID (252,493)......................1.25		1.50	1.75	18.00

☐	2440	**25c Love,** 1/18/90, Romance, AR.............................1.25	1.50	1.75	
☐	2441	**25c Love,** booklet single, 1/18/90, Romance, ID.......1.25			
☐	2441a	**Love,** booklet pane of 10 ....7.00			
		Total for Scott 2440-2441a was 257, 788.			
☐	2440-2441a	**Love,** sheet stamp & booklet pane, Romance, AR...			6.00
☐	2442	**25c Ida B. Wells,** 2/1/90, Chicago, IL (229,226) 1.25	1.50	1.75	12.00
☐	2443	**25c Beach Umbrella,** booklet single, 2/3/90,			
		Sarasota, FL...1.50			
☐	2443a	**Beach Umbrella,** booklet pane of 10 (72,286) 8.00			6.00
☐	2444	**25c Wyoming Statehood,** 2/23/90, Cheyenne, WY			
		(317,654)...1.25	1.50	1.75	6.00
☐	2445	**25c The Wizard of Oz,** 3/23/90, Hollywood, CA 3.00			18.00
☐	2446	**25c Gone with the Wind,** 3/23/90, Hollywood,CA 3.00			18.00
☐	2447	**25c Beau Geste,** 3/23/90, Hollywood, CA 1.25			18.00
☐	2448	**25c Stagecoach,** 3/23/90, Hollywood, CA 1.25			18.00
☐	2448a	**Se-tenant** (863,079)	7.00	9.00	14.00
☐	2449	**25c Marianne Moore,** 4/18/90, Brooklyn, NY			
		(390,535)...1.25	1.50	1.75	6.00

1990-95 Transportation Coil

☐	2451	**4c Steam Carriage,** 1/25/91, Tucson, AZ (100,393).....— pr 1.00	
☐	2452	**5c Circus Wagon,** 8/31/90, Syracuse, NY (71,806).......— pr 1.00	8.00
☐	2452B	**5c Circus Wagon,** photogravure, 12/8/92	
		Cincinnati, OH ....— pr 1.25	
☐	2452D	**5c Circus Wagon,** photogravure, with cent sign,	
		3/20/95, Kansas City, MO (20,835) ....— pr 1.25	
☐	2453	**5c Canoe,** engraved, 5/25/91, Secaucus, NJ	
		(108,634)...— pr 1.25	10.00
☐	2454	**5c Canoe,** photogravure, 10/22/91,	
		Secaucus, NJ...— pr 1.25	
☐	2457	**10c Tractor Trailer,** 5/25/91, Secaucus, NJ	
		(84,717) ....— pr 1.25	10.00
☐	2458	**10c Tractor Trailer,** photogravure, 5/25/94 (15,431) ..— pr 1.25	
☐	2463	**20c Cog Railway,** 6/9/95, Dallas, TX (28,883)..............— pr 1.25	
☐	2464	**23c Lunch Wagon,** 4/12/91, Columbus, OH	
		(115,830) ....— pr 1.25	
☐	2466	**32c Ferry Boat,** 6/2/95, McLean, VA 1.25	
☐	2468	**$1 Seaplane,** 4/20/90, Phoenix, AZ ....3.00 pr 4.00	10.00

1990

☐	2470	**25c Admiralty Head,** WA, 4/26/90, DC.....................1.75	
☐	2471	**25c Cape Hatteras,** NC, 4/26/90, DC 1.75	
☐	2472	**25c West Quoddy Head,** ME, 4/26/90, DC...............1.75	
☐	2473	**25c American Shoals,** FL, 4/26/90, DC 1.75	
☐	2474	**25c Sandy Hook,** NJ, 4/26/90, DC.............................1.75	8.00
☐	2474a	**Booklet pane of 5** (805, 133) 4.50	10.00
☐	2475	**25c Flag,** plastic self-adhesive, 5/18/90, Seattle, WA	
		(97,567)...1.25	6.00

1991-95 Flora & Fauna

☐	2476	**1c Kestrel,** 6/22/91, Aurora, CO (77,781) ....—	1.25	12.00
☐	2477	**1c Kestrel** with cent sign, 5/10/95, Aurora, CO		
		(21,767) ....—	1.25	
☐	2478	**3c Eastern Bluebird,** 6/22/91, Aurora, CO (76,149) ....—	1.25	
☐		Scott **2476 and 2478** on one cover.....................3.00		
☐	2479	**19c Fawn,** 3/11/91, DC (100,212) 1.25		

cover binders

Padded, durable, 3-ring binder will hold up to 100 covers. Features the "D" ring mechanism on the right hand side of album so you don't have to worry about creasing or wrinkling covers when opening or closing binder.

Item	Description	Retail
CBRD	Cover Binder - Red	$7.95
CBBL	Cover Binder - Blue	$7.95
CBGY	Cover Binder - Gray	$7.95
CBBK	Cover Binder - Black	$7.95
	Cover pages sold separately.	
T2	Cover Pages Black (25 per pckg)	$4.95
CBBL	Cover Pages Clear (25 per pckg)	$4.95

The cover binders and pages are available from your favorite stamp dealer or direct from:

SCOTT

P.O. Box 828 Sidney OH 45365-0828

to order call 1-800-572-6885

163

2434-2438

2440-2441,
2535-2536, 2618

2444

2475, 2522

2449

2439

2543

2445-2448

2470-2474

2481-2494

2476

2501-2505

OLYMPIAN

2496-2500

2506-2507

2508-2511

2513

2517-2520
2524-2527

2521

2523, 2523A

2529

2530

2528

2531

2532

2533

164

☐ 2480	30c **Cardinal**, 6/22/91, Aurora, CO (101,290)..........1.25				
☐ 2481	45c **Pumpkinseed Sunfish**, 12/2/92, DC (38,696).....1.75				6.00
☐ 2482	$2 **Bobcat**, 6/1/90, Arlington, VA (49,660)................7.00		11.00	15.00	10.00
☐ 2483	20c **Blue Jay**, booklet single, 6/15/95,				
	Kansas City, MO (16,847) ....—		1.25		
☐ 2483a	**Booklet pane of 10** 8.00				
☐ 2484	29c **Wood Duck**, black denomination, 4/12/91,				
	Columbus, OH 1.25				
☐ 2484a	**Booklet pane of 10** 9.00				
☐ 2485	29c **Wood Duck**, red denomination, 4/12/91,				
	Columbus, OH 1.25				
☐ 2485a	**Booklet pane of 10** 9.00				

First day cancel was applied to 205,305 covers bearing one or more of Nos. 2484-2485 2484a-2485a.

☐ 2486	29c **African Violet**, 10/8/93, Beaumont, TX (40,167)1.25				
☐ 2486a	**Booklet pane of 10** 5.00				
☐ 2487	32c **Peach**, bklt single, 7/8/95, Reno, NV..............1.25				
☐ 2488	32c **Pear**, bklt single, 7/8/95, Reno, NV...................1.25				
☐ 2488a	**Booklet pane of 10, 5 each #2487-2488** 8.00				
☐ 2488b	**Pair 2487-2488** 1.50				
☐ 2489	29c **Red Squirrel**, 6/25/93, Milwaukee, WI (48,546)1.25				6.00
☐ 2489a	**Booklet pane of 18** 14.00				
☐ 2490	29c **Red Rose**, 8/19/93, Houston, TX (37,916)..........1.25				
☐ 2490a	**Booklet pane of 18** 14.00				
☐ 2491	29c **Pine Cone**, 11/5/93, Kansas City, MO (110,929).1.25				
☐ 2491a	**Booklet pane of 18** 14.00				
☐ 2492	29c **Pink Rose**, 6/2/95, McLean, VA..........................1.25				

First Day cancel was applied to 59,100 covers bearing one or more of Nos. 2466, 2492

☐ 2493	32c **Peach**, serpentine, die cut, 7/8/95, Reno, NV 1.25				
☐ 2494	32c **Pear**, serpentine die cut, 7/8/95, Reno,NV.........1.25				
☐ 2495	32c **Peach**, serpentine die cut, vert., 7/8/95,				
	Reno, NV..1.25				
☐ 2495A	32c **Pear**, serpentine die cut vert., 7/8/95, Reno, NV1.25				

First Day cancels was applied to 71,086 covers bearing Nos. 2487-2488, 2488a, 2493-2495A

1990

☐ 2496	25c **Jesse Owens**, 7/6/90, Minneapolis, MN..............1.25				8.00
☐ 2497	25c **Ray Ewry**, 7/6/90, Minneapolis, MN...................1.25				
☐ 2498	25c **Hazel Wightman**, 7/6/90, Minneapolis, MN.......1.25				
☐ 2499	25c **Eddie Eagan**, 7/6/90, Minneapolis, MN..............1.25				
☐ 2500	25c **Helene Madison**, 7/6/90, Minneapolis, MN........1.25				
☐ 2500a	**Strip of 5, Olympians**, (1,143,404) 5.00	5.00	6.00	10.00	
☐ 2501	25c **Assiniboin**, 8/17/90, Cody, WY 1.25				
☐ 2502	25c **Cheyenne**, 8/17/90, Cody, WY 1.25				
☐ 2503	25c **Comanche**, 8/17/90, Cody, WY 1.25				
☐ 2504	25c **Flathead**, 8/17/90, Cody, WY 1.25				
☐ 2505	25c **Shoshone**, 8/17/90, Cody, WY 1.25				
☐ 2505a	**Booklet pane of 10**, 2 each, #2501-2505 (979,580).6.00				6.00
☐ 2506	25c **Federated States of Micronesia**, 9/28/90, DC				
	(3 types)*...1.25				8.00*
☐ 2507	25c **Republic of the Marshall Islands**, 9/28/90,DC ..1.25				

☐ 2507a **Se-tenant Pair, Nos. 2506-2507** 2.50   3.00
    Total for Scott 2506-2507a was 343,816.
☐   Scott 2506-2507 with Micronesia and Marshall Islands stamps
     dual cancel...15.00
☐ 2508   25c **Killer Whales,** 10/3/90, Baltimore, MD..............1.25   10.00
☐ 2509   25c **Northern Sea Lions,** 10/3/90, Baltimore, MD....1.25
☐ 2510   25c **Sea Otter,** 10/3/90, Baltimore, MD....................1.25
☐ 2511   25c **Common Dolphin,** 10/3/90, Baltimore, MD........1.25
☐ 2508-2511   with Russia stamps 5.00
☐ 2508-2511   with Russia stamps, dual cancels 15.00
☐ 2511a   **Se-tenant,** Sea Creatures, (706,047)
     Baltimore, MD, Grand Rapids, MI....................   4.00   4.50   10.00
☐ 2512   25c **Grand Canyon,** 10/12/90, Grand Canyon, AZ
     (164,190)..1.25   1.50   1.75   16.00
☐ 2513   25c **Dwight D. Eisenhower,** 10/13/90, Abilene, KS
     (487,988)..1.25   1.50   1.75   8.00
☐ 2514   25c **Christmas (Madonna & Child),** 10/18/90,
     DC (378,383) 1.25   1.50   1.75   8.00
     Error program (2514 only) 12.00
☐ 2514a **Booklet pane of 10,** 10/18/90 ....10.00
☐ 2515   25c **Christmas (Tree),** sheet stamp, 10/18/90,
     Evergreen, CO...1.25   1.50   1.75   8.00
     Error program (2515 only) 12.00
☐ 2516   25c **Christmas (Tree),** booklet single, 10/18/90,
     Evergreen, CO...1.25
☐ 2516a **Booklet pane of 10** 6.00
     Total for Scott 2515-2516a was 230,586.

1991-92

☐ 2517   (29c) **Flower,** non-denominated sheet stamp,
     1/22/91, DC..1.25   1.50   1.75
☐ 2518   (29c) **Flower,** non-denominated coil stamp,
     1/22/91, DC..1.25
☐ 2519   (29c) **Flower,** non-denominated booklet single
     (printed by BEP), 1/22/91, DC 1.25
☐ 2519a **Booklet pane of 10** 6.00
☐ 2520   (29c) **Flower,** non-denominated booklet single
     (printed by KCS), 1/22/91, DC 1.25
☐ 2520a **Booklet pane of 10** 6.00
☐ 2521   (4c) **Make-up rate,** non-denominated, text only,
     1/22/91, DC..1.25   1.50   1.75
☐ 2522   (29c) **Flag,** non-denominated ATM single,
     self-adhesive, 1/22/91, DC...............................1.25
☐ 2523   29c **Flag over Mt. Rushmore,** engraved, 3/29/91,
     Mt. Rushmore, SD (233,793)...........................1.25   1.50   6.00
☐ 2523A 29c **Flag over Mt. Rushmore,** photogravure, 7/4/91,
     Mt. Rushmore, SD (80,662)..............................1.25   1.50
☐ 2524   29c **Flower,** 4/5/91 Rochester, NY (132,233)..........1.25   1.50   1.75   12.00
☐ 2525   29c **Flower,** roulette 10 coil, 8/16/91, Rochester, NY
     (144,750)..1.25   1.50
☐ 2526   29c **Flower,** perf. 10 coil, 3/3/92, Rochester, NY
     (35,877)..1.25   1.50
☐ 2527   29c **Flower,** bklt. single, 4/5/91, Rochester, NY 1.25   1.50
☐ 2524, 2527   **Flower,** sheet & booklet, 4/5/91 ....   12.00
☐ 2527a **Booklet pane of 10** 6.00

167

First day cancel was applied to 16,975 covers
bearing one or more of Nos. 2527-2527a.

☐ 2528　29c **Flag and Olympic Rings**, bklt. single, 4/21/91, Atlanta, GA..1.25 — — 10.00

☐ 2528　29c **Flag and Olympic Rings**, (not 1st day), 4/22/91 Austin, TX .... — — 15.00

Ceremony Programs (not 1st day), 4/22/91, Bismarck, ND (set of 7)

☐ 2528a **Booklet pane of 10** 5.00

☐ 2529　19c **Fishing Boat**, two loops 8/8/91, DC (82,698)........— 1.25

☐ 2529C 19c **Fishing Boat**, one loop, 6/25/94, Arlington, VA (14,538) ....— 1.25

☐ 2530　19c **Balloon**, 5/17/91, Denver, CO 1.25

☐ 2530, C129, UC63, UC63a, 19c **Balloon**, 40c William Piper, 45c Eagle aerograms, 5/17/91, Denver CO 12.00

☐ 2530a **Booklet pane of 10** 6.00

First day cancel was applied to 96,351 covers
bearing one or more of Nos. 2530-2530a.

☐ 2531　29c **Flags on Parade**, 5/30/91, Waterloo, NY (104,046)...1.25 1.50 1.75 6.00

☐ 2531A 29c **Liberty Torch**, 6/25/91 New York, NY (68,456) .1.25

1991-93

☐ 2532　50c **Switzerland**, 2/22/91, DC (316,047)...................1.35 1.75 2.50 6.00
☐ 　　　Scott 2532 with Switzerland stamp, dual cancel....15.00
☐ 2533　29c **Vermont**, 3/1/91, Bennington, VT (308,105)......1.25 1.50 1.75 6.00
☐ 2534　29c **Savings Bonds**, DC 4/30/91 (341,955) 1.25 1.50 1.75 6.00
☐ 2535　29c **Love**, 5/9/91, Honolulu, HI (336,132).................1.25 1.50 1.75
☐ 2536　29c **Love**, bklt. single, 5/9/91, Honolulu, HI..............1.25
☐ 2536a **Booklet pane of 10** 5.00

First day cancel was applied to 43,336 covers
bearing one or more of Nos. 2536-2536a.

☐ 2537　52c **Love**, 5/9/91, Honolulu, HI (90,438)...................1.35 1.75 2.00
☐ 2535, 2537, U621 29c **Love** stamps & envelope......................... 6.00
☐ 2538　29c **William Saroyan**, 5/22/91, Fresno, CA (334,373)1.25 1.50 1.75 6.00
☐ 　　　Scott 2538 with Russian stamp, dual cancel 15.00
☐ 2539　$1 **Eagle & Olympic Rings**, 9/29/91, Orlando, FL (69,241)...3.00 6.00 7.50 6.00
☐ 2540　$2.90 **Eagle & Olympic Rings**, 7/7/91, San Diego, CA (79,555)...10.00 40.00 50.00 15.00
☐ 2541　$9.95 **Eagle & Olympic Rings**, 6/16/91, Sacramento, CA (68,657) 25.00 85.00 100.00 25.00
☐ 2542　$14 **Eagle**, 8/31/91, Hunt Valley, MD (54,727)........30.00 125.00 150.00
☐ 2543　$2.90 **Futuristic Space Shuttle**, 6/3/93, Kennedy Space Center, FL 8.00 40.00 50.00 15.00
☐ 2544　$3 **Challenger Shuttle**, 6/22/95, Anaheim, CA 8.00 15.00 17.00 14.00
☐ 2544A $10.75 **Endeavour Shuttle**, Express Mail, 8/4/95, Irvine, CA 25.00 45.00 50.00 22.00
☐ 2549a 29c **Fishing Flies booklet pane of 5**, 5/31/91, Cuddebackville, NY (1,045,726)........................3.00 12.00
☐ 2545-2549, any single...1.25
☐ 2550　29c **Cole Porter**, 6/8/91, Peru, IN (304,363) 1.25 1.50 1.75 6.00
☐ 2551　29c **Desert Storm/ Desert Shield**, 7/2/91, DC 2.00 2.50 3.00 10.00

SCOTT NUMBER	DESCRIPTION	SGL	CACHETED BLK	PL BLK

☐ 2552 **29c Desert Storm/ Desert Shield,** bklt. single,
7/2/91, DC (cerm. prog. includes No. 2551)......2.00   50.00

☐ 2552a Booklet pane of 5 ....4.00   8.00
     First day cancel was applied to 860,455 covers
     bearing one or more of Nos. 2551-2552, 2552a.

☐ 2557a **29c Summer Olympics,** 7/12/91, Los Angeles, CA
(886,984)..3.00   8.00

☐ 2553-2557, any single 1.25

☐ 2558 **29c Numismatics,** 8/13/91, Chicago, IL (288,519)....1.25   1.50   1.75   6.00

2534

2537

2559, 2697, 2765

2545-2549

2540-2542

2539

2543

2550

2551-2552

2558

2560

2561

2562-2566

2568-2577

2594, 2594B

2595-2597

2604-2606

2607

2608-608B

2609

2616

2619

2620-2629

		SINGLE	BLOCK	BLOCK	PROG
☐ 2559	29c **World War II Souvenir block of 10,** 9/3/91,				
	Phoenix, AZ (1,832,967) 10.00				12.00
☐ 2559a-2559j, any single 1.25					
☐ 2560	29c **Basketball,** 8/28/91, Springfield, MA (295,471).2.00		2.50	3.50	12.00
☐ 2561	29c **District of Columbia,** 9/7, DC (299,989) (2 types)*1.25		1.50	1.75	12.00*
☐ 2566a	29c **Comedians booklet pane of 10,** 8/29/91,				
	Hollywood, CA..6.00				8.00
☐ 2562-2566, any single..1.50					
	First day cancel was applied to 954,293 covers				
	bearing one or more of Nos. 2562-2566a.				
☐ 2567	29c **Jan Matzeliger,** 9/15/91, Lynn, MA (289,034) ...1.25		1.50	1.75	8.00
☐ 2577a	29c **Space Exploration booklet pane of 10,** 10/1/91,				
	Pasadena, CA 5.00				10.00
☐ 2568-2577, any single..1.25					
	First day cancel was applied to 1,465,111 covers				
	bearing one or more of Nos. 2568-2577a.				
☐ 2578	(29c) **Christmas (religious),** 10/17/91, Houston, TX 1.25		1.50	1.75	6.00
☐ 2579	(29c) **Christmas (secular),** 10/17/91, Santa, ID				
	(169,750)..1.25		1.50	1.75	
☐ 2579, 2980-2985 29c **Contemporary Christmas**					6.00
☐ 2581b	(29c) **Christmas booklet pane of 4,** 10/17/91,				
	Santa, ID...2.50				
☐ 2580-2581, any single..1.25					
☐ 2582	(29c) **Christmas,** bklt. single, 10/17/91, Santa, ID....1.25				
☐ 2582a	**Booklet pane of 4** 2.50				
☐ 2583	(29c) **Christmas,** bklt. single, 10/17/91, Santa, ID....1.25				
☐ 2583a	**Booklet pane of 4** 2.50				
☐ 2584	(29c) **Christmas,** bklt. single, 10/17/91, Santa, ID....1.25				
☐ 2584a	**Booklet pane of 4** 2.50				
☐ 2585	(29c) **Christmas,** bklt. single, 10/17/91, Santa, ID....1.25				
☐ 2585a	**Booklet pane of 4** 2.50				
☐ 2587	32c **Polk,** 11/2/95, Columbia, TN 2.00		2.25	2.50	8.00
☐ 2590	$1 **Surrender at Saratoga,** 5/5/94, New York, NY ...3.50		4.50	5.00	8.00
☐ 2592	$5 **Washington & Jackson,** 8/19/94, Pittsburgh, PA.17.50		24.00	30.00	12.00
☐ 2593	29c **Pledge of Allegiance,** black denomination,				
	9/8/92, Rome, NY 1.25				6.00
☐ 2593a **Booklet pane of 10** 5.00					
	First day cancel was applied to 61,464 covers				
	bearing one or more of Nos. 2594-2594a.				
☐ 2595	29c **Eagle & Shield,** brown denomination, 9/25/92,				
	Dayton, OH...1.25				
☐ 2596	29c **Eagle & Shield,** green denomination, 9/25/92,				
	Dayton, OH...1.25				
☐ 2597	29c **Eagle & Shield,** red denomination, 9/25/92,				
	Dayton, OH...1.25				
	First day cancel was applied to 65,822 covers				
	bearing one or more of Nos. 2595-2597.				
☐ 2595-2597 **Eagle & Shield** 4.00					10.00
☐ 2598	29c **Eagle ATM,** 2/4/94, Sarasota, FL (67,300).........1.25				6.00
☐ 2599	29c **Statue of Liberty,** 6/24/94, Haines City, FL(39,810)1.25				6.00
☐ 2602	(10c) **Eagle & Shield,** Bulk Rate USA, 12/13/91,				
	Kansas City, MO 1.25		1.50		
☐ 2603	(10c) **Eagle & Shield,** USA Bulk Rate, 5/29/93,				
	Secaucus, NJ 1.25		1.50		

☐ 2604	**(10c) Eagle & Shield,** gold eagle, 5/29/93, Secaucus, NJ 1.25	1.50	
☐ 2605	**23c Flag,** 9/27/91, DC..1.25	1.50	10.00
☐ 2606	**23c Reflected Flag,** 7/21/92, Kansas City, MO (35,673)..1.25	1.50	
☐ 2607	**23c Reflected Flag,** 7mm "23" 10/9/92, Kansas City, MO 1.25	1.50	
☐ 2608	**23c Reflected Flag,** 8 1/2mm "First Class" 5/14/93, Denver, CO 1.25	1.50	
☐ 2609	**29c Flag over White House,** 4/23/92 , DC (56,505)..1.25	1.50	

1992

☐ 2615a	**29c Winter Olympics,** strip of 5, 1/11/92, Orlando, FL (1,062,048)..3.00			
☐ 2611-2615, any single 1.25				
☐ 2616	**29c World Columbian Stamp Expo,** 1/24/92, Rosemont, IL (309,729)...................................1.25	1.50	1.75	10.00
☐	1st Info cachet 25.00			
☐ 2617	**29c W.E.B. Du Bois,** 1/31/92, Atlanta, GA (196,219)1.25	1.50	1.75	18.00
☐ 2618	**29c Love,** 2/6/92, Loveland, CO (218,043)..............1.25	1.50	1.75	10.00
☐ 2619	**29c Olympic Baseball,** 4/3/92, Atlanta, GA (105,996)4.00	5.00	7.00	
☐ 2623a	**29c Voyages of Columbus,** block of 4, 4/24/92, Christiansted, VI (509,170) 2.75			
☐ 2620-2623, any single 1.25				8.00
☐	Scott 2620-2623 with Italy stamps, dual blue cancel 450.00			
☐ 2624	**First Sighting of Land Souvenir Sheet of 3,** 5/22/92, Chicago, IL 5.00			
☐ 2624a	**1c** 1.25			
☐ 2624b	**4c** 1.25			
☐ 2624c	**$1** 3.00			
☐ 2625	**Claiming a New World Souvenir Sheet of 3,** 5/22/92, Chicago, IL 12.00			
☐ 2625a	**2c** 1.25			
☐ 2625b	**3c** 1.25			
☐ 2625c	**$4** 10.00			
☐ 2626	**Seeking Royal Support Souvenir Sheet of 3,** 5/22/92, Chicago, IL 4.00			
☐ 2626a	**5c** 1.25			
☐ 2626b	**30c** 1.25			
☐ 2626c	**50c** 2.00			
☐ 2627	**Royal Favor Restored Souvenir Sheet of 3,** 5/22/92, Chicago, IL 12.00			
☐ 2627a	**6c** 1.25			
☐ 2627b	**8c** 1.25			
☐ 2627c	**$3** 8.00			
☐ 2628	**Reporting Discoveries Souvenir Sheet of 3,** 5/22/92, Chicago, IL 15.00			
☐ 2628a	**10c** 1.25			
☐ 2628b	**15c** 1.25			
☐ 2628c	**$2** 6.00			
☐ 2629	**$5 Christopher Columbus Souvenir Sheet,** 5/22/92, Chicago, IL 15.00			
☐ 2624-2629 Columbian Souvenir Sheets				60.00

First day cancel was applied to 211,142 covers
bearing one or more of Nos. 2624-2629.

2630

2631

2635

Kentucky 1792
2636

2637

2642

2647

2698

2699

2700

2704

2705

2710

2711

2720

2721

2741

2746

2747

174

SCOTT NUMBER	DESCRIPTION	SINGLE	BLOCK	PLATE BLOCK	CERM PROG
☐ 2630	29c New York Stock Exchange, 5/17/92, New York, NY (261,897)..........................1.25		1.50	1.75	6.00
☐ 2634a	29c Space Accomplishments, block of 4, 5/29/92, Chicago, IL 2.75				6.00
☐ 2631-2634, any single 1.25					
	First day cancel was applied to 277,853 covers bearing one or more of Nos. 2631-2634a.				
☐ 2531-2634	with Russia stamps, dual cancels 15.00				
☐ 2635	29c Alaska Highway, 5/30/92, Fairbanks, AK (186,791)..1.25		1.50	1.75	6.00
☐ 2635	With Canada No. 1413, dual cancels,...........15.00				
☐ 2636	29c Kentucky, 6/1/92, Danville, KY (251,153)..........1.25		1.50	1.75	6.00
☐ 2641a	29c Summer Olympics, strip of 5, 6/11/92, Baltimore, MD (713,942)..3.00				
☐ 2637-2641, any single 1.25					
☐ 2646a	29c Hummingbirds booklet pane of 5, 6/15/92, DC...4.00				22.00
☐ 2642-2646, any single 1.25					
	First day cancel was applied to 995,278 covers bearing one or more of Nos. 2642-2646a.				
☐ 2696a	29c Wildflowers, pane of 50, 7/24/92, Columbus, OH (3,693,972) (2 types)*.....................................30.00				8.00*
☐ 2647-2696, any single 1.25					
☐ 2697	29c World War II Souvenir block of 10, 8/17/92, Indianapolis, IN (1,734,880) 8.00				10.00
☐ 2697a-2697j, any single 1.50					
☐ 2698	29c Dorothy Parker, 8/22/92, West End, NJ (266,323)..1.25		1.50	1.75	6.00
☐ 2699	29c Theodore von Karman, 8/31, DC (256,986) 1.25		1.50	1.75	28.00
☐ 2699	With Hungary No. 3353, dual cancels,...........15.00				
☐ 2703a	29c Minerals, DC 9/17/92 (681,416)........................2.75				10.00
☐ 2700-2703, any single 1.25					10.00
☐ 2704	29c Juan Rodriguez Cabrillo, 9/28/92, San Diego, CA (290,720)..1.25		1.50	1.75	
☐ 2709a	29c Wild Animals booklet pane of 5, 10/1/92, New Orleans, LA 3.25		8.00		6.00
☐ 2705-2709, any single 1.50					
	First day cancel was applied to 604,205 covers bearing one or more of Nos. 2705-2709a.				
☐ 2710	29c Christmas (religious), 10/22/92, DC 1.25		1.50	1.75	6.00
☐ 2710a Booklet pane of 10 ....7.25					
	First day cancel was applied to 201,576 covers bearing one or more of Nos. 2710-2710a.				
☐ 2714a	29c Christmas (secular), 10/22/92, Kansas City, MO..2.75				
☐ 2711-2714, any single 1.25					
☐ 2718a	29c Christmas (secular) booklet pane of 4, 10/22/92, Kansas City, MO 2.75				6.00
☐ 2715-2718, any single 1.25					
☐ 2715-2718	29c Contemporary Christmas................................				6.00
	First day cancel was applied to 461,937 covers bearing one or more of Nos. 2711-2714, 2715-2718 and 2718a.				
☐ 2719	29c Christmas (secular), self-adhesive, 10/28/92, New York, NY (48,873) 1.25				8.00
☐ 2720	29c Chinese New Year, 12/30/92, San Francisco, CA..1.25		1.50	1.75	6.00

1993

☐ 2721	29c Elvis (Presley), 1/8/93, Memphis, TN, AM cancellation..2.00		2.50	4.00	14.00

Scott Number	Description	Single	Block	Plate Block	Cerm Prog
☐	Any city, PM cancellation	1.75	2.00	2.25	
☐ 2722	29c Oklahoma!, 3/30/93, Oklahoma City, OK	1.25	1.50	1.75	25.00
☐ 2723	29c Hank Williams, 6/9/93, Nashville, TN	1.25	1.50	1.75	
☐ 2730a	29c Rock & Roll/Rhythm & Blues Musicians, strip of 7,				
	6/16/93, Cleveland, OH or Santa Monica, CA	5.00			10.00
☐	Any other city	5.00			
☐ 2724-2730, any single		1.25			
☐	Any single, any other city	1.25			
	Value for No. 2730a is also for any se-tenant				
	configuration of seven different stamps.				
☐ 2737a	29c Rock & Roll/Rhythm & Blues Musicians booklet				
	pane of 8, 6/16/93, Cleveland, OH or				
	Santa Monica, CA	5.25			
☐	Any other city	5.25			
☐ 2731-2737, any single		1.25			
☐	Any single, any other city	1.25			
☐ 2737b	29c Rock & Roll/Rhythm & Blues Musicians booklet				
	pane of 4, 6/16/93, Cleveland, OH or				
	Santa Monica, CA	3.00			
☐	Any other city	3.00			
☐ 2745a	29c Space Fantasy booklet pane of 5, 1/25/93,				
	Huntsville, AL	3.25			8.00
☐ 2741-2745, any single		1.25			
☐ 2746	29c Percy Lavon Julian, 1/29/93, Chicago, IL	1.25	1.50	1.75	12.00
☐ 2747	29c Oregon Trail, 2/12/93, Salem, OR	1.25	1.50	1.75	6.00
	No. 2747 was also available on the first day of issue				
	in 36 cities along the route of the Oregon Trail.				
☐ 2748	29c World University Games, 2/25/93, Buffalo, NY	2.00	2.25	2.50	6.00
☐ 2749	29c Grace Kelly, 3/24/93, Beverly Hills, CA	1.25	1.50	1.75	20.00
☐ 2749	With Monaco No. 1851, dual cancels,	15.00			
☐ 2753a	29c Circus, block of 4, 4/6/93, DC	3.50			15.00
☐ 2750-2753, any single		1.50			
☐ 2754	29c Cherokee Strip Land Run, 4/17/93, Enid, OK	1.25	1.50	1.75	6.00
☐ 2755	29c Dean Acheson, 4/21/93, DC	1.25	1.50	1.75	6.00
☐ 2759a	29c Sporting Horses, 5/1/93, Louisville, KY	3.50			8.00
☐ 2756-2759, any single		1.75			
☐ 2764a	29c Garden Flowers booklet pane of 5, 5/15/93,				
	Spokane, WA	3.25			6.00
☐ 2760-2764, any single		1.25			
☐ 2774a	29c Country Music, 9/25/93, Nashville, TN	2.75			
☐ 2771-2774, any single, 9/25/93		1.25			
☐ 2778a	29c Country Music bklt pane of 4, 9/25/93,				
	Nashville, TN	2.75			
☐ 2775-2778 any single		1.25			
☐ 2765	29c World War II Souvenir block of 10, 5/31/93, DC	7.00			15.00
☐ 2765a-2765j, any single		1.50			
☐ 2766	29c Joe Louis, 6/22/93, Detroit, MI	1.25	1.50	1.75	25.00
☐ 2770a	29c Broadway Musicals booklet pane of 4,				
	7/14/93, New York, NY	3.25			25.00
☐ 2767-2770, any single		1.25			
☐ 2782a	29c National Postal Museum, block of 4,				
	7/30/93, DC	2.75			6.00
☐ 2779-2782, any single		1.25			
☐ 2784a	29c Deafness/Sign Language, se-tenant pair, 9/20/93,				
	Burbank CA	2.00			8.00

cover sleeves

Protect your covers with 2 mil crystal clear
polyethylene sleeves. (Sold in packages of 100.)

U.S. Postal Cards

Item		Retail
CV005	5 7/8" x 3 3/4"	$3.95

U.S. First Day Cover #6

Item		Retail
CV006	6 3/4" x 3 3/4"	$3.95

Continental
Postcard

Item		Retail
CV007	6 1/4" x 4 1/4"	$4.95

European
Standard Envelope

Item		Retail
CV008	7 1/4" x 4 5/8"	$4.95

European FDC

Item		Retail
CV009	7 " x 5 3/8"	$4.95

#10 Business Envelope

Item		Retail
CV010	10 1/8" x 4 1/2"	$5.95

P.O. Box 828 Sidney OH 45365-0828

to order call 1-800-572-6885

2748

2749

2750

2754

2755

2756

2760

2779

2783

2785

2789

2791

2804

2805

2806

2807

2812

2813

2814

2815

SCOTT NUMBER	DESCRIPTION	SINGLE	BLOCK	PLATE BLOCK	CERM PROG
☐ 2783-2784, any single		1.25			6.00
☐ 2788a	29c **Classic Books,** block of 4, 10/23/93, Louisville, KY	2.75			25.00
☐ 2785-2788, any single		1.25			
☐ 2789	29c **Christmas (religious)**, 10/21/93, Raleigh, NC	1.25	1.50	1.75	6.00
☐ 2790	29c **Christmas (religious)**, booklet single, 10/21/93, Raleigh, NC	1.25			
☐ 2790a	**Booklet pane of 4**	2.00			
☐ 2794a	29c **Christmas (secular)**, sheet stamps, 10/21/93, New York, NY	2.75			
☐ 2791-2794, any single		1.25			
☐ 2798a	29c **Christmas (secular)** booklet pane of 10, 10/21/93, New York, NY	6.50			
☐ 2798b	29c **Christmas (secular)** booklet pane of 10, 10/21/93, New York, NY	6.50			
☐ 2795-2798, any single		1.25			
☐ 2799	29c **Christmas (snowman)**, large self-adhesive, 10/28/93, New York, NY	1.25			
☐ 2799-2802	**Contemporary Christmas,** self-adhesive				6.00
☐ 2800	29c **Christmas (soldier)**, self-adhesive, 10/28/93, New York, NY	1.25			
☐ 2801	29c **Christmas (jack-in-the-box)**, self-adhesive, 10/28/93, New York, NY	1.25			
☐ 2802	29c **Christmas (reindeer)**, self-adhesive, 10/28/93, New York, NY	1.25			
☐ 2799-2802 on one cover		2.50			6.00
☐ 2803	29c **Christmas (snowman)**, small self-adhesive, 10/28/93, New York, NY	1.25			
☐ 2804	29c **Mariana Islands**, 11/4/93, Saipan, MP	1.25	1.50	1.75	6.00
☐ 2805	29c **Columbus' Landing in Puerto Rico**, 11/19/93, San Juan, PR	1.25	1.50	1.75	6.00
☐ 2806	29c **AIDS Awareness**, 12/1/93, New York, NY	1.25	1.50	1.75	14.00
☐ 2806a	29c **AIDS Awareness**, booklet single, perf. 11 vert., 12/1/93, New York, NY	1.25			
☐ 2806b	**Booklet pane of 5**	3.25			

1994

SCOTT NUMBER	DESCRIPTION	SINGLE	BLOCK	PLATE BLOCK	CERM PROG
☐ 2811a	29c **Winter Olympics**, strip of 5, 1/6/94, Salt Lake City, UT	3.00			6.00
☐ 2807-2811, any single		1.25			
☐ 2812	29c **Edward R. Murrow**, 1/21/94, Pullman, WA	1.25	1.50	1.75	6.00
☐ 2813	29c **Love**, self-adhesive, 1/27/94, Loveland, OH	1.25			6.00
☐ 2814	29c **Love**, booklet single, 2/14/94, Niagara Falls, NY	1.25			6.00
☐ 2814a	**Booklet pane of 10**	6.50			
☐ 2814C	29c **Love**, 6/11/94, Niagara Falls, NY	1.25	1.50	1.75	
☐ 2815	52c **Love**, 2/14/94, Niagara Falls, NY	1.35	2.75	3.00	6.00
☐ 2816	29c **Dr. Allison Davis**, 2/1/94, Williamstown, MA	1.25	1.50	1.75	6.00
☐ 2817	29c **Chinese New Year**, 2/5/94, Pomona, CA	1.25	1.50	1.75	12.00
☐ 2818	29c **Buffalo Soldiers**, 4/22/94, Dallas, TX	1.25	1.50	1.75	15.00
☐	1st Dynamite Cover	20.00			

No. 2818 was also available on the first day of issue in forts in Kansas, Texas and Arizona.

2816   2817   2818   2819

2829   2834   2839   2841a

2842   2843   2848

2849   2854   2862   2863

2867   2871   2872   2873   2874

☐ 2828a	29c **Silent Screen Stars,** block of 10, 4/27/94,				
	San Francisco, CA 7.00				10.00
☐ 2819-2828, any single 1.50					
☐ 2833a	29c **Garden Flowers** booklet pane of 5, 4/28/93,				
	Cincinnati, OH 3.25				10.00
☐ 2829-2833, any single 1.25					
☐ 2834	29c **World Cup Soccer,** 5/26/94, New York, NY........1.25	1.50	1.75	12.00
☐ 2835	40c **World Cup Soccer,** 5/26/94, New York, NY........1.25	2.25	2.50	12.00
☐ 2836	50c **World Cup Soccer,** 5/26/94, New York, NY........1.35	2.50	2.75	12.00
☐ 2837	**World Cup Soccer,** Souvenir Sheet, 5/26/94,				
	New York, NY..				12.00
☐ 2838	29c **World War II** Souvenir block of 10, 6/6/94,				
	USS Normandy 10.00				12.00
☐ 2838a-2838j, any single.......................................1.50					
	No. 2838 was also available on the first day of				
	issue in 13 other locations.				
☐ 2839	29c **Norman Rockwell,** 7/1/94, Stockbridge, MA 1.25	1.50	1.75	10.00
☐ 2840	50c **Norman Rockwell** Souvenir Sheet of 4, 7/1/94,				
	Stockbridge, MA 5.00				10.00
☐ 2840a-2840d, any single.......................................1.60					
☐ 2841	29c **Moon Landing** Sheet of 12, 7/20/94, DC 10.00				12.00
☐ 2841a	single stamp 1.35				
☐ 2842	**$9.95 Moon Landing,** 7/20/94, DC........................25.00	85.00	100.00	
☐ 2847a	29c **Locomotives** booklet pane of 5, 7/28/94,				
	Chama, NM 3.25				8.00
☐ 2843-2847 Any single...1.25					
☐ 2848	29c **George Meany,** 8/16/94, DC 1.25	1.50	1.75	6.00
☐ 2853a	29c **American Music Series,** 9/1/94, New York, NY 4.00				
☐ 2849-2853 Any single 1.25					
☐ 2861a	29c **American Music,** 9/17/94, Greenville MS 6.00				10.00
☐ 2854-2861 Any single 1.25					
☐ 2862	29c **James Thurber,** 9/10/94, Columbus, OH 1.25	1.50	1.75	6.00
☐ 2866a	29c **Wonders of the Sea,** 10/3/94, Honolulu, HI 3.50				10.00
☐ 2863-2866 Any single..1.25					
☐ 2868a	29c **Cranes,** 10/9/94, DC 2.00				10.00
☐ 2867-2868 Any single..1.25					
☐ 2867-2868 with China stamp, dual cancels....................20.00					
☐ 2869	29c **Legends of the West,** pane of 20,10/18/94,				
	Laramie, WY, Tucson, AZ or Lawton, OK, ...30.00				12.00
☐ 2869a-2869t Any single 1.25					
☐ 2869	Any other city, any single 1.75				
☐ 2871	29c **Christmas, religious,** 10/20/94, DC 1.25	1.50	1.75	8.00
☐ 2871A	Perf. 9 3/4 x 11 ....1.25				
☐ 2872	**Christmas** (stocking), 10/20/94, Harmony, MN....1.25	1.50	1.75	
☐ 2873	**Christmas** (Santa), 10/20/94, Harmony, MN 1.25				
☐ 2874	**Christmas** (cardinal), 10/20/94, Harmony, MN........1.25				
☐ 2875	**$2 Bureau of Engraving & Printing,** souvenir sheet				
	of 4, 11/3/94, New York, NY 25.00				25.00
☐	Major Double Transfer, 11/3/94 1,500				
☐ 2876	29c **Chinese New Year,** 12/30/94, Sacramento, CA..1.50	1.75	2.00	12.00

1994-97

☐ 2877	(3c) **Dove, bright blue,** 12/13/94, DC........................1.50				
☐ 2878	(3c) **Dove, dark blue,** 12/13/94, DC...........................1.50				
☐ 2879	(20c) **G, black,** 12/13/94, DC...................................1.50				
☐ 2880	(20c) **G, red,** 12/13/94, DC.....................................1.50				

2876

2877

2879

2881

2888

2897

2902

2905

2908

2911

2919

2948

2949

2950

2951

2955

2956

2976

2980

2983

2993

2998

☐ 2881	(32c) G, **black**, 12/13/94, DC	1.50			
☐ 2881a	**Booklet pane of 10**	6.00			
☐ 2882	(32c) G, **red**, 12/13/94, DC	1.50			
☐ 2883	(32c) G, **black**, perf 10x9.9 booklet stamp, 12/13/94, DC	1.50			
☐ 2883a	**Booklet pane of 10**	6.00			
☐ 2884	(32c) G, **black**, perf 10.9 booklet stamp, 12/13/94, DC	1.50			
☐ 2884a	**Booklet pane of 10**	6.00			
☐ 2885	(32c) G, **red**, booklet stamp,12/13/94, DC	1.50			
☐ 2885a	**Booklet pane of 10**	6.00			
☐ 2886	(32c) G, **gray, blue, light blue, red & black**, self-adhesive, 12/13/94, DC	1.50			
☐ 2887	(32c) G, **black, blue & red**, self-adhesive, 12/13/94, DC	1.50			
☐ 2888	(25c) G, **black**, coil stamp, 12/13/94, DC	1.50			
☐ 2889	(32c) G, **black**, coil stamp, 12/13/94, DC	1.50			
☐ 2890	(32c) G, **blue**, coil stamp, 12/13/94, DC	1.50			
☐ 2891	(32c) G, **red**, coil stamp, perforated, 12/13/94, DC	1.50			
☐ 2892	(32c) G, **red**, coil stamp, rouletted, 12/13/94, DC	1.50			
☐ 2893	(5c) G coil, nonprofit, 12/31/94, DC	2.00			
☐ 2897	32c Flag over porch, 5/19/95, Denver, CO	1.25	1.50	1.75	
☐ 2902	(5c) Butte, coil, 3/10/95 State College, PA	1.25			
☐ 2902B	(5c) Butte, self-adhesive coil, 6/15/96 San Antonio, TX	1.25			
☐ 2903	(5c) **Mountain**, purple & multi coil, 3/16/96 San Jose, CA	—pr 1.25			8.00
☐ 2904	(5c) **Mountain**, blue & multi coil, 3/16/96 State College, PA	—pr 1.25			
☐ 2904A	(5c) **Mountain**, self-adhesive coil, 6/15/96, San Antionio, TX	1.25			
☐ 2904B	(5c) **Mountain**, Self-adhesive, inscription outlined, 1/24/97, Tuscon, AZ	1.25			
☐ 2905	(10c) **Auto**, coil, 3/10/95, State College, PA	—pr 1.25			
☐ 2906	(10c) **Auto**, self-adhesive coil, 6/15/96, San Antonio, TX	1.25			
☐ 2907	(10c) **Eagle & Shield**, USA Bulk Rate, self-adhesive coil, 5/21/96, DC	1.25			
☐ 2908	(15c) **Auto tail fin**, orange dk yellow, coil, 3/17/95, New York, NY	—pr 1.25			
☐ 2909	(15c) **Auto tail fin**, buff, coil, 3/17/95, New York, NY	—pr 1.25			
☐ 2910	(15c) **Auto tail fin**, buff, self-adhesive coil, 6/15/96, San Antonio, TX	1.25			
☐ 2911	(25c) **Juke Box**, coil, 3/17/95, New York, NY	—pr 1.25			
☐ 2912	(25c) **Juke Box**, coil, 3/17/95, New York, NY	—pr 1.25			
☐ 2912A	(25c) **Juke Box**, self-adhesive coil, serpentine die cut, 11.5 vert., 6/15/96, New York, NY	1.25			
☐ 2912B	(25c) **Juke Box**, self-adhesive coil, serpentine die cut 9.8 vert., 1/24/97, Tuscon, AZ	1.25			
☐ 2913	32c **Flag over porch**, coil, 5/19/95, Denver, CO	1.25			
☐ 2914	32c **Flag over porch**, coil, 5/19/95, Denver, CO	1.25			
☐ 2915	32c **Flag over porch**, self-adhesive, serpentine die cut 8.7, 4/18/95, DC	1.25			
☐ 2915A	32c **Flag over porch**, serpentine die cut 9.8 vert., 11 teeth, 5/21/96, DC	1.25			

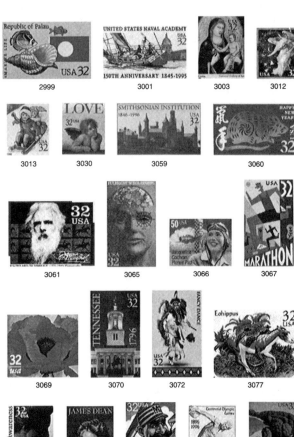

2999

3001

3003

3012

3013

3030

3059

3060

3061

3065

3066

3067

3069

3070

3072

3077

3081

3082

3083

3087

3088

		SINGLE	PLATE BLOCK	CERM PROG	
☐ 2915B	**32¢ Flag over porch,** self adhesive, serpentine die cut 11.5, 6/15/95, San Antonio, TX 1.25				
☐ 2915C	**32c Flag over porch,** serpentine die cut 10.9, 5/21/96, DC...1.25				
☐ 2915D	**32c Flag over porch,** serpentine die cut 9.8 vert., 9 teeth btwn cuts, 1/24/97, Tuscon, AZ 1.25				
☐ 2916	**32c Flag over porch,** booklet single, 5/19/95, Denver, CO 1.25				
☐ 2916a	booklet pane of 10 ....7.50				
☐ 2919	**32c Flag over field,** self-adhesive, 3/17/95...............1.25				
☐ 2920	**32c Flag over porch,** self-adhesive, 4/18/95, Washington, DC...1.25				
☐ 2921	**32c Flag over porch,** booklet single, serpentine die cut 9.8 on 2 or 3 adjacent sides, 5/21/96, DC 1.25				
☐ 2933	**32c Milton Hershey,** 7/11/95, Hershey, PA 1.25	1.50	1.75	8.00	
☐ 2934	**32c Cal Farley,** 4/26/96, Amarillo, TX 1.25			8.00	
☐ 2935	**32c Henry Luce,** 4/3/98, New York...........................1.25	1.50	1.75	10.00	
☐ 2936	**32c Lila & DeWitt Wallace,** 7/16/98, Pleasantville, Ny1.25	1.50	1.75	12.00	
☐ 2938	**46c Ruth Benedict,** 10/20/95, Virginia Beach, VA.....1.35	1.60	1.85		
☐ 2940	**55c Alice Hamilton,** 7/11/95, Boston, MA 1.35	1.60	1.85	8.00	
☐ 2941	**55c Justin S. Morrill,** self-adhesive, 6/17/99, Strafford, VT..1.50				
☐ 2942	**77c Mary Breckinridge,** self-adhesive, 11/9/98, Troy, NY..1.75	4.00	4.50		
☐ 2943	**78c Alice Paul,** 8/18/95, Mount Laurel, NJ...............1.50	1.75	2.00	8.00	

1995

		SINGLE	PLATE BLOCK	CERM PROG	
☐ 2948	**(32c) Love,** 2/1/95, Valentines, VA 1.25	1.50	1.75		
☐ 2949	**(32c) Love,** self adhesive, 2/1/95, Valentines, VA 1.25	1.50	1.75	8.00	
☐ 2950	**32c Florida Statehood,** 3/3/95, Tallahassee, FL.........1.25	1.50	1.75	10.00	
☐ 2954a	**32c Earth Day,** 4/20/95, DC 2.75				
☐ 2951-2954, block of 4, any single...1.25					
☐ 2955	**32c Richard Nixon,** 4/26/95, Yorba Linda, CA 1.25	1.50	1.75	10.00	
☐ 2956	**32c Bessie Coleman,** 4/27/95, Chicago, IL................1.25	1.50	1.75	10.00	
☐ 2957	**32c Love,** 5/12/95, Lakeville, PA..............................1.25	1.50	1.75		
☐ 2958	**55c Love,** 5/12/95, Lakeville, PA..............................1.35				
☐ 2959	**32c Love,** booklet single, 5/12/95, Lakeville, PA.......1.25				
☐ 2959a	booklet pane of 10 ....7.50				
☐ 2960	**55c Love,** self adhesive, 5/12/95, Lakeville, PA 1.35				
☐ 2965a	**32c Recreational Sports,** 5/20/95, Jupiter, FL 3.25				
☐ 2961-2965, any single...1.50				12.00	
☐ 2966	**32c Prisoners of War & Missing in Action,** 5/29/95, DC...2.00	2.25	2.50	12.00	
☐ 2967	**32c Marilyn Monroe,** 6/1/95, Universal City, CA 1.25	1.50	1.75	12.00	
☐	Any other city..1.25	1.50	1.75	8.00	
☐ 2968	**32c Texas Statehood,** 6/16/95, Austin, TX 1.25	1.50	1.75		
☐ 2973a	**32c Great Lakes Lighthouses,** booklet pane of 5, 6/17/96, Cheboygan, MI 5.00				
☐ 2969-2973, any single...1.75				12.00	
☐ 2974	**32c UN, 50th Anniv.,** 6/26/95, San Francisco...........1.25	1.50	1.75	10.00	
☐ 2974	**With UN Nos. 663-664, dual cancels,** 15.00				
☐ 2975	**32c Civil War sheet of 20,** 6/29/95, Gettysburg, PA13.00			10.00	
☐	Any other city..13.00				
☐ 2975a-2975t, any single, Gettysburg, PA...............................1.25					
☐	Any other city..1.25			12.00	
☐ 2979a	**32c Carousel Horses,** 7/21/95, Lahaska, PA....................	3.25			
☐ 2976-2979, any single...1.25				10.00	

3090

3091

3096

3100

3104

3106

3107

3108

3109

3110

3111

3117

3118

3120

3121

3122

3123

3124

3125

☐ 2980	32c Women Suffrage, 8/26,95, DC	1.25	1.50	1.75	12.00
☐ 2981	32c World War II Souvenir block of 10, 9/2/95,				
	Honolulu, HI	7.00			
☐ 2981a-2981j, any single		1.50			
☐ 2982	32c American Music Series, 9/1/95,				
	New Orleans, LA	1.25	1.50	1.75	14.00
☐ 2992a	32c American Music Series, 9/16/95, Monterey, CA	6.50			18.00
☐ 2983-2992, any single		1.25			
☐ 2997a	32c Garden Flowers booklet pane of 5,				
	9/19/96, Encintas, CA	4.00			12.00
☐ 2993-2997, any single		1.25			
☐ 2998	60c Eddie Rickenbacker, 9/25/95, Columbus, OH	1.50	1.75	2.00	8.00
☐ 2999	32c Republic of Palau, 9/29/95, Agana, GU	1.25	1.50	1.75	8.00
☐ 2999	With Palau No. 378, dual cancels,	15.00			
☐ 3000	32c Comic Strips Pane of 20, 10/1/95,				
	Boca Raton, FL	20.00			18.00
☐ 3000a-3000t, any single		2.00			
☐ 3001	32c US Naval Academy, 10/10/95, Annapolis, MD	1.25	1.50	1.75	8.00
☐ 3002	32c Tennessee Williams, 10/13/95, Clarksdale, MS.	1.25	1.50	1.75	8.00
☐ 3003	32c Christmas Madonna, 10/19/95, DC	1.25	1.50	1.75	8.00
☐ 3003A	Perf. 9.8x10.9	1.25	1.50	1.75	
☐ 3003Ab Booklet pane of 10		7.25			
☐ 3007a	32c Christmas (secular) sheet, 9/30/95,				
	North Pole, NY		3.25		10.00
☐ 3004-3007, any single		1.25			
☐ 3007b Booklet pane of 10, 3 #3004, etc.		7.25			
☐ 3007c Booklet pane of 10, 2 #3004, etc.		7.25			
☐ 3008	32c Christmas (Santa, Sled) self-adhesive bklt.,				
	9/30/95, North Pole, NY	1.25			
☐ 3009	32c Christmas (Jumping Jack) self-adhesive bklt.,				
	9/30/95, North Pole, NY	1.25			
☐ 3010	32c Christmas (Santa, Chimney) self-adhesive bklt.,				
	9/30/95, North Pole, NY	1.25			
☐ 3011	32c Christmas (Child, Tree) self-adhesive bklt.,				
	9/30/95, North Pole, NY	1.25			
☐ 3008-3011 on one cover		1.25			
☐ 3012	32c Angel, 10/19/95, Christmas, FL	1.25			12.00
☐ 3013	32c Children sledding, 10/19/95, Christmas, FL.	1.25			
☐ 3014	32c Christmas (Santa, Sled), self-adhveive coil,				
	9/30/95, North Pole, NY	1.25			
☐ 3015	32c Christmas (Jumping Jack), self-adhesive coil,				
	9/30/95, North Pole, NY	1.25			
☐ 3016	32c Christmas (Santa, Chimney), self-adhesive coil,				
	9/30/95, North Pole, NY	1.25			
☐ 3017	32c Christmas, (Child, Tree), self-adhesive coil,				
	9/30/95, North Pole, NY	1.25			
☐ 3014-3017 on one cover		3.25			8.00
☐ 3018	32c Angel, Self adhesive coil, 10/19/95,				
	Christmas, FL	1.25			
☐ 3023a	32c Antique Automobiles, 11/3/95, New York , NY.	3.25			12.00
☐ 3019-3023, any single		1.25			
☐ 3024	32c Utah Statehood Cent.,1/4/96, Salt Lake City, UT	1.25	1.50	1.75	8.00
☐ 3029a	32c Garden Flowers booklet pane, 1/19/96,				
	Kennett Square, PA	4.00			12.00
☐ 3025-3029, any single		1.25			

☐ 3030	**32c Love self-adhesive,** 1/20/96, New York , NY 1.25				
☐ 3032	**2c Red-headed woodpecker,** 2/2/96, Sarasota, FL....1.25		1.50	1.75	10.00
☐ 3033	**3c Eastern Bluebird,** 4/3/96, DC 1.25		1.50	1.75	10.00
☐ 3036	**$1 Red Fox,** self-adhesive, 8/14/98, DC 2.00				
☐ 3044	**1c American Kestrel,** coil, 1/20/96, New York, NY ..1.25		1.50	1.75	8.00
☐ 3045	**2c Red-headed Woodpecker,** self-adhesive,				
	6/22/99, DC..1.25				
☐ 3048	**20c Blue Jay,** booklet stamp, self-adhesive, 8/2/96,				
	St. Louis, MO..1.25				
☐ 3049	**32c Yellow Rose,** booklet stamp, self-adhesive, 10/24/96,				
	Pasadena, CA (7,849)..1.25				8.00
☐ 3050	**20c Ring-necked Pheasant,** booklet stamp, self-adhesive,				
	7/31/98, Somerset, NJ 1.25pr				
☐ 3052	**33c Coral Pink Rose,** booklet stamp, self-adhesive, 8/13/99,				
	Indianapolis, IN..1.25				
☐ 3053	**20c Blue Jay,** coil stamp, self-adhesive, 8/2/96,				
	St. Louis, MO..1.25				
	First day cancel was applied to 32,633 covers bearing one				
	or more of Nos. 3048-3053.				
☐ 3054	**32c Yellow Rose,** self-adhesive coil, 8/1/97,				
	Falls Church, VA 1.25				
☐ 3055	**20c Ring-necked Pheasant,** coil stamp, self-adhesive,				
	7/31/98, Somerset, NJ 1.25pr				
☐ 3058	**32c Ernest E. Just,** 2/1/96, DC..............................1.25		1.50	1.75	8.00
☐ 3059	**32c Smithsonian, 150th anniv.,** 2/7/96, DC............1.25		1.50	1.75	14.00
☐ 3060	**32c Chinese New Year,** 2/8/96, San Francisco, CA ..1.25		1.50	1.75	14.00
☐ 3064a	**32c Pioneers of Commuication,** 2/22/96,				
	New York, NY..		3.25		12.00
☐ 3061-3064, any single...1.25					
☐ 3065	**32c Fulbright Scholarships,** 2/28/96,				
	Fayetteville, AR...1.25		1.50	1.75	8.00
☐ 3066	**50c Jacquline Cochran,** 3/9/96, Indio, CA...............1.35		1.75	2.00	8.00
☐ 3067	**32c Marathon,** 4/11/96, Boston, MA 1.25		1.50	1.75	12.00
☐ 3068	**32c Olympics, pane of 20,** 5/2/96, DC 20.00				
☐ 3068a-3068t, any single...1.25			1.50	1.75	15.00
☐ 3069	**32c Georgia O'Keeffe,** 5/23/96, Santa Fe, NM 1.25		1.50	1.75	12.00
☐ 3070	**32c Tennessee Statehood, Bicen.,** 5/31/96,				
	Knoxville, Memphis or Nashville, TN................1.25		1.50	1.75	14.00
☐ 3071	**32c Tennessee,** self-adhesive, 5/31/96,				
	Knoxville, Memphis or Nashville, TN................1.25				
☐ 3070-3071 on one cover 1.75					
☐ 3076a	**32c American Indian Dances, strip of 5,** 6/7/96,				
	Oklahoma City, OK 3.50				
☐ 3072-3076, any single..1.25					15.00
☐ 3080a	**32c Prehistoric Animals,** 6/8/96, Toronto, Canada.........		4.00		
☐ 3077-3080, any single...1.25					15.00
☐ 3081	**32c Breast Cancer Awareness,** 6/15/96, DC 1.25		1.50	1.75	14.00
☐ 3082	**32c James Dean,** 6/24/96, Burbank, CA..................1.25		1.50	1.75	14.00
☐ 3086a	**32c Folk Heroes,** 7/11/96, Anaheim, CA..................3.25				
☐ 3083-3086, any single...1.25					15.00
☐ 3087	**32c Centennial Olympic Games,** 7/19/96,				
	Atlanta, GA..1.25		1.50	1.75	12.00
☐ 3088	**32c Iowa Statehood, 150th Anniv.,** 8/1/96,				
	Dubuque, IA..1.25		1.50	1.75	8.00
☐ 3089	**32c Iowa Statehood,** self-adhesive, 8/1/96,				
	Dubuque, IA..1.25				

☐ 3088-3089 on one cover 1.75
    First day cancel was applied to 215,181 covers bearing one or
    more of Nos. 3088-3089

☐ 3090   32c **Rural Free Delivery**, 8/7/96,
         Charleston, WV (192,070) 1.25   1.50   1.75   8.00

☐ 3095b 32c **Riverboats** strip of 5, 8/22/96, Orlando, FL 3.50
☐ 3091-3095 on one cover 3.50
☐ 3091-3095, **any single** 1.25   14.00
    First day cancel was applied to 770,384 covers bearing one
    or more of Nos. 3091-3095

☐ 3099a 32c **Big Band Leaders**, block of 4, 9/11/96,
         New York, NY 5.00
☐ 3096-3099, **any single** 1.25   15.00
☐ 3103a 32c **Songwriters**, block of 4, 9/11/96, New York, NY 5.00
☐ 3100-3103, **any single** 1.25   15.00
    First day cancel was applied to 1,235,166 covers bearing one or
    more of Nos. 3096-3103a

☐ 3104   23c **F. Scott Fitzgerald**, 9/27/96, St. Paul, MN (150,783) 1.25   1.50   1.75
☐ 3105   32c **Endangered Species**, pane of 15, 10/2/96,
         San Jose, CA 7.50
☐ 3105a-3105o, **any single** 1.25   15.00
    First day cancel was applied to 941,442 covers bearing one or
    more of Nos. 3105a-3105o

☐ 3106   32c **Computer Technology**, 10/8/96, Aberdeen Proving
         Ground, MD (153,688) 1.25   1.50   1.75   8.00
☐ 3107   32c **Christmas Madonna**, 11/1/96, Richmond, VA 1.25   1.50   1.75   8.00
☐ 3111a 32c **Christmas (Secular)**, 10/8/96, North Pole, AK 3.25   10.00
☐ 3108-3111, **any single** 1.25
☐ 3112   32c **Christmas Madonna**, self-adhesive, 11/1/96,
         Richmond, VA 1.25   10.00
    First day cancel was applied to 164,447 covers bearing one or
    more of Nos. 3107, 3112.

☐ 3113   32c **Family at fireplace**, self-adhesive, 10/8/96,
         North Pole, AK 1.25
☐ 3114   32c **Decorating Tree**, self-adhesive, 10/8/96,
         North Pole, AK 1.25
☐ 3115   32c **Dreaming of Santa**, self-adhesive, 10/8/96,
         North Pole, AK 1.25
☐ 3116   32c **Holiday shopping**, self-adhesive, 10/8/96,
         North Pole, AK 1.25
☐ 3113-3116 on one cover 3.25
☐ 3117   32c **Skaters**, self-adhesive, 10/8/96,
         North Pole, AK 1.25
    First day cancel was applied to 884,339 covers bearing one or more
    of Nos. 3108-3111, 3111a, 3113-3117.

☐ 3118   32c **Hanukkah**, 10/22/96, DC, (179,355) 1.25   15.00
☐ 3119   50c **Cycling** souvenir sheet of 2, 11/1/96,
         New York, NY 2.50   14.00
☐ 3119   with Hong Kong stamp, dual cancels 15.00
☐ 3119a-3119b, **any single** 1.50
    First day cancel was applied to 290,091 covers bearing one or
    more of Nos. 3119, 3119a-3119b.

1997

☐ 3120   32c **Chinese New Year**, 1/5/97, Honolulu, HI 1.50   1.75   2.00   12.00
☐ 3121   32c **Benjamin O. Davis, Sr.**, 1/28/97, DC 1.25   8.00

3126   3127   3130

3134   3137a

3139a   3140a   3141

3152   3166   3174   3179   3181

3198   3203   3211   3221

SCOTT NUMBER	DESCRIPTION	SINGLE	PLATE BLOCK	CERM BLOCK PROG
☐ 3122	32¢ **Statue of Liberty,** serpentine die cut 11, 2/1/97, San Diego, CA 1.25			
☐ 3123	32¢ **Love (Swans),** 2/4/97, Los Angeles, CA..............1.25			
☐ 3124	55¢ **Love (Swans),** 2/4/97, Los Angeles, CA..............1.50			
☐ 3123-3124	on one cover 2.00			10.00
☐ 3125	32¢ **Helping Children Learn,** 2/18/97, DC................1.25			8.00
☐ 3126	32¢ **Merian Prints, Citron** (large size), 3/3/97, DC...1.25			
☐ 3127	32¢ **Merian Prints, Pineapple** (large size), 3/3/97, DC..1.25			
☐ 3126-3127	on one cover 1.75			8.00
☐ 3128	32¢ **Merian prints, Citron** (small size), 3/3/97, DC...1.25			
☐ 3128a	Mixed die cut...1.25			
☐ 3129	32¢ **Merian Prints, Pineapple** (small size),3/3/97, DC1.25			
☐ 3129a	Mixed die cut...1.25			
☐ 3128-3129	on one cover 1.75			
☐ 3131a	32¢ **Pacific 97 pair,** 3/13/97, New York, NY	2.00	2.25	
☐ 3130-3131	any single..1.25			12.00
☐ 3132	(25¢) **Juke Box,** self-adhesive imperf., 3/14/97, New York, NY 1.25pr			
☐ 3133	32¢ **Flag over porch,** self-adhesive, serpentine die cut 9.9 vert., 3/14/97.......................................1.25			
☐ 3134	32¢ **Thornton Wilder,** 4/17/97, Hamden, CT 1.25	1.50	1.75	8.00
☐ 3135	32¢ **Raoul Wallenberg,** 4/24/97, DC 1.25	1.50	1.75	10.00
☐ 3136	32¢ **Dinosaurs,** pane of 15, 5/1/97, Grand Junction, CO..7.50			
☐ 3136a-3136o,	any single..1.25			14.00
☐ 3137a	32¢ **Bugs Bunny,** die cut single, 5/22/97, Burbank, CA..1.75			16.00
☐ 3138c	32¢ **Bugs Bunny,** imperf pane, 5/22/97, Burbank, CA..250.00			
☐ 3139	50¢ **Franklin,** pane of 12, 5/29/97, San Francisco, CA...			14.00
☐ 3139a	single stamp 2.00			
☐ 3140	60¢ **Washington,** pane of 12, 5/30/97, San Francisco, CA...			16.00
☐ 3140a	single stamp 2.50			
☐ 3141	32¢ **Marshall Plan,** 6/4/97, Cambridge, MA 1.25	1.50	1.75	8.00
☐ 3141	**With Germany No. 1970, dual cancels,**..........15.00			
☐ 3142	32¢ **Classic American Aircraft,** pane of 20, 7/19/97, Dayton, OH...9.50			
☐ 3142a-3142t,	any single 1.25			
☐ 3146a	32¢ **Legendary Football Coaches,** 7/25/97, Canton, OH...	4.00		10.00
☐ 3143-3146,	any single..1.50	1.75	2.00	
☐ 3147	32¢ **Vince Lombardi,** 8/5/97, Green Bay, WI............1.50	1.75	2.00	10.00
☐ 3148	32¢ **Bear Bryant,** 8/7/97, Tuscaloosa, AL.................1.50	1.75	2.00	10.00
☐ 3149	32¢ **Pop Warner,** 8/8/97, Philadelphia, PA................1.50	1.75	2.00	10.00
☐ 3150	32¢ **George Halas,** 8/16/97, Chicago, IL...................1.50	1.75	2.00	10.00
☐ 3151	32¢ **Classic American Dolls,** pane of 15, 7/28/97, Anaheim, CA...13.00			18.00
☐ 3151a-3151t,	any single..1.25			
☐ 3152	32¢ **Humphrey Bogart,** 7/31/97, Los Angeles, CA....1.25	1.50	1.75	12.00
☐ 3153	32¢ **"The Stars and Stripes Forever!",** 8/21/97, Milwaukee, WI...1.25	1.50	1.75	10.00
☐ 3157a	32¢ **Opera Singers,** 9/10/97, New York, NY....................	3.25		15.00

☐	3154-3157, any single 1.25				
☐	3165a 32c **Classical Composers and Conductors,** 9/12/97,				
	Cincinnati, OH..		5.25		14.00
☐	3158-3165, any single 1.25				
☐	3166 32c **Padre Felix Varela,** 9/15/97, Miami, FL 1.25		1.50	1.75	10.00
☐	3167 32c **Department of the Air Force,** 9/18/97, DC........1.25		1.50	1.75	10.00
☐	3172a 32c **Movie Monsters,** strip of 5, 9/30/97,				
	Universal City, CA..3.75				
☐	3168-3172, any single 1.25				
☐	3173 32c **Supersonic Flight,** self-adhesive, 10/14/97,				
	Edwards AFB, CA				10.00
☐	3174 32c **Women in the Military Service,** 10/18/97, DC...1.25		1.50	1.75	10.00
☐	3175 32c **Kwanzaa,** self-adhesive, 10/22/97,				
	Los Angeles, CA				14.00
☐	3176 32c **Holiday Traditional,** self-adhesive, 10/27/97,				
	DC..1.25				10.00
☐	3177 32c **Holiday Contemporary,** self-adhesive, 10/30/97,				
	New York, NY..				12.00
☐	3178 $3 **Mars Pathfinder,** 12/10/97, Pasadena, CA 10.00				

1998

☐	3179 32c **Chinese New Year,** 1/5/98, Seattle, WA 1.25		1.50	1.75	12.00
☐	3180 32c **Alpine Skiing,** 1/22/98, Salt Lake City, UT.........1.25		1.50	1.75	12.00
☐	3181 32c **Madam C. J. Walker,** self-adhesive, 1/28/98,				
☐	Indianapolis, IN...1.25				12.00
☐	3182 32c **1900-1909,** pane of 15, 2/3/98, DC 15.00				
☐	3182a-3182o, any single..1.25				
☐	3183 32c **1910-1919,** pane of 15, 2/3/98,DC 15.00				
☐	3183a-3183o, any single..1.25				20.00
☐	3184 32c **1920-1929,** pane of 15, 5/28/98, Chicago. IL...15.00				
☐	3184a-3184o, any single..1.25				20.00
☐	3185 32c **1930-1939,** pane of 15, 9/10/98, Cleveland, OH 15.00				
☐	3185a-3185o, any single..1.25				
☐	3186 33c **1940-1949,** pane of 15, 2/18/99, Dobbins AFB, GA15.00				
☐	3186a-3186o, any single..1.25				18.00
☐	3187 33c **1950-1959,** pane of 15, 5/26/99, Springfield, MA15.00				
☐	3187a-3187o, any single..1.25				18.00
☐	3188 33c **1960-1969,** pane of 15, 9/17/99, Green Bay, WI15.00				
☐	3188a-3188o, any single..1.25				
☐	3189 33c **1970-1979,** pane of 15, 11/18/99, New York, NY15.00				
☐	3189a-3189o any single..1.25				
☐	3190 33c **1980-1989,** pane of 15, 1/12/00,				
	Kennedy Space Center, FL................................10.00				
☐	3190a-3190o any single..1.25				
☐	3191 33c **1990-1999,** pane of 15, 5/2/00,				
	Escondido, CA..10.00				
☐	3191a-3191o any single..1.25				
☐	3192 32c **Remember the Maine,** 2/15/98, Key West, FL....1.25		1.50	1.75	10.00
☐	3193-3197 32c **Flowering Trees,** 3/19/98, New York, NY..6.00				
☐	3193-3197 any single..1.25				12.00
☐	3202a 32c **Alexander Calder** strip of 5, 3/25/98, DC 3.75				5.00
☐	3198-3202, any single..1.25				12.00
☐	3203 32c **Cinco de Mayo,** self-adhesive, 4/16/98,				
	San Antonio, TX...1.25				
☐	3204a 32c **Sylvester & Tweety,** self-adhesive, 4/27/98.				
	New York, NY..1.50				15.00

☐ 3205c	32c Sylvester & Tweety, self-adhesive, imperf. pane, 4/27/98, New York, NY .... –				
☐ 3206	32c Wisconsin, self-adhesive, 5/29/98, Madison, WI 1.25				10.00
☐ 3207	(5c) Wetlands, 6/5/98, McLean, VA 1.25				
☐ 3207A	(5c) Wetlands, self-adhesive coil, 12/14/98, DC 1.25				
☐ 3208	(25c) Diner, 6/5/98, McLean, VA .... 1.25 pr				
☐ 3208A	(25c) Diner, self-adhesive coil, 6/5/99, DC 1.25				
☐ 3209	Trans-Mississippi Centennial, pane of 9, 6/18/98, Anaheim, CA 20.00				16.00
☐ 3209a-3209f, 1c-10c, any single 1.25					
☐ 3209g	50c 1.50				
☐ 3209h	$1 .... 2.00				
☐ 3209i	$2 .... 4.00				
☐ 3210	$1 Trans-Mississippi Centennial pane of 9, 6/18/98, Anaheim, CA 16.00				
☐ 3211	32c Berlin Airlift, 6/26/98, Berlin, Germany 1.25	1.50	1.75	10.00
☐ 3215a	32c Folk Musicians, 6/26/98. DC	3.25		
☐ 3212-3215, any single 1.25					12.00
☐ 3219a	32c Gospel Musicians, 7/15/98, New Orleans, LA	3.25		
☐ 3216-3219, any single 1.25					12.00
☐ 3220	32c Spanish Settlement of Southwest, 7/11/98, Espanola, NM 1.25	1.50	1.75	12.00
☐ 3221	32c Stephan Vincent Benet, 7/22/98, Harpers Ferry, WV 1.25	12.00		12.00
☐ 3225a	32c Tropical Birds, 7/29/98, Ponce, PR	3.25		
☐ 3222-3225, any single 1.25					14.00
☐ 3226	32c Alfred Hitchcock, 8/3/98, Los Angeles, CA 1.25			
☐ 3227	32c Organ & Tissue Donation, self-adhesive, 8/5/98, Columbus, OH 1.25			12.00
☐ 3228	(10c) Modern Bicycle, self-adhesive coil, 8/14/98, DC 1.25			
☐ 3229	(10c) Modern Bicycle, coil, 8/14/98, DC 1.25			
☐ 3230-3234	32c Bright Eyes, self-adhesive, 8/20/98, Boston, MA 3.25			14.00
☐ 3230-3234, any single 1.25					
☐ 3235	32c Klondike Gold Rush, Centennial, 8/21/98, Nome or Skagway, AK 1.25	1.50	1.75	12.00
☐ 3236	32c American Art, pane of 20, 8/27/98, Santa Clara, CA 9.50			15.00
☐ 3236a-3236t, any single 1.25					
☐ 3237	32c American Ballet, 8/16/98, New York, NY 1.25	1.50	1.75	14.00
☐ 3242a	32c, Space Discovery, strip of 5, 10/1/98, Kennedy Space Center, FL 3.75			12.00
☐ 3238-3242, any single 1.25					
☐ 3243	32c Giving And Sharing, 10/7/98, Atlanta, GA 1.25	1.50	1.75	10.00
☐ 3244	32c Christmas - Madonna And Child, booklet stamp, self-adhesive, 10/15/98, DC 1.25			12.00
☐ 3245-3248	32c Christmas Wreaths, booklet stamp, self-adhesive, Christmas, MI 3.25			12.00
☐ 3245-3248, any single 1.25					
☐ 3249-3252	32c Christmas Wreaths, size: 23x30mm, booklet stamps, self-adhesive, Christmas, MI ... 3.25			
☐ 3245-3248, any single 1.25					
☐ 3257	(1c) Weather Vane, white USA, 11/9/98, Troy, NY ... 1.25	1.50	1.75	
☐ 3258	(1c) Weather Vane, pale blue USA, 11/9/98, Troy, NY 1.25	1.50	1.75	
☐ 3259	22c Uncle Sam, self-adhesive, 11/9/98, Troy, NY 1.25			12.00

3222

3226

3230

3237

3238

3259

3260

3262

3270

3276

3277

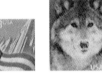

3292

3297

3306

3310

3316

3317

3321

		SINGLE	BLOCK	PLATE BLOCK	CERM PROG
☐ 3260	(33c) **Uncle Sam's Hat**, self-adhesive, 11/9/98, Troy, NY	1.25			
☐ 3261	$3.20 **Space Shuttle Landing**, self-adhesive Priority Mail rate, 11/9/98, DC,	8.00			
☐ 3262	$11.75 **Piggyback Space Shuttle**, self-adhesive Express Mail rate, 11/9/98, New York, NY,	25.00			40.00
☐ 3263	22c **Uncle Sam**, self-adhesive coil, 11/9/98, Troy, NY	1.25			
☐ 3264	(33c) **Uncle Sam's Hat**, coil, 11/9/98, Troy, NY	1.25			
☐ 3265	(33c) **Uncle Sam's Hat**, self-adhesive coil, die cut 9.9, round corners, 11/9/98, Troy, NY	1.25			
☐ 3266	(33c) **Uncle Sam's Hat**, self-adhesive coil, die cut 9.9, square corners, 11/9/98, Troy, NY	1.25			
☐ 3267	(33c) **Uncle Sam's Hat**, self-adhesive booklet single, die cut 9.9, 11/9/98, Troy, NY	1.25			
☐ 3268	(33c) **Uncle Sam's Hat**, self-adhesive booklet single, die cut 11.2x11.1, 11/9/98, Troy, NY	1.25			
☐ 3269	(33c) **Uncle Sam's Hat**, self-adhesive booklet single, die cut 8, 11/9/98, Troy, NY	1.25			
☐ 3270	(10c) **Eagle & Shield**, coil, presorted std., 12/14/98, DC	1.25			
☐ 3271	(10c) **Eagle & Shield**, self-adhesive coil, presorted std., 12/14/98, DC	1.25			

1999

		SINGLE	BLOCK	PLATE BLOCK	CERM PROG
☐ 3272	33c **Chinese New Year - Year of the Rabbit**, 1/5/99, Los Angeles, CA	1.25	1.50	1.75	12.00
☐ 3273	33c **Malcolm X - Black Heritage**, 1/20/99, New York, NY	1.25	1.50	1.75	16.00
☐ 3274	33c **Love**, self-adhesive booklet, 1/28/99, Loveland, CO	1.25			
☐ 3275	55c **Love**, self-adhesive, 1/28/99, Loveland, CO	2.00			
☐ 3274-3275	on one cover	3.25			
☐ 3276	33c **Hospice Care**, 2/9/99, Largo, FL	1.25	1.50	1.75	12.00
☐ 3277	33c **Flag and City**, 2/25/99, Orlando, FL	1.25	1.50	1.75	
☐ 3278	33c **Flag and City**, self-adhesive, die cut 9.8, 2/25/99, Orlando, FL	1.25			
☐ 3279	33c **Flag and City**, self-adhesive,[red date,] die cut 11.1, 2/25/99, Orlando, FL	1.25			
☐ 3280	33c **Flag and City**, coil, perf. 9.8 vert., 2/25/99, Orlando, FL	1.25			
☐ 3281	33c **Flag and City**, self-adhesive coil, die cut 9.8 vert., square corners, 2/25/99, Orlando, FL	1.25			
☐ 3282	33c **Flag and City**, self-adhesive coil, die cut 9.8 vert., round corners, 2/25/99, Orlando, FL	1.25			
☐ 3283	33c **Flag and Chalkboard**, self-adhesive booklet, die cut 7.9, 3/13/99, DC	1.25			
☐ 3286	33c **Irish Immigration**, 2/26/99, Boston, MA	1.25	1.50	1.75	12.00
☐ 3287	33c **Alfred Lunt and Lynn Fontanne**, 3/2/99, New York, NY	1.25	1.50	1.75	10.00
☐ 3292a	33c **Arctic Animals**, 3/12/99, Barrow, AK	3.75			
☐ 3288-3292	any single	1.25			12.00
☐ 3293	33c **Sonoran Desert**, pane of 10, 4/6/99, Tucson, AZ	6.75			
☐ 3293a-3293j	any single	1.25			14.00
☐ 3294-3297	33c **Berries**, self-adhesive, die cut 11.2x11.7, 4/10/99, Ponchatoula, LA	3.25			
☐ 3294-3297	any single	1.25			

3329

3334

3338

3341

3352

3355

3356

3369

3370

3371

3372

3389

3390

3420

3426

3438

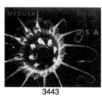
3443

3444

3445

3446

		SINGLE	BLOCK	BLOCK	PROG
☐ 3298-3301	33c **Berries,** self-adhesive, die cut 91/2x10,				
	4/10/99, Ponchatoula, LA	3.25			
☐ 3298-3301,	any single	1.25			
☐ 3302-3305	33c **Berries,** self-adhesive coil, die cut 8.5 vert.,				
	4/10/99, Ponchatoula, LA	3.25			
☐ 3302-3305,	any single	1.25			
☐ 3306a	33c **Daffy Duck,** self-adhesive, single stamp, 4/16/99,				
	Los Angeles, CA	1.25			14.00
☐ 3308	33c **Ayn Rand - Literary Arts,** 4/22/99,				
	New York, NY	1.25	1.50	1.75	28.00
☐ 3309	33c **Cinco De Mayo,** self-adhesive, 4/27/99,				
	San Antonio, TX	1.25			
☐ 3310-3313	33c **Tropical Flowers,** self-adhesive booklet,				
	5/1/99, Honolulu, HI	3.75			12.00
☐ 3310-3313,	any single	1.25			
☐ 3314	33c **John & William Bartram,** self-adhesive,				
	5/18/99, Philadelphia PA	1.25			10.00
☐ 3315	33c **Prostate Cancer Awareness,** self-adhesive,				
	5/28/99, Austin TX	1.25			10.00
☐ 3316	33c **California Gold Rush,** 6/22/99, Sacramento, CA	1.25	1.50	1.75	10.00
☐ 3317-3320	33c **Aquarium Fish,** self-adhesive, 6/24/99,				
	Anaheim, CA	3.75			
☐ 3317-3320,	any single	1.25			12.00
☐ 3321-3324	33c **Extreme Sports,** self-adhesive, 6/25/99,				
	San Francisco, CA	3.75			
☐ 3321-3324,	any single	1.25			12.00
☐ 3328a	33c **American Glass,** 6/29/99, Corning NY	1.25			
☐ 3325-3328,	any single	1.25			14.00
☐ 3329	33c **James Cagney - Legends of Hollywood,**				
	7/22/99, Burbank, CA	1.25			12.00
☐ 3330	55c **Gen. "Billy" Mitchell,** 7/30/99, Milwaukee, WI	1.50	2.75	3.00	
☐ 3331	33c **Honoring Those Who Served,** 8/16/99,				
	Kansas City, MO	1.50	2.00	2.25	10.00
☐ 3332	45c **Universal Postal Union,** 8/25/99, Beijing, China	1.40			10.00
☐ 3332	**With UN No. 767a, dual cancels**	15.00			
☐ 3337a	33c **Famous Trains,** booklet pane, 8/26/99,				
	Cleveland, OH	3.75			14.00
☐ 3333-3337,	any single	1.25			
☐ 3338	33c **Frederick Law Olmstead,** 9/12/99, Boston, MA	1.25	1.50	1.75	10.00
☐ 3344a	33c **Hollywood Composers,** 9/16/99,				
	Los Angeles, CA	3.75			
☐ 3339-3344,	any single	1.25			15.00
☐ 3350a	33c **Broadway Songwriters,** 9/21/99,				
	New York, NY	3.75			
☐ 3345-3350	any single, New York, NY	1.25			
☐ 3351	33c **Insects & Spiders,** 10/1/99, Indianapolis, IN	8.50			
☐ 3351a-3351t	any single	1.25			
☐ 3352	33c **Hanukkah,** 10/8/99, Washington, DC	1.25			
☐ 3353	22c **Uncle Sam perforated coil,** 10/8/99,				
	Washington, DC	1.25			
☐ 3354	33c **NATO,** 10/13/99, Brussels, Belgium	1.25			
☐ 3355	33c **Christmas Madonna,** 10/21/99, Washington, DC.	1.25			
☐ 3356-3359	33c **Christmas Deer,** narrow frame (sheet),				
	10/20/99, Rudolph, WI	3.25			
☐ 3356-3359	any single	1.25			

3447   3448   3451   3457   3468

3472   3473   3491   3496

3503   3504   3507

3508   3509   3511   3520

3521   3523   3524   3528   3532

☐ **3360-3363** **33c Christmas Deer, thick frame (booklet)**,
10/20/99, Rudolph, WI 3.25
☐ **3360-3363** any single 1.25
☐ **3364-3367** **33c Christmas Deer, smaller size (booklet)**,
10/20/99, Rudolph, WI 3.25
☐ **3364-3367** any single 1.25
☐ **3368** **33c Kwanzaa**, 10/29/99, Los Angeles, CA...1.25
☐ **3369** **33c Year 2000**, 12/27/99, Washington, DC 1.25
☐ **3370** **33c Chinese New Year**, 1/6/00, San Francisco, CA ..1.25
☐ **3371** **33c Patricia Roberts Harris**, 1/27/00, Washington, DC1.25
☐ **3372** **33c Los Angeles Class Submarine**, with
microprinting, 3/27/00, Groton, CT 1.25
☐ **3373** **22c S Class Submarine**, 3/27/00, Groton, CT 1.25
☐ **3374** **33c Los Angeles Class Submarine**, no microprinting,
3/27/00, Groton, CT 1.25
☐ **3375** **55c Ohio Class Submarine**, 3/27/00, Groton, CT......1.50
☐ **3376** **60c USS Holland**, 3/27/00, Groton, CT.....................1.50
☐ **3377** **$3.20 Gato Class Submarine**, 3/27/00, Groton, CT ..6.00
☐ **3377a** Booklet pane of 5, #3373-3377, either selvage..7.50
☐ **3378** **33c Pacific Coast Rain Forest**, pane of 10,
3/29/00, Seattle, WA 6.75
☐ **3378a-3378j** any single.......................................1.25
☐ **3383a** **33c Louise Nevelson**, 4/6/00, New York, NY 3.25
☐ **3379-3383** any single 1.25
☐ **3388a** **33c Hubble Space Telescope**, 4/10/00, Greenbelt, MD 3.25
☐ **3384-3388** any single 1.25
☐ **3389** **33c American Samoa**, 4/17/00, Pago Pago, AS 1.25
☐ **3390** **33c Library of Congress**, 4/24/00, Washington, DC .1.25
☐ **3391a** **33c Road Runner & Wile E. Coyote**, 4/26/00,
Phoenix, AZ..1.25
☐ **3396a** **33c Distinguished Soldiers**, 5/3/00, Washington, DC ..3.25
☐ Any other city..3.25
☐ **3393-3396** any single, Washington, DC................................1.25
☐ Any other city..1.25
☐ **3397** **33c Summer Sports**, 5/5/00, Spokane, WA...............1.25
☐ **3398** **33c Adoption**, 5/10/00, Beverly Hills, CA.................1.25
☐ **3402a** **33c Youth Team Sports**, 5/27/00,
Lake Buena Vista, FL 3.25
☐ **3399-3402** any single 1.25
☐ **3403** **33c The Stars and Stripes**, pane of 20, 6/14/00,
Baltimore, MD 9.50
☐ **3403a-3403t** any single 1.25
☐ **3404-3407** **33c Berries**, coils, die cut 8 1/2 horiz.,
6/16/00, Buffalo, NY 3.25
☐ **3404-3707** any single 1.25
☐ **3408** **33c Legends of Baseball**, 7/6/00, Atlanta, GA.........9.50
☐ **3408a-3708t** any single...1.25
☐ **3409** **60c Probing the Vastness of Space**, 7/10/00,
Anaheim, CA 6.00
☐ **3409a-3409f** any single..1.50
☐ **3410** **$1 Exploring the Solar System**, 7/11/00,
Anaheim, CA 9.00
☐ **3410a-3410e** any single..2.00
☐ **3411** **$3.20 Escaping the Gravity of Earth**, 7/9/00,
Anaheim, CA 10.00
☐ **3411a-3411b** any single..3.75
☐ **3412** **$11.75 Space Achievement and Exploration**,
7/7/00, Anaheim, CA 17.50
☐ **3413** **$11.75 Landing on the Moon**, 7/8/00, Anaheim, CA17.50

☐ **3414-3417 33c Stampin' The Future**, 7/13/00, Anaheim, CA 3.25
☐ **3414-3417** any single 1.25
☐ **3420** 10c Joseph W. Stilwell, 8/24/00, Providence, RI 1.25
☐ **3426** 33c Claude Pepper, 9/7/00, DC....................................1.25
☐ **3431** 76c Sen. Hattie Caraway, 2/21/2001, Little Rock, AR.1.75
☐ **3438** 33c California Statehood, 9/8/00, Sacramento, CA.... 1.25
☐ **3443a** 33c Deep Sea Creatures, 10/2/00, Monterey, CA 3.75
☐ **3439-3443** any single 1.25
☐ **3444** 33c Thomas Wolfe, 10/3/00, Asheville, NC................1.25
☐ **3445** 33c White House, 10/18/00, DC...................................1.25
☐ **3446** 33c Edward G. Robinson, 10/24/00, Los Angeles, CA ..1.25
☐ **3447** (10c)New York Public Library Lion, 11/9/00,
        New York, NY..1.25
☐ **3448** (34c)Flag Over Farm, perf, 12/15/00, DC..................1.25
☐ **3449** (34c)Flag Over Farm, litho. self-adhesive,
        12/15/00, DC...1.25
☐ **3450** (34c)Flag Over Farm, photo. self-adhesive,
        12/15/00, DC...1.25
☐ **3451** (34c)Statue of Liberty, booklet stamp,
        12/15/00, DC...1.25
☐ **3452** (34c)Statue of Liberty perforated coil,
        12/15/00, DC...1.25
☐ **3453** (34c)Statue of Liberty self-adhesive coil,
        12/15/00, DC...1.25
☐ **3454-3457** (34c) Flowers, booklet stamps, 12/15/00, DC.....3.25
☐ **3454-3457** any single...1.25
☐ **3462-3465** (34c) Flowers, coil stamps, 12/15/00, DC...........3.25
☐ **3462-3465** any single...1.25
☐ **3466** 34c Statue of Liberty coil (rounded corners),
        1/7/01, DC...1.25
☐ **3468** 21c American Buffalo, self-adhesive sheet stamp,
        2/22/01, Wall, SD..1.25
☐ **3469** 34c Flag Over Farm, perforated sheet stamp,
        2/7/01, New York, NY......................................1.25
☐ **3470** 34c Flag Over Farm, self-adhesive sheet stamp,
        3/6/01, Lincoln, NE..1.25
☐ **3471** 55c Eagle, 2/22/01, Wall, SD......................................1.5
☐ **3472** $3.50 Capitol Dome, 1/29/01, DC 6.25
☐ **3473** $12.25 Washington Monument, 1/29/01, DC 14
☐ **3475** 21c American Buffalo coil stamp, 2/22/01, Wall, SD....1.25
☐ **3476** 34c Statue of Liberty, perforated coil stamp,
        2/7/01, New York, NY......................................1.25
☐ **3477** 34c Statue of Liberty coil stamp (right angle corners),
        2/7/01, New York, NY......................................1.25
☐ **3478-3481 34c Flower coil stamps**, 2/7/01, New York, NY...3.25
☐ **3478-3481** any single...1.25
☐ **3482** 20c George Washington booklet stamp,
        2/22/01, Wall, SD...1.25
☐ **3483** 21c George Washington booklet stamp,
        2/22/01, Wall, SD...1.25
☐ **3485** 34c Statue of Liberty booklet stamp, 2/7/01,
        New York, NY..1.25
☐ **3487-3490 34c Flower** booklet stamps, 2/7/01,
        New York, NY..3.25
☐ **3487-3490** any single...1.25
☐ **3491-3492 34c Apple & Orange** booklet stamps, 2/7/01,
        Lincoln, NE...2.25
☐ **3491-3492** any single...1.25

☐ 3496 (34c)**Love Letter**, 1/19/01, Tucson, AZ...................1.25
☐ 3497 34c Love Letter, 2/14/01, Lovejoy, GA 1.25
☐ 3498 34c Love Letter, die cut 11 1/2x10 3/4, 2/14/01,
　　　　 Lovejoy, GA 1.25
☐ 3499 55c Love Letter, 2/14/01, Lovejoy, GA 1.50
☐ 3500 34c **Chinese New Year**, 1/20/01, Oakland, CA 1.25
☐ 3501 34c **Roy Wilkins**, 1/24/01, Minneapolis, MN 1.25
☐ 3502 34c **American Illustrators** pane of 20, 2/1/01,
　　　　 New York, NY 9.50
☐ 3502a-3502t any single 1.25
☐ 3503 34c **Diabetes Awareness**, 3/16/01, Boston, MA 1.25
☐ 3504 34c **Nobel Prize Centenary**, 3/22/01, DC 1.25
☐ 3505 **Pan-American Expo Invert Stamps**, Cent., Pane,
　　　　 3/29/01, New York, NY 6.00
☐ 3505a 1c **Pan-American Expo Invert Stamps**, Cent. -
　　　　 Reproduction of Scott 294a 1.25
☐ 3505b 2c **Pan-American Expo Invert Stamps**, Cent. -
　　　　 Reproduction of Scott 295a 1.25
☐ 3505c 4c **Pan-American Expo Invert Stamps**, Cent. -
　　　　 Reproduction of Scott 296a 1.25
☐ 3505d 80c **Pan-American Expo Invert Stamps**, Cent. -
　　　　 Commemorative (cinderella) stamp depicting
　　　　 a buffalo. 1.75
☐ 3506 34c **Great Plains Prairie**, Pane of 10, 4/19/01,
　　　　 Lincoln, NE 7.00
☐ 3507 34c **Peanuts**, 5/17/01, Santa Rosa, CA 1.25
☐ 3508 34c **Honoring Veterans**, 5/23/01, DC 1.25
　　　　 any other city..1.25
☐ 3509 34c **Frida Kahlo**, 6/21/01, Phoenix, AZ................1.25
☐ 3519a 34c **Legendary Playing Fields**, 6/27/01, New York, NY,
　　　　 Boston, MA, Chicago, IL or Detroit, MI..........6.50
☐ 3510-3519 Any single, New York, NY, Boston, MA,
　　　　 Chicago, IL or Detroit, MI.............................1.25
☐ 3520 (10c)**Atlas Statue**, 6/29/01, New York, NY............ 1.25
☐ 3521 34c **Leonard Bernstein**, 7/10/01, New York, NY... 1.25
☐ 3522 (15c)**Woody Wagon**, 8/3/01, Denver, CO 1.25
☐ 3523 34c **Lucille Ball**, 8/6/01, Los Angeles, CA.............. 1.25
☐ 3527a 34c **Amish Quilts**, 8/9/01, Nappanee, IN 3.25
☐ 3524-3527 any single 1.25
☐ 3528-3532 34c **Carnivorous Plants**, 8/23/01,
　　　　 Des Plaines, IL 3.25
☐ 3528-3532 any single 1.25
☐ 3532 34c **EID**, 9/01/01, Des Plaines, IL 1.25

☐ _____

☐ _____

☐ _____

☐ _____

☐ _____

☐ _____

☐ _____

☐ _____

☐ _____

☐ _____

☐ _____

☐ _____

☐ _____

☐ _____

☐ _____

☐ _____

☐ _____

☐ _____

☐ _____

☐ _____

☐ _____

☐ _____

☐ _____

☐ _____

☐ _____

☐ _____

☐ _____

☐ _____

☐ _____

☐ _____

☐ _____

☐ _____

Semi-Postal Stamp

☐ B1   **(32c+8c) Breast Cancer Awareness,** self-adhesive,
7/29/98, DC..1.25

C1-C3

C7-C9

C10

AIR POST
1918

☐ C1	6c Jenny, 12/10/18, DC ....27,500.	—	
☐	Washington, DC 12/16/18 ....2,500.	—	
☐	Philadelphia, PA 12/16/18 ....2,500.	—	
☐	New York, NY 12/16/18 ....2,500.	—	
☐ C2	16c Jenny, 7/11/18, DC 2 known ....27,500.	—	
☐	Washington, DC 7/15/18 ....800.00	—	
☐	Philadelphia, PA 7/15/18 ....800.00	—	
☐	New York, NY 7/15/18 ....800.00	—	
☐ C3	24c Jenny, 5/13/18, DC ....27,500.	—	
☐	Washington, DC 5/15/18 ....750.00	—	
☐	Philadelphia, PA 5/15/18 ....750.00	—	
☐	New York, NY 5/15/18 ....750.00	—	

*The earliest date listed under C1-C3 is the first day of
issue. The other date is the first flight for the three
different air mail rates of 1918.*

1923

☐ C4	8c Propeller, 8/15/23, DC.................................500.00	700.00
☐ C5	16c Insignia, 8/17/23, DC.................................725.00	1,150.
☐ C6	24c Biplane, 8/21/23, DC 900.00	2,000.

1926-27

☐ C7	10c Map, 2/13/26, DC.. 80.00	150.00	—	—
☐	Chicago, IL..85.00	160.00	—	—
☐	Cleveland, OH...125.00	200.00	—	—
☐	Dearborn, MI..125.00	200.00	—	—
☐	Detroit, MI..90.00	160.00	—	—
☐	Unofficial city 150.00	—	—	—

*FDC/first flight covers on 2/15/26 sell for 25% more
than values listed.*

☐ C8	15c Map, 9/18/26, DC..90.00	150.00	500.00	—
☐ C9	20c Map, 1/25/27, DC..100.00	175.00	—	—
☐	New York, NY 125.00	200.00	—	—
☐	1st Albert E. Gorham cachet.............................		250.00	—
☐ C10	10c Lindbergh's Plane, 6/18/27, DC 30.00	35.00	175.00	—
☐	Detroit, MI..35.00	40.00	175.00	—
☐	Little Falls, MN 35.00	40.00	175.00	—
☐	St. Louis, MO 25.00	30.00	175.00	—
☐	Air Mail Field, Chicago, unofficial...........150.00	—	—	—
☐	Any other unofficial city 160.00	—	200.00	—
☐	1st Milton Mauck cachet		300.00	—
☐ C10a	Lindbergh's Plane, booklet pane of 3,			
☐	5/26/28, DC..875.00	—		
☐	Cleveland Mid. Phil. Sta 800.00	—		
☐	Plus Scott 645, Cleveland Mid. Phil. Sta...1,000.	—		

C11

C12, C16, C17, C19

C13-C15

C18

C20-C22

C23

C24

C25, C35

C32

C33, C37, C39, C41

C34

C38

C40

C42

C45

C46

C47

C48, C50

C49

C51, C52, C60, C6

**Values for various cachet makers can be determined
by using the Cachet Calculator which begins on page 52A.**

SCOTT NUMBER	DESCRIPTION	UNCACHETED SINGLE	BLOCK	CACHETED SINGLE	BLOCK
☐ C10a	**Lindbergh's Plane**, booklet single, DC	110.00		1000.	
☐	Cleveland Mid. Phil. Sta	100.00		1000.	
☐	Plus Scott 645	150.00		1200.	
☐	Unofficial city	150.00			

Lindbergh booklet pane FDC's and Scott C10a plus 645 FDC's are both known on Garfield Perry Shield Eagle and Biplane general purpose cacheted envelopes. These sell for a 10% to 20% premium over uncacheted FDCS.

1928

☐ C11	**5c Beacon**, 7/25/28, DC (pair)	50.00	60.00	200.00	—
☐	With single stamp and postage due stamp	100.00	—	250.00	—
☐	Unofficial city (pair)	175.00	—	250.00	—
☐	Single stamp with no postage due	150.00	—	350.00	—
☐	Predate	1,500.			

1930

☐ C12	**5c Winged Globe**, 2/10/30, DC	15.00	20.00	100.00	—
☐ C13	**65c Zeppelin**, 4/19/30, DC	1,200.	2,400.	2,500.	4,000.
☐ C14	**$1.30 Zeppelin**, 4/19/30, DC	1,000.	1,800.	2,500.	3,000.
☐ C15	**$2.60 Zeppelin**, 4/19/30, DC	1,000.	2,400.	2,500.	3,000.
☐ C13-C15	complete set on one cover	16,000.	—	—	—
☐ C13-C15	complete set of pl# sgl on one cover	20,000.	—	—	—

FDC's flown on Zeppelin flights sell for a premium.

1931-32

☐ C16	**5c Winged Globe**, 8/19/31, DC	175.00	300.00	350.00	—
☐ C17	**8c Winged Globe**, 9/26/32, DC	15.00	18.00	60.00	65.00

1933

☐ C18	**50c Zeppelin**, 10/2/33, New York, NY (3,500)	175.00	225.00	250.00	450.00
☐	Akron, OH 10/4/33	275.00	400.00	425.00	650.00
☐	Washington, DC, 10/5/33	225.00	350.00	425.00	575.00
☐	Miami, FL, 10/6/33	200.00	250.00	325.00	450.00
☐	Chicago, IL, 10/7/33	275.00	375.00	400.00	550.00

FDC's flown on a Zeppelin flight sell for a premium.

1934

☐ C19	**6c Winged Globe**, Baltimore, MD, 6/30/34	175.00	—	600.00	—
☐	New York, NY	800.00	—	1,700.	—
☐	Brooklyn, NY	1200.	—	1,700.	—
☐	San Fransico, CA	1500.	—	—	—
☐	7/1/34, DC	10.00	12.50	35.00	45.00
☐	Unofficial city	20.00	—	—	—
☐	On Scott UC3	60.00			

1935

☐ C20	**25c China Clipper**, 11/22/35, San Francisco, CA (15,000)	17.50	20.00	45.00	55.00
☐	DC (10,910)	20.00	22.50	50.00	60.00

1937

☐ C21	**20c China Clipper**, 2/15/37, DC	20.00	22.50	50.00	55.00
☐ C22	**50c China Clipper**, 2/15/37, DC	20.00	22.50	55.00	60.00
☐	Both on one cover	37.50	40.00	125.00	165.00

Total for Scott C21 and C22 is 40,000.

C53

C54

C55

C56

C57, C59, C62, C63

C64-C65

C67

C68

C66

C69

C70

C72-C73

C74

C77

C71

C78, C82

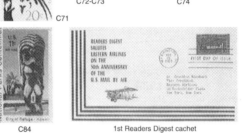

C84

1st Readers Digest cachet

C79, C83

**Values for various cachet makers can be determined
by using the Cachet Calculator which begins on page 52A.**

208

1938

☐ C23	6c Eagle Holding Shield, 5/14/38, Dayton, OH (116,443)	10.00	12.00	25.00	30.00
☐	St. Petersburg, FL (95,121)	10.00	12.00	25.00	30.00
☐	DC, 5/15/38	3.50			

1939

☐ C24	30c Winged Globe, 5/16/39, New York, NY (63,634)	20.00	30.00	50.00	75.00

SCOTT NUMBER	DESCRIPTION	SINGLE	BLOCK	PLATE BLOCK	CERM PROG

1941-44

☐ C25	6c Plane, 6/25/41, DC (99,986)	5.00	6.00	8.00	
☐ C25a	**Plane**, booklet pane of 3, 3/18/43, DC (50,216)	30.00			
☐ C25a	**Plane**, booklet single	10.00			
☐ C26	8c Plane, 3/21/44, DC (147,484)	5.00	6.00	8.00	
☐ C27	10c Plane, 8/15/41, Atlantic City, NJ (87,712)	8.00	10.00	15.00	
☐ C28	15c Plane, 8/19/41, Baltimore, MD (74,000)	10.00	15.00	25.00	
☐ C29	20c Plane, 8/27/41, Philadelphia, PA (66,225)	12.50	17.50	25.00	
☐ C30	30c Plane, 9/25/41, Kansas City, MO (57,175)	20.00	25.00	35.00	30.00
☐ C31	50c Plane, 10/29/41, St. Louis, MO (54,580)	40.00	50.00	100.00	

1946

☐ C32	5c DC-4, 9/25/46, DC	3.00	4.00	6.00	80.00
☐	1st William W. Bayless cachet	15.00		—	—
	Total for Scott C32 and UC14 is 396,639.				

1947

☐ C33	5c DC-4, 3/26/47, DC (342,634)	3.00	4.00	5.00	
☐ C34	10c Pan Am. Bldg., 8/30/47, DC (265,773)	3.00	4.00	5.00	50.00
☐	1st Glenn L. Martin Co. cachet	20.00			
☐ C35	15c N.Y. Skyline, 8/20/47, New York, NY (230,338)	3.00	4.00	6.00	45.00
☐ C36	25c Bay Bridge, 7/30/47, San Francisco, CA (201,762)	3.00	5.75	8.50	45.00

1948

☐ C37	5c DC-4, coil, 1/15/48, DC (192,084)	2.00	pr3.50	1p4.50	
☐ C38	5c Map, 7/31/48, New York, NY (371,265)	1.75	2.75	3.75	

1949

☐ C39	6c DC-4, 1/18/49, DC (266,790)	1.50	2.50	3.50	
☐ C39a	DC-4, booklet pane of 3, 11/18/49, New York, NY	9.00			
☐ C40	6c Alexandria Bicentennial, 5/11/49, Alexandria, VA (386,717)	1.25	2.00	3.00	40.00
☐ C41	6c DC-4, coil, 8/25/49, DC (240,386)	1.25	pr2.50	1p4.00	
☐ C42	10c P.O. Bldg., 11/18/49, New Orleans, LA (270,000)	2.00	3.00	3.75	45.00
☐ C43	15c Globes & Doves, 10/7/49, Chicago, IL (246,833)	3.00	4.50	7.00	45.00
☐	1st Jack Knight Air Mail Society cachet	30.00			

SCOTT NUMBER	DESCRIPTION	SINGLE	BLOCK	PLATE BLOCK	CERM PROG
☐ C44	25c **Boeing Stratocruiser**, 11/30/49, Seattle, WA				
	(220,215)..4.00	5.00		7.00	45.00
☐ C45	6c **Wright Bros.**, 12/17/49, Kitty Hawk, NC				
	(378,585)..3.50	5.00		8.00	50.00

1952

☐ C46	80c **Diamond Head**, 3/26/52, Honolulu, HI				
	(89,864)..18.00	25.00		50.00	60.00

1953

☐ C47	6c **Powered Flight**, 5/29/53, Dayton, OH (359,050)...1.50	2.50		3.50	35.00

1954

☐ C48	4c **Eagle**, 9/3/54, Philadelphia, PA (295,720)............1.00	1.50		2.50	45.00

1957

☐ C49	6c **Air Force**, 8/1/57, DC (356,683)............................1.75	2.75		3.75	

1958

☐ C50	5c **Eagle**, 7/31/58, Colorado Springs, CO, (207,954)...1.00	2.50		3.50	
☐	1st United States Air Force Academy cachet...18.00				
☐ C51	7c **Blue Jet**, 7/31/58, Phila. PA, (204,401)................1.00	2.50		3.50	30.00
☐ C51a	**Blue Jet**, booklet pane of 6, 7/31/58, San Antonio,				
	TX (119,769) 9.50				
☐ C52	7c **Blue Jet**, coil, 7/31/58, Miami, FL(181,603)..........1.00	pr2.00	lp3.00		25.00

1959

☐ C53	7c **Alaska**, 1/3/59, Juneau, AK (489,752) 1.00	1.75		2.75	20.00
☐	1st Gastineau Stamp Club cachet 15.00				
☐ C54	7c **Balloon**, 8/17/59, Lafayette, IN (383,556)............1.10	2.75		3.75	40.00
☐ C55	7c **Hawaii**, 8/21/59, Honolulu, HI (533,464) 1.00	2.50		3.50	30.00
☐ C56	10c **Pan Am. Games**, 8/27/59, Chicago, IL				
	(302,206) (2 types)*..1.00	2.00		3.00	20.00*

1959-66

☐ C57	10c **Liberty Bell**, 6/10/60, Miami, FL (246,509)				
	(2 types, uncanceled)*......................................1.25	2.00		4.00	20.00*
☐ C58	15c **Statue of Liberty**, 11/20/59, New York, NY				
	(259,412)..1.25	2.00		4.00	25.00
☐ C59	25c **Lincoln**, 4/22/60, San Francisco, CA (211,235) .1.75	2.75		4.75	30.00
☐ C59a	**Lincoln**, tagged, 12/29/66, DC (3,000) 60.00	—		—	

1960

☐ C60	7c **Red Jet**, 8/12/60, Arlington, VA (247,190)............1.00	1.00		2.50	20.00
☐ C60a	**Red Jet**, booklet pane of 6, 8/19/60, St. Louis, MO				
	(143,363)..9.50				20.00
☐ C61	7c **Red Jet**, coil, 10/22/60, Atlantic City, NJ				
	(197,995)..1.00	pr1.25	lp3.00		30.00

1961-67

☐ C62	13c **Liberty Bell**, 6/28/61, New York, NY (316,166) .1.00	1.00		2.75	18.00
☐ C62a	**Liberty Bell**, tagged, 2/15/67, DC 60.00	—		—	
☐ C63	15c **Statue of Liberty**, 1/13/61, Buffalo, NY				
	(192,976)..1.00	2.50		3.50	25.00
☐ C63a	**Statue of Liberty**, tagged, 1/11/67, DC...................60.00	—		—	

1962-65

☐ C64	**8c Capitol**, 12/5/62, DC (288,355) (2 types)*	1.00	1.00	2.50	30.00*
☐ C64a	**8c Capitol**, tagged, 8/1/63, Dayton, OH (262,720)	4.50	5.50	6.50	
☐	1st National Cash Register Co. cachet	15.00			
☐ C64b	**Capitol**, booklet pane of 5 + label, 12/5/62, DC (146,835)	3.50			
☐ C64c	**Capitol**, booklet tagged single w/zip slogan, 11/23/64.	150.00			
☐ C65	**8c Capitol**, coil, 12/5/62, DC(220,173)	1.00	pr1.00	lp2.75	
☐ C65a	**Capitol**, coil, tagged, 1/14/65, New Orleans, LA	60.00	—	—	

1963

☐ C66	**15c Montgomery Blair**, 5/3/63, Silver Spring, MD (260,031)	1.10	2.50	3.50	12.00
☐ C67	**6c Bald Eagle**, 7/12/63, Boston, MA (268,265)	1.00	1.00	2.50	14.00
☐ C67a	**Bald Eagle**, tagged, 2/15/67, DC	60.00	—	—	
☐ C68	**8c Amelia Earhart**, 7/24/63, Atchison, KS (437,996)	2.25	2.75	3.25	18.00
☐	1st The Ninety-Nines, Inc., cachet	15.00			

1964

☐ C69	**8c Robert H. Goddard**, 10/5/64, Roswell, NM (421,020)	2.25	2.75	3.25	10.00

1967

☐ C70	**8c Alaska**, 3/30/67, Sitka, AK (554,784)	1.00	1.00	2.50	15.00
☐	1st Sheldon Jackson College cachet	15.00			
☐ C71	**20c Audubon**, 4/26/67, Audubon, NY (227,930) (2 types)*	2.00	3.50	4.50	12.00*

1968

☐ C72	**10c 50-Star Runway**, 1/5/68, San Francisco, CA	1.00	1.00	2.50	14.00
☐ C72b	**50-Star Runway**, booklet pane of 8, 1/5/68, DC	3.50			
☐ C72c	**50-Star Runway**, booklet pane of 5 plus Mail Early Tab, 1/6/68, DC	125.00			
☐ C72c	**50-Star Runway**, booklet pane of 5 plus Zip Tab, 1/6/68, DC	125.00			
☐ C73	**10c 50-Star Runway**, coil 1/5/68 San Francisco, CA.	1.00	pr1.50	lp2.50	
	Total for Scott C72- C73 is 814, 140.				
☐ C74	**10c Jenny**, 5/15/68, DC (521,084) (5 types)*	1.50	2.75	3.75	12.00
☐	1st Readers Digest cachet	20.00	—	—	
☐ C75	**20c "USA,"** 11/22/68, New York, NY (276,244)	1.10	2.75	3.75	14.00

1969

☐ C76	**10c First Man on Moon**, 9/9/69, DC (8,743,070) (2 types)*	4.50	6.00	9.00	30.00*
☐	1st Dow-Unicover cachet	15.00			

1971-73

☐ C77	**9c Delta Plane**, 5/15/71, Kitty Hawk, NC (2 types)*	1.00	1.25	2.50	18.00*
	Total for Scott C77 and UXC10 is 379,442.				
☐ C78	**11c Jet**, 5/7/71, Spokane, WA	1.00	1.25	2.50	25.00
☐ C78a	**Jet**, booklet pane of 4 + 2 labels, 5/7/71, Spokane, WA	1.75			45.00
☐ C79	**13c Winged Envelope**, 11/16/73, New York, NY (282,550) (2 types)*	1.00	1.25	2.50	10.00

USA 20c
UNITED STATES AIR MAIL
C75, C81

FIRST MAN ON THE MOON
C76

C85

Progress in Electronics
C86

18c AIRMAIL
USA
C87

26c AIRMAIL
USA
C88

USAirmail 25c
C89

USAirmail 31c
C90

USAirmail
Blanche Stuart Scott
Pioneer Pilot
C99

Philip Mazzei
Patriot Remembered
USAirmail 40c
C98

Glenn Curtiss
Aviation Pioneer
USAirmail 35c
C100

USA 40c
Airmail
C105-C108

USA 28c
Airmail
C101-C104

USAirmail
Alfred V. Verville
Aviation Pioneer
33
C113

Lawrence and
Elmer Sperry
Aviation
Pioneers
USAirmail 39
C114

C115

Junipero
Serra
USAirmail
44
C116

Samuel P. Langley
Aviation Pioneer
45
USAirmail
C118

36 USAirmail
Igor Sikorsky
C119

SCOTT NUMBER	DESCRIPTION	SINGLE	BLOCK	PLATE BLOCK	CERM PROG
☐ C79a	**Winged Envelopes**, booklet pane of 5 + label, 12/27/73, Chicago, IL 1.75				30.00
☐ C80	**17c Statue of Liberty**, 7/13/71 Lakehurst, NJ (172,269)..................1.00		1.25	2.50	20.00
☐ C81	**21c "USA,"** 5/21/71, DC (293,140) (2 types)*............1.00		1.25	2.50	18.00*
☐ C82	**11c Jet**, coil, 5/7/71, Spokane, WA..........1.00 pr1.25 lp2.50 35.00				
	Total for Scott C78, C78a and C82 is 464, 750.				
☐ C83	**13c Winged Envelope**, coil 12/27/73, Chicago, IL 1.00		1.25	2.00	
	Total for Scott C79a and C83 is 204,756.				

1972

☐ C84	**11c City of Refuge**, 5/3/72, Honaunau, HI (364,816).................1.00		1.25	2.50	35.00
☐ C85	**11c Olympics**, 8/17/72, DC.........................1.00		1.25	2.50	
	Total for Scott 1460-1462 and C85 is 971,536.				

1973

☐ C86	**11c Electronics**, 7/10/73, New York, NY 1.00		1.25	2.50	30.00
	Total for set Scott 1500-1502 and C86 is 1,197,700.				

1974

☐ C87	**18c Statue of Liberty**, 1/11/74, Hempstead, NY (216,902)............................1.00		1.25	2.50	20.00
☐	1st James Hogg cachet 15.00				
☐ C88	**26c Mt. Rushmore**, 1/2/74, Rapid City, SD (210,470)...........................1.25		1.50	2.75	

1976

☐ C89	**25c Plane and Globes**, 1/2/76, Honolulu, HI 1.25		1.50	2.75	
☐ C90	**31c Plane**, Globe and Flag, 1/2/76, Honolulu, HI 1.25		1.50	3.00	
☐	Scott C89 & C90 on one 3.00				25.00

1978

☐ C91	**31c Wright Bros.**, 9/23/78, Dayton, OH 3.00				
☐ C92	**31c Wright Bros.**, 9/23/78, Dayton, OH 3.00				
☐ C92a	**Se-tenant pair** 4.00		5.00	6.00	14.00

1979

☐ C93	**21c Octave Chanute**, 3/29/79, Chanute, KS..............3.00				
☐ C94	**21c Octave Chanute**, 3/29/79, Chanute, KS..............3.00				
☐ C94a	**Se-tenant pair** 4.00		5.00	6.00	14.00
	Total for Scott C93 and C94 is 459,235.				
☐ C95	**25c Wiley Post**, 11/20/79, Oklahoma City, OK 3.00				
☐ C96	**25c Wiley Post**, 11/20/79, Oklahoma City, OK 3.00				
☐ C96a	**Se-tenant pair** 4.00		5.00	6.00	14.00
☐ C97	**31c Olympics**, 11/1/79, Colorado Springs, CO 1.25		1.65	2.35	14.00

1980

☐ C98	**40c Philip Mazzei**, 10/13/80, DC................................1.75		2.75	4.00	8.00
☐ C99	**28c Blanche Stuart Scott**, 12/30/80, Hammondsport, NY (238,502) 1.25		1.50	2.75	15.00
☐ C100	**35c Glenn Curtiss**, 12/30/80, Hammondsport, NY (208,502)...........................1.25	1.75		3.00	
☐	Scott C99 & C100 on one 2.50	—		—	15.00

1983

		SINGLE	BLOCK	PLATE BLOCK	CERM PROG
☐ C101	**28c Gymnastics**, 6/17/83, San Antonio, TX	1.25	—	—	
☐ C102	**28c Hurdles**, 6/17/83, San Antonio, TX	1.25	—	—	
☐ C103	**28c Basketball**, 6/17/83, San Antonio, TX	1.25	—	—	
☐ C104	**28c Soccer**, 6/17/83, San Antonio, TX	1.25	—	—	
☐ C104a	**Se-tenant**, (901,028)	—	3.75	4.50	15.00
☐ C105	**40c Shot Put**, 4/8/83, Los Angeles, CA	1.75	—	—	
☐ C106	**40c Gymnastics**, 4/8/83, Los Angeles, CA	1.75	—	—	
☐ C107	**40c Swimming**, 4/8/83, Los Angeles, CA	1.75	—	—	
☐ C108	**40c Weight Lifting**, 4/8/83, Los Angeles, CA	1.75	—	—	
☐ C108a	**Se-tenant**, (1,001,657)	—	5.00	6.00	18.00
☐ C109	**35c Fencing**, 11/4/83, Colorado Springs, CO	1.75	—	—	
☐ C110	**35c Cycling**, 11/4/83, Colorado Springs, CO	1.75	—	—	
☐ C111	**35c Volleyball**, 11/4/83, Colorado Springs, CO	1.75	—	—	
☐ C112	**35c Pole Vaulting**, 11/4/83, Colorado Springs, CO	1.75	—	—	
☐ C112a	**Se-tenant**, (897,729)	—	4.50	5.50	18.00

1985

☐ C113	**33c Alfred Verville**, 2/13/85, Garden City, NY	1.75	2.00	2.50	8.00
☐ C114	**39c Lawrence & Elmer Sperry**, 2/13/85, Garden City, NY	1.75	2.00	2.50	8.00
☐ C113-C114	**33c Verville & Sperry**, 2/13/85, Garden City, NY				8.00
☐ C115	**44c Transpacific Air Mail**, 2/15/85, San Francisco, CA (269,229)	1.75	2.00	2.50	8.00
☐ C116	**44c Junipero Serra**, 8/22/85, San Diego, CA (254,977)	1.75	2.00	2.50	8.00

1988

☐ C117	**44c Settling of New Sweden**, 3/29/88, Wilmington, DE (213,445)	1.75	2.00	2.50	14.00
☐	**With Finland No. 768 and Sweden No. 1672, multiple cancels**	20.00			
☐ C118	**45c Samuel P. Langley**, 5/14/88, San Diego, CA	1.75	2.00	2.50	12.00
☐ C119	**36c Igor Sikorsky**, 6/23/88, Stratford, CT (162,986)	1.50	2.00	2.50	12.00

1989

☐ C120	**45c French Revolution Bicentennial**, 7/14/89, DC (309,975)	1.75	2.50	3.00	8.00
☐ C121	**45c America**, 10/12/89, San Juan, PR (93,569)	1.75	2.50	3.00	
☐ C122	**45c Spacecraft**, 11/27/89, DC	1.75	—	—	
☐ C123	**45c Hover Car**, 11/27/89, DC	1.75	—	—	
☐ C124	**45c Moon Rover**, 11/27/89, DC	1.75	—	—	
☐ C125	**45c Space Shuttle**, 11/27/89, DC	1.75	—	—	
☐ C125a	**Se-tenant**, (765,479)	—	6.00	7.00	10.00
☐ C126	**45c Futuristic Mail Delivery**, souvenir sheet, 11/24/89, DC (237,826)	6.00	—	—	10.00

1990

☐ C127	**45c America**, 10/12/90, Grand Canyon, AZ (137,068)	2.00	2.25	2.50	10.00

SCOTT NUMBER	DESCRIPTION	SINGLE	PLATE BLOCK	CERM BLOCK	PROG

1991

☐ C128	50c Harriet Quimby, 4/27/91, Plymouth, MI	2.00	2.25	2.50	
☐ C129	40c William T. Piper, 5/17/91, Denver, CO	2.00	2.25	2.50	
☐ C130	50c Antarctic Treaty, 6/21/91, DC	2.00	2.25	2.50	6.00
☐ C131	50c Bering Land Bridge, 10/12/91, Anchorage, AK	2.00	2.25	2.50	6.00

1999

☐ C133	48c Niagara Falls, 5/12/99, Niagara Falls, NY	1.40	2.25	2.50	10.00
☐ C134	40c Rio Grande, 7/30/99, Milwaukee	1.50	2.25	2.50	

2000

☐ C135	60c Grand Canyon, 1/20/00, Grand Canyon, AZ, Self-adhesive	1.50			
☐ C136	70c Nine-Mile Prairie, 2/22/01, Lincoln, NE, Self-adhesive	1.60			
☐ C137	80c Mt. McKinley, 4/17/01, Fairbanks, AK, Self-adhesive	1.75			
☐ C138	60c Acadia National Park, 5/30/01, Bar Harbor, ME, Self-adhesive	1.50			

Cachet values in this catalogue are for an average cacheted First Day Cover. Some FDC's, depending on the cachet, can sell for many times the catalogue value, while others sell for less. The Cachet Calculator lists cachetmakers, the dates they produced FDC's and a market value multiplier. The Calculator begins on page 52A.

AIRPOST SPECIAL DELIVERY

CE1-CE2

E1

E12-E13, E15-E18

E14, E19

E22-E23

E20-E21

FA1

1934

☐ CE1	**16c Great Seal,** 8/30/34, Chicago, IL (AAMS Convention Sta.) (40,171)	30.00	35.00	40.00
☐	DC, 8/31/34	15.00	17.50	22.50
	For Scott CE1 design imperforate, see Scott 771.			

1936

☐ CE2	**16c Great Seal,** 2/10/36, DC (72,981)	25.00	27.50	32.50

SPECIAL DELIVERY
1885

☐ E1 **10c Messenger,** at special delivery offices, 10/1/1885....8,500.

1888

☐ E2 **10c Messenger,** at any post office, 12/18/1888, earliest known use ....—

1893

☐ E3 **10c Messenger,** 2/11/1893, earliest known use ....—

1894

☐ E4 **10c Messenger,** unwmkd, 11/21/1894, earliest known use ..—

1895-99

☐ E5 **10c Messenger,** wmk USPS, 10/3/1895, earliest known use .—

1903

☐ E6 **10c Bicycle,** perf. 12, dbl-line wmk, 1/22/03, earliest known use ....—

1908

☐ E7 10c **Mercury**, 12/14/08, earliest known use ....—

1911

☐ E8 10c **Bicycle**, perf. 12, sgl-line wmk, 1/14/11,
earliest known use ....—

1914

☐ E9 10c **Bicycle**, perf. 10, sgl-line wmk, 10/26/14,
earliest known use ....—

1916

☐ E10 10c **Bicycle**, perf. 10, unwmk, 11/4/16, earliest known use..—

1917

☐ E11 10c **Bicycle**, perf. 11, unwmk, 6/12/17, earliest known use..—

1922

☐ E12 10c **Motorcycle**, perf. 11, 7/12/22 ....400.00

1925

☐ E13 15c **Motorcycle**, perf. 11, 4/11/25 ....225.00   375.00
☐ E14 20c **P.O. Truck**, perf. 11, 4/25/25 ....100.00   200.00

1927-41

☐ E15 10c **Motorcycle**, perf. 11 x 10 1/2, 11/29/27, DC 90.00   200.00
☐ E15 **Motorcycle**, electric eye, perf 11 x 10 1/2, 9/8/41, DC.....25.00   35.00
*Values given for Scott E15 Electric Eye are for covers
with sheet salvage with Electric Eye markings.*

1931

☐ E16 15c **Motorcycle**, perf. 11 x 10 1/2, 8/13/31, DC 125.00   200.00
☐ Easton, PA, 8/6/31 ....2000.   —
*8/6/31 is the earliest known use of Scott E16,
8/13/31 is the first day of sale at the Philatelic Agency.*

1944

☐ E17 13c **Motorcycle**, 10/30/44, DC 12.50   15.00
☐ E18 17c **Motorcycle**, 10/30/44, DC 12.50   15.00
☐ Scott E17 & E18 on one cover ....15.00   —
Total for Scott E17 and E18 is 158,863

1951

☐ E19 20c **P.O. Truck**, 11/30/51, DC (33,139)..............................5.00   8.00

1954-57

☐ E20 20c **Letter**, 10/13/54, Boston, MA (194,043)......................3.00   5.00   45.00
☐ E21 30c **Letter**, 9/3/57, Indianapolis, IN (111,451)...................2.25   4.25   30.00

1969-71

☐ E22 45c **Arrows**, 11/21/69, New York, NY (192,391)................3.50   6.00   20.00
☐ E23 60c **Arrows**, 5/10/71, Phoenix, AZ (129,562).....................3.50   6.00   20.00

CERTIFIED MAIL/REGISTRATION

☐ FA1 **15c Certified Mail**, 6/6/55, DC (176,308) 3.25   5.00
☐ F1   **10c Registry**, 12/1/11, any city...12,000.

SPECIAL HANDLING

QE1-QE4   Q2   J68   J88

SCOTT NUMBER	DESCRIPTION	UNCACHETED SINGLE	BLOCK	CACHETED SINGLE
☐ QE1a	**10c Special Handling**, 6/25/28 ....50.00		65.00	200.00
☐ QE2a	**15c Special Handling**, 6/25/28 ....50.00		65.00	200.00
☐ QE3a	**20c Special Handling**, 6/25/28 ....50.00		65.00	200.00
☐ QE4a	**25c Special Handling**, 4/11/25 ....225.00		275.00	300.00
☐	Scott QE4a & E13 on one cover, 4/11/25 ....1,300.			1,500.

PARCEL POST

Parcel Post Service (fourth class) began January 1, 1913, and these stamps were issued
for that service only. The 1c, 2c, 4c and 5c are known with January 1, 1913, postmarks
— the 2c undoubtedly for fourth class usage, the others possible but unproven. Beginning
July 1, these stamps could be used for any purpose, thus a few first class FDCs were prepared for some of the lower denominations. There was not an official first day city for
either date.

		4th Class (1/1/13)	1st Class (7/1/13)
☐ Q1	**1c Post Office Clerk**, any city ....3,500.		2,500.
	Scott Q1 known on picture postcard.		
☐ Q2	**2c City Carrier**, any city..4,500.		2,500.
☐ Q3	**3c Railway Postal Clerk**, any city ....—		4,500.
☐ Q4	**4c Rural Carrier**, any city ....—		5,000.
☐ Q5	**5c Mail Train**, any city...4,000.		7,000.
	Scott Q4 & Q5 on wrapper...—		8,000

SCOTT NUMBER	DESCRIPTION	CACHETED SINGLE	BLOCK	CERM PROG

OFFICIALS
1983-85

☐ O127	**1c Great Seal**, 1/12/83, DC..1.00			1.25
☐ O128	**4c Great Seal**, 1/12/83, DC..1.00			1.25
☐ O129	**13c Great Seal**, 1/12/83, DC...1.00			1.25
☐ O129A	**14c Great Seal**, 5/15/85 DC..1.00			1.25
☐ O130	**17c Great Seal**, 1/12/83, DC...1.00			1.25
☐ O132	**$1 Great Seal**, 1/12/83, DC 3.00			6.00
☐ O133	**$5 Great Seal**, 1/12/83, DC..15.00			20.00
☐ O135	**20c Great Seal Coil**,1/12/83, DC 1.00			pr1.25
☐	Scott O127-O129, O130-O135 on one cover..........15.00			
☐	Scott O127-O129, O130-O135 on Official Postal Card (Scott UZ2) or envelope (Scott UO73)....................20.00			

SCOTT NUMBER	DESCRIPTION	CACHETED SINGLE	BLOCK	CERM PROG
☐ 0136	22c Great Seal Coil, 5/15/85, DC	1.00	pr1.25	
☐ 0138	(14c) Great Seal, 2/4/85, DC	1.00	1.25	

SCOTT NUMBER	DESCRIPTION	CACHETED SINGLE	PAIR	CERM PROG

1988

☐ 0138A	15c Great Seal Coil, 6/11/88, Corpus Christi, TX	1.00	1.25	
☐ 0138A & 0141				8.00
☐ 0138B	20c Great Seal Coil, with frame line, 5/19/88, DC	1.00	1.25	
☐ 0139	(22c) Great Seal, 2/4/85, DC	1.00	1.25	
☐ 0140	(25c) Great Seal Coil, 3/22/88, DC	1.75	2.00	
☐ 0141	25c Great Seal Coil, 6/11/88, Corpus Christi, TX	1.75	2.00	

SCOTT NUMBER	DESCRIPTION	CACHETED SINGLE	BLOCK	CERM PROG

1989

☐ 0143	1c Great Seal, lithographed, 7/5/89, DC	1.00	1.10	

1991-95

☐ 0144	(29c) Great Seal, non-denominated, 1/22/91, DC	1.75	2.00	
☐ 0145	29c Great Seal, 5/24/91, Seattle, WA	1.75	2.00	
☐ 0146	4c Great Seal, 4/6/91, Oklahoma City, OK	1.75	2.00	
☐ 0146A	10c Great Seal, 10/19/93, DC	1.25	2.00	
☐ 0147	19c Great Seal, 5/24/91, Seattle, WA	1.75	2.00	
☐ 0148	23c Great Seal, 5/24/91, Seattle, WA	1.75	2.00	
☐ 0152	(32c) G, Great Seal, 12/13/94, DC	1.25		
☐ 0153	32c Great Seal, 5/9/95, DC	1.25		
☐ 0154	1c Great Seal, microscopic text, 5/9/95, DC	1.25	2.00	
☐ 0155	20c Great Seal, microscopic text, 5/9/95, DC	1.25	2.00	
☐ 0156	23c Great Seal, microscopic text, 5/9/95, DC	1.25	2.00	
☐ 0157	33c Great Seal, microscopic text, 10/8/99, DC	1.00	2.00	
☐ 0158	34c Great Seal, Coil stamp, 2/27/01, DC	1.25		

SCOTT NUMBER	DESCRIPTION	SINGLE	CERM PROG

POSTAGE DUE
1925

☐ J68	1/2c Dull Red, 4/15/25, earliest known use, Philadelphia, PA	900.00	
☐	Raway, NJ	2,000.	

1959

☐ J88	1/2c Red and Black, 6/19/59	75.00	
☐ J89	1c Red and Black, 6/19/59	75.00	
☐ J89-J101	1/2c -$5 Postage Due 6/19/59 (without due stamps)		35.00
☐ J90	2c Red and Black, 6/19/59	75.00	
☐ J91	3c Red and Black, 6/19/59	75.00	
☐ J92	4c Red and Black, 6/19/59	75.00	
☐ J93	5c Red and Black, 6/19/59	100.00	
☐ J94	6c Red and Black, 6/19/59	100.00	
☐ J95	7c Red and Black, 6/19/59	100.00	
☐ J96	8c Red and Black, 6/19/59	100.00	
☐ J97	10c Red and Black, 6/19/59	100.00	
☐ J98	30c Red and Black, 6/19/59	100.00	
☐ J99	50c Red and Black, 6/19/59	100.00	
☐ J100	$1 Red and Black, 6/19/59	100.00	
☐ J101	$5 Red and Black, 6/19/59	150.00	

1978-85

☐ J102	**11c Red and Black**, 1/2/78	5.00	
☐ J103	**13c Red and Black**, 1/2/78	5.00	
☐ J104	**17c Red and Black**, 6/10/85	5.00	

POSTAL NOTES

☐ PN1	**1c Black**, 2/1/45, on complete 3 part money order form	45.00	
☐ PN1-PN18	**1c to 90c Black**, 2/1/45 on 18 money order forms	600.00	

*Last day covers of this service also exist, dated 3/31/51.
These sell for $15-$20.*

POSTAL SAVINGS
1941

☐ PS11	**10c Red**, 5/1/41, any city	175.00	

REVENUES

These examples of Revenue FD's are postmarked with fiscal
rather than postal cancellations.

1898

☐ R154	**1c Green**, Franklin, 7/1/98	—	
☐ R155	**2c Washington**, 7/1/98	1000.	
☐ R166	**4c Rose Battleship**, 7/1/98	—	

HUNTING PERMIT STAMPS

The following are not postage stamp items. They are listed here only for collectors'
interest. Ceremony Program prices are for programs without a stamp affixed.

☐ RW3	**$1 Canada Geese**, 7/1/36, Warren, NJ	700.00	
☐ RW43	**$5 Canada Geese**, 7/1/76, any city	150.00	
☐ RW46	**$7.50 Green-winged Teal**, 7/1/79, any city	150.00	
☐ RW47	**$7.50 Mallards**, 7/1/80, any city	150.00	
☐ RW48	**$7.50 Ruddy Ducks**, 7/1/81, any city	75.00	
☐ RW49	**$7.50 Canvas Backs**, 7/1/82, any city	55.00	
☐ RW50	**$7.50 Pintail**, 7/1/83, any city	50.00	
☐ RW51	**$7.50 Wigeons**, 7/1/84, any city	50.00	
☐ RW52	**$7.50 Cinnamon Teal**, 7/1/85, any city	45.00	
☐ RW53	**$7.50 Fulvous Whistling Duck**, 7/1/86, any city	45.00	
☐ RW54	**$10 Redheads**, 7/1/87, any city	45.00	15.00
☐ RW55	**$10 Snow Goose**, 7/1/88, any city	45.00	20.00
☐ RW56	**$12.50 Lesser Scaup**, 6/30/89, any city	45.00	25.00
☐ RW57	**$12.50 Black Bellied Whistling Duck**, 6/30/90, any city	45.00	35.00
☐ RW58	**$15 Elders**, 7/1/91, DC	35.00	30.00
☐ RW59	**$15 Spectacled Eider**, 7/1/92, DC	35.00	30.00
☐ RW60	**$15 Canvasback**, 7/1/93	35.00	30.00
☐ RW61	**$15 Mergansers**, 7/1/94	35.00	30.00
☐ RW62	**$15 Mallard**, 6/30/95, DC	35.00	30.00
☐ RW63	**$15 Surf Scoter**, 6/27/96, DC	35.00	25.00
☐ RW64	**$15 Canada Goose**, 6/21/97, DC	35.00	25.00
☐ RW65	**$15 Barrow's Goldeneye**, 7/1/98, DC	35.00	25.00
☐ RW65	**$15 Barrow's Goldeneye**, 7/1/98, DC	35.00	25.00
☐ RW65A	**$15 Barrow's Goldeneye**, self-adhesive, 7/1/98, DC	35.00	
☐ RW66	**$15 Greater Scaup**, 7/1/99, DC	35.00	25.00
☐ RW66A	**$15 Greater Scaup**, self-adhesive, 7/1/99, DC	35.00	
☐ RW67	**$15 Mottled Duck**, 6/30/00, DC	35.00	25.00
☐ RW67A	**$15 Mottled Duck**, 6/30/00, DC	35.00	
☐ RW68	**$15 Northern Pintail** - Inscribed 'Void after June 30, 2002'	35.00	25.00
☐ RW68A	**$15 Northern Pintail**, 6/30/02, Self-Adhesive	35.00	

ENVELOPES

Sizes of U.S. Envelope FD's are as follows: Size 5 — 89x160mm, Size 6 3/4 - 92x165mm, Size 7 - 98x225mm, Size 7 1/2 — 99x190mm, Sizes 8 and 10 — 105x240mm, Size 13 — 95x171mm. Where a paper difference is shown, the watermark of "Standard Quality" is similar to Watermark 28 and "Extra Quality" is similar to Watermark 29.

All FDC's prior to 1946 have normal cancels.

** Denotes: Does not exist with either a standard FDOI cancel or with any other cancel used specifically for that First Day, (1946 and later)

U481, U436-9,
U529-U531

U522

U523-U528

U532-U534,
U536, U544

U541-U542

U543

U546

1861

☐ U35 3c George Washington, pink, 8/10/1861,
earliest known use ....—

1876

☐ U221 3c Centennial, green, 5/10/1876, earliest known use,
Centennial cancel, size 3, wmk 3 ....3,500.

1883

☐ U227 2c George Washington, 10/2/1883, size 5, wmk 6,
earliest known use 350.00

1886

☐ U293 2c U.S. Grant, letter sheet, 8/18/1886,
earliest known use ....—

1916-32

☐ U436a 3c George Washington, white paper, extra quality,
6/16/32, DC, size 5, die 1, wmk 29 ....75.00   —
☐   size 8, die 1, wmk 29...25.00   75.00
☐ U436e 3c George Washington, white paper, extra quality,
6/16/32, DC, size 5, die 7, wmk 29 ....35.00   50.00
☐   size 13, die 7, wmk 29...35.00   50.00

			UNCACH	CACH	PROG
☐ U436f	3c **George Washington**, white paper, extra quality,				
	6/16/32, DC, size 5, die 9, wmk 29	12.00	30.00	
☐	size 13, die9, wmk 29	15.00	30.00	
☐ U437a	3c **George Washington**, amber paper, 7/13/32, DC, size			
	5, wmk 28, standard quality	50.00	—	
☐	7/19/32, DC, size 5, wmk 29, extra quality	35.00	—	
☐ U439a	3c **George Washington**, blue paper, 7/13/32, DC, size 5,			
	wmk 28, standard quality	40.00	—	
☐	size 13, wmk 28, standard quality	65.00	—	
☐	9/9/32, DC, size 8, wmk 28, standard quality	85.00	—	

1921

☐ U446	2c on 3c **George Washington**, 5/21/21,				
	earliest known use	—		

1925

			UNCACH	CACH	PROG
☐ U481	1 1/2c **George Washington**, 3/19/25, DC, size 5,				
	wmk 27	35.00	—	
☐	size 8, wmk 27	70.00	—	
☐	size 13, wmk 26	50.00	—	
☐	size 5 or 13, with Scott 553, 582, or 598	60.00	—	
☐	Any size with 553, 582 and 598	200.00	—	
☐ U495	1 1/2c on 1c **Benjamin Franklin**, 6/1/25, DC size 5	50.00	—	
☐	6/3/25, DC, size 8	65.00	—	
☐	6/2/25, DC, size 13	60.00	—	
☐ U515	1 1/2c on 1c **Benjamin Franklin**, 8/1/25, Des Moines,			
	IA, size 5, die 1	50.00	—	
☐ U521	1 1/2c on 1c **Benjamin Franklin**, 10/22/25, DC, size 5,			
	die 1, wmk 25	100.00	—	

1926

☐ U522a	2c **Liberty Bell**, 7/27/26, Philadelphia, PA, size 5,				
	wmk 27**	20.00	30.00	
☐	7/27/26, DC, size 5, wmk 27	22.50	32.50	
☐	7/27/26, unofficial city, size 5, wmk 27	35.00	45.00	

1932

			UNCACH	CACH	PROG
☐ U523	1c **Mount Vernon**, 1/1/32, DC, size 5, wmk 29	8.00	20.00	
☐	size 8, wmk 29	10.00	20.00	
☐	size 13, wmk 29	8.00	20.00	
☐ U524	1 1/2c **Mount Vernon**, 1/1/32, DC, size 5, wmk 29	8.00	20.00	
☐	size 8, wmk 29	10.00	20.00	
☐	size 13, wmk 29	8.00	20.00	
☐ U525	2c **Mount Vernon**, 1/1/32, DC, size 5, wmk 29	8.00	20.00	
☐	size 8, wmk 29	10.00	20.00	
☐	size 13, wmk 29	8.00	20.00	
☐ U526	3c **Mount Vernon**, 6/16/32, DC, size 5, wmk 29	15.00	20.00	
☐	size 8, wmk 29	25.00	40.00	
☐	size 13, wmk 29	20.00	30.00	
☐ U527	4c **Mount Vernon**, 1/1/32, DC, size 8, wmk 29	15.00	25.00	
☐ U528	5c **Mount Vernon**, 1/1/32, DC, size 5, wmk 29	10.00	22.00	
☐	size 8, wmk 29	12.00	22.00	
☐ U529	6c **George Washington**, white paper, 8/18/32, Los			
	Angeles, CA, size 8, wmk 29	15.00	—	

SCOTT NUMBER	DESCRIPTION	UNCACH	CACH	CERM PROG
☐	8/19/32, DC, size 7, wmk 29 ....20.00		—	
☐	8/19/32, DC, size 9, wmk 29 ....20.00		—	
☐ U530	6c George Washington, amber paper, 8/18/32, Los Angeles, CA, size 8, wmk 29....................15.00		—	
☐	8/19/32, DC, size 7, wmk 29 ....20.00		—	
☐	8/19/32, DC, size 9, wmk 29 ....20.00		—	
☐	size 8, wmk 29, with Scott 723 pair 25.00		—	
☐ U531	6c George Washington, blue paper, 8/18/32, Los Angeles, size 8, wmk 29....................15.00		—	
☐	8/19/32, DC, size 7, wmk 29 ....20.00		—	
☐	8/19/32, DC, size 9, wmk 29 ....20.00		—	

1950

SCOTT NUMBER	DESCRIPTION	UNCACH	CACH	CERM PROG
☐ U532	1c Benjamin Franklin, 11/16/50, New York, NY, size 13, wmk 42.......................1.50		2.50	
☐ U533a	2c George Washington, 11/17/50, New York, NY, size 13, wmk 42.......................1.50		2.50	
☐ U534a	3c George Washington, die 1, 11/18/50, New York, NY, size 13, wmk 42.......................1.50		2.50	
☐ U534b	3c George Washington, die 2, 11/19/50, New York, NY, size 8, wmk 42**.......................5.00		10.00	

1952

SCOTT NUMBER	DESCRIPTION	UNCACH	CACH	CERM PROG
☐ U535	1 1/2c George Washington, 10/21/52, Dover or Kenvil, NJ, size 13, wmk 42, earliest known use 75.00		—	

1958

SCOTT NUMBER	DESCRIPTION	UNCACH	CACH	CERM PROG
☐ U536	4c Benjamin Franklin, 7/31/58, Montpelier, VT (163,746), size 6 3/4, wmk 46....................1.00		1.50	
☐	size 8, wmk 46**.......................60.00		—	
☐	size 13, wmk 46**.......................60.00		—	
☐	7/31/58, Wheeling, WV, size 6 3/4, wmk 46 with Scott 1036a**.......................35.00		—	
☐	size 13, window**.......................35.00		—	
☐ U540	3c + 1c George Washington (U534c), 7/22/58, Kenvil, NJ, size 8, wmk 46, die 3, earliest known use** 50.00		—	

1960

SCOTT NUMBER	DESCRIPTION	UNCACH	CACH	CERM PROG
☐ U541	1 1/4c Benjamin Franklin, 6/25/60, Birmingham, AL (211,500), size 6 3/4, wmk 46....................1.00		1.25	25.00
☐ U542	2 1/2c George Washington, 5/28/60, Chicago, IL (196,977), size 6 3/4, wmk 46....................1.00		1.25	30.00
☐ U543	4c Pony Express Rider, 7/19/60, St. Joseph, MO (407,160), size 6 3/4, wmk 46....................1.00		1.25	30.00
☐	7/19/60, Sacramento, CA, with Scott 1154, size 6 3/4, wmk 46.......................3.50		5.00	

1962

SCOTT NUMBER	DESCRIPTION	UNCACH	CACH	CERM PROG
☐ U544	5c Abraham Lincoln, 11/19/62, Springfield, IL (163,258), size 6 3/4, wmk 48....................1.00		1.25	15.00

Values for various cachet makers can be determined by using the Cachet Calculator which begins on page 52A.

U547, U548,
U548A, U556

U549, U552

U550, U553

U551, U561

U554

U555, U562

U557

U563

U564

U565

U567

U569

U568

U571-U575

U576

U581

U584

224

SCOTT NUMBER	DESCRIPTION	UNCACH	CACH	CERM PROG
☐ U546	5c New York World's Fair, 4/22/64, World's Fair, NY (466,422), size 6 3/4, wmk 48 .... 1.00		1.25	18.00

1965-69

☐ U547	1 1/4c Liberty Bell, 1/6/65, DC, size 6 3/4, wmk 49 .... 1.00		1.00	
☐	1/8/65, DC, size 10, wmk 48** 10.00		20.00	
☐	cerm. prog. includes U549			18.00
☐ U548	1 4/10c Liberty Bell, 3/26/68, Springfield, MA (134,832), size 6 3/4, wmk 49 .... 1.00		1.00	18.00
☐	3/27/68, DC, size 10, wmk 48** 5.00		8.00	
☐ U548A	1 6/10c Liberty Bell, 6/16/69, DC, size 6 3/4, wmk 47 (130,109) 1.00		1.00	
☐	size 10, wmk 49** 1.25		1.75	
☐ U549	4c Old Ironsides, 1/6/65, DC, size 6 3/4, wmk 49 .... 1.00		1.00	
☐	1/8/65, DC, size 6 3/4, window, wmk 49** 10.00		20.00	
☐	size 10, wmk 49** 10.00		20.00	
☐	size 10, window, wmk 49 ** 10.00		20.00	
	Total for Scott U547 and U549 is 451,960.			
☐ U550	5c Eagle, 1/5/65, Williamsburg, PA (246,496), size 6 3/4, wmk 49 .... 1.00		1.00	18.00
☐	1/8/65, DC, size 6 3/4, window, wmk 49** 10.00		20.00	
☐	size 10, wmk 49** 10.00		20.00	
☐	size 10, window, wmk 49** 10.00		20.00	
☐ U550a	Eagle, tagged, 8/15/67, DC & Dayton, OH, size 6 3/4, wmk 50** 3.50		5.00	
☐	size 6 3/4, window, wmk 48 .... 3.50		5.00	
☐	size 10, wmk 48 .... 3.50		5.00	
☐	size 10, wmk 49, Dayton only 4.50		7.50	
☐	size 10, window, wmk 49 .... 3.50		5.00	
	There were no FDOI cancels for any sizes or formats of U550a			
☐ U551	6c Statue of Liberty, 1/4/68, New York, NY (184,784), size 6 3/4, wmk 47 or 48 .... 1.00		1.25	15.00
☐	1/5/68, DC, size 6 3/4, window, wmk 48 or 49** 7.50		15.00	
☐	size 10, wmk 47** 5.00		10.00	
☐	size 10, window, wmk 49** 5.00		10.00	
☐	11/15/68, DC, new shiny plastic window, size 6 3/4, window, wmk 48** 3.00		10.00	

1968

☐ U552	4c + 2c Old Ironsides, 2/5/68, DC, size 6 3/4, wmk 50 ..... 3.50		7.50	
☐	size 6 3/4, window, wmk 48 .... 3.50		5.00	
☐	size 10, wmk 47 .... 3.50		7.50	
☐	size 10, window, wmk 49 .... 3.50		7.50	
☐ U553	5c + 1c Eagle, 2/5/68, DC, size 6 3/4, wmk 49 .... 3.50		5.00	
☐	size 10, window, wmk 49 .... 3.50		7.50	
☐ U553a	Eagle, tagged, 2/5/68, DC, size 6 3/4, wmk 48 .... 3.50		5.00	
☐	size 10, wmk 47 or 49 .... 3.50		7.50	
☐	size 10, window, wmk 49 .... 3.50		7.50	
	There were no FDOI cancels for any sizes or formats of U552, U553, U553a			

1970

☐ U554	6c Moby Dick, 3/7/70, New Bedford, MA (433,777) size 6 3/4, wmk 47 .... 1.00		1.25	12.00

1971

☐ U555	6c Youth Conference, 2/24/71, DC, (264,559), size 6 3/4, wmk 49 .... 1.00		1.00	25.00

☐ **U556** **1 7/10c Liberty Bell**, 5/10/71, Baltimore, MD (150,767),
size 6 3/4, wmk 48A 1.00 1.00
☐ 5/10/71, DC, size, 6 3/4, wmk 49** 9.00 15.00
☐ 5/11/71, DC, size10, wmk 47 or 49** 7.50 12.00
☐ 5/11/71, DC, size 10, wmk 48A** 3.50 6.00

☐ **U557** **8c Eagle**, 5/6/71, Williamsburg, PA (193,000), size 6 3/4,
wink 48A 1.00 1.00 20.00
☐ size 6 3/4 window, wmk 49** ....10.00 —
☐ size 10, wmk 49** ....10.00 —
☐ size 10, window, wmk 47** ....10.00 —

☐ **U561** **6c + (2c) Statue of Liberty**, 5/16/71, DC, size 6 3/4,
wmk 47 ....2.00 4.00
☐ size 6 3/4, wmk 48A, (25 known) 15.00 25.00
☐ size 6 3/4, wmk 49 ....2.50 4.00
☐ size 6 3/4, window, wmk 47 ....2.50 4.00
☐ size 10, wmk 48A 2.00 3.00
☐ size 10, wmk 49 ....3.50 6.00
☐ size 10, window, wmk 47 ....2.50 4.00
☐ size 10, window, wmk 49 ....2.50 4.00

☐ **U562** **6c + (2c) Youth Conference**, 5/16/71, DC, size 6 3/4,
wmk 47 ....20.00 30.00
☐ size 6 3/4, wmk 49 ....2.50 5.00
There were no FDOI cancels for any sizes or formats of U561 and U562

☐ **U563** **8c Bowling**, 8/21/71, Milwaukee, WI (267,029),
size 6 3/4, wmk 49 ....1.00 1.25 18.00
☐ size 10, wmk 49 ....1.00 2.00

☐ **U564** **8c Aging Conference**, 11 / 15/71, DC (125,000),
size 6 3/4, wmk 48A 1.00 1.00 25.00

1972

☐ **U565** **8c International Transportation Exposition**, 5/2/72, DC,
size 6 3/4, wmk 47 ....2.50 3.00 18.00
☐ size 6 3/4, wmk 49 ....1.00 1.00

1973

☐ **U566** **8c + 2c Eagle**, 12/1/73, DC, size 6 3/4, wmk 47 or 49 ....1.50 2.50
☐ size 6 3/4, window, wmk 48A ....7.50 —
☐ size 6 3/4, window, wmk 49 ....4.00 7.50
☐ size 10, wmk 47 ....3.00 4.50
☐ size 10, window, wmk 49 ....4.00 7.50
There were no FDOI cancels for any sizes or formats of U566

☐ **U567** **10c Liberty Bell**, 12/5/73, Philadelphia, PA (142,141),
☐ size 6 3/4, wmk 47, old knife depth 58mm 1.00 1.50 25.00
☐ size 6 3/4, wmk 47, new knife depth 51mm 1.00 1.50
☐ size 6 3/4 window, wmk 47** 10.00
☐ size 10, wmk 47** ....10.00 —
☐ size 10, window, wmk 47** ....10.00 —

1974

☐ **U568** **1 8/10c Volunteer Yourself**, 8/23/74, Cincinnati, OH,
size 6 3/4, wmk 47 ....1.00 1.00 12.00
☐ size 10, wmk 47 ....1.00 1.50

☐ **U569** **10c Tennis Centenary**, 8/31/74, Forest Hills, NY
(245,000), size 6 3/4, wmk 49 ....1.00 1.25

☐	size 10, wmk 49 ....1.00		3.00	
☐	9/3/74, DC, size 6 3/4, window, wmk 49** 2.50		5.00	
☐	size 10, window, wmk 49** 2.50		5.00	

Note: Window envelopes were sold and canceled on the first day, contrary to regulations.

1975-76 Bicentennial Era

☐ U571	**10c Seafaring Tradition**, 10/13/75, Minneapolis, MN (255,304), size 6 3/4...1.00		1.00	12.00
☐	size 10 ....1.00		1.25	
☐ U572	**13c American Homemaker**, 2/2/76, Biloxi, MS (196,647), size 6 3/4...1.00		1.00	12.00
☐	size 10 ....1.00		1.25	
☐ U573	**13c American Farmer**, 3/15/76, New Orleans, LA (214,563), size 6 3/4...1.00		1.00	15.00
☐	size 10 ....1.00		1.25	
☐ U574	**13c American Doctor**, 6/30/76, Dallas, TX, (251,272) size 6 3/4...1.00		1.00	12.00
☐	size 10 ....1.00		1.25	
☐ U575	**13c American Craftsman**, 8/6/76, Lunesboro, MA, (215,000) size 6 3/4...1.00		1.00	12.00
☐	size 10 ....1.00		1.25	

1975

☐ U576	**13c Liberty Tree**, 11/8/75, Memphis, TN (226,824)			
	size 6 3/4, wmk 48A..1.00		1.00	12.00
☐	size 10, wmk 47 ....1.00		1.25	

1976-78

☐ U577	**2c Star and Pinwheel**, 9/10/76, Hempstead, NY (81,388), size 6 3/4, wmk 48A or 49..........................1.00		1.00	10.00
☐	size 10, wmk 48A...1.00		1.25	
☐ U578	**2.1c (Non-Profit)**, 6/3/77, Houston, TX (120,280) size 6 3/4, wmk 47 ....1.00		1.00	10.00
☐	size 10, wmk 47 ....1.00		1.25	
☐ U579	**2.7c (Non-Profit)**, 7/5/78, Raleigh, NC (92,687), size 6 3/4, wmk 47 ....1.00		1.00	
☐	size 10, wmk 47 ....1.00		1.25	
☐ U580	**(15c) "A" & Eagle**, 5/22/78, Memphis, TN, size 6 3/4 wmk 47 ....1.00		1.50	
☐	size 6 3/4, wmk 48A..1.00		1.00	
☐	size 6 3/4, window, wmk 47 or 48A..........................1.25		2.00	
☐	size 10, wmk 47 or 49 ....1.00		1.25	
☐	size 10, window, wmk 47 or 49 ....1.25		2.00	
☐	size 6 3/4, wmk 48A with sheet, coil & booklet pane 5.00		10.00	
☐ U581	**15c Uncle Sam**, 6/3/78, Williamsburg, PA (176,000), size 6 3/4, wmk 47 or 49 ....1.00		1.00	
☐	size 6 3/4, window, wmk 47......................................4.00		5.00	
☐	size 10, wmk 47 or 48A 1.00		1.25	
☐	size 10, window, wmk 48A or 49...............................4.00		5.00	

1976

☐ U582	**13c Bicentennial**, 10/15/76, Los Angeles, CA (277,222), size 6 3/4, wmk 48A...2.00		3.00	12.00

U587

U590

U593

U595

U598

U602

U606

U607

U608

U609

SCOTT NUMBER	DESCRIPTION	UNCACH	CACH	CERM PROG
☐	size 6 3/4, wmk 49	1.00	1.00	
☐	size 6 3/4, wmk 49, dark green	—	7.50	
☐	size 10, wmk 49	1.00	1.25	

1977

☐ U583	**13c Golf**, 4/7/77, Augusta, GA (252,000), size 6 3/4, wmk 49	1.00	7.00	
☐	size 10, wmk 49	1.00	7.00	
☐	4/8/77, DC, size 6 3/4, window, wmk 49**	2.00	7.50	
☐	size 10, window, wmk 49**	2.00	7.50	
☐ U584	**13c Energy Conservation**, 10/20/77, Ridley Park, PA, San Francisco, CA, size 6 3/4, wmk 49	1.00	1.00	
☐	size 6 3/4, window, wmk 49	2.00	4.00	
☐	size 10, wmk 49	1.00	1.25.	
☐	size 10, window, wmk 49	2.00	4.00	
☐	10/20/77, DC, with Scott 1723-1724, all sizes	3.50	4.00	
☐ U585	**13c Energy Development**, 10/20/77, Ridley Park, PA, San Francisco, CA, size 6 3/4, wmk 49	1.00	1.00	
☐	size 6 3/4, window, wmk 49	2.00	4.00	
☐	size 10, wmk 49	1.00	1.25	
☐	size 10, window, wmk 49	2.00	4.00	
☐	10/20/77, DC, with Scott 1723-1724, all sizes	3.50	4.00	
	Total for Scott U584 and U585 is 353,515.			

1978

☐ U586	**15c on 16c USA**, 7/28/78, Williamsburg, PA, (193,153), size 6 3/4, wmk 47	1.00	1.00	
☐	size 10, wmk 47	1.00	1.25	
☐	size 6 3/4 window**	10.00	—	
	size 10 window **	10.00	—	
☐ U587	**15c Auto Racing**, 9/2/78, Ontario, CA (209,147), size 6 3/4, wmk 49	1.00	1.00	14.00
☐	size 10, wmk 49	1.00	1.25	
☐ U588	**15c on 13c Liberty Tree**, 11/28/78, Williamsburg, PA (137,500), size 6 3/4, wmk 47	1.00	1.00	
☐	size 10, wmk 47	1.00	1.25	
☐	size 6 3/4, window, wmk 47**	10.00	—	
☐	size 10, window, wmk 48A**	10.00	—	

1979- 82

☐ U589	**3.1c (Non-Profit)**, 5/18/79, Denver, CO (117,575) size 6 3/4, wmk 48A	1.00	1.00	10.00
☐	size 6 3/4, window, wmk 48	3.00	7.50	
☐	size 10, wmk 49	1.00	1.25	
☐	size 10, window, wmk 49	3.00	7.50	
☐ U590	**3.5c (Non-Profit)**, 6/23/80, Williamsburg, PA, size 6 3/4, wmk 49	1.00	1.00	
☐	size 10, wmk 48A or 49	10.00	—	
☐	size 6 3/4, window	1.00	2.00	
☐	size 10, window	10.00	—	
☐ U591	**5.9c (Non-Profit)**, 2/17/82, Wheeling, WV, size 6 3/4, wmk 47, 48A or 49	1.00	1.25	
☐	size 6 3/4, window, wmk 47	2.50	5.00	
☐	size 10, wmk 47, 48A or 49	1.00	1.50	
☐	size 10, window	2.50	5.00	

		UNCACH	CACH	CERM PROG
☐ U592	**(18c) "B" & Eagle**, 3/15/81, Memphis, TN (179,171),			
	size 6 3/4, wmk 47, 48A, or 49 ....1.00		1.00	
☐	size 6 3/4, window, wmk 47, 48A, or 49...................2.50		5.00	
☐	size 10, wmk 47 or 49 ....1.00		1.25	
☐	size 10, window, wmk 47 or 49 ....2.50		5.00	
☐	3/15/81, San Francisco, CA, With Scott 1818-1820 on			
	any of the above..1.50		2.00	
☐ U593	**18c Star**, 4/2/81, Star City, IN (160,439), size 6 3/4,			
	wmk 47 or 49 ....1.00		1.00	
☐	size 10, wmk 47, 48A or 49 ....1.00		1.25	
☐	size 6 3/4, window 2.50		5.00	
☐	size 10, window 2.50		5.00	
☐ U594	**(20c) "C" & Eagle**, 10/11/81, Memphis, TN			
	size 6 3/4, wmk 47 or 49 ....1.00		1.25	
☐	size 6 3/4 window 7.50		10.00	
☐	size 10, wmk 47, 48A or 49 ....1.00		1.50	
☐	size 10 window 4.00		5.00	
	Note: Window envelopes were sold and canceled with			
	the "FDOI" cancel contrary to announced policy.			

1979

☐ U595	**15c Veterinary Medicine**, 7/24/79, Seattle, WA			
	(209,658), size 6 3/4, wmk 49....................................1.00		1.00	10.00
☐	size 10, wmk 49 ....1.00		1.25	
☐	size 6 3/4 window** 10.00		—	
☐	size 10 window** 10.00		—	
☐ U596	**15c Olympic Games**, 12/10/79, E. Rutherford, NJ			
	(179,336), size 6 3/4, wmk 49....................................1.00		1.25	
☐	size 10, wmk 49 ....1.00		1.50	

1980

☐ U597	**15c Bicycling**, 5/16/80, Baltimore, MD (173,978)			
	size 6 3/4, wmk 49 ....1.00		1.25	10.00
☐	size 10, wmk 49 ....1.00		1.50	
☐ U598	**15c America's Cup Yacht Races**, 9/15/80, Newport, RI,			
	(192,220), size 6 3/4, wmk 49....................................1.00		1.25	15.00
☐	size 10, wmk 49 ....1.00		1.50	
☐ U599	**15c Honey Bee**, 10/10/80, Paris, IL, (202,050) size 6 3/4,			
	wmk 49 ....1.00		1.00	18.00
☐	size 10, wmk 49 ....1.00		1.25	

1981-82

☐ U600	**18c Remember the Blinded Veteran**, 8/13/81, Arlington,			
	VA (175,966), size 6 3/4, wmk 49 ....1.00		1.00	8.00
☐	size 10, wmk 49 ....1.00		1.25	
☐ U601	**20c Capitol Dome**, 11 /13/81, Los Angeles, CA,			
	size 6 3/4, wmk 48A or 49 ....1.00		1.25	
☐	size 10, wmk 47 or 49, size 10 ....1.00		1.50	
☐ U602	**20c Great Seal**, 6/15/82, DC, (163,905), size 6 3/4,			
	wmk 49 ....1.00		1.25	10.00
☐	size 10, wmk 49 ....1.00		1.50	
☐ U603	**20c Purple Heart**, 8/6/82, DC, (110,679), size 6 3/4,			
	wmk 49 ....1.00		1.25	10.00
☐	size 10, wmk 49 ....1.00		1.50	

1983

☐ U604	**5.2c (Non-Profit)**, 3/21/83, Memphis, TN, size 6 3/4,			
	wmk 47, 48A or 49 ....1.00		1.25	

		size 6 3/4, window, wmk 49	2.50	5.00	
		size 10, wmk47	1.00	1.50	
		size 10, window, wmk 47	2.50	5.00	
☐ U605	20c Paralyzed Veterans, 8/3/83, Portland, OR,				
		size 6 3/4	1.00	1.25	6.00
☐		size 10	1.00	1.50	

1984

| ☐ U606 | 20c Small Business, 5/7/84, DC, (77,665) size 6 3/4 | 1.00 | 1.25 | 8.00 |
| ☐ | | size 10 | 1.00 | 1.50 | |

1985

☐ U607	(22c) "D" & Eagle, 2/1/85, Los Angeles, size 6 3/4, wmk 47,			
	48A or 49	1.00	1.25	
☐	size 6 3/4, window, wmk 47, 48A or 49	2.50	5.00	
☐	size 10, wmk 47, 48A or 49	1.00	1.50	
☐	size 10, window, wmk 47	2.50	5.00	
☐ U608	22c Bison, 2/25/85, Bison, SD, (105,271)			
	size 6 3/4, wmk 47, 48A or 49	1.00	1.25	
☐	size 6 3/4, window, wmk 47, 48A or 49	2.50	5.00	
☐	size 10, wmk 47, 48A or 49	1.00	1.50	
☐	size 10, window, wmk 48A or 49	2.50	5.00	
☐	11/4/86 (First Day sold) DC, precanceled, size 10			
	window, unwmk.	25.00	—	
	11/1/86 (pre-date), DC, precanceled, size window,			
	unwmk	5.00	7.50	
☐ U609	6c U.S.S. Constitution, 5/3/85, Boston, MA, (170,425)			
	size 6 3/4, wmk 47, 48A or 49	1.00	1.25	8.00
☐	size 10, wmk 47, 48A or 49	1.00	1.50	
☐	size 6 3/4, window	2.00	4.00	
☐	size 10, window	2.00	4.00	

1986

☐ U610	8.5c The Mayflower, 12/4/86, Plymouth, MA (105,164),			
	size 6 3/4, wmk 48A, 49 or 50	1.00	1.25	
☐	size 6 3/4 with window, wmk 48A, 49 or 50	2.50	5.00	
☐	size 10, wmk 48A,49 or 50	1.00	1.50	
☐	size 10 with window, wmk 48A, 49 or 50	2.50	5.00	

1988

☐ U611	25c Stars, 3/26/88, Star, MS, (29,393) size 6 3/4	1.25	1.25	
☐	size 6 3/4, window	2.50	4.00	
☐	size 10	1.00	1.50	
☐	size 10 window	2.50	4.00	
☐	size 10 double window, wmk 50, (25,171),, 8/18/88,	1.25	1.50	
☐ U612	8.4c Sea Gulls & U.S. Frigate Constellation, 4/12/88,			
	Baltimore, MD, size 6 3/4 (41,420)	1.00	1.25	
☐	size 10	1.00	1.50	
☐	size 6 3/4, window	2.50	4.00	
☐	size 10, window	2.50	4.00	
☐ U613	25c Snowflake, 9/8/88, Snowflake, AZ, (32,601) wmk 50	1.25	2.00	

1989

☐ U614	25c Stars in "perforated" square, 3/10/89 Cleveland,			
	OH, (33,461) size 9, wmk 50	1.25	2.00	8.00
☐ U615	25c Stars in circle, 7/10/89, DC, size 9, unwmk	1.25	2.00	

	FDOI cancellation at Washington, D.C., 12/29/89			
☐	size 9 left window 3.00		7.50	
☐	size 9 right window....................................3.00		7.50	
☐ U616	25c **Love**, 9/22/89, McLean, VA (69,498), size 9, unwmk ..1.25		1.50	6.00
☐ U617	25c **Space Station**, hologram, 12/3/89, DC, (131,245)			
	size 9, unwmk 1.25		1.50	10.00

1990

☐ U618	25c **Football**, hologram, 9/9/90, Green Bay, WI			
	(54,589), size 10, unwmk...........................1.25		1.50	

1991

☐ U619	29c **Star**, 1/24/91, DC, (33,025) size 6 3/4,			
	wmk 48A, 49 or 50 ....1.25		1.50	
☐	size 6 3/4 window, wmk 48A, 49 or 50.....................2.00		3.00	
☐	size 10, wmk 48A, 49 or 50 ....1.25		1.50	
☐	size 10 window, wmk 48A, 49 or 50 ....2.00		3.00	
☐ U620	11.1c **Birds**, 5/3/91, Boxborough, MA, (20,720)			
	size 6 3/4, wmk 48A, 49 or 50...............................1.25		1.50	10.00
☐	size 6 3/4 window, wmk 48A, 49 or 50.....................2.00		3.00	
☐	size 10, wmk 48A, 49 or 50 ....1.25		1.50	
☐	size 10 window, wmk 48A, 49 or 50 ....2.00		3.00	
☐ U621	29c **Love**, 5/9/91, Honolulu, HI, (40,110)			
	size 6 3/4, unwmk 1.25		1.50	
☐	size 10, unwmk 1.25		1.50	
	exists on recycled paper, issued 5/1/1992, Kansas City, MO			
☐ U622	29c **Magazine Industry**, 10/7/91, Naples, FL,			
	size 10, unwmk..1.25		1.50	6.00
☐ U623	29c **Star**, 7/20/91, DC, (16,038), size 9 regular 1.25		1.50	
☐	size 9 left window 2.00		3.00	
☐	size 9 right window....................................5.00		10.00	
☐ U624	29c **Geese**, 11/8/91, Virginia Beach, VA, (21,031)			
	size 6 3/4, wmk 49 or 50 ....1.25		1.50	
☐	1/21/92, size 10, wmk 49 or 50 (37,424) 1.25		1.50	

1992

☐ U625	29c **Space Station**, 1/21/92, Virginia Beach, VA, (37,646)			
	size 10, unwmk 1.25		1.50	
☐ U626	29c **Western Americana**, 4/10/92, Dodge City, KS, (34,268)			
	size 10, unwmk 1.25		1.50	
☐ U627	29c **Environment**, 4/22/92, Chicago, IL, (29,432) size 10,			
	unwmk 1.25		1.50	22.00
☐ U628	19.8c **Bulk Rate Star**, 5/19/92, Las Vegas, NV,			
	size 10, unwmk 1.25		1.50	
☐ U629	29c **Disabled Americans**, 7/22/92, DC, (28,218)			
	size 6 3/4, unwmk 1.25		1.50	
☐	size 10, unwmk 1.25		1.50	6.00

1993-96

☐ U630	29c **Kitten**, 10/2/93, King of Prussia, PA, (49,406)			
	size 10, unwmk 1.25		1.50	14.00
☐ U631	29c **Football**, 9/17/94, Canton, OH, (44,711)			
☐	size 10, unwmk..1.25		1.50	

SCOTT NUMBER	DESCRIPTION	UNCACH	CACH	CERM PROG
☐ U632	32c **Liberty Bell**, 1/3/95, Williamsburg, VA		1.25	
☐	size 6 3/4	1.25	1.50	
☐	size 6 3/4, window	2.00	3.00	
☐	size 10	1.25	1.50	
☐	size 10, window	2.00	3.00	
☐ U633	(32c) **Old Glory**, 12/13/94 size 6 3/4,	1.00	1.25	
☐	6 3/4 window, Cancel, released 1/12/95	1.00	1.25	
☐ U634	(32c) **Old Glory** 12/13/94, size 10, 10 window cancel, released 1/12/95	1.00	1.25	
☐ U635	(5c) **Sheep**, 3/10/95, State College, PA, size 6 3/4	1.00	1.25	
☐	size 6 3/4, window	2.50	5.00	
☐	size 10	1.00	1.25	
☐	size 10, window	2.50	5.00	
☐ U636	(10c) **Eagle**, 3/10/95, State College, PA, size 10	1.25	1.50	
☐ U637	32c **Spiral Heart**, 5/12/95, Lakeville, PA	1.25	1.50	
☐	size 10	1.25	1.50	
☐ U638	32c **Liberty Bell**, Security Size 9, 5/15/95, DC	1.00	1.25	
☐ U639	32c **Space Hologram**, 9/22/95, Milwaukee, WI	1.25	1.50	
☐	size 10	1.25	1.50	
☐ U640	32c **Environment**, 4/20/96, Chicago, IL	1.25	1.50	8.00
☐ U641	32c **Paralympics**, 5/2/96, DC	1.25	1.50	10.00
☐	size 10	1.25	1.50	
☐ U642	33c **Flag**, 1/11/99, DC, sizes 6 3/4, 6 3/4 window, 10 and 10 window	1.25	1.50	
☐ U643	33c **Flag**, 1/11/99, DC, sizes 9 and 9 window	1.25	1.50	
☐ U644	33c **Victorian Love**, 1/28/99, Loveland, CO, sizes 6 3/4 and 10	1.25	1.50	
☐ U645	33c **Lincoln**, 6/5/99, Springfield, IL, sizes 6 3/4. 6 3/4 window, 10, and 10 window	1.25	1.50	
☐ U646	34c **Eagle**, 1/7/01, DC	1.25		
☐ U647	34c **Lovebirds**, 2/14/01, Lovejoy, GA	1.25		
☐ U648	34c **Community Colleges**, Cent., 2/20/01, Joliet, IL	1.25		

SCOTT NUMBER	DESCRIPTION	UNCACHETED SINGLE BLOCK	CACHETED SINGLE BLOCK
☐			
☐			
☐			
☐			
☐			
☐			
☐			
☐			
☐			
☐			
☐			
☐			
☐			
☐			
☐			
☐			
☐			
☐			
☐			
☐			
☐			
☐			
☐			
☐			
☐			
☐			
☐			
☐			
☐			
☐			
☐			
☐			
☐			

☐ _____

☐ _____

☐ _____

☐ _____

☐ _____

☐ _____

☐ _____

☐ _____

☐ _____

☐ _____

☐ _____

☐ _____

☐ _____

☐ _____

☐ _____

☐ _____

☐ _____

☐ _____

☐ _____

☐ _____

☐ _____

☐ _____

☐ _____

☐ _____

☐ _____

☐ _____

☐ _____

☐ _____

☐ _____

☐ _____

UC1-UC7

UC14, UC18, UC26

UC16

UC25

UC17

UC32

UC33-34

UC36

UC35

UC37

UC38-UC39

UC42

UC40, UC45

UC43

UC44-UC44a

HOW TO USE THIS BOOK
The number in the first column is its Scott number or identifying number. Following that is the denomination of the stamp, description, date of issue, and the value.

236

AIR POST ENVELOPES & AIR LETTER SHEETS

1929

☐	UC1	**5c Blue**, 1/12/29, DC, size 13, wmk 28 ....35.00	—	
☐		2/1/29, DC, size 5, wmk 28 ....55.00	—	
☐		Size 8, wmk 28 ....75.00	—	

1934

☐	UC3	**6c Orange**, 7/1/34, DC, size 8, wmk 33 ....25.00	100.00	
☐		Size 13, wmk 33 ....15.00	75.00	

1932

☐	UC7	**8c Olive green**, 9/26/32, DC, size 8, wmk 30a............35.00	—	
☐		Size 13, wmk 30a 20.00	—	

1946

☐	UC10	**5c on 6c Orange**, 10/1/46, Aiea Heights, HI, size 13, die 2a, wmk 41** 100.00	—	
☐	UC11	**5c on 6c Orange**, 10/1/46, Aiea Heights, HI, size 13, die 2b, wmk 41** 150.00	—	
☐	UC12	**5c on 6c Orange**, 10/1/46, Aiea Heights, HI, APO & New York, NY, size 13, die 2c, wmk 41** 75.00	—	
☐	UC13	**5c on 6c Orange**, 10/1/46, Aiea Heights, HI, size 13, die 3, wmk 41** 75.00	—	
☐	UC14	**5c Skymaster**, 9/25/46, DC, size 13, wmk 41 ....1.50	2.50	

1947

☐	UC16	**10c Skymaster Letter Sheet**, 4/29/47, DC (162,802) ...2.00	3.00	
☐	UC17	**5c Stamp Cent. - Type I**, 5/21/47, New York, NY size 13, wmk 41 ....1.25	2.50	
☐	UC17a	**5c Stamp Cent. - Type II**, 5/21/47, New York, NY (421,232) size 13, wmk 41 ....1.25	2.50	
		Total for Scott UC17 and UC17a is 306,660.		

1950

☐	UCI8	**6c Skymaster**, 9/22/50, Phila. PA (74,006), size 13, wmk 43 ....1.00	1.50	40.00

1952

☐	UC22	**6c on 5c Carmine (UC15)**, die 2, 8/29/52, Norfolk, VA,** size 13, wmk 41 ....20.00	30.00	

1956

☐	UC25	**6c FIPEX**, 5/2/56, New York, NY (363,239), size 13, wmk 45, with short clouds 1.00	1.50	
☐		Size 13, wmk 45, with long clouds 1.00	1.50	

1958

☐	UC26	**7c Skymaster**, 7/31/58, Dayton, OH (143,428), size 6 3/4, wink 46, straight left wing 1.50	1.00	
☐		Size 6 3/4, wmk 46, swollen left wing 1.00	2.00	
☐		Size 8, wmk 46** 35.00	—	

☐   **UC32a 10c Jet Airliner letter sheet**, Type I, 9/12/58,
     St. Louis, MO (92,400)...1.25   2.00

☐   **UC33 7c Blue**, 11/21/58, New York, NY (208,980), size 6 3/4,
     wmk 46 ....1.00   1.25   35.00

1960

☐   **UC34 7c Jet**, carmine, 8/18/60, Portland, OR (196,851),
     size 6 3/4, wmk 46 ....1.00   1.25   30.00

1961

☐   **UC35 11c Jet Airliner letter sheet**, 6/16/61, Johnstown, PA
     (163,460) (2 types)*...1.00   1.75   35.00*

1962

☐   **UC36 8c Jet**, 11/17/62, Chantilly, VA (194,810), size 6 3/4,
     wmk 47 ....1.00   1.25

1965-67

☐   **UC37 8c Jet Triangle**, 1/7/65, Chicago, IL (226, 178)
     size 6 3/4, wmk 49 (2 types)*.............................1.00   1.25   25.00*
☐   1/8/65, DC, size 10, wmk 49**............................10.00   20.00
☐   **UC37a Jet Triangle**, tagged, 8/15/67, Dayton, OH & DC,
     size 6 3/4, wmk 48**...3.50   5.00
☐   Size 10, wmk 49**...3.50   5.00

1965

☐   **UC38 11c Kennedy letter sheet**, 5/29/65, Boston, MA
     (337,422)...1.00   1.75   15.00

1967

☐   **UC39 13c Kennedy letter sheet**, 5/29/67, Chicago, IL
     (211,387)...1.00   1.75   20.00
☐   5/29/67, Boston, MA**..5.00   7.50
☐   5/29/67, Brookline, MA with # 1246...................5.00   7.50
     Above actually FDC of #1246

1968

☐   **UC40 10c Jet Triangle**, 1/8/68, Chicago, IL (157,553),
     size 6 3/4, wmk 48 ....1.00   1.25   15.00
☐   1/9/68, DC, size 10, wmk 49**...........................4.50   7.50
☐   **UC41 8c + 2c Jet Triangle**, 2/5/68, DC, size 6 3/4, wmk 49**3.50   5.00
☐   size 10, wmk 49 ....3.50   7.50
☐   **UC42 13c Human Rights letter sheet**, 12/3/68, DC (145,898)1.25   2.50   18.00

1971

☐   **UC43 11c Jet**, 5/6/71, Williamsburg, PA (187,000), size 6 3/4,
     wmk 49 ....1.00   1.25
☐   Size 10, wmk 49**...10.00   —
☐   **UC44 15c Birds letter sheet**, 5/28/71, Chicago, IL (130,669)1.00   1.25   18.00
☐   **UC44a 15c Birds letter sheet**, "Aerogramme" added, 12/13/71,
     Philadelphia, PA 1.00   1.25
☐   **UC45 10c + 1c Jet Triangle**, 6/28/71, DC, size 6 3/4 wmk 47,
     48A, or 49**...4.00   7.50
☐   Size 10, wmk 49**...4.00   15.00

SCOTT NUMBER	DESCRIPTION	UNCACH	CACH	CERM PROG

1973

☐	UC46	15c Ballooning letter sheet, 2/10/73, Albuquerque, NM (210,000)	1.00	1.25	15.00
☐	UC47	13c Bird in Flight, 12/1/73, Memphis, TN (132,658) size 6 3/4, wmk 47	1.00	1.25	15.00
☐		12/28/73, size 10, earliest known use	15.00	—	

1974

| ☐ | UC48 | 18c "USA" letter sheet, 1/4/74, Atlanta, GA (119,615) | 1.00 | 1.25 | |
| ☐ | UC49 | 18c NATO letter sheet, 4/4/74, DC | 1.00 | 1.25 | |

1976

| ☐ | UC50 | 22c "USA" letter sheet, 1/16/76, Tempe, AZ (118,303) | 1.00 | 1.25 | 10.00 |

1978

| ☐ | UC51 | 22c "USA" letter sheet, 11/3/78, St. Petersburg, FL (86,099) | 1.00 | 1.25 | 10.00 |

1979

| ☐ | UC52 | 22c Olympics letter sheet, 12/5/79, Bay Shore, NY (129,221) | 1.00 | 1.25 | |

1980

| ☐ | UC53 | 30c "USA" letter sheet, 12/29/80, San Francisco, CA | 1.25 | 1.50 | 15.00 |

1981

| ☐ | UC54 | 30c "USA" letter sheet, 9/21/81, Honolulu, HI | 1.25 | 1.50 | 18.00 |

1982

| ☐ | UC55 | 30c "USA" & Globe letter sheet, 9/16/82, Seattle, WA (209,210) | 1.25 | 1.50 | 14.00 |

1983

| ☐ | UC56 | 30c World Communications letter sheet, 1/7/83, Anaheim, CA | 1.25 | 1.50 | 14.00 |
| ☐ | UC57 | 30c Olympics letter sheet, 10/14/83, Los Angeles, CA | 1.25 | 1.50 | 12.00 |

1985

☐	UC58	36c Landsat letter sheet, 2/14/85, Goddard Flight Center, MD (84,367)	1.25	1.50	8.00
☐	UC59	36c Urban Skyline letter sheet, 5/21/85, DC (94,388)	1.25	1.50	
☐	UC60	36c Comet Tail letter sheet, 12/4/85, Hannibal, MO (83,125)	1.25	1.50	10.00

1988

| ☐ | UC61 | 39c Envelope letter sheet, 5/9/88, Miami, FL (27,446) | 1.25 | 1.50 | |

1989

| ☐ | UC62 | 39c Montgomery Blair letter sheet, 11/20/89, DC (48,529) (2 types)* | 1.25 | 1.50 | 10.00* |

1991

| ☐ | UC63 | 45c Eagle letter sheet, 5/17/91, Denver, CO, blue paper | 1.50 | 2.00 | |
| ☐ | UC63a | , white paper | 1.50 | 2.00 | |

239

UC46

UC47

UC48

UC49

UC50

UC52

UC53-54

UC58

UC59

1995

☐ UC64 **50c Ballooning letter sheet**, 9/23/95, Tampa, FL 1.50 2.00

1999

☐ UC65 **60c Voyageurs Natl. Park MN**, 5/15/99,
Denver, CO 1.50 1.75

OFFICIAL MAIL
1983

☐ U073 **20c Eagle**, 1/12/83, DC, size 10, wmk 47 ....1.25 1.50
☐ Size 10, window, wmk 47 ....2.00 3.00

1985

☐ U074 **22c Eagle**, 2/26/85, DC, (79,788)
size 10, wmk 47, 48A or 49 ....2.50 3.50
☐ Size 10, window, wmk 47, 48A or 49 ....2.50 3.50

1987

☐ U075 **22c Eagle**, 3/2/87, DC, (34,799) savings bond size 2.50 3.00

1988

☐ U076 **(25c)"E" Eagle**, 3/22/88, DC, savings bond size...........1.50 2.00
☐ U077 **25c Eagle**, 4/11/88, DC, size 10, wmk 48A, 49 or 50...1.25 1.50
☐ Window, wmk 48A, 49 or 50 ....2.00 3.00
☐ U078 **25c Savings Bond**, 4/11/88, DC,
savings bond size, plain back flap 1.25 1.50
☐ U078 **25c Savings Bond**, Washington, DC, 11/28/88,
with printing on back flap (Legend 1) 1.50 1.75
Total for Scott U077 and U078 was 12,017.

1990

☐ U079 **45c Eagle**, 3/17/90, Springfield, VA (5,956),
passport size, Cerm. includes U080..........................1.50 2.00 6.00
☐ U080 **65c Eagle**, 3/17/90, Springfield, VA (6,922),
passport size 1.75 2.25
☐ U081 **45c Eagle**, self-sealing, 8/10/90, DC (7,160),
passport size 1.50 2.00
☐ U082 **65c Eagle**, self-sealing, 8/10/90, DC (6,759),
passport size 1.75 2.25

1991

☐ U083 **(29c) "F" Savings Bond**, 1/22/91, (30,549)
savings bond size, printing on backflap (Legend 2)...1.25 1.50
☐ U084 **29c Eagle**, 4/6/91, (27,841)
size 10, wmk 48A, 49 or 50 ....1.25 1.50
☐ Size 10, window, wmk 48A, 49, or 50 ....2.00 3.00
☐ U085 **29c Eagle**, 4/17/91, savings bond size, wmk 51 ....1.25 1.50

1992

☐ U086 **52c Consular Service**, DC, 7/10/92, (25,563) passport size,
logo on back at left, unwmk, heavy weight paper.....1.75 2.25
☐ 3/2/94, passport size, logo on back at right, unwmk.7.50 10.00
☐ U087 **75c Consular Service**, 7/10/92, passport size, logo on
back at left, unwmk, heavy weight paper.................2.00 2.50
☐ 3/2/94, passport size, logo on back at right, unwmk.7.50 10.00

1995

| ☐ | UO88 | 32c Eagle, 5/9/95, DC, size 10 ....1.25 | 2.00 | |
| ☐ | | size 10, window ....2.00 | 3.00 | |

1999

| ☐ | UO89 | **33c Eagle**, 2/22/99, DC.............................1.25 | |
| ☐ | UO90 | **34c Eagle**, 2/27/01, DC ....1.25 | |

POSTAL CARDS
1873

| ☐ | UX1 | **1c Liberty**, 5/13/1873, Boston, New York or DC.........2250. |

1875

| ☐ | UX5 | **1c Liberty**, unwmk, 9/30/1875 ....1200. |

1910

| ☐ | UX21 | **1c William McKinley**, 2/13/10, any city...................250.00 |

1926

| ☐ | UX37 | **3c William McKinley**, 2/1/26, DC ....200.00 | — |

1951

| ☐ | UX38 | **2c Benjamin Franklin**, 11/16/51, New York, NY |
| | | (170,000)...1.25 | 2.50 |

1952

☐	UX39	**2c on 1c Thomas Jefferson** (UX27), 1/1/52, DC.........12.50	25.00
☐	UX40	**2c on 1c Abraham Lincoln**, (UX28), 3/22/52, DC.......35.00	—
		Scott UX40 went on sale at the Philatelic Agency
		3/22/52 and some were canceled that day. It is
		believed that the 1/1/52 cancels are not legitimate.
☐	UX43	**2c Abraham Lincoln**, 7/31/52, DC (125,400)................1.00	1.75

1956

☐	UX44	**2c FIPEX**, 5/4/56, New York, NY (537,474) 1.00	1.25
☐	UX45	**4c Statue of Liberty**, 11/16/56, New York.(129,841) ...1.00	1.25
☐		**UX45 & UY16 4c Statue of Liberty and 4c Statue of Liberty**
		paid reply postal card (2 types)*.......................................	60.00*

1958

☐	UX46	**3c Statue of Liberty**, 8/1/58, Philadelphia, PA
		(180,610)...1.00	1.25
☐		**UX46a Statue of Liberty "N God We Trust"**, 8/1/58,
		Philadelphia, PA...................................175.00	250.00

1961

| ☐ | | **UX46c Statue of Liberty**, precanceled, 9/15/61, |
| | | Philadelphia, PA.....................................50.00 | — |

1962-66

☐	UX48	**4c Abraham Lincoln**, 11/19/62, Springfield, IL
		(162,939)..1.00	1.00
☐		**UX48a Abraham Lincoln**, tagged, 6/25/66, Bellevue, OH **..25.00	30.00
☐		7/6/66, DC**.......................................1.50	2.50
☐		Toledo, OH** 7.50	12.50

☐		Overlook, OH**	4.50	7.50	
☐		Columbus, OH**	7.50	12.50	
☐		Bellevue, OH**	15.00	25.00	
☐		Cleveland, OH**	6.00	10.00	
☐		Cincinnati, OH**	4.50	7.50	
☐		Dayton, OH**	3.50	6.00	
☐		Indianapolis, IN**	7.50	2.50	
☐		Louisville, KY**	7.50	12.50	

1963

| ☐ | UX49 | 7c Map, 8/30/63, New York, NY | 1.00 | 1.25 | 18.00 |

1964

☐	UX50	4c Flags, Map & "Customs," 2/22/64, DC (313,275)	1.00	1.25	20.00
☐	UX51	4c Social Security, 9/26/64, DC (293,650)	1.00	1.25	20.00
☐		with official government printed cachet	—	12.00	
☐		with blue hand cancel & government cachet	—	20.00	

1965

| ☐ | UX52 | 4c Coast Guard Flag, 8/4/65, Newburyport, MA (338,225) | 1.00 | 1.25 | 20.00 |
| ☐ | UX53 | 4c Census Bureau, 10/21/65, Philadelphia, PA (272,383) | 1.00 | 1.25 | 30.00 |

1967

| ☐ | UX54 | 8c Map, 12/4/67, DC | 1.00 | 1.25 | 15.00 |

1968

| ☐ | UX55 | 5c Abraham Lincoln, 1/4/68, Hodgenville, KY | 1.00 | 1.25 | 20.00 |
| ☐ | UX56 | 5c Women Marines, 7/26/68, San Francisco, CA (203,714) | 1.00 | 1.25 | 20.00 |

1970

| ☐ | UX57 | 5c Weather Vane, 9/1/70, Ft. Myer, VA (285,800) | 1.00 | 1.25 | 15.00 |

1971

☐	UX58	6c Paul Revere, 5/15/71, Boston, MA	1.00	1.25	12.00
☐	UX59	10c Map, 6/10/71, New York, NY	1.00	1.25	
☐		cerm. prog. includes UXC11			15.00
		Total for Scott UX59 and UXC11 is 297,000.			
☐	UX60	6c America's Hospitals, 9/16/71, New York, NY (218,200)	1.00	1.25	22.00

1972

☐	UX61	6c U.S. Frigate Constellation, 6/29/72, any city	1.25	1.50	
☐	UX62	6c Monument Valley, 6/29/72, any city	1.25	1.50	
☐	UX63	6c Gloucester, MA 6/29/72, any city	1.25	1.50	
☐	UX64	6e John Hanson, 9/1/72, Baltimore, MD (156,000)	1.00	1.25	12.00

1973

☐	UX65	6c Centenary of Postal Card, 9/14/73, DC(276,717)	1.00	1.25	20.00
☐	UX66	8c Samuel Adams, 12/16/73, Boston, MA (147,522)	1.00	1.25	12.00
☐	UX67	12c Ship's Figurehead, 1/4/74, Miami, FL (138,500)	1.00	1.25	
☐		cerm. prog. includes UXC15			15.00

UX1, UX3, UX65

UX21

UX37

UX38

UX43

UX44

UX45, UY16

UX46, UY17

UX48

UX49, UX54, UY19, UY20

UX50

UX51

UX52

UX53

UX56

UX58, UY22

UX62

UX63

UX67

HOW TO USE THIS BOOK
The number in the first column is its Scott number or identifying number. Following that is the denomination of the stamp, description, date of issue, and the value.

1975

☐ **UX68** **7c Charles Thomson**, 9/14/75, Bryn Mawr, PA 1.00 1.25 10.00
Total for Scott UX68 and UY25 is 321,910.

☐ **UX69** **9c John Witherspoon**, 11/10/75, Princeton, NJ...............1.00 1.25 10.00
Total for Scott UX69 and UY26 is 254,239.

1976

☐ **UX70** **9c Caesar Rodney**, 7/1/76, Dover, DE.............................1.00 1.25 10.00
Total for Scott UX70 and UY27 is 307,061.

1977

☐ **UX71** **9c Federal Court House**, 7/20/77, Galveston, TX
(245,535)..1.00 1.25 20.00

☐ **UX72** **9c Nathan Hale**, 10/14/77, Coventry, CT 1.00 1.25 10.00
Total for Scott UX72 and UY28 is 304,592.

1978

☐ **UX73** **10c Cincinnati Music Hall**, 5/12/78, Cincinnati, OH
(300,000)...1.00 1.25 15.00

☐ **UX74** **(10c) John Hancock**, 5/19/78, Quincy, MA 1.00 1.25 12.00

☐ **UX75** **10c John Hancock**, 6/20/78, Quincy, MA 1.00 1.25

☐ **UX76** **14c U.S. Coast Guard Eagle**, 8/4/78, Seattle, WA (196,400)1.00 1.25 10.00

☐ **UX77** **10c Molly Pitcher**, 9/8/78, Freehold, NJ (180,280) 1.00 1.25 12.00

1979

☐ **UX78** **10c George Rogers Clark**, 2/23/79, Vincennes, IN
(260,110)..1.00 1.25 12.00

☐ **UX79** **10c Casimir Pulaski**, 10/11/79, Savannah, GA (210,000) 1.00 1.25 18.00

☐ **UX80** **10c Olympic Games**, 9/17/79, Eugene, OR 1.00 1.25 12.00

☐ **UX81** **10c Iolani Palace**, 10/1/79, Honolulu, HI (242,804) 1.00 1.25 20.00

1980

☐ **UX82** **14c Winter Olympic Games**, 1/15/80, Atlanta, GA
(160,977)...1.00 1.25 15.00

☐ **UX83** **10c Salt Lake Temple**, 4/5/80, Salt Lake City, UT
(325,260)...1.00 1.25 15.00

☐ **UX84** **10c Landing of Rochambeau**, 7/11/80, Newport, RI
(180,567)...1.00 1.25 18.00

☐ **UX85** **10c Battle of Kings Mountain**, 10/7/80, Kings Mountain,
NC (136,130) 1.00 1.25 14.00

☐ **UX86** **19c Golden Hinde**, 11/21/80, San Rafael, CA (290,547)...1.00 1.25 15.00

1981

☐ **UX87** **10c Battle of Cowpens**, 1/17/81, Cowpens, SC (160,000).1.00 1.25 18.00

☐ **UX88** **(12c) Eagle**, 3/15/81, Memphis, TN 1.00 1.25

☐ **UX89** **12c Isaiah Thomas**, 5/5/81, Worcester, MA 1.00 1.25 8.00

☐ **UX90** **12c Nathaniel Greene**, 9/8/81, Eutaw Springs, SC
(115,755)..1.00 1.25 14.00

☐ **UX91** **12c Lewis & Clark Expedition**, 9/23/81, St. Louis, MO....1.00 1.25 10.00

☐ **UX92** **(13c) Robert Morris**, 10/11/81, Memphis, TN 1.00 1.25

☐ **UX93** **13c Robert Morris**, 11/10/81, Philadelphia, PA...............1.00 1.25 10.00

UX73

UX76

UX79

UX91

UX82

UX86

UX88, UY31

HOW TO USE THIS BOOK

The number in the first column is its Scott number or
identifying number. Following that is the denomination
of the stamp, description, date of issue, and the value.

SCOTT NUMBER	DESCRIPTION	UNCACH	CACH	CERM PROG

1982

☐ UX94	13c Francis Marion, 4/3/82, Marion, SC (141,162)......1.00		1.25	12.00
☐ UX95	13c LaSalle Claims Louisiana, 4/7/82, New Orleans, LA (157,691).........................1.00		1.25	10.00
☐ UX96	13c Philadelphia Academy of Music, 6/18/82, Philadelphia, PA (193,089)..........................1.00		1.25	10.00
☐ UX97	13c Old Post Office, 10/14/82, St. Louis, MO 1.00		1.25	12.00

1983

☐ UX98	13c Oglethorpe, 2/12/83, Savannah, GA (165,750)......1.00		1.25	12.00
☐ UX99	13c Old Post Office, 4/19/83, DC (125,056)(2 types)*...1.00		1.25	8.00*
☐ UX100	13c Olympics (Yachting), 8/5/83, Long Beach, CA (132,232) 1.00		1.25	10.00

1984

☐ UX101	13c The Ark and the Dove, 3/25/84, St. Clement's Island, MD 1.00		1.25	8.00
☐ UX102	13c Olympics (Torch), 4/30/84, Los Angeles, CA 1.00		1.25	10.00
☐ UX103	13c Frederic Baraga, 6/29/84, Marquette, MI (100,156)1.00		1.25	8.00
☐ UX104	13c Historic Preservation, 9/16/84, Compton, CA 1.00		1.25	6.00

1985

☐ UX105	(14c) Charles Carroll, 2/1/85, New Carrollton, MD......1.00		1.25	
☐ UX106	14c Charles Carroll, 3/6/85, Annapolis, MD.................1.00		1.25	6.00
☐ UX107	25c Clipper Flying Cloud, 2/27/85, Salem, MA (95,559)1.25		1.50	6.00
☐ UX108	14c George Wythe, 6/20/85, Williamsburg, VA 1.00		1.25	6.00

1986

☐ UX109	14c Settling of Connecticut, 4/18/86, Hartford, CT (76,875)................................1.00		1.25	6.00
☐ UX110	14c Stamps, 5/23/86, Chicago, IL (75,548)...................1.00		1.25	8.00
☐ UX111	14c Francis Vigo, 5/24/86, Vincennes, IN (100,141) 1.00		1.25	6.00
☐ UX112	14c Settling of Rhode Island, 6/26/86, Providence, RI (54,559) 1.00		1.25	6.00
☐ UX113	14c Wisconsin Territory, 7/3/86, Mineral Point, WI (41,224)...........................1.00		1.25	6.00
☐ UX114	14c National Guard Heritage, 12/12/86, Boston, MA (72,316)....................................1.00		1.25	6.00

1987

☐ UX115	14c Self-Scouring Steel Plow, 5/22/87, Moline, IL (160,099)...................................1.00		1.25	8.00
☐ UX116	14c Constitutional Convention, 5/25/87, Philadelphia, PA (138,207)........................1.00		1.25	6.00
☐ UX117	14c Flag, 6/14/87, Baltimore, MD.................................1.00		1.25	6.00
☐ UX118	14c Take Pride in America, 9/22/87, Jackson, WY (47,281)......................................1.00		1.25	8.00
☐ UX119	14c Timberline Lodge, 9/28/87, Timberline Lodge, OR (63,595)......................................1.00		1.25	8.00

1988

☐ UX120	15c Bison and Prairie, 3/28/88, Buffalo, WY (52,075).1.00		1.25	
☐ UX121	15c Blair House, 5/4/88, DC (52,188).........................1.00		1.25	10.00
☐ UXI22	28c Yorkshire, Square-rigged Packet, 6/29/88, Mystic, CT (46,505) 1.25		1.50	12.00
☐ UX123	15c Iowa Territory, 7/2/88, Burlington, IA (45,565) 1.00		1.25	12.00

"Swamp Fox" Francis Marion, 1782

UX94

UX55, UY21

UX96

UX71

UX107

HOW TO USE THIS BOOK

The number in the first column is its Scott number or identifying number. Following that is the denomination of the stamp, description, date of issue, and the value.

		UNCACH	CACH	CERM PROG
☐	**UX124 15c Settling of Ohio**, Northwest Territory, 7/15/88, Marietta, OH (28,778) 1.00		1.25	12.00
☐	**UX125 15c Hearst Castle**, 9/20/88, San Simeon, CA (84,786) .1.00		1.25	10.00
☐	**UX126 15c The Federalist Papers**, 10/27/88, New York, NY (37,661) 1.00		1.25	10.00

1989

☐	**UX127 15c Red-tailed Hawk Sonora Desert**, 1/13/89, Tucson, AZ (51,891) 1.00		1.25	6.00
☐	**UX128 15c Healy Hall**, Georgetown University, 1/23/89, DC (54,897) 1.00		1.25	6.00
☐	**UX129 15c Great Blue Heron**, Marsh, 3/17/89, Okefenokee, GA (58,208) 1.00		1.25	6.00
☐	**UX130 15c Settling of Oklahoma**, 4/22/89, Guthrie, OK (68,689) 1.00		1.25	
☐	**UX131 15c Canada Geese and Mountains**, 5/5/89, Denver, CO (59,303) 1.00		1.25	6.00
☐☐	**UX132 15c Seashore**, 6/17/89, Cape Hatteras, NC (67,073) 1.00		1.25	6.00
☐	**UX133 15c Deer Beside Woodland Waterfall**, 8/26/89, Cherokee, NC (67,878) 1.00		1.25	6.00
☐☐	**UX134 15c Hull House**, 9/18/89, Chicago, IL (53,773) 1.00		1.25	6.00
☐	**UX135 15c Independence Hall**, 9/25/89, Philadelphia, PA (61,659) 1.00		1.25	
☐	**UX136 15c Inner Harbor Baltimore**, 10/7/89, Baltimore, MD (58,746) 1.00		1.25	
☐	**UX137 15c 59th Street Bridge**, 11/8/89, New York, NY (48,044)..1.00		1.25	
☐	**UX138 15c Capitol**, 11/26/89, DC (47,146)..............................1.00		1.25	10.00
☐	**UX139 15c Independence Hall** 12/1/89, DC...........................2.00		3.00	12.00
☐	**UX140 15c Inner Harbor Baltimore**, 12/1/89, DC 2.00		3.00	
☐	**UX141 15c 59th Street Bridge**, 12/1/89, DC...........................2.00		3.00	
☐	**UX142 15c Capitol**, 12/1/89, DC...2.00		3.00	
	Scott UX135-UX138 have inscription and copyright symbol at lower left. Scott UX139- UX142 do not and are rouletted on 2 or 3 sides.			
☐	**UX143 15c White House**, 11/30/89, DC (52,090) 1.25		1.50	10.00
☐	**UX144 15c Jefferson Memorial**, 12/2/89, DC (59,568) 1.25		1.50	10.00

1990

☐	**UX145 15c Rittenhouse Paper Mill**, 3/13/90, New York, NY (9,866) (2 types)*..1.00		1.25	18.00*
☐	**UX146 15c World Literacy Year**, 3/22/90, DC (11,163) 1.00		1.25	6.00
☐	**UX147 15c Fur Traders Descending the Missouri**, 5/4/90, St. Louis, MO (13,632)...1.25		1.50	6.00
☐	**UX148 15c Isaac Royall House**, 6/16/90, Medford, MA (21,708)..1.00		1.25	6.00
☐	**UX150 15c Quadrangle**, Stanford University, 9/30/90, Stanford, CA (28,430)..1.00		1.25	6.00
☐	**UX151 15c Constitution Hall**, 10/11/90, DC (33,254) 1.25		1.50	6.00
☐	**UX152 15c Chicago Orchestra Hall**, 10/19/90, Chicago, IL (28,546) 1.00		1.25	6.00

1991

☐	**UX153 19c Flag**, 1/24/91, DC (26,690) 1.00		1.25	
☐	**UX154 19c Carnegie Hall**, 4/1/91, New York, NY (27,063) 1.00		1.25	6.00
☐	**UX155 19c "Old Red,"** Univ. of Texas, 6/14/91, Galveston, TX (24,308) 1.00		1.25	6.00

☐ UX156 19c Bill of Rights, 9/25/91, Richmond, VA (27,457) 1.00 1.25 6.00
☐ UX157 19c Notre Dame, 10/15/91, Notre Dame, IN (34,325).....1.00 1.25 6.00
☐ UX158 30c Niagara Falls, 8/21/91, Niagara Falls, NY (29,762) .1.25 2.00
☐ UX159 19c Old Mill, Univ. of Vermont, 10/29/91,
　　　　　Burlington, VT (23,965)...1.00 1.25 6.00

1992

☐ UX160 19c Wadsworth Atheneum, 1/16/92, Hartford, CT.........1.00 1.25 6.00
☐ UX161 19c Cobb Hall, Univ. of Chicago, 1/23/92, Chicago, IL ...1.00 1.25 6.00
☐ UX162 19c Waller Hall, 2/1/92, Salem, OR..................................1.00 1.25 6.00
☐ UX163 19c America's Cup, 5/6/92, San Diego, CA.....................1.25 1.50
☐ UX164 19c Columbia River Gorge, 5/9/92, Stevenson, WA........1.00 1.25 6.00
☐ UX165 19c Great Hall, Ellis Island, 5/11/92, Ellis Island, NY....1.00 1.25 6.00

1993

☐ UX166 19c National Cathedral, 1/6/93, DC.................................1.00 1.25
☐ UX167 19c Wren Building, 2/8/93, Williamsburg, VA 1.00 1.25 6.00
☐ UX168 19c Holocaust Memorial, 3/23/93, DC............................1.25 1.50 6.00
☐ UX169 19c Ft. Recovery, 6/13/93, Fort Recovery, OH 1.00 1.25 6.00
☐ UX170 19c Playmaker's Theater, 9/14/93, Chapel Hill, NC 1.00 1.25 6.00
☐ UX171 19c O'Kane Hall, 9/17/93, Worcester, MA......................1.00 1.25
☐ UX172 19c Beecher Hall, 10/9/93, Chicago, IL...........................1.00 1.25 6.00
☐ UX173 19c Massachusetts Hall, 10/14/93, Brunswick, ME........1.00 1.25 6.00
☐ UX174 19c Lincoln Home, 2/12/94, Springfield, IL.....................1.00 1.25 6.00

1994-96

☐ UX175 19c Myers Hall (Wittenberg Univ.) , 3/11/94,
　　　　　Springfield, OH...1.00 1.25 6.00
☐ UX176 19c Canyon de Chelly, 8/11/94, Chinle, AZ 1.00 1.25 6.00
☐ UX177 19c St. Louis Union Station,9/3/94, St. Louis, MO 1.00 1.25 6.00
☐ UX178-UX197 19c Legends of the West (20 different), 10/18/94,
　　　　　Laramie, WY, Lawton,OK, Tuscon, AZ, set of 20........20.00 35.00
☐ UX198 20c Red Barn, 1/3/95, Williamsburg, PA.......................1.00 1.25
☐ UX199 (20c) "G" Old Glory, 12/13/94,cancel, released 1/12/95 .1.00 1.25
☐ UX200-UX219 20c Civil War, 6/29/95, Gettysburg, PA
　　　　　set of 20 ....20.00 35.00
☐ UX220 20c Clipper Ship,9/23/95, Hunt Valley, MD 1.00 1.25
☐ UX221-UX240 20c Comic Strips of 20, 10/1/95, Boca Raton, FL20.00 35.00
☐ UX241 20c Winter Farm Scene, 2/23/96, Watertown, NY..........1.00 1.25 8.00
☐ UX242-UX261 20c Olympics, Set of 20, 5/2/96, DC.................20.00 35.00
☐ UX262 20c St. John's College, 6/1/96, Annapolis, MD (8,793) ...1.00 1.25
☐ UX263 20c Alexander Hall, 9/20/96, Princeton, NJ (11,621) 1.00 8.00
☐ UX264-UX278 20c Endangered Species, set of 15, 10/2/96,
　　　　　San Diego, CA 20.00 35.00

1997

☐ UX280 20c City College of New York, 5/7/97, New York, NY.....1.00 1.25 8.00
☐ UX281 20c Bugs Bunny, 5/22/97, Burbank, CA 1.25 1.50
☐ UX282 20c Golden Gate (Day), 6/2/97, San Francisco, CA........1.00 1.25 8.00
☐ UX283 50c Golden Gate (Night), 6/2/97, San Francisco, CA......1.25 1.50
☐ UX284 20c Fort McHenry, 9/7/97, Baltimore, MD 1.00 1.25
☐ UX285-UX289 20c Movie Monsters, 9/30/97, any card,
　　　　　Universal City, CA 1.75 2.00

1998

☐ UX290 20c University of Mississippi, 4/20/98, University, MS ...1.00 1.25

☐ **UX291 20c Sylvester & Tweety**, 4/27/98, New York, NY 1.75 2.00
☐ **UX292 20c Girard College**, 5/1/98, Philadelphia, PA...................1.00 1.25
☐ **UX293-UX296 20c Tropical Birds**, set of 4, 7/29/98, Ponce, PR 4.00 5.00
☐ **UX297 20c Ballet**, 9/16/98, New York , NY................................1.00 1.25
☐ **UX298 20c Northeastern University**, 10/3/98, Boston, MA 1.00 1.25
☐ **UX299 20c Brandeis University**, 10/17/98, Waltham, MA..........1.00 1.25

1999

☐ **UX300 20c Victorian Love**, 1/28/99, Loveland, CO 1.00 1.25
☐ **UX301 20c University of Wisconsin**, 2/5/99, Madison, WI 1.00 1.25
☐ **UX302 20c Washington & Lee University**, 1/11/99,
      Lexington, VA...1.00 1.25 10.00
☐ **UX303 20c Redwood Library & Athenaeum**, 3/11/99,
      Newport, RI...1.00 1.25 10.00
☐ **UX304 20c Daffy Duck**, 4/16/99, Los Angeles, Ca.......................1.00 1.25 10.00
☐ **UX305 20c Mt. Vernon**, 5/14/99, Mount Vernon, VA...................1.00 1.25 10.00
☐ **UX306 20c Block Island Lighthouse**, 7/24/99, Block Island, RI .1.00 1.25 10.00
☐ **UX307-UX311 20c Famous Trains**, Set of 20, 8/26/99,
      Cleveland, OH uncacheted....................................20.00 35.00

2000

☐ **UX312 20c University of Utah**, 2/28/00, Salt Lake City, UT 1.00 1.50
☐ **UX313 20c Ryman Auditorium**, 3/18/00, Nashville, TN 1.00 1.50
☐ **UX314 20c Road Runner & Wile E. Coyote**, booklet of 10 cards,
      4/26/00, Phoenix, AZ..................................15.00 22.50
☐ **UX315 20c Adoption**, 5/10/00, Beverly Hills, CA 1.40 1.75
☐ **UX316 20c Old Stone Row**, Middlebury College, 5/19/00,
      Middlebury, VT 1.00 1.50
☐ **UX317-UX336 20c Stars and Stripes**, set of 20, 6/14/00,
      Baltimore, MD 20.00 35.00
☐ **UX337-UX356 20c Legends of Baseball**, Atlanta, GA
      set of 20, 7/6/00...20.00 35.00
☐ **UX357-UX360 Christmas Deer Type of 1999**, 10/12/00,
      any card, Rudolph, WI 1.75
☐ **UX361 20c Connecticut Hall**, Yale University, 3/30/01,
      New Haven, CT 1.00
☐ **UX362 20c University of South Carolina**, 4/26/01, Columbia, SC 1.00
☐ **UX363 20c Northwestern University**, Sesquicentennial, 4/28/01,
      Evanston, IL 1.00
☐ **UX364 20c University of Portland**, Waldschmidt Hall, 5/1/01,
      Portland, OR...1.00

REPLY POSTAL CARDS
1892

☐ **UY1** 1c + 1c U.S. Grant 10/25/92, any city 350.00

1926

☐ **UY12** 3c + 3c William McKinley, 2/1/26, any city ....250.00   —

1951

☐ **UY13** 2c + 2c George Washington, 12/29/51, DC (49,294).......1.25 2.50

1952

☐ **UY14** 2c on 1c + 2c on 1c George Washington, 1/1/52,**
      any city 50.00 75.00

UXC1

UXC4

UXC5, UXC8, UXC11

UXC9-10

UXC6

UXC7

UXC14

UXC16

UXC18

UXC20

UXC22

HOW TO USE THIS BOOK

The number in the first column is its Scott number or
identifying number. Following that is the denomination
of the stamp, description, date of issue, and the value.

1956

☐ UY16 **4c + 4c Statue of Liberty**, 11/16/56, New York, NY
(127,874)..1.00 1.25

☐ UY16a **4c + 4c Statue of Liberty**, message card printed on
both halves, 11/16/56, New York,NY 75.00100.00

☐ UY16b **4c + 4c Statue of Liberty**, reply card printed on both
halves, 11/16/56, New York, NY 50.00 75.00

1958

☐ UY17 **3c + 3c Statue of Liberty**, 7/31/58, Boise, ID (136,768)1.00 1.25

1962-67

☐ UY18 **4c + 4c Abraham Lincoln**, 11/19/62, Springfield, IL
(107,746)..1.00 1.25

☐ UY18a **Abraham Lincoln**, tagged, 3/7/67, Dayton, OH,
earliest known use** ....50.00   —

1963

☐ UY19 **7c + 7c Map**, 8/30/63, New York, NY 1.00 1.25

1967

☐ UY20 **8c + 8c Map**, 12/4/67, DC 1.00 1.25

1968

☐ UY21 **5c + 5c Abraham Lincoln**, 1/4/68, Hodgenville, KY 1.00 1.25

1971

☐ UY22 **6c + 6c Paul Revere**, 5/15/71, Boston, MA 1.00 1.25

1972

☐ UY23 **6c + 6c John Hanson**, 9/1/72, Baltimore, MD
(105,708)..1.00 1.25

1973

☐ UY24 **8c + 8c Samuel Adams**, 12/16/73, Boston, MA
(105,369)..1.00 1.25

1975

☐ UY25 **7c + 7c Charles Thomson**, 9/14/75, Bryn Mawr, PA 1.00 1.25
☐ UY26 **9c + 9c John Witherspoon**, 11/10/75, Princeton, NJ ...1.00 1.25

1976

☐ UY27 **9c + 9c Caesar Rodney**, 7/1/76, Dover, DE..................1.00 1.25

1977

☐ UY28 **9c + 9c Nathan Hale**, 10/14/77, Coventry, CT 1.00 1.25

1978

☐ UY29 **(10c + 10c) John Hancock**, 5/19/78, Quincy, MA 1.75 3.50
☐ UY30 **10c + 10c John Hancock**, 6/20/78, Quincy, MA............1.00 1.25

1981

☐ UY31 **(12c + 12c) Eagle**, 3/15/81, Memphis, TN 1.00 1.25
☐ UY32 **12c + 12c Isaiah Thomas**, 5/5/81, Worcester, MA........1.00 1.25
☐ UY32a **Isaiah Thomas**, Small Die 3.00 5.00
☐ UY33 **(13c + 13c) Robert Morris**, 10/11/81, Memphis, TN 1.25 1.25
☐ UY34 **13c + 13c Robert Morris**, 11/10/81, Philadelphia, PA..1.25 1.25

1985

☐ UY35 **(14c + 14c) Charles Carroll**, 2/1/85,
New Carrollton, MD 1.25   1.50

☐ UY36 **14c + 14c Charles Carroll**, 3/6/85, Annapolis, MD.......1.25   1.50

☐ UY37 **14c + 14c George Wythe**, 6/20/85, Williamsburg, VA ..1.25   1.50

1987

☐ UY38 **14c + 14c Flag**, 9/1/87, Washington, DC, (22,314) 1.25   1.50

1988

☐ UY39 **15c + 15c Bison and Prairie**, 7/11/88, Buffalo, WY
(24,338)..1.25   1.50

1991-95

☐ UY40 **19c + 19c Flag**, 3/27/91, DC (25,562) 1.25   1.50

☐ UY41 **20c+20c Red Barn**, 2/1/95, Williamsburg, PA 1.25   1.50

1999

☐ UY42 **20c+20c Block Island Lighthouse**, 11/10/99, ...1.25   1.50

AIR POST POSTAL CARDS
1949

☐ UXC1 **4c Eagle in Flight**, 1/10/49, DC, (236,620) 1.00   1.50

1958

☐ UXC2 **5c Eagle in Flight**, 7/31/58, Wichita, KS (156,474)......1.00   1.25   50.00

1960

☐ UXC3 **5c Eagle in Flight**, bi-colored border, 6/18/60,
Minneapolis, MN (228,500).......................................1.00   1.75   25.00

☐   With thin dividing line at top 2.50   5.00

1963

☐ UXC4 **6c Bald Eagle**, 2/15/63, Maitland, FL (216,203)...........1.00   1.25   20.00

1966

☐ UXC5 **11c Flag & "VISIT THE USA"**, 5/27/66, DC (272,813)
(2 types)*...1.00   1.25   20.00*

1967

☐ UXC6 **6c Virgin Islands**, 3/31/67, Charlotte Amalie, VI,
(346,906)..1.00   1.25   20.00

☐ UXC7 **6c World Boy Scout Jamboree**, 8/4/67,
Farragut State Park, ID (471,585) 1.00   1.25   35.00

☐ UXC8 **13c Flag & "VISIT THE USA"**, 9/8/67, Detroit, MI
(178,789) (2 types)*...1.00   1.25   15.00

1968-69

☐ UXC9 **8c Eagle**, 3/1/68, New York, NY...................................1.00   1.25   15.00

☐ UXC9a **Eagle**, tagged, 3/19/69, DC** 10.00   15.00

1971

☐ UXC10 **9c Eagle**, 5/15/71, Kitty Hawk, NC, (167,000 est.) 1.00   1.25

☐ UXC11 **15c Flag & "VISIT THE USA"**, 6/10/71, New York, NY 1.00   1.25

1972

☐ **UXC12 9c Grand Canyon**, 6/29/72, any city 1.25   1.50

☐ **UXC13 15c Niagara Falls**, 6/29/72, any city..........................1.25   1.50

☐ **UXC13a Niagara Falls**, address side blank ....600.00   —

1974

☐ **UXC14 11c Stylized Eagle**, 1/4/74, State College, PA,
     (160,500) 1.00   1.25   10.00

☐ **UXC15 18c Eagle Weather Vane**, 1/4/74, Miami, FL (132,114)..1.00   1.25

1975

☐ **UXC16 21c Angel Weather Vane**, 12/17/75, Kitty Hawk, NC
     (113,191)..1.00   1.25   15.00

1978

☐ **UXC17 21c Curtiss Jenny**, 9/16/78, San Diego, CA (174,886)..1.00   1.25   10.00

1979

☐ **UXC18 21c Olympics (Gymnast)**, 12/1/79, Fort Worth, TX
     (150,124)..1.25   1.50   10.00

1981

☐ **UXC19 28c First Transpacific Flight**, 1/2/81, Wenatchee, WA...1.25   1.50   10.00

1982

☐ **UXC20 28c Gliders**, 3/5/82, Houston, TX (106,932) 1.25   1.50   8.00

1983

☐ **UXC21 28c Olympics (Speedskating)**, 12/29/83,
     Milwaukee, WI (108,397)..1.25   1.50   6.00

1985

☐ **UXC22 33c China Clipper Seaplane**, 2/15/85,
     San Francisco, CA 1.25   1.50

1986

☐ **UXC23 33c Chicago Skyline**, 2/1/86, Chicago, IL (84,480).......1.25   1.50   6.00

1988

☐ **UXC24 36c DC-3**, 5/14/88, San Diego, CA 1.25   1.50   6.00

1991-95

☐ **UXC25 40c Yankee Clipper**, 6/28/91, Flushing, NY (24,865)...1.50   2.00   6.00

☐ **UXC26 50c Eagle**, 8/24/95, St. Louis, MO................................1.50   2.00   8.00

☐ **UXC27 55c Mt. Rainier National Park**, 5/15/99, Denver, CO...1.00   1.25

☐ **UXC28 70c Badlands Natl. Park**, South Dakota, 2/22/01, Wall, SD 1.50

OFFICIAL POSTAL CARDS
1983-96

☐ UZ2   **13c Eagle**, 1/12/83, DC 1.00   1.25

☐ UZ3   **14c Eagle**, 2/26/85, DC (62,396) 1.00   1.25

☐ UZ4   **15c Eagle**, 6/10/88, New York, NY (133,498) 1.00   1.25

☐ UZ5   **19c Eagle**, 5/24/91, Seattle, WA (23,097) 1.00   1.50

☐ UZ6   **20c Eagle**, 5/9/96, DC 1.00   1.50

SCOTT NUMBER	DESCRIPTION	UNCACH	CACH	CERM PROG
☐				
☐				
☐				
☐				
☐				
☐				
☐				
☐				
☐				
☐				
☐				
☐				
☐				
☐				
☐				
☐				
☐				
☐				
☐				
☐				
☐				
☐				
☐				
☐				
☐				
☐				
☐				
☐				
☐				
☐				

SCOTT NUMBER	DESCRIPTION		UNCACH	CACH	CERM PROG
☐					
☐					
☐					
☐					
☐					
☐					
☐					
☐					
☐					
☐					
☐					
☐					
☐					
☐					
☐					
☐					
☐					
☐					
☐					
☐					
☐					
☐					
☐					
☐					
☐					
☐					
☐					
☐					
☐					
☐					
☐					

PLATE NUMBER COIL FDC

Since early 1981, nearly all coil stamps issued by the United States have plate numbers printed on the stamps at regular intervals. The tiny digits printed in the stamps' bottom margins have given rise to the fastest growing area of modern United States stamp collecting — plate number coils (PNC).

Not all plate numbers exist on FDC's — only the ones that are printed before the

stamp is issued or very shortly after the first day, during the grace period for submitting covers to be canceled.

Because some PNC first-day covers are scarce and expensive, and some forgeries have already appeared on the philatelic market, collectors are advised to have costly FDC's expertized.

SCOTT NUMBER	DESCRIPTION	PLATE NUMBER	PAIR VALUE	STRIP OF 3 VALUE
☐ 1891	18c Flag, 4/24/81	1	75.00	150.00
☐		2	225.00	425.00
☐		3	325.00	525.00
☐		4	200.00	350.00
☐		5	125.00	—
☐ 1895	20c Flag over Supreme Court, 12/17/81	1	20.00	40.00
☐		2	100.00	200.00
☐		3	200.00	400.00
☐ 1897	1c Omnibus, 8/19/83	1	9.00	13.00
☐		2	9.00	13.00
☐ 1897A	2c Locomotive, 5/20/82	3	12.00	20.00
☐		4	12.00	20.00
☐ 1898	3c Handcar, 3/25/83	1	10.00	20.00
☐		2	10.00	20.00
☐		3	10.00	20.00
☐		4	10.00	20.00
☐ 1898A	4c Stagecoach, 8/19/82	1	10.00	18.50
☐		2	10.00	18.50
☐		3	10.00	18.50
☐		4	10.00	18.50
☐ 1899	5c Motorcycle, 10/10/83	1	10.00	15.00
☐		2	10.00	15.00
☐		3	2,000.	—
☐		4	1,200.	1,800.
☐ 1900	5.2c Sleigh, 3/21/83	1	15.00	30.00
☐		2	15.00	30.00

SCOTT NUMBER	DESCRIPTION	PLATE NUMBER	PAIR VALUE	STRIP OF 3 VALUE
☐	**1900a** **Sleigh**, untagged (Bureau precanceled), 3/21/83	1	500.	500.
☐		2	500.	500.
☐	**1901** 5.9c Bicycle, 2/17/82	3	15.00	25.00
☐		4	15.00	25.00
☐	**1901a** **Bicycle**, untagged (Bureau precanceled), 2/17/82	3	2,000.	2,000.
☐		4	2,000.	2,000.
☐	**1902** 7.4c Baby Buggy, 4/7/84	2	10.00	20.00
☐	**1902a** **Baby Buggy**, untagged (Bureau precanceled), 4/7/84	2	2,000.	2,000.
☐	**1903** 9.3c Mail Wagon, 12/15/81	1	20.00	40.00
☐		2	20.00	40.00
☐		3	2,000.	2,000.
☐		4	2,000.	2,000.
☐	**1903a** **Mail Wagon**, untagged Bureau precanceled), 12/15/81	1	2,500.	
	One cover known to exist			
	One cover known to exist	2	2,500.	
☐		3	2,000.	2,000.
☐		4	2,000.	2,000.
☐	**1904** 10.9c Hansom Cab, 3/26/82	1	17.50	35.00
☐		2	17.50	35.00
☐	**1904a** **Hansom Cab**, untagged (Bureau precanceled), 3/26/82	1	2000.	2000.
☐		2	2000.	2000.
☐	**1905** 11c Caboose, 2/3/84	1	15.00	35.00
☐	**1905a** 11c Caboose, "B" Press, 9/25/91	2	-	350.00**

This price is for a cacheted cover with dial UO cancellation. There was no FDOI cancel although some exist where the stamps had been added to a postal card with the FDOI for the postal card. These sell for consideralby less.

Warning: Other covers are on the market with an earlier date **but no location. These are not **legitimate** since the stamps were first sold in Washington, DC on 9/25/91 and had not been shipped to other locations for sale.

☐	**1906** 17c Electric Auto, 6/25/82	1	17.50	30.00
☐		2	17.50	30.00
☐	**1907** 18c Surrey, 5/18/81	1	20.00	45.00
☐		2	20.00	45.00
☐		3	700.00	1500.
☐		4	700.00	1500.
☐		5	100.00	200.00
☐		6	100.00	200.00
☐		7	400.00	800.00
☐		8	100.00	200.00
☐		9	450.00	900.00
☐		10	450.00	900.00
☐	**1908** 20c Fire Pumper, 12/10/81	1	75.00	150.00
☐		2	150.00	300.00
☐		3	15.00	40.00
☐		4	15.00	40.00
☐		5	100.00	175.00
☐		6	100.00	175.00
☐		7	1,000.	—
☐		8	1,000.	—
☐		10	2,500.	—

	Scott Number	Description	Plate Number	Pair Value	Strip of 3 Value
☐	2005	20c Consumer Education, 4/27/82	1	25.00	40.00
☐			2	25.00	40.00
☐			3	25.00	40.00
☐			4	25.00	40.00
☐	2112	(22c)"D" & Eagle, 2/1/85	1	10.00	17.50
☐			2	10.00	17.50
☐	2115	22c Flag over Capitol Dome, 3/29/85	1	35.00	65.00
☐			2	15.00	25.00
☐			5		2500.
		One cover known to exist			
☐	2115b	22c Flag over Capitol Dome, inscribed "T" at bottom, 5/23/87	1		15.00
☐	2123	3.4c School Bus, 6/8/85	1	6.50	12.50
☐			2	6.50	12.50
☐	2124	4.9c Buckboard, 6/21/85	3	7.50	13.50
☐			4	7.50	13.50
☐	2124a	Buckboard, untagged (Bureau precanceled), 6/21/85	3	2,000.	2,000.
☐			4	2,000.	2,000.
☐	2125	5.5c Star Route Truck, 11/1/86	1	7.50	12.50
☐	2125a	Star Route Truck, untagged (Bureau precanceled), 11/1/86	1		40.00
☐	2126	6c Tricycle, 5/6/85	1	6.50	10.00
☐	2126a	Tricycle, untagged (Bureau precanceled), 5/6/85	1	—	—
		FDC's of the 6c Tricycle untagged are not believed to be legitimate, but are listed here for reference.			
☐	2127	7.1c Tractor, 2/6/87	1	—	12.50
☐	2127a	Tractor, untagged (Bureau precancel "Nonprofit Org."in black), 2/6/87	1		30.00
☐	2127a	Tractor, untagged (Bureau precancel), ("Nonprofit 5-Digit Zip + 4" in black), 5/26/89	1	—	10.00
☐	2128	8.3c Ambulance, 6/21/86	1	7.50	12.50
☐			2	7.50	12.50
☐	2128a	Ambulance, untagged (Bureau precanceled), 6/21/86	1	2,000.	—
☐			2	2,000.	—
☐	2129	8.5c Tow Truck, 1/24/87	1	—	10.00
☐	2129a	Tow Truck, untagged (Bureau precanceled), 1/24/87	1		15.00
☐	2130	10.1c Oil Wagon, 4/18/85	1	7.50	10.00
☐	2130a	Oil Wagon, untagged (red Bureau precancel), 6/27/88	2		8.50
☐	2131	11c Stutz Bearcat, 6/11/85	3	12.50	17.50
☐			4	12.50	17.50
☐	2132	12c Stanley Steamer, 4/2/85	1	7.50	12.50
☐			2	7.50	12.50
☐	2132a	Stanley Steamer, untagged (Bureau precanceled), 4/2/85	1	2,500.	—
		One cover known to exist			
☐	2132a	Stanley Steamer, B Press, untagged (Bureau precanceled)	1	2,000.	2,000.
		The price is for the postally used EKU, prices for the covers with the Philatelic Center cancellation are $750.00			
		There was no official first day of issue for the B Press version of this			

stamp. Cacheted covers exist canceled September 3, 1987, the date the stamp was placed on sale at the Philatelic Sales Unit in Washington, DC, currently the earliest known postmark. The stamp had been shipped to other locations prior to that date so there is a possibility of an earlier date.

☐	2133	**12.5c Pushcart**, 4/18/85 ....1...................7.50		12.50
☐	2134	**14c Iceboat**, 3/23/85 ....1...................15.00		20.00
☐		2...................15.00		20.00
☐		3............................		2500.
		One cover known to exist		
☐		4............................		2,500.
		One cover known to exist		
☐	2134b	**Iceboat**, B Press, 9/30/86 ....2............................		2,000.

There was no official first day of issue for the B Press version of this stamp. The earliest known use was September 30, 1986, but no cacheted covers are known.

☐	2135	**17c Dog Sled**, 8/20/86 ....2...................—		10.00
☐	2136	**25c Bread Wagon**, 11/22/86 ....1...................—		12.50
☐	2149	**18c George Washington**, 11/6/85 ....1112...................20.00		35.00
☐		3333...................20.00		35.00
☐	2149a	**George Washington**, untagged		
		(Bureau precanceled), 11/6/85 ....11121...................45.00		75.00
☐		33333...................45.00		75.00
☐	2150	**21.1c Letters**, 10/22/85 ....111111...................15.00		25.00
☐	2150a	**21.1c Letters**, untagged		
		(Bureau precanceled), 10/22/85 ... 111111...................35.00		65.00
☐	2225	**1c Omnibus**, re-engraved, 11/26/86 ....1...................7.50		12.50
☐	2226	**2c Locomotive**, re-engraved, 3/6/87 1		8.50
☐	2228	**4c Stagecoach**, re-engraved, 8/15/86 1		350.00

There was no official first day of issue for Scott 2228, but cacheted covers exist canceled August 15, 1986, the earliest known use.

☐	2231	**8.3c Ambulance**, B Press, untagged		
		(Bureau precanceled), 8/29/86 1		1,000.

There was no official first day of issue for the B Press version of this stamp, but cacheted covers exist canceled August 29, 1986, the earliest known use.

☐	2252	**3c Conestoga Wagon**, 2/29/88 1		7.50
☐	2253	**5c Milk Wagon**, 9/25/87 1		7.50
☐	2254	**5.3c Elevator**, 9/16/88 1		7.50
☐	2255	**7.6c Carreta**, 8/30/88 1		7.50
☐		2............................		1000.
☐	2256	**8.4c Wheel Chair**, 8/12/88 1		7.50
☐		2............................		750.00
☐	2257	**10c Canal Boat**, 4/11/87 1		8.50
☐	2258	**13c Patrol Wagon**, 10/29/88 1		7.50
☐	2259	**13.2c Coal Car**, 7/19/88 1		7.50
☐	2260	**15c Tugboat**, 7/12/88 1		7.50
☐	2261	**16.7c Popcorn Wagon**, 7/7/88 1		7.50
☐	2262	**17.5c Racing Car**, 9/25/87 1		8.50
☐	2262a	**Racing Car**, untagged		
		(Bureau precanceled), 9/25/87 1		10.00
☐	2263	**20c Cable Car**, 10/28/88 1		7.50
☐		2		60.00
☐	2264	**20.5c Fire Engine**, 9/28/88 1		7.50

	Scott Number	Description	Plate Number	Pair Value	Strip of 3 Value
☐	2265	21c Railroad Mail Car, 8/16/88 1			7.50
☐		2			1,500.
☐	2266	24.1c Tandem Bicycle, 10/26/88 1			7.50
☐	2279	(25c) "E" & Earth, 3/22/88 1111			7.50
☐		1211			10.00
☐		1222			7.50
☐		2222			25.00
☐	2280	25c Flag Over Yosemite, 5/20/88 1			10.00
☐		2			10.00
☐		3			150.00
☐		4			150.00
☐	2280	25c Flag Over Yosemite, pre-phosphored paper, 2/14/89 5			20.00
☐		6			40.00
☐		7			8.50
☐		8			8.50
☐		9			60.00
☐		10			1,500.
☐	2281	25c Honeybee, 9/2/88 1			10.00
☐		2			30.00
☐	2451	4c Steam Carriage, 1/25/91 1			6.50
☐	2452	5c Circus Wagon, engr., 8/31/90 1			6.50
☐	2452B	5c Circus Wagon, photo., 12/8/92 ....A1			6.50
☐		....A2			8.00
☐	2452D	5c Circus Wagon, SV, 3/20/95 ....S1			6.50
☐	2453	5c Canoe, engr., 5/25/91 1			6.50
☐	2454	5c Canoe, photo., 10/22/91 ....S11			6.50
☐	2457	10c Tractor Trailer, engr., 5/25/91 1			6.50
☐	2458	10c Tractor Trailer 11			6.50
☐		22			6.50
☐	2463	20c Cog Railroad, 6/9/95...........................1			7.50
☐		2			25.00
☐	2464	23c Lunch Wagon, 4/12/91 2			8.50
☐		3			7.50
☐	2466	32c Ferry Boat, 6/2/95 2			7.50
☐		3			7.50
☐		4			15.00
☐		5			35.00
☐	2468	$1 Seaplane, 4/20/90 1			10.00
☐	2480	29c Pine Cone (self adhesive), 11/5/93 ....B1			10.00
☐	2492	32c Rose (self adhesive), 6/2/95 ....S111			10.00
☐	2495A	32c Peaches and Pears (self adhesive), 7/8/95 ....V11111			10.00
☐	2518	(29c) "F", 1/22/91 1111			10.00
☐		1211			100.00
☐		1222			10.00
☐		2211			25.00
☐		2222			10.00
☐	2523	29c Flag over Mt. Rushmore, engr., 3/29/91 1			7.50
☐		2			7.50
☐		3			7.50
☐		4			7.50
☐		5			7.50
☐		6			7.50
☐		7			7.50

SCOTT NUMBER	DESCRIPTION	PLATE NUMBER	PAIR VALUE	STRIP OF 3 VALUE
☐	2523A	29c Flag over Mt. Rushmore, photo., 7/4/91	11111		7.50
☐	2525	29c Flower, rouletted, 8/16/91	S1111		7.50
☐	2526	29c Flower, perf., 3/3/92	2222		7.50
☐	2529	19c Fishing Boat, 8/8/91	1111		7.50
☐			1112		15.00
☐			1212		7.50
☐			1424		250.00
☐	2529C	19c Fishing Boat, 6/25/94	S11		7.50
☐	2598	29c Eagle (self adhesive), 2/4/94	111		10.00
☐	2599	29c Statue of Liberty (self adhesive), 6/24/94	D1111		10.00
☐	2602	(10c) Eagle & Shield, ABNC, 12/13/91	A11111		7.50
☐			A11112		7.50
☐			A12213		30.00
☐			A21112		7.50
☐			A21113		7.50
☐			A22112		7.50
☐			A22113		7.50
☐			A32333		125.00
☐			A33333		7.50
☐			A33334		750.00
☐			A33335		7.50
☐			A34424		350.00
☐			A34426		350.00
☐			A43324		15.00
☐			A43325		15.00
☐			A43326		15.00
☐			A43334		15.00
☐			A43335		15.00
☐			A43426		25.00
☐			A53335		25.00
☐			A54444		50.00
☐			A54445		50.00
☐			A77777		750.00
☐	2603	(10c) Eagle & Shield, BEP, 5/29/93	11111		6.50
☐			22221		250.00
☐	2604	(10c) Eagle & Shield, Stamp Venturers, 5/29/93	S11111		6.50
☐	2605	23c Flag Pre-sort, 9/27/91	A111		7.50
☐			A112		250.00
☐			A122		250.00
☐			A212		7.50
☐			A222		7.50
☐	2608	23c Reflected Flag Pre-sort, ABNC, 7/21/92	A1111		7.50
☐			A2222		7.50
☐	2608A	23c Reflected Flag Pre-sort, BEP, 10/9/92	1111		7.50
☐	2608B	23c Reflected Flag Pre-sort, Stamp Venturers, 5/14/93	S111		7.50
☐	2609	29c Flag over White House, 4/23/92	1		7.50
☐			2		7.50
☐			3		7.50
☐			4		7.50
☐			5		7.50
☐			6		7.50

☐		7		7.50
☐		8		1,000.00
☐	**2799-2802 29c Christmas (self adhesive),**			
	10/28/93	...................................V1111111		10.00
☐	2813	**29c Love (self adhesive),** 1/27/94	....................B1	10.00
☐	2873	**29c Santa (self adhesive),** 10/20/94	..............V1111	10.00
☐	2888	**(25c) "G" Flag,** 12/13/94	...........................S11111	7.50
☐	2886	**(32c) "G" Flag, (self adhesive),**		
	12/13/94	...................................V11111		7.50
☐	2888	**(32c) "G" Flag,** 12/13/94	...........................S11111	7.50
☐	2889	**(32c) "G" Flag,** 12/13/94	1111	7.50
		2222		7.50
☐	2890	**(32c) "G" Flag,** 12/13/94	............................A1111	10.00
☐		....A1112		10.00
☐		....A1113		10.00
☐		....A1211		10.00
☐		....A1212		10.00
☐		....A1222		10.00
☐		....A1311		10.00
☐		....A1313		10.00
☐		....A1314		10.00
☐		....A1324		10.00
☐		....A1417		10.00
☐		....A1433		10.00
☐		....A2211		10.00
☐		....A2212		10.00
☐		....A2213		10.00
☐		....A2214		10.00
☐		....A2223		10.00
☐		....A2313		10.00
☐		....A3113		10.00
☐		....A3114		10.00
☐		....A3314		10.00
☐		....A3315		10.00
☐		....A3323		10.00
☐		....A3423		10.00
☐		....A3324		10.00
☐		....A3426		10.00
☐		....A3433		10.00
☐		....A3435		10.00
☐		....A3536		10.00
☐		....A4426		10.00
☐		....A4427		10.00
☐		....A4435		250.00
☐		....A5327		10.00
☐		....A5417		10.00
☐		....A5427		10.00
☐		....A5437		10.00
	Note: The full set of 36 ABN covers is valued at $1,000.00			
☐	2891	**(32c) "G" Flag, perf.,** 12/13/94	...............S1111	10.00
☐	2892	**(32c) "G" Flag, rouletted,** 12/13/94	...........S1111	10.00
		....S2222		10.00
☐	2893	**(32c) "G" Flag,** 12/13/94	.........................A11111	10.00
		....A21111		10.00
☐	2902	**(5c) Butte,** SV, 3/10/95	........................S111	7.50
☐	2902B	**(5c) Butte,** SV, (self-adhesive), 6/15/96. S111		6.50

SCOTT NUMBER	DESCRIPTION	PLATE NUMBER	PAIR VALUE	STRIP OF 3 VALUE
☐ 2903	(5c) Mountains, BEP, 3/16/96	11111		6.50
☐ 2904	(5c) Mountains, SV, 3/16/96	S11		6.50
☐ 2904A	(5c) Mountains, (self-adhesive), 6/15/96	V222222		6.50
☐		V333333		6.50
☐		V333323		6.50
☐		V333342		6.50
☐		V333343		6.50
☐ 2905	(10c) Auto, 3/10/95	S111		7.50
☐ 2906	(10c) Auto, (self-adhesive), 6/15/96	S111		6.50
☐ 2907	(10c) Eagle & Shield, (self-adhesive), 5/21/96	S1111		6.50
☐ 2908	(15c) Auto Tail Fin, BEP, 3/17/95	11111		7.50
☐ 2909	(15c) Auto Tail Fin, SV, 3/17/95	S11111		7.50
☐ 2911	(25c) Juke Box, BEP 3/17/95	111111		7.50
☐ 2912	(25c) Juke Box, SV, 3/17/95	S11111		7.50
☐ 2912A	(25c) Juke Box, SV, (self-adhesive), 6/15/96	S11111		7.50
☐ 2912B	(25c) Juke Box, BEP, (self-adhesive), 6/15/96,	11111		7.50
☐ 2913	32c Flag over Porch, BEP, 5/19/95	11111		10.00
☐		22221		15.00
☐		22222		10.00
☐		33333		10.00
☐		44444		10.00
☐		45444		35.00
☐		66646		35.00
☐ 2914	32c Flag over Porch, SV, 5/19/95	S11111		10.00
☐ 2915A	32c Flag over Porch, BEP, (self-adhesive), 5/21/96,	55555		10.00
☐		66666		10.00
☐		78777		10.00
☐		87888		50.00
☐		87898		10.00
☐		88888		10.00
☐		88898		500.00
☐		89878		10.00
☐		89888		50.00
☐		89898		20.00
☐		97898		10.00
☐		99999		10.00
☐ 2915B	32c Flag over Porch, SV, (self-adhesive), 6/15/96	S11111		10.00
☐ 2915C	32c Flag over Porch, BEP, (self-adhesive), 5/21/96, serpentine die cut 11	66666		25.00
☐ 3017	32c Christmas, (self adhesive) 9/30/95	V1111		10.00
☐ 3018	32c Christmas Angel, (self adhesive) 10/31/95	B1111		10.00
☐ 3044	1c Kestrel, 1/20/96	1111		6.50
☐ 3045	2c Red Headed Woodpecker, 6/22/99	11111		6.50
☐ 3053	20c Blue Jay, (self-adhesive), 8/2/96	S111		7.50
☐ 3054	32c Yellow Rose, (self-adhesive), 8/1/97	1111		7.50
☐		1112		7.50
☐		1122		7.50
☐		2222		7.50

SCOTT NUMBER	DESCRIPTION	PLATE NUMBER	PAIR VALUE	STRIP OF 3 VALUE
☐		.............2223.............		7.50
☐		.............2233.............		900.00
☐		.............2333.............		7.50
☐		.............3344.............		7.50
☐		.............3444.............		7.50
☐		.............4455.............		7.50
☐		.............5455.............		7.50
☐		.............5555.............		7.50
☐		.............5556.............		7.50
☐		.............5566.............		7.50
☐		.............5666.............		7.50
☐ 3055	20c Ring-Necked Pheasant, 7/31/98....1111.............			7.00
☐ 3207	(5c) Wetland, 6/5/98 ....S1111.............			6.50
☐ 3207A	(5c) Wetlands, (self-adhesive), 12/14/981111.............			6.50
☐ 3208	(25c) Diner, 9/30/98 ....S11111.............			7.50
☐ 3208A	(25c) Diner, (self-adhesive), 9/5/98.....11111.............			7.50
☐ 3228	(10c) Bicycle (self-adhesive), 8/14/98 ....111.............			6.75
☐		.............221.............		6.75
☐		.............222.............		6.75
☐		.............333.............		6.75
☐ 3229	(10c) Bicycle, 8/14/98 ....S111.............			6.75
☐ 3263	22 Uncle Sam, 11/9/98 ....111.............			7.25
☐ 3264	(33c) "H", 11/9/98 ....1111.............			7.50
☐		.............3333.............		7.50
☐		.............3343.............		7.50
☐		.............3344.............		7.50
☐		.............3444.............		7.50
☐ 3265	(33c) "H" (self-adhesive), 11/9/98 ....1111.............			7.50
☐		.............1131.............		7.50
☐		.............2222.............		7.50
☐		.............3333.............		7.50
☐ 3266	(33c) "H" (self-adhesive spaced), 11/9/98 ....1111.............			8.00
☐ 3270	(10c) Eagle & Shield, 12/14/98 ....11111.............			6.50
☐ 3271	(10c) Eagle & Shield (self-adhesive), 12/14/98 ....11111.............			6.50
☐ 3280	33c City Flag, 2/25/99 ....1111.............			7.50
☐		.............2222.............		7.50
☐ 3281	33c City Flag (self-adhesive), 2/25/99 ..1111.............			7.50
☐		.............2222.............		7.50
☐		.............3333.............		7.50
☐		.............3433.............		7.50
☐		.............4443.............		7.50
☐		.............4444.............		7.50
☐		.............5555.............		7.50
☐ 3282	33c City Flag (self-adhesive spaced), 2/25/99 ....1111.............			8.00
☐		.............1222.............		8.00
☐ 3302-3305	33c Fruit Berries, 4/10/99 ....B1111.............			7.50
☐		.............B1112.............		7.50
☐		.............B2211.............		7.50
☐		.............B2221.............		7.50
☐		.............B2222.............		7.50
☐ 3404-3407	33c Fruit Berries, die cut horiz., 6/16/00............G1111.............			7.50

SCOTT NUMBER	DESCRIPTION	STRIP OF 3 VALUE
☐ 3447	10c NYC Public Library Lion, 11/9/00, ...	7.50
☐ 3452	34c Statue of Liberty, 12/15/00, ...	7.50
☐ 3453	34c Statue of Liberty (self adhesive), 12/15/00, ...	7.50
☐ 3462-65	34c Flowers, 12/15/00, ...	7.50
☐ 3466	34c Statue of Liberty (self adhesive spaced), 1/7/01, ...	7.50
☐	34c Statue of Liberty (self adhesive), 2/7/01, ...	7.50
☐	34c Statue of Liberty, 2/7/01, ...	7.50
☐	34c Flowers (self adhesive), 2/7/01, ...	7.50

☐ _____

☐ _____

☐ _____

☐ _____

☐ _____

☐ _____

☐ _____

☐ _____

☐ _____

☐ _____

☐ _____

☐ _____

☐ _____

☐ _____

☐ _____

☐ _____

☐ _____

☐ _____

☐ _____

☐ _____

☐ _____

☐ _____

☐ _____

☐ _____

SCOTT NUMBER	DESCRIPTION	PLATE NUMBER	PAIR VALUE	STRIP OF 3 VALUE

OFFICIAL STAMPS

☐	O135	20c Official, 1/12/83	1	30.00	75.00
☐	O139	(22c) "D" 2/4/85	1	35.00	80.00

COMPUTER VENDED POSTAGE

☐	31	29c ECA GARD, 8/20/92	1	7.50
☐	31	29c Variable Rate, 8/20/92, 1st print	1	7.50
☐	31b	29c Variable Rate, 8/20/92, (2nd print)	1	25.00
☐	32	29c Variable Rate, 8/20/92	A11	7.50

c o v e r   b o x

10.5"

4.25"

7.5"

Item	Description	Retail
CVBOX	Marble Cover Box	$6.95

INAUGURATION, RESIGNATION, AND DEATH IN OFFICE COVERS

All values given are for cacheted covers postmarked on the date of the presidents' inauguration, resignation or death in office. Uncacheted covers sell for about one-half of the catalogue value. Values for covers after 1945 are for unaddressed cacheted covers. Addressed covers after 1949 sell for about one-half of the catalogue value.

- [ ] **McKinley** Mar. 4, 1901 ....1,500.
- [ ] **McKinley** Sept. 14, 1901, Assassination cover Death in Office ....1,500.
- [ ] **T. Roosevelt** Mar. 4, 1905 ....500.00
- [ ] **Taft** Mar. 4, 1909 ....250.00
- [ ] **Wilson** 1st Term Mar. 4, 1913 ....500.00
- [ ] **Wilson** 2nd Term, Mar. 5, 1917 ....450.00
- [ ] **Harding** Mar. 4, 1921 ....—
- [ ] **Harding** Death, Aug. 2, 1923 ....—
- [ ] **Coolidge** Inauguration, Aug. 3, 1923 ....400.00
- [ ] **Coolidge** 2nd Term, Mar. 4, 1925 ....300.00
- [ ] **Hoover** Mar. 4, 1929 ....250.00
- [ ] **F.D. Roosevelt** 1st Term, Mar. 4, 1933 ....60.00
- [ ] **F.D. Roosevelt** 2nd Term, Jan. 20, 1937 ....225.00
- [ ] **F.D. Roosevelt** 3rd Term, Jan. 20, 1941 ....225.00
- [ ] **F.D. Roosevelt** 4th Term, Jan. 20, 1945 ....200.00
- [ ] **F.D. Roosevelt** Date of Death, Apr. 12, 1945, canceled at Roosevelt, NY 65.00
- [ ] **Truman** 1st Term, Apr. 12, 1945 ....200.00
- [ ] **Truman** 2nd Term, Jan. 20, 1949 ....70.00
- [ ] **Eisenhower** 1st Term, Jan. 20, 1953 ....20.00
- [ ] **Eisenhower** 2nd Term, Jan. 21, 1957 ....20.00
      Note: 1/20/57 was a Sunday. However, some Artcraft and Fluegel
      cacheted covers do have the 1/20/57 cancel.
- [ ]   With Artcraft cachet 35.00
- [ ]   With Fluegel cachet 75.00
- [ ] **Kennedy** Jan. 20, 1961 ....20.00
- [ ]   With Fluegel cachet 35.00
- [ ] **Kennedy** Assassination cover, Nov. 22, 1963 ....40.00
- [ ] **Kennedy** Assassination cover, Nov. 22, 1963, with FDC of
          Scott 1246 on May 29, 1964 ....65.00
- [ ] **L.B. Johnson** Jan. 20, 1965 ....10.00
- [ ]   With Fluegel cachet 35.00
- [ ] **Nixon** 1st Term, Jan. 20, 1969 ....10.00
- [ ] **Nixon** 2nd Term, Jan. 20, 1973 ....8.00
- [ ] **Nixon** Announces resignation, canceled Aug 8, 1974 on same cover
          canceled Jan. 20, 1973 ....20.00
- [ ] **Nixon** Resigns to Congress, Aug. 9, 1974 ....8.00
- [ ] **Nixon** Resigns to Congress, canceled Aug. 9, 1974 on same cover
          canceled Jan. 20, 1973 ....10.00
- [ ] **Ford**, V.P. Dec. 6, 1973 ....8.00
- [ ] **Ford** Aug. 9, 1974 ....5.00
- [ ] **Carter** Jan. 20, 1977 ....4.00
- [ ] **Reagan** 1st Term, Jan. 20, 1981 ....3.00
- [ ] **Reagan** 2nd Term, Jan. 21, 1985 ....3.00
- [ ] **Bush** Jan. 20, 1989 ....3.00
- [ ] **Clinton** 1st Term, Jan. 20, 1993 ....3.00
- [ ] **Clinton** 2nd Term, Jan.20,1997...3.00
- [ ] **Bush** Jan. 20, 2001...3.00

PATRIOTIC COVERS OF WW II

Listed below are significant World War II patriotic dates. Values are for related, printed-cacheted covers, canceled on the appropriate date. The listed values reflect the work of the following cachet makers: Crosby, Fidelity, Fleetwood/Knapp, Fleetwood/Staehle, Fluegel, Richardson/Knapp, Smartcraft, and Teixeria.

In addition, Minkus and several other cachet makers made a group of general purpose patriotic covers such as "Win the War" and "Sink the Japs". These covers generally have a value of $3.00 each, while uncanceled covers have a value of 75c each.

WWII COVERS DESCRIPTION	CACHETED SINGLE
☐ Pearl Harbor, 12/7/41	150.00
☐ U.S. Declares War on Japan, 12/8/41	75.00
☐ Germany and Italy Declare War on U.S., 12/11/41	75.00
☐ U.S Declares War on Germany and Italy, 12/11/41	75.00
☐ Churchill arrives at the White House, 12/22/41	60.00
☐ Manila and Cavite Fall, 1/2/42	60.00
☐ Roosevelt's Diamond Jubilee Birthday, 1/30/42	60.00
☐ Singapore Surrenders, 2/15/42	60.00
☐ Japan takes Java, 3/10/42	60.00
☐ Marshall Arrives in London, 4/8/42	60.00
☐ Dedication of MacArthur Post Office, 4/15/42	60.00
☐ Doolittle Air Raid of Tokyo, 4/18/42	60.00
☐ Air Raid on Tokyo by Doolittle, 4/18/42	60.00
☐ Fort Mills Corregidor Island Surrenders, 5/6/42	60.00
☐ Madagascar Occupied by U.S, 5/9/42	60.00
☐ Mexico at War with Axis, 5/23/42	60.00
☐ Bombing of Cologne, 6/6/42	60.00
☐ Japan Bombs Dutch Harbor, AK, 6/6/42	60.00
☐ Six German Spies Sentenced to Death, 8/7/42	60.00
☐ Brazil at War, 8/22/42	55.00
☐ Battle of El Alamein, 10/23/42	45.00
☐ Invasion of North Africa (Operation Torch), 11/8/42	45.00
☐ Gas rationing is Nationwide, 12/1/42	45.00
☐ The Casablanca Conference, 1/22/43	45.00
☐ The Casablanca Conference (You must remember this!), 1/22/43	40.00
☐ Point Rationing, 3/1/43	50.00
☐ Battle of the Bismarck Sea, 3/13/43	40.00
☐ U.S. Planes Bomb Naples, 4/5/43	40.00
☐ Bizerte & Tunis Occupied, 5/8/43	40.00
☐ Invasion of Attu, 5/11/43	40.00
☐ Sicily Invaded, 7/14/43	35.00
☐ Italy Invaded, 9/3/43	40.00
☐ The Quebec Conference, 8/14/43	45.00
☐ Italy Surrenders, 9/8/43	40.00
☐ Mussolini Escapes, 9/18/43	40.00
☐ U.S. Drives Germans out of Naples, 10/2/43	40.00
☐ Italy Declares War on Germany, 10/13/43	40.00
☐ Hull Eden Stalin Conference, 10/25/43	40.00
☐ U.S. Government Takes over Coal Mines, 11/3/43	40.00
☐ The Cairo Meeting, 11/25/43	35.00
☐ The Teheran Meeting, 11/28/43	35.00
☐ Roosevelt, Churchill, Chiang Kai-Shek at Cairo, 12/2/43	40.00

☐ FDR, Stalin, Churchill Agree on 3 fronts, 12/2/43 ....40.00
☐ Soviets Reach Polish Border, 1/4/44 ....30.00
☐ U.S Captures Cassino, 3/15/44 ....35.00
☐ Invasion of Dutch New Guinea, 4/24/44 ....35.00
☐ Rome Falls, 6/4/44..35.00
☐ D-Day Single Face Eisenhower, 6/6/44 ....125.00
☐ Invasion of Normandy D-Day, 6/6/44 ....35.00
☐ B29's Bomb Japan, 6/15/44...35.00
☐ Cherbourg Surrenders, 6/7/44...40.00
☐ Paris Revolts, 6/23/44 ....35.00
☐ Caen Falls to Allies, 7/10/44 ....35.00
☐ Marines Invade Guam, 7/21/44..35.00
☐ Yanks Enter Brest, etc., 8/7/44 ....35.00
☐ U.S. Bombs Philippines, 8/10/44 ....35.00
☐ Invasion of Southern France, 8/16/44 ....25.00
☐ Liberation of Paris, 8/23/44 ....30.00
☐ Florence Falls to Allies, 8/23/44 ....30.00
☐ Liberation of Brussels, 9/4/44 ....30.00
☐ U.S. Invades Holland, Finland Quits, 9/5/44 ....30.00
☐ Russians Invade Yugoslavia, 9/6/44 ....30.00
☐ Russians Enter Bulgaria, 9/9/44 ....30.00
☐ Liberation of Luxembourg, 9/10/44 ....30.00
☐ Albania Invaded, 9/27/44...35.00
☐ Philippines, We Will Be Back, 9/27/44 ....25.00
☐ Greece Invaded, 10/5/44 ....35.00
☐ Liberation of Athens, 10/14/44 ....30.00
☐ Liberation of Belgrade, 10/16/44 ....30.00
☐ Russia Invades Czechoslovakia, 10/19/44 ....30.00
☐ Invasion of the Philippines, 10/20/44 ....30.00
☐ The Pied Piper of Leyte-Philippine Invasion, 10/21/44 ....45.00
☐ Invasion of Norway, 10/25/44..**25.00**
☐ Liberation of Tirana, 11/18/44 ....25.00
☐ 100,000 Yanks Land on Luzon, 1/10/45 ....25.00
☐ Liberation of Warsaw, 1/17/45 ....30.00
☐ Russians Drive to Oder River, 2/2/45 ....25.00
☐ Liberation of Manila, 2/4/45 ....25.00
☐ Yalta Conference, 2/12/45 ....25.00
☐ Budapest Liberated, 2/13/45 ....25.00
☐ Corregidor is Ours, 2/17/45 ....25.00
☐ Turkey Wars Germany and Japan, 2/23/45..25.00
☐ Yanks Enter Cologne, 3/5/45..25.00
☐ Cologne is Taken, 3/6/45 ....20.00
☐ Historical Rhine Crossing, 3/8/45 ....20.00
☐ Bombing of Tokyo, 3/10/45 ....25.00
☐ Russia Crosses Oder River, 3/13/45 ....20.00
☐ Capture of Iwo Jima, 3/14/45 ....20.00
☐ Battle of the Inland Sea, 3/20/45 ....20.00
☐ Crossing of the Rhine, 3/24/45 ....20.00
☐ Danzig Invaded, 3/27/45 ....25.00
☐ Okinawa Invaded, 4/1/45 ....25.00
☐ Japanese Cabinet Resigns, 4/7/45 ....25.00
☐ Liberation of Vienna, 4/10/45 ....25.00

☐	U.S. Invades Bremen etc., 4/10/45	25.00
☐	FRD Dies-Truman beomes President, 4/12/45	50.00
☐	Liberation of Vienna, 4/13/45	25.00
☐	Patton Invades Czechoslovakia, 4/18/45	25.00
☐	Berlin Invaded, 4/21/45	25.00
☐	Berlin is Encircled, 4/25/45	25.00
☐	GI Joe and Ivan Meet at Torgau-Germany, 4/26/45	25.00
☐	Mussolini Executed, 4/28/45	25.00
☐	Hitler Dead, 5/1/45	35.00
☐	Liberation of Italy, 5/2/45	25.00
☐	Berlin Falls, 5/2/45	25.00
☐	Liberation of Rangoon, 5/3/45	25.00
☐	5th and 7th Armies Meet at the Brenner Pass, 5/4/45	25.00
☐	Liberation of Copenhagen, 5/5/45	25.00
☐	Liberation of Amsterdam, 5/5/45	25.00
☐	Liberation of Oslo, 5/8/45	25.00
☐	Liberation of Prague, 5/8/45	25.00
☐	V-E Day, 5/8/45	35.00
☐	Atomic Bomb Test, 5/16/45	25.00
☐	Invasion of Borneo, 6/11/45	25.00
☐	Eisenhower Welcomed Home, 6/18/45	20.00
☐	Okinawa Captured, 6/21/45	25.00
☐	United Nations Conference, 6/25/45	25.00
☐	American Flag Raised Over Berlin, 7/4/45	25.00
☐	Big Three Meet at Potsdam, 8/1/45	25.00
☐	Atomic Bomb, 8/6/45	75.00
☐	Russia Declares War on Japan, 8/8/45	25.00
☐	Japan Capitulates, 8/14/45	25.00
☐	Japan Signs Peace Treaty, 9/1/45	50.00
☐	Liberation of China, 9/2/45	35.00
☐	V-J Day, 9/2/45	35.00
☐	Liberation of Korea, 9/2/45	25.00
☐	Flag Raising over Tokyo-MacArthur takes over, 9/8/45	25.00
☐	Gen. Wainwright Rescued from the Japanese, 9/10/45	25.00
☐	Nimitz Post Office, 9/10/45	25.00
☐	Marines Land in Japan, 9/23/45	40.00
☐	Nimitz Day-Wshington, 10/5/45	25.00
☐	War Crimes Commission, 10/18/45	25.00
☐	Premier Laval Executed as Traitor, 10/15/45	25.00
☐	Fleet Reviewed by President Truman, 10/27/45	35.00
☐	Trygve Lie Elected, 1/21/46	25.00
☐	2nd Anniversary of D-Day, 6/6/46	25.00
☐	Operation Crossroads, 6/3/46	100.00
☐	Bikini Atomic Bomb Test, 7/1/46	125.00
☐	Independence of the Philippines, 7/4/46	100.00
☐	Atomic Age, 7/10/46	25.00
☐	Victory Day, 8/14/46	25.00
☐	Opening of UN Post Office at Lake Success, 9/23/46	25.00
☐	Goering Commits Suicide, 10/16/46	40.00
☐	Opening Day of UN in Flushing, NY, 10/23/46	25.00
☐	Marshall is Secretary of State, 1/21/47	25.00
☐	Moscow Peace Conference, 3/10/47	25.00

SCOTT NUMBER	DESCRIPTION	UNCACH	CACH	CERM PROG
☐	_____			
☐	_____			
☐	_____			
☐	_____			
☐	_____			
☐	_____			
☐	_____			
☐	_____			
☐	_____			
☐	_____			
☐	_____			
☐	_____			
☐	_____			
☐	_____			
☐	_____			
☐	_____			
☐	_____			
☐	_____			
☐	_____			
☐	_____			
☐	_____			
☐	_____			
☐	_____			
☐	_____			
☐	_____			
☐	_____			
☐	_____			
☐	_____			
☐	_____			
☐	_____			
☐	_____			
☐	_____			
☐	_____			
☐	_____			

INDEX TO ADVERTISERS